ISLAMIC GENDER APARTHEID:
Exposing A Veiled War Against Women

ISLAMIC GENDER APARTHEID:
Exposing A Veiled War Against Women

PHYLLIS CHESLER

Published by New English Review Press
a subsidiary of World Encounter Institute
PO Box 158397
Nashville, Tennessee 37215
&
27 Old Gloucester Street
London, England, WC1N 3AX

Cover Art and Design by Kendra Mallock

ISBN: 978-1-943003-12-9

First Edition

NEW ENGLISH REVIEW PRESS
newenglishreview.org

Praise for Phyllis Chesler

On *The Death of Feminism:*

"With great talent and in a vivid style, Phyllis Chesler observes every aspect of today's American culture, politics, and society with humor and through a feminist lens. This enlightening picture unveils the most dramatic domestic and international problems of our times, including that of Islamic gender apartheid, analyzed by a daring and politically incorrect lover of truth."—**Bat Ye'or**

"Phyllis Chesler brings an eloquent and righteous anger to bear against Western feminists for their dual habit of overlooking the plight of Muslim women and blaming Israel, by far the Middle East's most feminist country, for the woes of that region. Chesler's focus on this topic, it turns out, is informed by an intensely personal experience; in *The Death of Feminism* she reveals her nightmare as a young wife in Afghanistan in 1961. That event, it turns out, was a crucible vital both to her general intellectual development and to the making of this powerful book."
—**Daniel Pipes**

"To read Phyllis Chesler is to encounter one of the most challenging and original minds in the world today. Every Chesler book takes on the conventional wisdoms and political correctness with verve and insight. *The Death of Feminism* is a tour de force, combining personal experience, brilliant analysis and heart-felt advocacy. Chesler demonstrates how anti-Israel bigotry, which has already damaged the credibility of many human rights organizations, is now endangering feminism. A must read."
—**Alan Dershowitz**

"Ms. Chesler's book is a welcome critique of the Feminist Left's willful and shameful neglect of their sisters' plight in the Islamic World. Rejecting cultural relativism or political correctness, Ms. Chesler paints a depressing but truthful picture of the world that women under Islam have to live in. One hopes Ms. Chesler's book will bring about not only a change in attitudes but some sort of political and social action on behalf of women suffering because of the totalitarian and misogynistic tenets of Islam." —**Ibn Warraq**

Acknowledgements

I am very grateful to Cornelia Foster Wood, for her loving friendship and long-term support; Dr. Daniel Pipes for his loyal and ongoing support; Susan L. Bender, Esq., for her quarter-century of powering the "wind beneath my sails;" Merle Hoffman for her extraordinary generosity and eclectic imagination; Ibn Warraq and Bat Ye'or for their company, kindness, and pioneering work; to all those who stood with me, early on, against Big Lies; and to my son, Ariel David Chesler, who has graced me with his rigorous legal genius, writing chops, and love.

I also wish to acknowledge my assistant, Emily Feldman, and my archivist, Evelyn Shunaman, for their superb support; my IT support, especially Matt Greenfield; and my team of health care-givers and maintainers, especially Dr. Tina Dobsevage and Beth Dobsevage.

Most of all, I wish to thank my publisher and editor, Rebecca Bynum, for her incredible professionalism, political sophistication, and courage.

Contents

Section Three: Should America Ban the Burqa? 129

Section Eight: The American Gulag 443

Introduction

These articles span a fourteen year period, from 2003-2016. I have tried to convey what Islamic gender apartheid is, both as an academic and as a journalist. It is a system of pernicious tribal, ethnic, and religious customs. Few contemporary feminist scholars have dared to name, document, and condemn this as a violation of women's and human rights—lest they be demonized as "racists;" this fear has trumped the Western intelligentsia's concern with barbarism and the feminist concern with misogyny.

The Collection opens with an excerpt from my 2005 book, *The Death of Feminism*, which first appeared in *Middle East Quarterly*. Here is where I consider the extent to which my American feminism might have been forged in the fires of my long-ago captivity in Kabul, Afghanistan; it is where I first experienced Islamic gender and religious apartheid long before the emergence of the Taliban.

Unlike many Western feminists, I do not view the Islamic veil or the burqa as either comfortable or sexy. It is, essentially, a sensory deprivation isolation chamber. It violates a woman's dignity and is gravely restricts her physical and social mobility.

Islamic gender apartheid includes some or all of the following practices: The masking of the female face, (niqab), body (burqa or chador), and head (hijab); child marriage; arranged marriage to a close cousin; polygamy; female segregation/sequestration (purdah); normalized honor-based violence, including the daily beating, monitoring, and stalking of daughters; forcing daughters to become family domestic servants; not allowing daughters to leave home unsupervised; forbidding daughters to befriend non-co-religionists or to talk to male non-relatives; forbidding daughters an advanced education; forbidding daughters to leave a dangerously violent husband; female genital mutilation; forbidding daughters to leave their religion of origin; and honor killing one's daughter—which is a family-of-origin conspiracy and in no way analogous to Western domestic violence.

In addition, those who practice gender apartheid may also engage in religiously and legally sanctioned sex slavery, concubinage, "temporary" marriage, and pedophilia, as well as the sanctioned sexual harassment and rape of naked-faced infidel women.

Gender apartheid is probably tribal in origin but worldwide, it is practiced mainly by Muslims. Hindus sexually harass women (it's called "Eve teasing") and also perpetrate honor killings, but only in India; they honor kill mainly for caste-related violations in terms of a spouse—not for the many and varied reasons that motivate Muslim honor killings. More important, Hindus do not bring this custom with them when they emigrate to the West, whereas Muslims do. Sikhs also perpetrate honor killings, but to a much lesser extent. As tribal people, Hindus and Sikhs practice some, but not all, of the apartheid practices listed above. Many Muslims perpetrate some, most, or all of these practices.

Some of these articles were originally speeches which I delivered at a Senate hearing, and in which I was beamed up, live, into Tehran; at a grassroots panel at the United Nations organized by Iranian and Afghan women against their respective regimes; at a G8 conference in Rome; and at the New York State Supreme Court for judges who were interested in the affidavits that I'd submitted on behalf of women in flight from honor-based violence and in search of political asylum.

I wrote some articles in order to assist those who were rescuing sex slaves from ISIS; to publicize the plight of women who were facing extreme punishment or execution in Muslim jails for having killed their rapists in self-defense; having tried to bring their rapists to justice; or for having worn trousers.

I've interviewed a number of experts, including Muslim free thinkers and reformers such as Asma'a Al-Gul, Nonie Darwish, Tarek Heggy, Asra Nomani, and Nadia Shahram. In addition, I document the extraordinary heroism of Lubna Ahmed Al-Hussein (Sudan), Nujood Ali (Yemen), Mukhtaran Bibi (Pakistan) Wajeda Huwaider (Saudi Arabia), Gulie Khalaf (Yazidi-Iraqi-American), Adoul Keijan (Yazidi-Iraqi American), Fauzia Koofi (Afghanistan), Kainat Soomro (Pakistan), Hans Erling Jensen (Scandinavia, Germany) and Sister Hatune Dogan (Turkey, Syria, Iraq).

Throughout, I express considerable anguish and anger about the relative silence of many Western feminists about gender apartheid. Here's why.

Second Wave Western feminists exposed, analyzed, and condemned rape. We pioneered rape crisis counseling and changed the laws about rape. Yet, by the 21st century, leading feminists became exceedingly cautious.

In our time and on our watch, rape became a full-fledged weapon—not merely a spoil—of war. Repeated and public gang rape is a form of gender cleansing. This happened in Pakistan-Bangladesh (1971), in Algeria (1992-1995), in the former Yugoslavia (1992-1995); Rwanda (1994), in Sudan (2004—) and in the Punjab (2002). It is happening now in Iraq and Syria.

ISIS kidnapped young girls and raped them nine-to-ten times a day—sometimes thirty times a day—every day. These infidels—Christians and Yazidis—were viewed by Islamists as religiously permitted sex slaves and are auctioned off in videotaped slave markets. Many girls killed themselves or attempted to do so. Such slaves begged for the bombing of the brothels in which they were being held captive—or to be rescued.

Professional Western feminists: our Women's Studies professors, politicians, journalists, and human rights activists are multi-cultural relativists and "postcolonial" scholars; thus, they are reluctant to accuse formerly colonized men of color of misogyny—not even when it is quite barbaric. They are not merely "politically correct;" they have become "Islamically correct."

May I suggest that we at least provide refuge to girls and women who live in the West and who are in flight from honor-based violence? Their blood should not be on our hands. We must also prosecute, not only their tormentors and honor killers, but their family-of-origin accomplices.

Today, my 21st century colleagues are Muslim and ex-Muslim, Sikh, Hindu, Christian, and Jewish feminists, dissidents, conservatives, and libertarians. With some precious exceptions, radical and liberal Second, Third, and Fourth Wave Western feminists are silent on the subject of Islamic gender apartheid.

Today, my colleagues and I are anti-Islamists or anti-Sharia-ists: As the feminists of yore, we share one universal standard of human rights. We support post-Enlightenment Western values such as the separation of religion and state, freedom from and freedom of religion, free speech, fact-based knowledge as opposed to mere opinion, intellectual diversity, the right to dissent, as well as individual and human rights. We oppose herd thinking and totalitarianism in all its forms.

Some of my allies write under pseudonyms. Others live with round-the-clock bodyguards. This Muslim and infidel anti-Islamist movement is the major resistance movement of our time. It has been marginalized and silenced by Western governments.

Gender apartheid and honor-based violence are crimes and cannot be justified in the name of multicultural relativism, political "correctness," tolerance, or anti-racism.

The battle for women's rights is central to the battle for Western values. It is a necessary part of true freedom and democracy. Here, then, is exactly where the greatest battle of the twenty-first century is joined.

****

I've edited these articles considerably and have often changed their original titles. They were originally published in the journal *Middle East Quarterly* and at the following websites: *American Thinker/Campus Watch; Breitbart; Feminist Theory; FrontPage Magazine; Huffington Post; Israel National News; Middle East Quarterly online; Newsmax; Newsrealblog; New York Post; New York Times; Pajamas Media; Playboy*, and *Times of Israel*. They were cross-posted at a variety of other venues.

I want to thank Mary Curtis of Transaction for taking me to the Plaza for tea and persuading me to undertake this Collection. I am deeply grateful for the support shown to my work by Dr. Daniel Pipes of the Middle East Education Forum; to Cornelia Foster Wood, who has been a loyal and loving supporter for more than a decade; to Joy Brighton, who supported this work at a time when it mattered; to my dear friend and supporter, Merle Hoffman of the Choices Global Institute of Healing and Education; to Abigail and Jerry Martin, who have been staunch supporters; and to my invaluable assistant, Emily G. Feldman; and to my partner, Susan L. Bender, who has been my mainstay. Finally, working with Rebecca Bynum has been a real pleasure.

—New York City, February 2017

Section One:
How Afghan Captivity Shaped My Feminism

- 1 -

How Afghan Captivity Shaped My Feminism

On December 21, 1961, when I returned from Afghanistan, I kissed the ground at New York City's Idlewild Airport. I weighed 90 pounds and had hepatitis. Although I would soon become active in the American civil rights, anti-Vietnam war, and feminist movements, what I had learned in Kabul rendered me immune to the Third World romanticism that infected so many American radicals. As a young bride in Afghanistan, I was an eyewitness to just how badly women are treated in the Muslim world. I was mistreated, too, but I survived. Perhaps my "Western" feminism was forged in that most beautiful and treacherous of countries.

In 1962, when I returned to Bard College, I tried to tell my classmates how important it was that America had so many free libraries, movie theatres, bookstores, universities, unveiled women, freedom of movement on the streets, freedom to leave our families of origin if we so chose, freedom from arranged marriages—and from polygamy, too. This meant that as imperfect as America may be, it was still the land of opportunity and of "life, liberty, and the pursuit of happiness."

My friends, future journalists, artists, physicians, lawyers, and intellectuals, wanted only to hear fancy Hollywood fairy tales, not reality. They wanted to know how many servants I had and whether I ever met the king. I had no way of communicating the horror, and the truth. My American friends could not or did not want to understand. As with my young college friends so long ago, today's leftists and progressives want to remain ignorant about the indigenous nature of barbarism in tribal societies and about Islam's long history of imperialism, colonialism, gender apartheid, and slavery.

FROM NEW YORK TO KABUL

My Afghan awakening began in New York in 1961 when I married my college sweetheart, Ali, a man from Afghanistan who had been away from home for more than a decade while studying at private schools in Europe and America.

My plan was to meet Ali's family in Kabul, stay there a month or two, study "History of Ideas" at the Sorbonne for a semester, then return to Bard College to complete my final semester.

When we landed in Kabul at least thirty members of his family were there to greet us. The airport officials smoothly confiscated my American passport. "It's just a formality, nothing to worry about," Ali assured me. "You'll get it back later." I never saw that passport again.

I was now the citizen of no country and the property of a large polygamous family.

Upon our arrival in Kabul, my Westernized husband simply became another person. For two years, in the United States, Ali and I had been inseparable. He had walked me to my classes. We did our homework together in the library. We talked constantly. In Afghanistan, everything changed. We were no longer a couple during the day. He no longer held my hand. He barely spoke to me. He only sought me out at night. He treated me the way his father and elder brother treated their wives: with annoyed embarrassment, coldness, distance.

My father-in-law, Amir, whom we knew as "Agha Jan" or "Dear Master," was a leading businessman and an exceedingly dapper man. In Afghanistan, he was a progressive. In his youth, he had supported Amanullah Khan (1919-29) who had boldly unveiled Afghan women, instituted the country's first educational and health care systems, and introduced European-style trolleys in the capital city. Nevertheless, he did not want an American or Jewish daughter-in-law. I was Ali's desperate rebellion. I was flesh-and-blood proof that, for years, Ali had actually been living in the twentieth century.

Ali had not told me that his father was polygamous until just before we had arrived in Kabul. Then he told me that, "actually," his father had two wives. Imagine my surprise when I discovered that Agha Jan actually had three wives. This reality was one that Ali would not or could not discuss. He and his brothers blamed their mother for this third marriage to Sultana, which had jeopardized their inheritance considerably; this was a risky, tabooed subject. This third marriage didn't "count" because it counted all too much.

Agha Jan was in his sixties and stood six feet tall. His black hair was thick and only flecked with gray at the temples. He had a broad, frank mustache, and velvet black eyes that matched his black Italian handmade shoes. Although he wore the jauntiest and most expensive of Afghan-style karakul hats, Agha Jan also wore European-made suits and coats. As a devout Muslim, he neither drank nor smoked. Agha Jan's grown and married children, both men and women, executed a cringing half-bow whenever they greeted him.

Agha Jan's current home, with his third wife, Sultana, had one great European-style room in which he received visitors and dined. He usually ate alone, in a sitting room hushed by thick maroon carpets and thick, European-style velvet drapes. Rozia, his fourteen-year-old daughter by his third wife, served him each dish, bowing in and out of the room, like a servant.

"How can you justify polygamy?" I'd ask Ali. "It's humiliating, cruel, unfair to the wives, it dooms them to sexual celibacy and emotional solitude at a very young age and for the rest of their lives. It also sets up fearful rivalries among the half-brothers of different mothers who have lifelong quarrels over their inheritances."

When he was being Eastern, Ali would say: "Don't be a silly American. You say you're a thinker, God knows, you're always reading, and I therefore expect more understanding and broadmindedness from you. Polygamy tries to give men what they need so that they will treat their wives and first children in a civilized way. In the West, men are serial polygamists. They leave their first wives and set of children without looking back. Here, we do not like the earlier wives to be abandoned, impoverished, and ripped from their social identities. If she is a good Muslim wife, accepts and obeys her husband's wishes, he will support her forever, she will always have her children near her which is all that matters to a woman, her world will remain whole."

When he was being Western, Ali would say, "Our country is not ready for personal freedoms. That's why I'm needed here, to help bring my poor countrymen into the twentieth century. It's my destiny and I need you to help me. Don't leave."

As to the burqa, my Western husband would say: "You are too impatient about this damn *chadari*.[1] Afghan women are not stupid. Give them some time. They will, in time, probably all adopt the more Western, freeing clothing."

---

1 The *chadari* is also known as the burqa. It is a covering worn by Afghan women.

But Eastern Ali tried to justify the burqa in other ways. He said: "The country is dusty and sometimes dangerous and a woman is better protected in many ways by the *chadari*. Anyway, country women do not wear *chadaris* when they farm. This is largely a phenomenon of the city and anyway it's dying out." This was not exactly true. Afghan country-women almost immediately turned their faces to the nearest available wall whenever a man to whom they were not related walked by. They tended to cover their heads and faces with their scarves.

We lived with Ali's oldest brother Abdullah, his wife Rabiah, and their two children, who all shared a home with my mother-in-law Aishah, or "Beebee Jan" (Dear Lady). Agha Jan had not lived with Bee-bee Jan for a very long time.

My life was that of an upper class Afghan woman. My experience was similar to—but hardly as constrained as—that which an increasing number of Arab and Muslim women face today. In this first decade of the twenty-first century, women living in Islamic societies are being forced back in time, re-veiled, more closely monitored, and more savagely punished than they were in the 1960s. That said, I had never expected my freedom and privacy to be so curtailed.

In Afghanistan, a few hundred wealthy families lived by European standards. Everyone else lived in a premodern style. And that's the way the king, his government, and the mullahs wanted it to remain. Western diplomats did not peg their foreign policies to how Afghanistan treated its women. Even before multicultural relativism kicked in, Western diplomats did not believe in "interfering."

The Afghanistan I knew was a prison, a feudal monarchy, and rank with fear, paranoia, and slavery. Individual Afghans were charming, funny, humane, tender, enchantingly courteous, and sometimes breath-takingly honest. Yet, their country was a bastion of illiteracy, poverty, and preventable disease. Women were subjected to domestic and psychological misery in the form of arranged marriages, polygamy, forced pregnancies, the *chadari*, domestic slavery and, of course, purdah (seclusion of women). Women led indoor lives and socialized only with other women. Most women were barely educated.

In Kabul, I met other foreign wives who loved having servants but whose own freedom had been curtailed. Some European wives, who had come in the late 1940s and early 1950s had converted to Islam and wore The Thing, as I called the cloaking *chadari*. Each had been warned, as had I, that whatever they did would become known, that there were eyes everywhere, and that their actions could endanger their families and themselves.

Afghans mistrusted foreign wives. Once, I saw an Afghan husband fly into a rage when his foreign wife not only wore a Western swimsuit to a swimming party—but actually plunged into the pool. The men expected to be the only ones who would swim; their wives were meant to chat and sip fruit drinks.

The concept of privacy is a Western one. When I would leave the common sitting room in order to read quietly in my own bedroom, all the women and children would follow me. They'd ask: "Are you unhappy?" No one spent any time alone. To do so was an insult to the family. The idea that a woman might be an avid reader of books and a thinker was too foreign to comprehend.

Like everyone else, Ali was under permanent surveillance. His career and livelihood depended upon being an obedient Afghan son and subject. How he treated me was crucial. He had to prove that his relationship to women was every bit as Afghan as any other man's; perhaps more so, since he had arranged his own marriage to a foreigner.

OUT AND ABOUT IN KABUL

After two weeks of marathon tea-drinking and pistachio-eating, my polite smile was stuck to my face. I could not understand what people were saying, I was bored, I wanted to get out on my own and see Kabul, visit the markets and the museum, and see the mountains closer-up. I was under a very polite form of house arrest. "It's not done," "People will talk," "Tell me what you need and I'll get it for you," were some of Ali's responses. And so, I began to "escape" from the house.

I never put on the headscarves and long coats and gloves pointedly left for me atop my bedroom bureau. I would take a deep breath, go out, and stride at a brisk, American pace. Always, a female relative or servant would run after me, bearing the scarves. I would smile, shake my head "no," and keep on going. Of course, I was also followed by a slow-moving family Mercedes. The driver would call out: "Madame, please get inside. We are worried that you will hurt yourself."

Sometimes, I'd walk faster, or I'd take a bus or a *gaudi*, a horse-drawn painted cart. The buses were quite colorful except inside, fully sheeted women sat apart from the men—literally at the back of the bus. The first time I saw this, I laughed out loud in disbelief and nervousness. In any event, as women moved onto the bus, men would jostle them, and make sneering remarks I could not understand.

My family was right. They knew their country. Barefaced and alone, I looked like an "uppity" Afghan woman and was thus fair game for catcalls, propositions, interminable questions, rough advances. Men would push themselves against me, knock me around, laugh, joke. But, I could easily have been kidnapped and held for ransom, taken to a cave, kept there for days, raped, then returned. Ali finally exploded at me and told me that this exact scenario had happened to the wife of an Afghan minister who had killed himself afterwards.

I had to be brought to heel. Ali's manhood and future depended upon this. A male servant would prevent me from going out. The family would call Ali and he would call me to yell, threaten, plead, or shame. I presented myself at the American embassy.

"I want to go home. I'm an American citizen," I said.

"Where is your passport?" The marine guard would ask.

"They took it away from me when our plane landed. But, they told me that I'd get it back."

Each time, the Marines would escort me back home. They told me that as the "wife of an Afghan national," I was no longer an American citizen entitled to American protection.

I did, on occasion, get to speak with diplomats. Not a single foreign voice was heard protesting the condition of women. The Western media didn't care about what Afghans did to one another, or what men did to "their" women. Gin-soaked diplomats told me that it would be "immoral" to preach to Afghans about their tribal violence or their oppression of women; these were sovereign, sacred, local customs. One American diplomat put it this way: "We can't impose our moral or cultural values on these people. We can't ask them about their system of government or justice, their treatment of women, their servants, their jails. These are very sensitive, very touchy, very proud men who happen to own a piece of land that's important to us. If we aren't careful, their kids would be learning Russian—or Chinese—instead of English and German. You've got to remember, we're guests here, not conquerors."

I was under house arrest in the tenth century. I had no freedom of movement, nothing with which to occupy myself. I was supposed to accept this.

Ali knew he was losing me. We fought bitterly every single night. Was he trying to make me pregnant so that I'd have to stay? I was afraid to go to bed. His eldest sister, Soraya, offered to sleep with me in our bedroom—an act of courage and kindness that I have never forgotten. She must have known what was going on.

28

Yes, my husband "loved" me and wanted to protect me, but I was, after all, a woman, which meant that he believed he owned me, and that his honor consisted of his ability to control me. Ali was also locked into a power struggle with his father and with his culture. I was the symbol of his freedom and independence, a reminder of his life lived apart. He did not want to lose such a valuable symbol. If I became pregnant, I would have to stay. His father would be forced to stop making things so hard for us.

MY ESCAPE

I devoted all my waking time to planning an escape. I gave up on the American embassy. I stopped confiding in Ali. I began to contact foreign wives, most of whom would not or could not help me. I could only meet people through Ali or through a relative. I was not allowed to talk privately to anyone. All the public tea-houses were for men-only. I could not drift in and strike up a conversation with a man.

I finally found a foreign wife who agreed to help me. She was the German-born second wife of the ex-mayor of Kabul. She promised to obtain a passport for me. I had agreed to reimburse her the moment I got home. Now, I only had to choose a flight and book a seat.

And then, I fainted. I had come down with hepatitis. I learned later that Beebee Jan had ordered the servants to stop boiling my water and washing my vegetables. Some Afghans seemed to enjoy the spectacle of Westerners succumbing to such illnesses; they took it as proof of foreign "weakness." I was finally taken to the new hospital and accompanied by at least ten family members. The American doctor said:

"Honey, you are very sick and you have to get out of here. Will they let you go? If you are strong enough to sit up and walk a bit, get on a plane, go home."

He gave me a pair of dark glasses to hide my jaundiced eyes from the flight attendants. And, he prescribed intravenous infusions of vitamins and nutrients. He sent a nurse to the house.

And then, Beebee Jan tried to pull out the IV and all hell broke loose. I called Agha Jan and begged him to come over. He was the Master of the Universe as far as his family was concerned.

He came. First, he prayed "for my recovery." Then, he asked everyone else to leave, after which he spoon-fed me milk custard. He was tender towards me; only afterwards did I understand that he could afford to be. My illness and probable departure meant that he had won the battle

29

with Ali. Perhaps he did not want a dead American daughter-in-law on his hands either. And, he'd be glad to see me gone. I only spelled trouble for his family, any foreign wife would, especially one who had tried to escape so many times.

"I know about your little plan with the German woman," he quietly said. "I think it will be best if you leave with our approval on an Afghan passport which I have obtained for you. You have been granted a six-month visa for "reasons of health."

And he gave it to me on the spot. He also handed me a plane ticket. "We will see you off. It is better this way."

Ali raged and swore—and begged me to stay but I remained adamant.

Thirty relatives dutifully came to see me off. Kabul was hidden in snow. I was booked on an Aeroflot flight to Moscow. The minute that plane took off a fierce joy seized me by the throat and would not let go. I was both jaundiced and pregnant. Had Ali discovered this while I was still in Afghanistan, I would never have been allowed to leave. Given my medical condition, it would have been my death sentence.

MY FEMINIST AWAKENING

I had experienced gender apartheid long before the Taliban made it headline news. I came to understand that once an American woman marries a Muslim, and lives in a Muslim country, she is no longer a citizen of any country. Never again could I romanticize foreign places or peoples in the Third World.

Once a Western woman marries a Muslim and lives with him in his native land, she is no longer entitled to the rights she once enjoyed. Only military mercenaries can rescue her. I have since heard many stories about Western women who have married Muslim men in Europe and America but whose children were then kidnapped by their fathers and kept forever after in countries such as Saudi Arabia,[2] Jordan, Egypt, Pakistan and Iran. The mothers were usually permitted no contact.

Westerners do not understand that Eastern men can blend into the West with ease while still remaining Eastern at their core. They can "pass" for one of us but, upon returning home, can also assume their original ways of being. Some may call this schizophrenic; others might see this as duplicitous. From a Muslim man's point of view, it is neither.

2 See, for example, "U.S. Department of State, Marriage to Saudis," *Middle East Quarterly*, Winter 2003, pp. 74-81.

It is merely Realpolitik. The transparency and seeming lack of guile that characterizes many ordinary Westerners make us seem childlike and stupid to those with multiple cultural personalities.

A woman dares not forget such lessons—not if she manages to survive and escape. What happened to me in Afghanistan must also be taken as a cautionary tale of what can happen when one romanticizes the "primitive" East.

Did Ali really think that I would be able to adjust to a medieval, Islamic way of life? Or that his family would ever have accepted a Jewish-American love-bride?

There are only two answers possible. Either he was not thinking or he viewed me as a woman, which meant that I did not exist in my own right, that I was destined to please and obey him and that nothing else was really important. He certainly helped shape the feminist that I was to become.

When I returned to the United States, there were few feminist stirrings. However, within seven years, I became a leader of America's Second Wave feminist movement. In 1967, I became active in the National Organization for Women, as well as in various feminist consciousness-raising groups and campaigns. In 1969, I pioneered women's studies classes for credit, cofounded the Association for Women in Psychology, and began delivering feminist lectures. In 1970, at the annual American Psychological Association meeting, I demanded one million dollars in "reparations" for having diagnostically pathologized, dangerously tranquilized, institutionalized—and then neglected women who were victims of violence and oppression. I also began work on my first book, *Women and Madness*,[3] which became a classic feminist text.

Firsthand experience of life under Islam as a woman held captive in Kabul has shaped the kind of feminist I became and have remained— one who is not politically "correct" or a multi-cultural relativist. By seeing how women interacted with men and then with each other, I learned how incredibly servile oppressed peoples could be and how deadly the oppressed could be toward each other. Beebee Jan was cruel to her female servants. She beat her elderly personal servant and verbally humiliated our young and pregnant housemaid. It was an observation that stayed with me.

While it has become increasingly popular, I never could accept cultural relativism. Instead, what I experienced in Afghanistan as a woman taught me the necessity of applying a single standard of human

3 New York: Doubleday, 1972.

rights, not one tailored to each culture.

In recent years, I fear that Western "progressives" have refused to understand how Islamism endangers Western values and lives, beginning with our commitment to women's rights and human rights. The jihadists who are beheading civilians, stoning Muslim women to death, jailing Muslim dissidents, and bombing civilians on every continent are now moving among us both in the East and in the West. While some feminist leaders and groups have publicized the atrocities against women in the Islamic world, they have not tied them to any foreign policy. Women's studies programs should have been the first to sound the alarm. They did not. More than four decades after I was a virtual prisoner in Afghanistan, I realize how far the Western feminist movement has to go.

Middle East Quarterly
12/31/05

- 2 -

The Brownshirts of Our Time

On Saturday evening, November 8, 2003, the eve of Kristall-nacht, I addressed a feminist "networking" conference of mainly African-American and Hispanic-American womanists at Barnard College. The conference was described as a grassroots, multi-cultural, multi-generational and multi-disciplinary organization for women in the arts. The women ranged in age from 20-65 and were dressed in corporate business suits, ever-colorful African/ethnic attire, youthful jeans.

Booths were arranged in a semi-circle—it was as if the panels and performances were taking place in an African marketplace. The conference was closed to men--but one of the organizers made a split second decision to allow my adult son in and seated him by himself at the very back of the room on a chair set apart. Growing up in a feminist household, he was used to this. Privately, we both sighed and wondered when feminist men would finally be welcome at a feminist conference.

I doubt that the organizers of this conference knew anything of my background but they were more than welcoming. They had real class and great soul. For example, when I'd explained that I was just in the midst of both a major move into Manhattan and a book tour, one organizer said: "We understand what it's like when a woman is jammed up doing too much. We'll love you anyway. You can let us know at the last minute." She was so damn upbeat and understanding that I decided I'd come no matter what.

A few days before the conference I had the following conversation with one of the organizers. She asked me what my most recent book was and I told her it was *The New Anti-Semitism*. I explained that Jew-hatred was a form of racism—only it was not being treated as such by anti-rac-

33

ist "politically correct" people. The organizer did not say: "I don't agree with you" nor did she say: "This won't play well to our constituency." She only said: "We need you to explain the ways in which women sabotage each other and remain divided so that we can understand and overcome it in order to come together. We need you to talk about your book *Woman's Inhumanity to Woman.* Your speech will precede our big Unity panel."

When I arrived, performers were rapping and singing and dancing and the energy was fabulous. They were running late and I waited patiently and happily. I whispered to my son: "There's still a whole world out there. And in ways, it's quite wonderful. Perhaps I have become too obsessed with The Jewish Cause, with Israel. Maybe I need to remember that I am also connected to more than one world."

As I spoke, the women in the audience sighed, cheered, applauded, nodded in agreement, laughed, groaned, nudged each other—it was a half hour of good vibes.

And then my first questioner blew it all to Hell. All it took was The Question and it only required one Questioner. I could not see who was speaking. A disembodied voice demanded to know where I stood on the question of the women of Palestine. Her tone was forceful, hostile, relentless, and prepared. I could have said: "The organizers have specifically asked me not to address such questions." I did not say that. I could also have said: "I am concerned with the women of Palestine but I am more concerned with the women of Rwanda, Bosnia, Guatemala, who have all been gang-raped by soldiers who used rape as a weapon of war; I am also concerned with the poverty and homelessness of women right here in America—and with the women of Israel who are being blown up in buses, at cafes, in their own bedrooms." I did not say this.

Instead, I took a deep breath and said that I did not respect people who hijacked airplanes or hijacked conferences or who, at this very moment, were trying to hijack this lecture. I pointed out that the subject of my talk was not Israel or Palestine. I did not want us to lose our focus. My Questioner grew even more hostile and demanding. "Tell this audience what you said on WBAI. I heard you on that program." Clearly, she wanted to "unmask" me before this audience as a Jew-lover and an Israel-defender.

I took the question head-on. "If you're really asking about apartheid, let me talk about it. Contrary to myth and propaganda, Israel is not an apartheid state. The largest practioner of apartheid in the world is Islam which practices both gender and religious apartheid. In terms of

34

gender apartheid, Palestinian women—and all women who live under Islam—are oppressed by "honor" killings, in which girls and women are then killed by family members for the sake of restoring the family "honor;" forced veiling, segregation, stonings to death for alleged adultery, seclusion/sequestration, female genital mutilation, polygamy, outright slavery, sexual slavery.

"Islam also specializes in religious apartheid as well. All non-Muslims (Christians, including Maronites and Melkites, Greek Orthodox, Catholics and Protestants, Jews, Assyrians, Hindus, Zoroastrians, Ba'hai, animists) have historically been viewed and treated as subhumans who must either convert to Islam or be mercilessly taxed, beaten, jailed, murdered, or exiled. The latest al-Qaeda attack in Saudi Arabia was primarily directed against Lebanese Christians and Americans.

"Today, the entire Middle East is *judenrein*, there are no Jews left in 22 Arab countries. And, the Arab leadership has backed the PLO strategy in which the 23rd state—Israel—remains under constant and perilous siege. Since 1948-1956, Arab Jews were forced to flee Arab Islamic lands. Most are living in Israel, the only Middle Eastern state in which Jews are allowed to live. Jews cannot become citizens of Jordan, Egypt, or Saudi Arabia, for example and yet no one accuses those nations of apartheid."

I told the truth. Clearly, they had not heard it before. The audience collectively gasped. Then, people went a little crazy.

Someone muttered darkly, coarsely, in a near-growl: "What about the humiliation at the checkpoints? What about the fence?" As if checkpoints and fences are the same as being killed by your brother or father or, most recently, in Ramallah, by your mother. I asked the audience if they thought that being detained at a checkpoint was really the same as having your clitoris sliced off, the same as being stoned to death for alleged adultery. The only response I got was from the first questioner who demanded that I denounce Ariel Sharon—but not Yasir Arafat—as a murderer.

I absolutely refused to do so.

The lightning rod of "Palestine" was enough to turn a very friendly audience quite hostile and a bit unhinged. Two or three women proceeded to ask aggressive questions in which they tried to get me to say that I had somehow "disrespected" poor women in my remarks.

As I left the podium, a young African-American woman stopped me to say that I'd "hurt" her by how I had "disrespected" a "brown" woman. "What brown woman?" I asked. "Your first questioner was a brown woman," she said, "and so are Palestinian women." I said: "Jewish women, especially in Israel also come in many colors including brown and black." She stopped me. "But you're a white Jew." As if this was proof of a crime.

I did not bother to tell her that without my glasses I could not see the face or color of a questioner so far away, that my answer to the question would have been the same no matter what color the questioner happened to be.

As I was trying to leave, one woman, who said her name was "Lupe," (she was dressed in a button-festooned serape, and had a cross tattooed between her eyebrows) loped after me and continued to demand that I deal with the Palestine question. She kept trying to get at me physically. One of the organizers kept putting her own body between Lupe and me. Lupe behaved like a trained operative, her rage was legitimized, empowered, by her politics.

The three young African-American women who had invited me were VERY supportive of me, they hugged me and thanked me for coming and looked rather embarrassed about what had happened.

What's important is this: Not one of them tried to stop what was happening, not one stood up and said: "Something good has just turned ugly and we must not permit this to happen." Thus, the "good" people did nothing to disperse the hostility or to address the issues. Perhaps they were simply unprepared on the issues; perhaps they agreed with the view that Israel is an apartheid state and that anyone who would dare defend it deserved to be treated as a traitor. Perhaps they simply lacked the courage to stand up to the fundamentalists in their midst.

Afterwards, my son told me that he was on his feet the minute The Questioner spoke and although I could not see him either, I was glad to know that he was in the room. Things could easily have turned much uglier. (By the way: Talk about gender apartheid! The conference confined him to his men-only single chair section.)

It seemed that The Questioner had at least one, and possibly two henchwoman with her. Clearly, she wanted to "get" the pro-Israel white Jew.

I reflected on my life's work against racism. For example, in 1963, I joined The Northern Student Movement and tutored Harlem students. This was the Northern branch of the civil rights movement. In the late 1960s, I was involved with both the Young Lords and the Black Panthers. I marched outside the Women's House of Detention when they jailed Angela Davis. I was involved in the Inez Garcia case and have written extensively about the cases of both Joanne Little and Yvonne Wanrow, two women of color who, like Garcia, had killed (white) men in self-defense. In the mid-70s, I interviewed Jews from India, Iran, Afghanistan, and North Africa, and Jews who had fled Arab lands about "cultural" or "ethnic" racism in Israel. By the early 1970s, I also began organizing against Jew-hatred on the left and among feminists in America. Over the years, I have lectured on the complexities of both racism and sexism in the Caribbean, Europe, the Middle East, and in Japan.

For nearly 30 years, I taught working-class and students of color at a public university. I admired and loved them and was sometimes able to help them in ways that changed their views and their lives.

Here's what's sad. Clearly, my speech touched hearts and minds; there was room for common ground and for civilized discourse. But not once the word "Palestine" was uttered, not when "Palestine" is seen as a symbol for every downtrodden group of color who are "resisting" the racist-imperialist American and Zionist Empires. Once the "Palestine" litmus test of political respectability was raised, everyone responded on cue, as if brainwashed. It immediately became a "white" versus "brown" thing, an "oppressed versus oppressor" thing.

These are the Brownshirts of our time. The fact that they are women of color, womanists/feminists is all the more chilling and tragic. And unbelievable. And to me: Practically unbearable.

Afterwards, my son, ever-wise, said: "Well mom, you have your answer. The Jew-haters will never allow you into their wider, wonderful world. You can't go back."

I should have seen this coming.

I first began to encounter Jew-hatred on the left in the late 1960's, especially after Israel successfully defended itself in the 1967 war. I spoke out about this right away and have never stopped doing so. All throughout the 1970's, I brought journalists and ideologues to Israel and courted countless celebrity signatures to oppose the resolutions equating Zionism with racism. I also worked for the United Nations, attended the Copenhagen conference, and was an eyewitness-participant in the Russian-P.L.O.-Arab-U.N. orchestrated orgy against Israel in which Israel was demonized as the whipping girl of the world.

Today, these same ideologues and their intellectual descendants are still not thundering against gender apartheid in the Islamic world; they are thundering against Israel as the apartheid state. Some of them are also wonderfully progressive Jews.

Thus, feminists and leftists, including Jews, are more concerned with the so-called occupation of Palestine than with the occupation of women's bodies, worldwide.

For example, a feminist rabbi recently had a representative of the P.L.O. address her congregation on Yom Kippur. Another Jewish feminist recently gave a speech about the future of Jewish feminism in which she said that "Jewish feminism would have no future if the Palestinians did not have a state and if Israel did not redress the wrongs done to the Palestinians."

An Israeli Jewish feminist rebuked me when I called for "equal compassion for the Israeli Jewish civilian victims of Islamist terrorism." She accused me of betraying the cause of both peace and women by calling for *rachmones* for other Jews. (Who could make this up?) An Israeli Jewish feminist psychiatrist described the Israelis as "batterers" and the Palestinians as "battered women."

A leading feminist described Israelis as the "Johns and pimps" and the Palestinians as the "prostituted women of the world."

Such condemnation by metaphor is what Jews, Israel and America have been suffering both in the media and in Western academia. Intellectuals have described Israelis as "worse than Nazis." In my view, this is a new form of Holocaust denial.

Let me be clear. There was no physical rioting at Barnard. I was not in physical danger—although toward the end even the otherwise passive organizers started to surround me to protect me; they gently hustled me out.

What happened at the conference was important for this reason: I was there as an authority, a leader. The audience was grooving on every word I said. But once I was "unmasked" as a Jew-lover and an Israel-defender, I was instantly seen as a traitor. There was no reserve of trust or respect toward me—not after I'd crossed over this "politically correct" line.

I hope this was an isolated instance. I fear it was not. Thus, if Jewish and non-Jewish educators were to speak out for Israel and for Judaism on campus, at rallies, they may risk just this kind of mistreatment at the hands of their peers and students. In fact, many professors and students have written to me and said that this is indeed the case.

We must create pockets of civility in which people can stand up to the Big Lies (the Jews control Wall Street, the media, the United States government; they killed Jesus and are now perpetrating a Holocaust on the Palestinians). We must be able to speak the truth—especially on college campuses and at conferences—without being mocked, scorned, silenced and intimidated.

FrontPage Magazine
11/19/03

- 3 -

Forced Female Suicide

Are Palestinian female suicide bombers active members of a Death Cult, or unwilling participants in it? Are they religious fanatics, Western-style revolutionaries, or clinically depressed human beings facing No Exit lives? Have they been indoctrinated and brainwashed by master seducers or have they been brutally forced into it?

These are necessary questions to ask when contemplating the emergence of a new female form of suicide bomber. Certainly, some female Palestinian suicide bombers have "freely" chosen the murderous martyr's path: most likely, such women have had close male relatives who have died in the war that the Palestinians have declared against the Israelis.

But evidence also suggests that the Palestinians have created yet another form of Arab honor killing. For some time now, reports have reached my desk about Palestinian girls and women being recruited, seduced, and trapped, by older male terrorists in very woman-specific ways.

For example, I have been told that in one instance, the chosen Palestinian girl was unmarried and pregnant. She was offered the chance to "cleanse" her honor by blowing herself and Jews up. Her family spirited her out of the West Bank to safety in Europe. I have also been told that some Palestinian masters of mass murder have themselves had affairs with vulnerable young Palestinian girls in order to compromise their "honor" and to season them, pimp-style, for martyrdom. Hard facts are hard to come by, anecdotes abound.

Journalist Barbara Victor, the author of the recent book about Palestinian female suicide bombers, *Army of Roses*, and playwright Glyn

40

O'Malley, whose play, *Paradise*, is on the same subject, have both dealt with some of the earliest Palestinian female suicide bombers whose lives were stunted by oppression.

Wafa Idris, the first Palestinian suicide bomber, was probably in a clinical depression. Her first and only child had been a stillborn and, as a result, she was now sterile. Her husband, who was also her first cousin, had divorced her over this and had already taken a second wife. She was mocked by family and friends and she understood that she had no future in Palestinian society. As a divorced and infertile woman, she was doubly "tainted." Her bleak prospects—due to Islamic and Palestinian misogyny and not to the Israeli-Palestinian conflict—were used to trap her into redeeming her dishonor by becoming a murdering martyr.

We cannot say that these women (or, for that matter, their male counterparts) are making "free" choices. No one is offering them the presidency of their country, an all-paid scholarship to a prestigious university—or, as a third choice, the opportunity to kill and die at a tender age. Their choices are "forced." They are probably not political extremists or revolutionaries in the Western sense. They have grown up in a tribal, Islamic society in which women are expected to sacrifice themselves in terrible and medieval ways.

Most recently, the case of Reem al-Riyashi suggests a similar and horrifying scenario. Several Israeli sources have discovered that this young mother of two very young children "was forced to carry out the suicide attack as punishment for cheating on her husband." Allegedly, al-Riyashi's husband was a Hamas activist and her lover was a Hamas operative who had carried out the love affair with the express purpose of recruiting her. According to the British *Sunday Times*, al-Riyashi's husband himself drove her to the border crossing.

This is unbelievable—and tragic. Had these men threatened to kill her children if she refused this mission? I would not be surprised.

Whatever the tragic circumstances, it is important to understand that the coercion of women by men to become suicide bombers is not an aberration in the Middle East. Myth aside, Islam is the largest and most savage practitioner of religious and gender apartheid on the planet. If you attend a college in the Western world, you'd have no way of knowing this—perhaps this is because many Western multi-cultural ideologues have muted their criticism of Islamic misogyny in order to propagandize for the victory of the Palestinians over the Zionists.

It is this context that compels us to stop romanticizing these homicide bombers—and presenting them as heroes.

41

I understand what the Israeli ambassador to Sweden felt when he saw the exhibit that glorified yet another Palestinian female suicide bomber: Hanadi Jaradat, who killed 22 innocent Israeli civilians, both Christian Arabs and Jews. Jaradat's smiling, serene face floated above a pool of civilian blood. The artwork had been done by an expatriate Israeli artist and installed at the entrance to a building that is to house an upcoming conference against genocide. The Swedes had promised the Israelis that the Middle East conflict was not going to be part of the conference.

But this art exhibit found a way to bring the Middle East conflict into the conference—in a way that justified and glorified homicidal/genocidal suicide bombers who, upon closer inspection, may be committing a "forced" suicide as their only way out.

FrontPage Magazine
1/22/04

- 4 -
The Psychoanalytic Roots of Islamic Terrorism

I n the ongoing battle for Fallujah, terrorists are using women and children as human shields against American soldiers. On April 27, 2004, in Jerusalem, Hamas used a Palestinian human bomb to kill two alleged Palestinian "collaborators." On April 28, 2004, even as UN envoy, Lakhdar Brahimi, was busy characterizing Israeli policy as the "great poison in the region," Jordanian police arrested al-Qaeda operatives who were quite literally trying to launch a chemical poison attack that might have killed 80,000 Jordanians and Americans. And, on May 1, 2004, in Gaza, Palestinian gunmen shot and killed a Jewish woman who was eight-months pregnant together with her four young daughters.

Despite enormous and continuing denial on the part of left and liberal ideologues and the media, we are facing an exceedingly pathological strain of Islamofascist terrorism. So a crucial question must be asked: from a psychological point of view, what kind of culture produces human bombs, glorifies mass murderers, and supports humiliation-based revenge?

According to Minnesota based psychoanalyst and Arabist, Dr. Nancy Kobrin, it is a culture in which shame and honor play decisive roles and in which the debasement of women is paramount. In an utterly fascinating and as-yet unpublished book, which I will be introducing, *The Sheik's New Clothes: the Psychoanalytic Roots of Islamic Suicide Terrorism*, Kobrin, and her Israeli co-author, counter-terrorism expert Yoram Schweitzer, describe barbarous family and clan dynamics in

43

which children, both boys and girls, are orally and anally raped by male relatives; infant males are sometimes sadistically over-stimulated or "soothed" by being masturbated; boys between the ages of 7-12 are publicly and traumatically circumcised; many girls are clitoridectomized; and women are seen as the source of all shame and dishonor and treated accordingly: very, very badly.

According to Dr. Kobrin, "The little girl lives her life under a communal death threat—the honor killing." Both male and female infants and children are brought up by mothers who are debased and traumatized women. As such, all children are forever psychologically "contaminated" by the humiliated yet all-powerful mother. Arab and Muslim boys must disassociate themselves from her in spectacularly savage ways. But, on a deep unconscious level, they may also wish to remain merged with the source of contamination—a conflict that suicide bombers both act out and resolve when they manfully kill, but also merge their blood eternally with that of their presumably most hated enemies, the Israeli Jews. In Kobrin's view, the Israeli Jews may actually function as substitutes or scapegoats for an even more primal, hated/ loved enemy: Woman.

Widespread child sexual abuse leads to paranoid, highly traumatized, and revenge-seeking adults. Based on my own experience in Afghanistan (a non-Arab, Muslim culture), a polygamous, patriarchal culture also leads to an infernal, fraternal competition for paternal favor and inheritance. It is brother against brother, full brothers against half-brothers, full and half brothers against first cousins—and thus, can entire families and clans remain locked in revenge-fueled mortal combat for generations.

Clearly, only the elevation of women can begin to change such dynamics.

Yesterday, further confirmation of Dr. Kobrin's thesis arrived at my door. The charming Walid Shoebat, a self-described ex-PLO terrorist, came to visit. He has been speaking about his renunciation of terrorism and conversion to evangelical Christianity. Shoebat has been touring the country speaking out for Israel and against the "occupation of Palestinian minds with Jew-hatred." Unlike the human bombs, Shoebat "merged" with his American-born mother by finally rescuing her from years of captivity and domestic abuse in Bethlehem/Beit Sahur. He also rescued his father, the man who imprisoned and abused her.

Shoebat confirmed the widespread sexual abuse of both boys and girls in Palestinian society. "It is a strange society. Homosexuality is forbidden but if you're the penetrator, not the penetrated, it's okay." He is describing prison sexuality. "If you're a teenage boy with no hair on your legs other boys your age will pinch your butt and tease you. Once, I saw a class of clothed teenage boys sexualize their gymnastics exercizes. And once, on a hiking trip, I saw a line of shepherd boys waiting for their turn to sodomize a five year old boy. It was unbelievable."

Shoebat's father also told him stories about starving Arab men who would barter sex for meat from Iraqi soldiers. According to Shoebat, teenage boys prey upon younger children; older male relatives prey upon pre-adolescent and adolescent boys and girls. They do not have intercourse with the girls since this would render them un-marriageable and bring shame upon their families. I heard many stories in both Afghanistan and Iran about the male preference for anal sex, even within marriage, either as a form of birth control or as a preferred homosexual practice.

Most Arabs and Muslims will deny that this is so. They will attack westerners who say so as "orientalists, colonialists, racists." Western intellectuals will agree with them. They have been well indoctrinated by—no, western academics were the ones who first glorified the work of the late Edward W. Said who, in my opinion, published his master work, *Orientalism*, in 1978 as a way of denying feminist ideas and refocusing academic attention away from women and onto brown, Muslim, Arab men as the truest victims of oppression. Neat trick.

Shoebat's grandfather was the Muktar of his village. Nevertheless, eleven to fifteen people lived cramped into two rooms with a huge balcony, a courtyard, and an outhouse. Once, when Shoebat's American-born Christian mother, (she was forced to convert to Islam), upended a backgammon board in front of his father Achmed's friends, Achmed took a hammer and cracked her skull. Shoebat, her youngest child, took her hand and walked with her to the nearest church where the nuns sewed up her head. There were no hospitals. Whenever his mother tried to escape, (always together with her three children) the Shoebat men would find and re-kidnap her, then subject her to further punishment.

The male sexual abuse of female children exists everywhere; it is one of the main means of traumatizing and shaming women into obedience and rendering them incapable of resistance or rebellion. However, the male sexual abuse of male children—denied, never admitted—may work differently and may turn boys into predatory, pedophilic men. Also, among Arabs and Muslims, revenge killings are uniquely prevalent.

Shoebat told me several extraordinary stories which illustrate Palestinian and Arab Middle Eastern mentality. One of his paternal uncles was supposedly having an affair with a married woman whose husband was the chief of police. His revenge consisted of throwing live grenades at Shoebat's family home. The home bore the unrepaired damage for years. The outraged husband wanted to not only kill his wife's lover but his entire family. "My father and his immediate family all had to die because of what his brother did."

Shoebat asked me how I would resolve this feud-unto-death. I foundered. Bride-exchange sacrifice? Blood money? I could not come up with the ingenious plan that Shoebat's uncle crafted—a plan which may also shed light, in part, upon the nature of the Arab war against the Jews. He persuaded the village that they had to attack, pogrom-style, a nearby Jewish community (Ramat Rachel). Once the Israelis opened fire in self-defense, most of the Arabs fled. However, the Arab attack upon the Jews provided cover for what his uncle had to do: He shot his lover's husband in the back. When the Israelis, as they always did, allowed the Arabs to safely retrieve their dead, his uncle proclaimed his rival a "shahid" and buried him in his bloody clothing. A "shahid" enters heaven more quickly, clothed in his own blood.

This characterizes an Arab way of thinking. From here, it is easy to create the kinds of doctored footage and photo-opportunity journalism that has dominated this latest Intifada against the Jews. It is also a way of thinking that the liberal western media does not comprehend.

FrontPage Magazine
5/03/04

- 5 -

"Gender Cleansing" in the Sudan

The images from the Sudan are horrific: Wounded, starving, diseased adults, skeletal, dying infants. Some people have referred to this as "ethnic cleansing." Indeed, an estimated two million black African Christians, Muslims, and animists have been massacred by ethnic Arab Muslims over the last 21 years. Today, an estimated 1.2 million people have been internally displaced, and 170,000 have fled across the border into Chad. At least 30,000 human beings have been massacred by the state-sanctioned Janjaweed ("men on horses") in the last six months.

The United Nations did nothing during this time except condemn Israel for crimes it did not commit. The French? They are too busy condemning Ariel Sharon to notice a real human rights atrocity. Thus, the French continue to oppose UN sanctions against the Sudan. To their credit, the American House and Senate have just passed a bi-partisan resolution that defines the massacres as "genocide."

Still, although we are overwhelmed with images of suffering, one image is missing. We have no photos of what I shall describe as "gender cleansing." The systematic use of repeated, public, gang rape as a weapon of war cannot be captured in a single photo.

According to Amnesty International, eyewitness-survivors have seen girls as young as eight repeatedly gang-raped; their captors break both their arms and their legs when they try to escape. Women and children have described being kidnapped and kept as domestic and sexual slaves, and of being gang-raped every night in captivity.

The damage to a woman's self-esteem and sanity is impossible to calculate. Suicide, life-long anxiety, depression, and nightmares are among the many symptoms. To rub salt into the wound, Amnesty International reports that Janjaweed women sing (!!) to cheer their men on when they rape other women; they also utter racial insults to the women being raped.

Those feminists who immediately condemned Lyndie England and the American military as "depraved" in the matter of the alleged torture or humiliation of Iraqi male prisoners in Abu Ghraib are, so far, noticeably silent. Mind you: I am only calling for even-handedness; I am not defending torture or prisoner abuse.

As the author of *Woman's Inhumanity to Woman*, I am not surprised by the behavior of the Janjaweed women—although their hard-heartedness is rather breathtaking. Like men, women also internalize sexist values and are capable of both cruelty and compassion. Like men, many women cling to the status quo, even to one that demeans them.

While rape has been used as a weapon, not merely as a spoil of war, before, most notably in Algeria, Bosnia, and Rwanda, there is something uniquely sadistic going on in Sudan. Here's what is: The women who are being gang-raped by Arab Islamists are also women who have been genitally mutilated (either clitoridectomized or infibulated). These crude, mutilating "surgeries," often conducted by village women, result in tissue scaring and loss of elasticity. (Infibulation involves leaving only a small opening for urination and menstruation. Normally, these women have to be cut open wide enough for intercourse when they marry).

Repeated rape must be excruciatingly painful and must cause severe physical and psychological damage. The rape victims (who are Muslims as well as Christians and animists), have been raised to view their genitalia as "unclean" and shameful. Tribal honor is bound up with female chastity—this is why rape as a tactic is being used to destroy not only the individual woman but also her entire social fabric. Many Sudanese women have been taught that sexual activity—including rape—is always the woman's fault. Some Sudanese tribes believe that a pregnancy cannot result from rape; thus, raped women who become pregnant will be suspected of having voluntary sex with the enemy; their families will never accept a baby born of rape.

Amnesty International believes that many raped women are not reporting their rapes. They fear their families will ostracize them; perhaps they also blame themselves for the shame they have brought on their families and tribes.

Honorably, the United States calls it genocide. The Sudan Campaign, A Coalition to Stop Genocide, Slavery, Starvation, and Religious Persecution has organized arrests and hunger strikes at the Sudanese

Embassy in Washington D. C.

But where are the leftists and feminists who are so quick to condemn both America and Israel for alleged "ethnic cleansing" and racism?

I'm on many feminist academic and activist listserv groups. During the last two months, the matter of the Sudan has not commanded much attention. What has? Defeating Bush, cosmetic surgery, discrimination against transgendered people, defeating Bush, gay marriage, abortion, defeating Bush.

Make no mistake. I am in favor of elective surgery and abortion, and against discrimination, but I am puzzled by the isolationism and self-involvement of activists who should be part of making a difference.

I understand that the situation in Sudan is politically and practically complicated. Technically, rebel groups did oppose the government which, in turn, set the Janjaweed militia loose on them. Can food and medicine be safely distributed without being siphoned off by corrupt warlords? Will sanctions only hurt the most vulnerable people? Will nothing short of a full-scale military invasion really stop the genocide and the "gender cleansing?" Dare America—which has been so defamed because of Afghanistan and Iraq—invade Sudan?

During the European Holocaust, people did not see the photos or receive reports of the genocide in process. In the matter of the Sudan, we cannot claim that "we did not know," or that "no one told us." We know. We've heard and seen everything. To do nothing renders us complicit in what is happening. Those who survive such torture in war are more haunted by what the presumably good people failed to do than they are by the criminals whose evil character is already well known to their victims.

May we never have to learn this from first-hand experience.

FrontPage Magazine
7/26/04

- 6 -

Gender Apartheid

In the fall of 2004 I found myself in conversation with a woman who in no way wished to offend or argue with me. Indeed, she assumed we stood on common ground (she was a feminist professor) and thus became agitated by my silence as she recited the usual litany: President Bush, not Bin Laden, is a terrorist; the war in Iraq is worse than the Vietnam war; America's reputation is ruined; we need to work in concert with the United Nations. I said nothing. Finally she blurted out, "But after what we did in Guatemala and all our other dirty doings in South America, you can't say we didn't deserve having it thrown back at us on 9/11. You do understand that America deserves being hated everywhere, don't you?"

I don't. I responded, "You can't possibly believe that Al Qaeda's jihadi terrorism is a form of retributive justice, can you?"

Ah, but she can and does. I tell this story to illustrate an important point.

She is not a bad woman; she is being a "good feminist." It gives me no pleasure, but someone must finally tell the truth about how feminists have failed their own ideals and their mandate to think both clearly and morally. Only an insider can do this, someone who cares deeply about feminist values and goals. I have been on the front lines for nearly 40 years, and I feel called upon to explain how many feminists—who should be first among freedom- and democracy-loving people—have become cowardly herd animals.

From the start, feminism has been unfairly, even viciously attacked. I do not want to do that here. The truth is that in less than 40 years a visionary feminism has managed to challenge, if not transform, world consciousness. Nevertheless, feminists are often perceived as marginal and irrelevant, and in some important ways the perception is accurate. Today the cause of justice for women around the world is as urgent as it has ever been.

The plight of both women and men in the Islamic world (and increasingly in Europe) requires a sober analysis of reality and a heroic response. World events have made feminism more important, yet at the same time feminism has lost much of its power. To my horror most Western academic and mainstream feminists have not focused on what I call gender apartheid in the Islamic world or on its steady penetration of Europe.

Islamic terrorists have declared jihad against the "infidel West" and against all those who yearn for freedom. Women in the Islamic world are treated like subhumans. Although some feminists have sounded the alarm about this, a much larger number have remained silent. Why have many of them misguidedly romanticized Islamist terrorists as freedom fighters and condemned both America and Israel as the real terrorists or as the root cause of terrorism?

In the name of multicultural correctness (all cultures are equal; formerly colonized cultures are more equal), the feminist academy and media appear to have all but abandoned vulnerable people—Muslims as well as Christians, Jews and Hindus—to the forces of Islamism.

A knee-jerk hatred for President Bush has all but blinded many feminists and progressives to the greater danger of Wahhabism, Salafist Islamism and terrorism. Because feminist academics and journalists are now so heavily influenced by leftist and post-colonial ways of thinking, many now believe that speaking out against head scarves (*hijabs*), face-veils (*niqabs*), chadors (*burqas*), arranged marriages, polygamy, forced pregnancies or female genital mutilations is either imperialist or Crusade-ist.

Post-modern ways of thinking have also led feminists to believe that confronting narratives on the academic page is as important and world-shattering as is confronting jihadists in the flesh and rescuing living beings from captivity.

I am disheartened by what has happened to feminism and by what I see as the new powerlessness of women. I did not foresee the extent to which feminists would, paradoxically, become both multicultural relativists and isolationists. Such cultural relativism is perhaps the greatest failing of the feminist establishment. Despite our opponents' fears that feminism would radicalize campuses and the world, most feminists refuse to take risky, real-world positions. In doing so, they have lost their individualism, radicalism and, potentially, some of their own freedom.

In an age when being entertained is confused with learning how to think and when books are not necessarily or primarily valued, feminist students and their teachers have increasingly become spectators at confessional theatrical events such as campus productions of *The Vagina Monologues*. I question whether what one learns as a function of public group catharsis is the same as what one learns from reading in solitude, listening to an expert lecture, and then participating in a focused and informed discussion or debate about the material. I question the highly theatrical and emotional nature of how information is being imparted.

I view this teaching technique as not only lazy but also proto-fascist.

Some may say I am being unnecessarily harsh on women who have indeed been sounding the alarm about the global rise in fundamentalist misogyny. Perhaps I am. But I think we can make a real difference. I want more of us to put our shoulder to freedom's wheel.

Many feminists enjoyed talking about the plight of Afghan women under the Taliban, and why not? This tragedy proved that Feminism 101 was right all along, that men really do oppress women. But safely railing against oppressors is one thing; actually going up against them personally, physically, risking anything, is something else. After all, many feminists are pacifists. An increasing number, however, are leftists. As such, they will happily and repeatedly talk about going up against America as an oppressor, but they will not even whisper words that oppose any (brown-skinned, formerly colonized) third world Muslim tyrant—not even when he is systematically slaughtering equally brown-skinned and formerly colonized women, children, men and Muslim feminists both male and female.

So what am I saying? I'm saying that feminists can no longer afford to navel-gaze—not if they want to play vital roles on the world-historical stage, not if they want to continue to struggle for women's and humanity's global freedom. American women can no longer allow themselves to be rendered inactive or anti-activist by outdated leftist and European views of colonial-era racism that are meant to trump and silence concerns about gender. This is precisely what Edward Said's book *Orientalism* accomplished. Published in 1978, it replaced academic views of woman as worthy victim with the brown-skinned Arab man as the worthiest victim of them all. Said stole our feminist thunder at its academic height. Ultimately even feminists came to believe that the "occupation of

Palestine"—a country that has never existed—was more important than the occupation of women's bodies worldwide.

Educated feminist Americans may not want to believe that Islamic jihad is here and that the survival of Western civilization is at stake. But how can educated feminist Americans not recognize the exceptionally bloody jihad that Islam has long declared against women, not only in Muslim countries but also in Europe and North America? How can feminists remain so morally and intellectually passive?

The way I see it, everything is at stake. This is not the time for nihilistic rhetoric or tedious party lines. I do not want to offend my good feminist friends; on the contrary, I would like to bring women and men together—from the right and the left—to make a real difference. This is a time when we, the good people, have to think clearly and boldly. I especially want intellectuals to acknowledge that Islamic terrorism is evil and has no justification. I would like us to support Muslim and Arab dissidents in their fight against Islamic gender and religious apartheid and against tyranny. To fail this opportunity betrays all that we believe in, both as good—and as a relatively free people.

This is an excerpt from my book *The Death of Feminism,* which appeared in *Playboy.*
11/1/05

- 7 -

Islamic Gender Apartheid: My Speech for a Senate Hearing

A speech for the 12/14/05 Senate hearing organized by the American Committee for Democracy in the Middle East.

According to one Iranian dissident, "being born female is both a capital crime and a death sentence." Today, the plight of both women and men in the Islamic world, and in an increasingly Islamized Europe, demands a sober analysis and a heroic response. In a democratic, modern, and feminist era, women in the Islamic world are treated as sub-human beings. Women in Iran and elsewhere in the Islamic world are viewed as the source of all evil. Their every move is brutally monitored and curtailed. The smallest infraction—a wanton wisp of hair escaping a headscarf—merits maximum punishment: flogging in public, or worse. This is happening in Iran even as we speak.

In 2005, a hospital in Tehran was accused of refusing entry to women who did not wear head-to-toe covering. In 2002, in Saudi Arabia, religious policemen prevented 14 year old schoolgirls from leaving a burning school building because they were not wearing their headscarves and abayahs. Fifteen girls died.

Today, George Orwell's Thought Police are, rather ominously, everywhere in the Arab and Islamic world. They pre-date the Afghan Taliban or Iran's or Saudi Arabia's Virtue-and-Vice squads, who arrest men and women for the smallest sign of "individuality," difference, or female-ness.

Women in Iran, Afghanistan, Saudi Arabia, and increasingly in

Egypt, are veiled from head to toe. They live in purdah and lead segregated lives. Women are also forced into arranged and polygamous marriages, often when they are children, and often to much older men or to first cousins.

Girls and women are routinely beaten. Woman-beating is normalized and culturally sanctioned and those who dare protest it are shamed, beaten savagely, and sometimes even honor-murdered by their own families. According to the Women's Forum Against Fundamentalism in Iran, two out of every three Iranian women have experienced serious domestic violence. Eighty one per cent of married women have experienced domestic violence in their first year of marriage. In addition, every year, millions of Muslim women are genitally mutilated—and this is not only happening in Muslim and pagan Africa. It is increasingly happening in Iran, Indonesia, and in Europe and in North America where the procedures are quietly carried out in private offices and hospitals, or in visits back home to the "old country."

In many Muslim countries, women are not allowed to vote, drive, leave the house, or leave the country without male permission and a male escort. Most runaway girls in Iran are raped within the first 24 hours of their departure. The majority of such runaway rape victims are rejected by their families after they're raped. When Iranian girls or women run away from abusive homes, they are quickly trafficked into prostitution, which has increased alarmingly in the last decade in Iran and which now includes temporary marriages that allow men to "marry for only an hour." Rape victims and suspected prostitutes are quickly jailed and repeatedly raped, and often impregnated, by their guards. In 2004, nearly 4,000 women were arrested in Tehran alone. Six hundred and forty nine were girls below the age of 14.

Iranian women are worn down every minute and in every way in their private lives. For example, in the summer of '05, a court in Tehran barred a young woman from working after her estranged husband complained that she was only allowed to be a housewife. This woman had been battered and she had fled the marriage two years earlier. But the court confirmed her husband's right to bar her from working outside the home. In November of '05, an 80-year-old husband clubbed his 50-year-old wife to death, "because he could not tolerate her wearing makeup outside the home." In October of '05, female civil servants at Iran's culture ministry were forced to leave the office by dusk "to be with their families." One female journalist, who works nightshifts at an Iranian newspaper said: "This decree means that I will be jobless soon."

And then there are the public and terrifying atrocities.

Increasingly in Iran, women are publicly hung or are slowly and painfully stoned to death for alleged adultery or for having been raped. Public amputations, floggings, and executions are "almost a daily spectacle." If women (and men) publicly protest such heartbreaking barbarities, they are slandered as "anti-Muslim," arrested, and often murdered by the state.

The bravery of Iranian demonstrators is therefore heart stopping. They know precisely what can and will happen to them and still they demonstrate. In Tehran this past summer of '05, women protested Iran's clerical rulers. They chanted "Freedom, freedom, freedom!" and called for a referendum on religious rule. They chanted "Unequal law means inhuman justice" and "Misogyny is the root of tyranny." Earlier in March of '05, demonstrators at Tehran University demanded that women have a right to choose what they wear; that women must be free to choose their husbands and to marry or to divorce; that any kind of sex trade and human trafficking should be forbidden; that polygamy should be illegal.

Many Muslim women are also honor murdered by their families—yes, by their mothers as well as by their fathers and older brothers for the crime of wanting to go to college, marry for love, end abusive marriages, or go to the movies. Honor murders are usually horrific, very primitive. The girls or women are beheaded or they are stabbed many times, or slowly choked to death. I write about this in my most recent book, *The Death of Feminism: What's Next in the Struggle for Women's Freedom*.

I call this systemic mistreatment: "Islamic gender apartheid."

If we do not oppose and defeat Islamic gender apartheid, democracy and freedom cannot flourish in the Arab and Islamic world. If we do not join forces with Muslim dissident and feminist groups, and above all, if we do not have one universal standard of human rights for all—then we will fail our own Judeo-Christian and western secular ideals. We will also inherit the whirlwind. If we do not stop Islamic gender and religious apartheid abroad, be assured: It is coming our way soon. Indeed, it is already here. I document Islamic gender apartheid in both Europe and North America in *The Death of Feminism*.

It is dangerous to say what I've just said on most campuses in Europe and North America. If one describes the barbaric human rights violations being carried out in the name of Islam, one is instantly accused of being a "racist," a "Zionist," an American "imperialist," and, the worse epithet of all, a "pro-war conservative." Islamic associations in the West, radical mullahs and Muslim leaders abroad, and culturally relativist western thinkers will sue you, shout you down, refuse to publish or refuse to listen to you.

Some personal disclosures are now in order.

First, I'm a feminist and an American patriot. Yes, one can be both. I'm also an internationalist. I believe in one universal standard of human rights for everyone. Finally, I am a religious Jew and am sympathetic to both religious and secular world-views. Being religious does not compromise my feminism. On the contrary, it gives me the strength and a necessarily humbled perspective to continue the struggle for justice.

Let us now return to the Islamic Republic of Iran. In 1990, Iranian journalist, Freidoune Sahebjam, published a haunting and carefully rendered account of how, on August 15, 1986, a 35-year-old woman was stoned to death in Kupayeh, Iran. It is titled: *The Stoning of Soraya M.* Soraya, (peace be upon her), was lynched by the villagers with whom she had lived all her life. Her own father, her two sons, and her lying, greedy, heartless, criminal-husband, Ghorban-Ali, all threw the first stones.

When Soraya was only 13, an arranged marriage with the 20-year-old Ghorban-Ali took place. Soraya was docile, obedient, and fertile. She did everything uncomplainingly. Her husband routinely insulted, beat, and then abandoned her and their children; he also consorted with prostitutes and brought them into the marital bed. Soraya dared not say a word. A "complaining" wife is easy to divorce.

On his say-so, she was sentenced to die—on the very day her husband accused her of adultery. The villagers chanted: "The whore has to die. Death to the woman." The villagers—who had known Soraya since her birth—cursed her, spit on her, hit her, and whipped her as she walked to her stoning. According to Sahebjam's account, a "shudder of pleasure and joy ran through the crowd," as their stones drew blood. Soraya died a slow and agonizing death. Afterwards, the villagers all literally danced on the spot where Soraya had been murdered.

I must emphasize that this ghastly, local stoning cannot be blamed on the alleged crimes of the American or Israeli Empire. Such barbaric customs are indigenous customs. The West has not caused them.

Dare to argue for military as well as humanitarian and educational intervention—and you will be slandered as a "racist"—even when you are arguing for the lives and dignity of brown- and black- and olive-skinned people.

If we, as Americans, want to continue the struggle for women's and humanity's global freedom, we can no longer allow ourselves to remain inactive, cowed by outdated left and European views of colonial-era racism that are meant to trump and silence concerns about gender. The Western academy has been thoroughly "Palestinianized." Even feminists have come to believe that the "occupation of Palestine" is far more important than the occupation and destruction of women's bodies, worldwide.

As I see it, everything is at stake. This is not the time for ideological party lines. It is a time for action, clarity, and unity. As Americans, we must acknowledge that Islamic religious and gender apartheid are evil and have no justification.

What must be done? We must combat the hate propaganda against women—and against America, and Israel that characterizes so much of the Arab and Muslim world today. This is a long educational process. We must defeat jihad. We must peg every peace and trade treaty with a Muslim country to the status of women in that country. I have a list of ten things that must be done in this regard vis à vis Iran. My esteemed colleague, Professor Donna Hughes, has begun to spell out what an American feminist foreign policy might be towards Iran.

American and Western leaders cannot turn their backs on Muslim dissidents, on the people in the Arab and Muslim world—or on the endangered Jews in Israel or on the Christians in Muslim countries. Our American vision of freedom and equality for women must also become part of American foreign policy. This is the feminist priority of the twenty-first century.

FrontPage Magazine
12/16/05

Section Two:
My Headscarf Headache

- 8 -
"White" Feminists Are Always to Blame

I thank the editors for allowing me to comment upon this article by Tanzanian-born Canadian sociologist, Sunera Thobani, which appears in this issue of *Feminist Theory*.[1] Thobani's article condemns myself and two other American feminist scholars (Judith Butler and Zillah Eisenstein) as racially "superior" white women who collaborate with the "imperial imaginary" and with "colonialism." Thobani also condemns us for daring to present "whiteness" as "vulnerable." She mocks the alleged "racial paranoia of imperial subjects" (that's us), claiming that in our work we three experience our own "imperial" aggression as a form of victimization which then allows us to justify the aggression as self defence.[2]

One might wonder why I am taking the time to respond to this inflammatory article. There are four reasons. First, her diatribe is typical but has rarely been answered in the pages of a feminist academic journal. Second, I could not allow her condemnation of three feminist theorists to pass unchallenged. Third, I had recently been invited to deliver a keynote address at Cambridge University as part of an international feminist conference in 2007. When I raised questions about security and

---

1 I assume that readers have already read through Sunera Thobani's paper titled "'White Wars', white feminism, and the 'War on Terror'" in *Feminist Theory* and thus will not summarize it here. Thobani studied in the UK and in Canada; spent a year as a volunteer in Palestine. She describes herself as "Southeast Asian."

2 Although the published version of Thobani's article is less personalized than the original version to which I was responding in this paper, she still ignores the fact that I call for Judaeo-Christian alliances with Muslim and ex-Muslim dissidents and feminists, and that in my view, the clash is not between civilizations but between civilization and barbarism.

about the utter absence of kindred spirits, and despite the fact that I had stressed that neither factor would keep me away —I was summarily dis-invited. (These feminists have invited me to lecture alone at some future date, but not within the context of an international conference.) I there-fore decided that responding to Thobani might be another way to be "heard" in the UK and in international feminist circles. Finally, I felt it was important to explain how Thobani's paper (and so many others like it) is the written equivalent of what happens today on campuses when genuine dissent or non-politically correct feminist speech dares appear.

Instead of a respectful hearing what ensues is this: the political-ly incorrect feminist speaker is peppered with hostile questions, then silenced by boos, catcalls, foot-stamping, and name-calling; she might even be physically menaced. Security might be required. This is hardly an atmosphere in which a free exchange of ideas can occur. Similarly, like the Mearsheimer-Walt[3] and Joan Wallach Scott[4] papers, Thobani's seemingly sophisticated paper, replete with footnotes, is trying to pass for an academic or intellectual work. But these are ideological, not schol-arly, views. The attempt to pretend that one is the other is what I have characterized as a new totalitarianism among Western intellectuals.

Thobani's article is an angry and self-righteous declaration of war. She does not have one positive thing to say about any of our work. Re-sponding to Thobani in kind—with rage and condemnation—gives me no pleasure for what do we gain? Two warriors growling, slicing the air with paper swords while millions of Third World women and men of di-verse skin colors and ethnicities are indeed being tormented and slaugh-tered—but mainly by other Third World men and women of diverse skin colors and ethnicities—while we do nothing because to intervene or even to acknowledge that this is happening is politically incorrect? (By the way, "white" folk have sorrows too but enough about that.)

Ethnic Arab Muslims are genocidally slaughtering black African Muslims, Christians, and animists in Darfur; Muslims are blowing each other up when they pray in mosques in Saudi Arabia, Iraq, Pakistan, and Indonesia; Muslim men are shooting down and beheading their own

3 Phyllis Chesler, "Academic Anti-Semitism," *National Review*, 30 May 2006 [http://article.nationalreview.com/?q=M2E3YzMzNGRmNzczMmE2Y2YxZmU3OTQ3Z-jZhZDA3MmU=]; Alan Dershowitz, "Debunking the Newest – and Oldest – Jewish Conspiracy: A Reply to the Mearsheimer-Walt 'Working Paper,'" Harvard Law School, April 2006 [http://www.ksg.harvard.edu/research/working_papers/dershowitzreply.pdf]
4 Phyllis Chesler et al., "The Lamentable Case of Joan Scott," *FrontPage Magazine*, 21 February 2006, [http://www.frontpagemag.com/Articles/ReadArticle.asp?ID=21369]

intellectuals and dissidents in unimaginable numbers. According to one source, such numbers far outpace anything the combined American and Israeli forces have done in the last 50 years. The estimated Third World Muslim violent deaths by other Third World Muslims, country by country, vastly exceeds that of Third World Muslim deaths in so-called "white imperial" wars.[5]

Thobani seems to believe in racial purity and therefore in the rights of racially oppressed victims to engage in apocalyptic "resistance." Thobani is not deterred by the fact that "white" and "colored" skin colors are not pure, have no significant scientific basis, and often have different meanings as a function of other variables such as class, caste, gender, sexual preference, ethnicity, religion, educational level, marital, national, and immigrant status, birth order, character, destiny, etc. (Haven't feminist academics said so over and over again?)

Reality does not conform to Thobani's ideological "imaginary." The American population (we three "white" feminists are American citizens), the victims of 9/11, the members of the American Armed Forces, and the large number of immigrants to America, including those from Muslim and Third World countries, are not all "white." As of 2005, over 73 million Americans (or 25 per cent of the population) were "non-white." An additional 40 million Hispanic-Americans do not identify themselves as either "black" or "white" but as "Latino".[6] (Latino skin color ranges from white to black.) Also, nearly 36 per cent of American soldiers are "nonwhite" Americans[7] and about 15 per cent of American soldiers are women.[8]

Thus, Thobani's alleged "white" perpetrators are not all white.[9] Nor

5 The article from which this information was drawn was written by Ben Dror Yemini for the Israeli newspaper *Maariv*. The original article can be found at [http://www.nrg.co.il/online/1/ART1/482/564.html]. This article may be dismissed by anti-Israel fanatics as mere propaganda, but it carefully goes through the history of each country and notes who both the perpetrators and victims were in different wars. I recommend that you read the article and decide for yourself.

6 2005 American Community Survey Data Profile Highlights, US Census Bureau. American Factfinder Website [http://factfinder.census.gov/servlet/ACSSAFFFacts?_submenuId=factsheet_1&_sse=on]

7 2003 Demographics; Profile of the Military Community, Military Family Resource Center. [http://www.militaryhomefront.dod.mil/dav/lsn/LSN/BINARY_RESOURCE/BINARY_CONTENT/1869841.swf]

8 See Solaro (2005).

9 But according to Thobani, all "imperial subjects" have agency and are therefore guilty of collaboration – just as we three theorists allegedly are. The fact that "imperial subjects" are actually non-white does not exempt them. Thus, Thobani cannot argue

are the victims of Islamic Holy War all white. For example, approximately 24 per cent of those murdered in the 2001 World Trade Center attacks were identified as "non-white."[10] In London, almost one-third of the population (which one assumes uses public transport) identified itself as "nonwhite."[11] On 7 July 2005, 52 people were murdered and nearly 800 injured by Islamic jihadist attacks on the London transportation systems. France's 2005 version of the Palestinian intifada against Israel was characterized by nearly two months of rioting, attacks on the police, and car burnings—and by the exceptionally horrific torture of one young North African-Jewish man, the olive-skinned Ilan Halimi (may his memory be for a blessing). Over a three-week period, black African and ethnic Arab North African criminals slowly tortured him to death, while many people came to watch or to participate.[12] One year later, in 2006, this France-based jihad was commemorated by bus and car burnings.[13] I am particularly haunted by the fate of one young, black-skinned French-African woman who was torched when the bus she was riding on was set on fire.[14] The rioting arsonists have yet to be tried. Although their ethnicity has, carefully, not been described, I predict that if and when we find out who they are, they will probably not be "white" feminists.

I wonder whether Thobani realizes that all three of her alleged, targeted "traitors" are not only major, original feminist theorists and activists but are also *Jews*. In George Orwell's novel *1984*, someone named "Goldstein" is designated as the permanent traitor whom Big Brother denounces for monstrous crimes, thereby brainwashing the masses into

---

that American people of "color" are being forced to do their Master's bidding while American "white" people freely choose to do so.

10 New York City Health Department, Summary of Vital Statistics 2000 [http://www. nyc.gov/html/doh/downloads/pdf/vs/2000sum.pdf, 2000], Special Report: World Trade Center Disaster Deaths, 45.

11 Office of National Statistics, 2001 Census [http://neighbourhood.statistics.gov.uk/ dissemination/, 2001], Key Statistics: London: Ethnic Groups.

12 Nidra Poller, "The Murder of Ilan Halimi," *Wall Street Journal*, 26 February 2005, *The Opinion Journal* [http://www.opinionjournal.com/ extra/?id=110008006&o-jrss=wsj]

13 *BBC News*, "Police Deployed in Paris Suburbs," 27 October 2006, Europe Section [http://news.bbc.co.uk/2/hi/europe/6093276.stm]

14 *BBC News*, "Five Held for Marseille Bus Blaze," 31 October 2006, Europe Section [http://news.bbc.co.uk/2/hi/europe/6101574.stm]; Nidra Poller, "Burning Buses: 'She Was Black but She Looked White, her Skin Was Peeled,'" *Pajamas Media*, 3 November 2006 [http://www.pajamasmedia.com/2006/11/burning_buses_she_was_black_bu.php]

extraordinary group hatred against him. Are we meant to be Thobani's version of "Goldstein?" Does she not understand that Jews come in all colors, and that even when we have white skins we are still not considered "white" but *other*, Oriental, Semitic? (This does not mean that anti-Semitism, which is primarily about Jews, is the same as or even analogous to "Islamophobia" which is a false concept of recent vintage and with a different historical trajectory.)

Thobani specializes in the postcolonial work that has increasingly come to dominate what once used to be called feminism or women's studies. I document this unfortunate, even tragic trend in *The Death of Feminism: What's Next in the Struggle for Women's Freedom* (2005). Westernized Third World feminists refuse to view any formerly colonized culture of "color" as barbaric, even when it is, because all cultures are presumably equal—except Western culture, which is worse.

Thobani views the cause of women as served only by a Marxist-Islamist critique of Western foreign policy and by virulent anti-Americanism. Here, she does not address any core or burning emergency issues that concern women.

Thobani is utterly silent about the international trafficking in women and children (female sexual slavery) that may far exceed all other illegal enterprises. She is also silent about female genital mutilation, wife- and daughter-beating, honor murders, forced veiling, purdah (segregation – sequestration), and arranged and polygamous marriage. These barbaric customs are normalized, not criminalized, and they characterize what I term Islamic gender apartheid. These practices are tribal, indigenous, and preceded Western imperialism and colonialism.

Thobani is also silent about the high rate of AIDS with which young girls and women are being infected by their male partners (especially in the Third World and in communities of color in the West); about sexual, reproductive and physical violence, including incest—especially in the Third World; about the repeated public gang-rapes of genitally infibulated girls and women in the Sudan which have been carried out against black African Muslims, Christians, and animists by ethnic Arab Muslims; about the history of African Muslim slave traders, and about the genocide against black Africans being carried out in the Sudan by ethnic Arab Muslims.

Thobani will condemn Third World deaths only if they have been perpetrated by "white" people, but not if those deaths have been caused by people of "color."

Thobani is free to criticize, even to demonize the West, because she is living in a Western democracy where academic freedom and free speech are (still) taken seriously. Were Thobani to dare criticize the barbarism, misogyny, and despotism of Third World countries, were she to do so in Afghanistan, Algeria, Iran, Bangladesh or Saudi Arabia (to name only a few such countries), she would be in serious danger of being shot to death in her own home, as happened recently to an Afghan woman journalist, or of being imprisoned, tortured, and murdered. This has happened to many Muslim dissidents and feminists. In 2003, Wajeha Al-Huwaider was barred from publishing in the Saudi Kingdom; in 2006 she was arrested, interrogated, and forced to sign a statement agreeing to cease her human rights activities.[15]

In *The Death of Feminism*, I describe what I mean by Islamic religious and gender apartheid in Muslim countries and I document how such customs have penetrated the West through immigrant communities. Feminists need to acknowledge that this is happening. We need to wrestle with it and take a stand against it. We need to make common cause with Third World and Muslim feminists and dissidents who want to create alliances.

Today, in Muslim countries, women are being more forcefully veiled. They are being imprisoned, raped and flogged; in Iran, they are often hung or stoned to death[16] when they allege rape or run away from unusually dangerous families.[17] Honor murders are either increasing or have become more visible—perhaps because Western and Western influenced feminists have begun to document them. In the fall of 2006, Human Rights Watch published a new report in which they documented that violence against Palestinian women is increasing and that it is primarily due to the rise of Islamic fundamentalism and the ascent of Hamas.[18]

Recently, in the fall of 2006 (the end of Ramadan), perhaps a thousand men conducted a "sexual wilding" in Cairo. They surrounded individual girls and women who were fully veiled, partly veiled, and unveiled, and groped and assaulted them. Individuals tried to help these women—who escaped from the male crowds naked and half-naked. The police refused to make any arrests and the media did not cover it. I

15 Sarah Leah Whitson and Human Rights Watch, Letter to Prince Naif bin Abdul Aziz, 20 October 2006 [http://hrw.org/english/docs/2006/10/20/saudia14461.htm]

16 Chesler, 2005: 58–9; Sahebjam, 1994.

17 Chesler, 2005: 187–8.

18 Human Rights Watch, A Question of Security, Vol. 18, No. 7(E), November 2006 [http://hrw.org/reports/2006/opt1106/opt1106webwcover.pdf]

and others only learned of this incident because some foreign journalists blogged about it—and because one brave Egyptian woman spoke about it on a live Egyptian television programme.[19]

But worse things happened during Ramadan 2006. In Indonesia, three Christian high school girls were beheaded as a "Ramadan trophy." Their heads were dumped in plastic bags in their village with a note: "Wanted. 100 more Christian heads." The man charged with this offence had, it has been reported, decided that beheading Christians would "qualify as an act of Muslim charity."[20]

I will not respond to the specific points Thobani raises about my book, *The New Anti-Semitism*. For the record, let me say that she draws highly biased conclusions and quotes from my work only in order to discredit it and in a particularly incendiary way. In doing so, she utterly misinforms the reader.[21]

Thobani writes, "Chesler's analysis pivots on her reproduction of Muslims as an absolute Other, whose actions cannot be comprehended rationally." How can this be true since I call for alliances with dissident and feminist Muslims in both recent books and in my articles? There is a difference between "Muslims" and "Islamist, terrorist, fundamentalists."

19 Anonymous, translation of "Mass Sexual Assault in Downtown Cairo," "Unnecessary, and Not Very Diverting, Musings," posted 15 November, 2006 [http://forsooth-sayer.blogspot.com/2006/10/mass-sexual-assault-in-downtown-cairo.html]; Mona El-Naggar and Michael Slackman, "Silence and Fury in Cairo after Sexual Attacks on Women," *New York Times*, 15 November 2006, World Section, Africa; "Cairo Street Crowds Target Women," *BBC News*, 1 November 2006, Middle East Section [http://news.bbc.co.uk/2/hi/middle_east/6106500.stm]

20 Stephen Fitzpatrick, "Beheaded Girls were Ramadan Trophies," *The Australian*, 9 November 2006, The World [http://www.theaustralian. news.com.au/story/0,20867,20726085-2703,00.html]

21 Thobani's expanded critique of one of my thirteen books, *The New Anti-Semitism*, is still very biased. Clearly, she is unaware that I have been a named-plaintiff in a landmark Israeli Supreme Court lawsuit in which I sued the Israeli state on behalf of Jewish women's religious rights. (I co-authored a book about this titled, *Women of the Wall: Claiming Sacred Ground at Judaism's Holy Site*.) Quite apart from the body of my feminist work, this would suggest that my reading of Israeli morality is nuanced, careful, fair. Alas, historical realities have tempered my original view that if Israel gave back land—as it has given back Gaza—that this would lead to peace and to the acceptance of the Jewish state by Jew-hating and anti-Zionist Muslim nation-states. Events on the ground from 2000–2007 have cured me of that dream and I explain this to some extent in *The New Anti-Semitism* and again in *The Death of Feminism*. I have not pronounced feminism "dead"; rather, I challenge what often passes for feminism (as this article by Thobani tries to do) and suggest that feminism ought to return to its original concepts of universalism.

Thobani also quotes my description of the 1980 United Nations conference in Copenhagen to prove that I see all Arab or Palestinian women negatively.

Not so. In the paragraph Thobani quotes, I am not describing "Muslim women." I am describing a Soviet-funded, Iranian, and Arab League orchestrated campaign under United Nations auspices to torpedo and hijack a conference that was supposed to be about women. The Soviets and Iranians trained and used female Iranian and PLO operatives whose choreographed hostility does not represent most "Muslim women" or Muslim feminists.

Again, let me thank the editors for giving me this opportunity to respond.

References:

Chesler, Phyllis (2005) *The Death of Feminism: What's Next in the Struggle for Women's Freedom.* New York: Palgrave Macmillan.

Hirsi Ali, Ayaan (2007) *Infidel.* New York: Free Press.

Nafisi, Azar (2003) *Reading Lolita in Tehran.* New York: Random House.

Sahebjam, Freidoune (1994) *The Stoning of Soraya M.* New York: Arcade Publishing.

Warraq, Ibn (2007) *Defending the West: A Critique of Edward Said's Orientalism.* Amherst, New York: Prometheus.

Feminist Theory
7/31/07

- 9 -

Muslim Women Activists in North America:
A Review

Western Feminists: At the Service of Radical Islam

One might expect Western feminists to take the lead in challenging Islamic gender apartheid, but sadly, this is not the case. Rather, they tend to be more concerned with Israel's alleged "occupation" of Palestine, aka, the disputed territories, or the U.S. "occupation" of Afghanistan than with the Islamist persecution of women. They consider it "racist" to condemn gender apartheid of the most savage sort, and "racism" trumps their concerns about gender.

Incredibly, those same Western feminists who condemn as patriarchal Western institutions of marriage, biological motherhood, heterosexuality, and religion now view Islamic face-and-body veiling, the hijab (head scarf), purdah (seclusion of women), arranged marriage, and polygamy as sacred religious rights.

Those same feminists who condemn Christianity and Judaism for more minor (but still serious) misogynist practices only whisper about major Islamic misogyny—lest it be viewed as politically incorrect and racist.

Like other academics, feminists will not characterize a culture as "barbaric" if it is an Arab or Muslim country—not even if that culture or country is perpetrating genocidal violence against Muslims and what I call gender-cleansing—as is the case in the Sudan. Western feminists and leftists do not feel it is their right to condemn Muslim-on-Muslim violence.

Katherine Bullock's *Muslim Women Activists in North America* and

Ann Chamberlin's *A History of Women's Seclusion in the Middle East: The Veil in the Looking Glass* take such thought disorders to new Orwellian heights. Both books are published by university or academic presses; both have many footnotes, and the latter volume has a long, somewhat outdated bibliography. These academic trappings notwithstanding, neither volume is a scholarly work, but each is a work of propaganda, in the latter case, of a rather fevered sort. Both volumes illustrate the worrisome trend of prestigious presses publishing non-scholarly works disguised as works of scholarship. (Other examples include the University of California Press publishing Norman Finkelstein, Oxford University Press publishing Tariq Ramadan, and Farrar, Strauss, and Giroux publishing John Mearsheimer and Stephen Walt.)

In *Muslim Women Activists*, when Bullock mentions Muhammad, she consistently follows his name with the phrase "peace be upon him," she refers to "Muslim religious theology" as "the Islamic sciences." Bullock views Muslim communities in North America as "under siege" and condemns imaginary, omnipresent "Muslim bashing" and "hate crimes" against Muslims. In her view, "covered" women are not oppressed because "many do positive volunteer activism." Paradoxically, Bullock herself notes that many such "covered" and "non-oppressed" Muslim women in this volume themselves write about "negative pressures" from within the Muslim community regarding a "woman's right to speak publicly, [and] be involved in community decision making." Such women have only been able to resist community pressures with the "help of a father or husband."

Bullock's authors also propound some chilling ideas. Nimat Hafez Barazangi, born in Syria and currently living in Ithaca, New York, views herself as a "feminist activist." But I see her as an Islamist exploring ways to use the American legal system to wrest some separate-but-equal gender justice for Muslim women and girls (and only for them, not for other groups of girls and women). I do not oppose such efforts, but they are far short of what Muslim women, even in Ithaca, probably need. Proudly, Barazangi reports how she used Title Nine and the Fourteenth Amendment to persuade Ithaca town officials to allow Muslim girls to swim separately from boys. However, she was unable to persuade Muslim families to allow their daughters and wives to swim at all.

Gul Joya Jafri, a Canadian Muslim and self-described activist, worked with an Afghan Women's Organization. She addressed the way in which the mainstream media portrays Muslim women. Her activism consisted of monitoring media outlets and fighting against "anti-Islam" forces. Joya Jafri's activism does not find it necessary to protest women's forced wearing of burqas or women's mistreatment by the Taliban. Instead, she laments that the media chooses to portray only these aspects and stories about Afghanistan. It is "true," she says, "but it doesn't need to be reported in that way." As a high school student, Joya Jafri "dreamily quoted the U.N.'s Universal Declaration on Human Rights: 'Everyone has a right to life, liberty and security of the person,'" but as an adult, she focuses on a portrayal of Muslims in the media—one that does not focus upon or condemn gender apartheid and honor murders but that, instead, focuses on a Muslim woman's right to practice Islam in a highly visible and separatist way in the West. Like Bullock and Barazangi, hers is a faith-based perspective—one that does not support a Muslim woman's right not to cover, become an "apostate," or to live a secular life.

Chamberlin's work in *A History of Women's Seclusion* amounts to a romantic hodgepodge moored in an American feminism of the 1970s. In effect, she argues that Western women who seek to integrate previously male-only space are far more "conservative" and "patriarchal" than are American lesbian separatists or veiled Muslim women who live in purdah. She sees women-only religious rituals and women-only space as equivalent to anti-patriarchal protest or resistance movements. She views purdah as a "feminist defense against exploitation and as an empowering force." True, very wealthy women may have "ruled" other women in the harem or household—but this is equivalent to a wife or mother-in-law ruling her female servants. Some may have influenced their sons or husbands in ways that had far-reaching consequences; however, this paradigm describes only a handful of Muslim women, not the masses.

Chamberlin's approach is seductive and dangerous. It caters to a woman's desire to feel morally superior, valued, and safe. Chamberlin claims that slave women in the pre-Islamic and pagan Middle East were forced to work naked and to be sexually available at any moment to all men. Thus, "covered" and secluded women were safer than slave or "uncovered" women—mainly because they only had one male master, not many. The distinction is similar to that between housewives and prostitutes. The conclusions Chamberlin draws are zany. In her own words:

> X million tons of toxic waste created per year or an astronomical national deficit are to the natural and economic resources of our children what the abstraction and exploitation of the individual—women in particular—are to their emotion-

al resources. When faced with exploitation similar to what American women—and more gravely, their children—stand on the brink of today, women in the Middle East millennia ago threw their veil over their faces, put up a wall of mystified honor, and said: 'So far you may exploit, but by God no further.'

The Islamization of America has begun. Pro-Islamist, anti-American, anti-Israeli, and anti-Jewish hate speech is protected on American campuses by concepts such as academic freedom and freedom of speech. False and often paranoid allegations of "Islamophobia" are taken seriously by Western intellectual elites who deny (or justify) the reality of the Islamist war against infidels. Doctrines of multicultural relativism and unspoken fears about "death by lawsuit" or physical acts of violence make it difficult for anyone to tell the truth about the Islamist war against Western values.

Western feminists are not alone in appeasing Islamization; the postcolonial and postmodern feminist academy is very much part of the problem.

Middle East Quarterly
Fall 2007

- 10 -
The Heroic Nonie Darwish Faces Muslim "Mean Girl" Power at Wellesley

"The radical Muslims on American campuses are getting more belligerent, far more militant," author and lecturer Nonie Darwish tells me. "They have perfected their intimidation and disruption techniques."

Darwish is an expressive, emotional orator, dramatically thrilling (as so many Arabs can be), but Darwish is also soft, almost maternal when she speaks. She is also very clear, very firm, and totally uncompromising. She grew up in Cairo and in Gaza and now lives in America. She has founded Arabs for Israel. She is pro-American and also concerned with women's rights. Her first book, *Now They Call Me Infidel: Why I Renounced Jihad for America, Israel, and the War on Terror*, is extremely brave.

Darwish is the daughter of a high-ranking Egyptian military officer who died in battle against the Israelis and who is considered a "shahid," or martyr. While she continues to love her father, she has "shaken off," renounced, the hate propaganda with which she was raised.

On October 18, 2007, Darwish spoke at the all-female Wellesley College as the guest of Hillel on campus. She was not treated as a hero; then again, maybe she was, maybe her treatment is precisely how heroes are greeted on American campuses today.

About 80-100 students came. Far more Muslim than Jewish students came and many of the Muslim girls were wearing head-scarves.

According to Darwish, the female students in head-scarves did the following: As she spoke, they made exaggerated, "mean girl" faces at her.

They rolled their eyes, practiced "disbelieving" facial expressions—did everything but stick out their tongues. And they continued to talk to each other in loud whispers while Darwish spoke: "How can she tell such lies!" "I was never, ever indoctrinated against Jews!" "Can you believe what she is saying?" "We do not call Jews pigs and apes, how can she lie about her own people?"

In addition to the "mean girl" faces and the continual loud whispering, one by one, at least four to five head-scarved girls, got up to leave the room during Darwish's speech. This meant that each girl took two minutes to move to the end of her row, physically causing the other students to get up or twist aside, causing the entire room to look at the departing student, not at their invited guest—and then each girl did precisely the same thing when she returned two minutes later, presumably from a bathroom break.

They quadruple-teamed Darwish and did not stop until Darwish ended her lecture. Twenty to thirty minutes of soft-core, well-choreographed, goon squad behavior. "They are Hamas-trained" says Darwish.

"And all the while," Darwish says, "the Jewish students cringed and cowered, so afraid that they might have hurt Muslim feelings. (Or rather, that the Muslims might physically hurt them afterwards. According to Darwish, one Jewish student told her that she "was locking her dorm-room door. I'm scared.")

She is probably right to be. During the Question and Answer period, many of the head-scarved students expressed calculated, injured outrage. "How dare (Hillel) bring this woman to our campus? How dare she insult Islam, tell lies about Islam" etc. "We are free under Islam, how can she deny this?"

Darwish had first been asked to speak about Muslim women who live under Muslim religious law. Then, at the last minute, Hillel had asked her to talk about something, anything else—about Israel, not about Islam. Apparently, the female Muslim chaplain on campus had warned the Hillel students not to allow Darwish to "say anything bad about Islam."

One must not expose Islam's long record of gender and religious apartheid and if one does, one is treated as a traitor and a liar and silenced in violent ways.

Ironically, the flyer describing Darwish's visit advertised her speech as one about "peace." Darwish was the last to know about it. Still, she rode the wave. "We can't have peace unless each group engages in self-criticism which is what I'm doing."

The Muslim chaplain at Wellesley herself wears a headscarf, and arrived accompanied by a bearded male companion. Darwish asks: "Who is paying for all these Muslim chaplains on every American campus? Why are they needed? What is their real role?"

In Darwish's view, "the happiest Muslims on earth are those who live under Judeo-Christian laws, not under Sharia law." These young girls are "disconnected from the reality of Islam." Or, they are exercising the "only power anyone, men or women, are allowed to have: the power to enforce the status quo and to further the Muslim jihadic mission."

Darwish repeated, many times, that "not all Muslims are terrorists, but so many terrorists are Muslims;" that she is "not speaking about peaceful Muslims or about each and every Muslim," but "about Muslims who uphold a reactionary status quo."

Darwish concludes: "Muslim girls like these are like gangsters. They know more about their rights in America than the Jewish girls do. The Muslim girls all have a chip on their shoulders."

And then she is silent. Softly, she says: "We are fighting an avalanche. We are too few. I am frightened by my culture of origin. I am scared of my own people."

I do not think that campus lecturers should have to face disruption and intimidation; such working conditions are far too hostile.

However, one of the approximately ten students who gratefully crowded around Darwish after her speech was over, wrote to thank her for her "powerful testimony." This student apologized for how "disrespectfully" so many Wellesley students had treated Darwish. But she ended her note this way: "You are giving me the hope and strength to stand against extremism."

All in all, it was a good day for heroes.

Pajamas Media
10/22/07

- 11 -
Afghan Kites: Fantasy and Reality

Last night I finally saw the film based on Khaled Hosseini's novel, *The Kite Runner*. I loved it—yes, even if it presents a pre-Taliban country more mythical than real. Nevertheless, the musical soundtrack, the recitation of classical poetry, the innocent kite-flying competitions in Kabul, (not to mention Homayoun Ershadi who strongly resembles Marcello Mastroianni), all comprise utterly charming scenes and characters carefully chosen and calibrated to help us distinguish between sophisticated and westernized Afghans who are non-violent, (I know many), and the barbarians amongst them.

I think that the film is also brave. First, it depicts a tall, thin, slightly effeminate, incredibly brutal pederast ("Assef") who, although he is an Afghan through and through, reminds one of none other than Osama bin Laden. Both figures walk languidly; both teach "harsh" lessons. The film also shows us how the Taliban publicly stone a sobbing woman in a pink burqa to death and how they kidnap or purchase Afghan orphans, mainly girls, but sometimes also boys, as "dancing" sex-objects.

As shown, wealthy and western-educated Afghans did have private, gender-integrated dancing parties in the 1970s in Kabul—but the nature of Afghan society is better represented in both the novel and the film in how they depict Afghan marriage and family customs in America. Even those immigrants who live in San Francisco guard their women, expect would-be suitors to ask a father for his daughter's hand in marriage. (The film has a wonderful Afghan Wedding scene every bit the equal of any Bollywood Indian Wedding.) And, Afghan immigrants continue to live with or geographically near their parents and to enjoy inter-generational, parent-centered adult social lives.

Not a bad idea at all.

Ah, but now I come to the hard part. Daily, I receive news of Islamic gender and religious apartheid, both in the Islamic East and as it has steadily penetrated the West. I write about this at length in my latest book *The Death of Feminism*.

But, the same continent (North America) and culture (the West) which is so proud of its multi-cultural sensitivity and tolerance—and whose people have embraced books such as *The Kite Runner* and *Reading Lolita in Tehran*, are more eager to embrace the immigrant "Other," (which is commendably open-hearted), but reluctant to take into account the cultural "baggage" that most immigrants bring with them into their new lives.

Although fewer immigrants arrive in the West from Iran or Saudi Arabia, these two countries have exported their versions of Islam to Muslims in very effective ways. In the last month:

IRAN

A top Muslim cleric, Hojatolislam Gholam Reza Hassani said that Muslim women who do not wear the hijab "should die." He went further: "These women and their husbands and their fathers must die."

The use of the word "women" has just been banned from Iranian state TV. They have begun using the word "family" instead. In recent weeks, Iran's Center for the Participation of Women changed its name to the Centre for Family Matters.

Two Kurdish women's rights activists, Ronak Safazadeh and Hana Abdi, were just arrested in Tehran and charged as "terrorists." These two feminists were collecting "a million signatures for equality" but have, instead, been charged with a car bomb.

PAKISTAN

Seventy one percent of the men polled in Pakistan "justify beating women." The survey documents that 80% of Pakistani women are the "victims of domestic violence." The report claims that "Women in Pakistan face death by shooting, burning, or killing with axes" in honor murders.

Also, a former Muslim in Pakistan who converted to Christianity has been receiving "death threats from his Muslim siblings" and is now in hiding together with his wife, their four daughters and son.

IRAQ

Religious vigilantes have killed at least 40 women in the southern city of Basra because their dress "violated Islamic teachings." Maj General Jalil Khalaf said: "The women of Basra are being horrifically murdered and then dumped in the garbage with notes saying they were killed for un-Islamic behavior."

SAUDI ARABIA

The parents of a nineteen year-old Saudi girl chained her by the feet in order to prevent her from meeting her fiancée whom her family would not accept.

Saudi women are not allowed to drive or change the color of their clothing or shake a man's hand (which some mullahs view as "adultery of the hand.") Women cannot marry without permission, retain custody of their children after a divorce, or "annoy" their husbands. They are also forbidden to "speak in public." A popular Saudi television preacher has stated that "a girl who is not beaten from an early age grows up to be a rebellious woman, difficult to control" and that "a woman who leaves her home without a veil is like a woman who goes out naked."

Those who emigrate into the West from these countries take these attitudes and customs along with them. So far, the West has been slow in noting or in trying to prevent what for us are crimes. On the other hand, the West has also offered refuge to and published the work of Islamic dissidents; appointed and elected pro-woman and anti-violence Muslims to public office; offered police protection and shelter to those in flight from Islamist violence in the West. Thus, also in the last month:

BRITAIN

The daughter of an imam who herself has converted to Christianity, is under serious police protection after receiving death threats from her family. She has, so far, had to move 45 times since she converted 15 years ago. She did so after she ran away from home to escape an arranged marriage.

Waris Dirie, who herself underwent female genital mutilation in her native Somalia has, together with Corinna Milborn, published a new book in Britain. They estimate that 500,000 girls and women have been genitally mutilated in Europe—even though it is illegal to do so. Dirie considers the "difficulties of bringing such cases to court, the culture of silence that keeps affected women quiet, and the muddled association of circumcision with Islam."

NORWAY

On the other hand: Norwegian author, Tor Erling Staff, has published a book in which he calls for "reduced sentences for honor murders." In his view, such Muslim men who kill are "betrayed by Norwegian society. They come from places where equality is an unknown concept. Where the thought of equality is a humiliation. Suddenly they land here, in the middle of equality paradise. It is clear there is stress…"

He is part of the problem.

HOLLAND

Dutch Minister of Integration, Ella Vogellar, admitted that the emancipation of immigrant women is expected to lead to more cases of honor related violence. A special task force has received about 470 such cases this year. Men are also the victims, either because they are homosexuals or because they try to help their sisters.

Not everyone is keeping their heads firmly down. In Amsterdam, Ehsan Jami, the founder of the Committee for Former Muslims, is about to release a film about the life of Mohammed. He says: "I show how violent and tyrannical Mohammed was. This man murdered three Jewish tribes, killed people who left the faith, and married a 6 year-old girl with whom he had sex when she was 9." Jami remains under heavy police protection and has offered EUR 50,000 to "anyone who can refute these facts."

Too many people in the West are misguided and believe that telling the truth about Islam is "Islamophobic" or simply dangerous. May we all begin to have the courage of Ehsan Jami (or Khaled Hosseini) because we are going to need it.

Pajamas Media
12/20/07

- 12 -

Iran's Ayatollah: West Abuses Women, Islam Honors Them

They are clever, these Iranian Islamists; subtle and sly. Deranged as no men have been before them. For example, just a few days ago, Iran's Supreme Ayatollah, Ali Khamenei, claimed that the West "abuses women" and that Islamic Iran "honors them." His proof? Islam forces women to "wear the hijab." Veiled women are entirely invisible to your average man-on-the-street whom, it is assumed, would otherwise sexually harass or rape every woman they see.

He said it. I didn't.

Khamenei is really a Second Wave American-born feminist in disguise. I kid you not. He agrees completely with the views of Ann Chamberlain. I reviewed her 2006 book, *A History of Women's Seclusion in the Middle East. The Veil in the Looking Glass* for *Middle East Quarterly*. Chamberlain writes that Western women who seek to integrate previously male-only space are far more "conservative" and "patriarchal" than are veiled Muslim women who live in purdah.

Chamberlain sees women-only space as equivalent to an anti-patriarchal resistance movement. She claims that pagan-era slave women in the Middle East were forced to work naked and to be sexually available at any moment to all men. Thus, "covered" and secluded women were safer than slave women. Wealthy women were veiled and the veil was a statement about their power and hence, unavailability.

Is Khameini trance-channeling Ann Chamberlain? According to Terence P. Jeffrey on the CBN, "Khamenei told the Iranian students' conference that in the Iranian vision of Islam, it was determined that poor women should be compelled to cover their entire bodies and faces in order to honor them and make their dress conform to the style adopted by aristocratic women. In ancient Iran, aristocratic women used to wear hijab," he said. "Women from lower classes did not bother. But when Islam came, it rejected such instances of discrimination. It said that all women must wear the hijab. In other words, it wanted to honor all women. Now, they [in the West] behave as if we are doing something wrong and they are doing the right thing! No, they are in the wrong. They must answer why they have been treating women like a commodity in order to gratify their own lust."

Khameini does not mention (or possibly even view) the practices of gender apartheid for alleging rape as "dishonoring" women. Instead, he focuses on the West's use of naked women (that hair, those elbows!) to sell products and the West's refusal to allow women to veil themselves in universities. He also insists that newly gathered statistics document that one-third of all men in the West batter women. A recent poll suggests that 12-16% of all women in Europe are battered at home. Does that figure soar when Third World communities are included?

I wonder what the statistics are in Iran: Closer to 90%? Maybe those abayas are not thick enough, dark enough, suffocating enough; maybe Iranian women have too many elbows? We've already seen Iran's rulers insist that women not swim, swim separately, or wear full body-bags when they swim in public . We have seen special outfits for riding bicycles. What next? Little eye-brow veils? Or just smother the whole face and be done with it?

Listen Mister: When you leave this much to the imagination of male jerks, a fully veiled woman can be pretty enticing. Why not give the men curfews (as Golda Meir once famously suggested)? They seem to be the problem. Not the women.

Pajamas Media
1/18/08

- 13 -
We Need a Prophet in the American Cabinet

I propose that the next American President appoint a Prophet to the Cabinet. We have entered an era where prophetic views and values are sorely required.

Prophets, (Jeremiah, Isaiah, Cassandra), see what's happening but the people and their leaders don't listen to them. Perhaps if prophets could once again assume official positions (with calling cards and press secretaries) their voices might be heard. Consigning prophets to the care and keeping of commercial or even academic publishing is a risk we can no longer afford to take.

I am not talking about False Prophets or lunatics but about the real deal.

The handwriting-on-the-sky has been alarmingly visible for quite some time. In the 1970s, French novelist Jean Raspail published a Swiftian novel, *The Camp of the Saints*, in which he envisioned a flotilla of millions of immigrants traveling from the Ganges to France. An all-powerful, politically correct intelligentsia that has taught Europe that it must atone for its racist, colonial guilt welcomes the invasion. Europe—European culture as we have known it—is destroyed.

In the 1980s and 1990s, the Egyptian-born scholar Bat Ye'or and Italy's finest journalist Oriana Fallaci tried to warn us in both learned and passionate ways. They continued this work right into the twenty-first century. In the beginning, they were dismissed as "paranoid" and "racist," viciously attacked, even sued.

From the mid-1990s on, other voices chimed in: the eminent Daniel Pipes for one, and the equally eminent Ibn Warraq, for another. Post 9/11, both men have continued this work and have been joined by

Robert Spencer, Steve Emerson, Ayaan Hirsi Ali, Nonie Darwish, Wafa Sultan, and scores of others (Pim Fortyn, Theo Von Gogh, Bruce Bawer, Carol Gould, Melanie Phillips, Fiamma Nierenstein, myself).

So far, what we have said has made little difference. We, too, have often been dismissed and attacked as "racists" and "reactionaries" by other westerners. Some of my prophet-friends say that the tide is turning, that both European governments and civilians now "get it."

Welcome news—although rather late in the day.

In my view, the signs are still there for all to see. My email this morning tells me:

In Iran, Hossein Shariatmadari, managing editor of 'Kayhan' (Universe), one of Iran's most influential newspapers, has "issued a strongly worded editorial inviting Muslims to topple moderate Islamic governments and attack US, European and Israeli interests." In the editorial, entitled "The enemy's shield," Shariatmadari argues that in Shia or Sunni Islam "It is legal to strike those who protect the enemy." "The real enemies," says Shariatmadari are "The barbaric Zionists, the ferocious Americans and their European allies."

Not to be outdone, Al-Qaeda has threatened to assasinate Gordon Brown and Tony Blair and to devastate Britain with a wave of suicide bombings unless all British troops are withdrawn from Iraq and Afghanistan and all Islamist prisoners are freed from British jails by the end of March. This threat appeared on a recognized jihadi website (al-ekhlass.net) but has now been taken down. It was also posted in English under "Al Qaeda in Britain" but has also been removed. Despite such threats, Britain continues to groan under the costs of subsidizing the precipitously rising birth rate among non-employed or minimally waged immigrants.

The upper house of the Afghan parliament supported a death sentence which was issued against a young Afghan journalist for blasphemy in northern Afghanistan. Pervez Kambaksh, 23, was convicted last week of downloading and distributing an article insulting Islam. (The article concerned women and Islam.) He has denied the charge. These Afghan Parliament members are America's and Europe's allies.

Turkey's governing political party agreed to lift the ban on Islamic headscarves for women attending university. This group almost made it into the European Union—and the Turkish military may stage a coup over this.

In Jordan, a 17 year-old girl was strangled to death by her brother in a Palestinian refugee camp in Jordan in what was reported to be an honor killing. But this must be due to the alleged Israeli Occupation—oh wait a minute, Israel does not occupy Jordan.

The same Hamas that invaded neighboring Egypt's sovereign space, has, since Israel withdrew from Gaza, bombarded the Israeli border town of Sderot with more than 4,000 rocket and mortar attacks, killing, injuring, and terrifying many innocent civilians. (Much thanks to Jennifer Lazlo Mizrahi of The Israel Project for publishing a Time-Line of these rocket attacks.)

And our trendy friends at al-Jazeera are trying to exert more control over the English-language outlet. The editor-in-chief, Ibrahim Hilal, was not pleased by how his mainly western journalists handled the infamous Mohammed-the-teddy-bear incident. According to one source, "Hilal sent an email banning the story from being run on al-Jazeera English because it would upset Muslims. It was only covered when there were riots in Sudan." (A British schoolteacher in Sudan was convicted of insulting Islam by allowing her class of six-year-olds to name a teddy bear "Muhammad.")

Yes, there are signs of resistance afoot as well: The Danish Royal Library is planning to exhibit the Mohammed cartoons—but the British decision to label all acts of Islamist terrorism as "anti-Islamic" (which columnist Mark Steyn labels as "Orwellian") is far more characteristic of our times.

Pajamas Media
1/30/08

- 14 -
My Headscarf Headache

My headscarf is giving me a headache! What I mean, is that the issue of the Islamic headscarf is a tricky, thorny one with no hard-and-fast solution in sight precisely when one is required. Just yesterday, a dear friend challenged me on this very subject.

She said: "How can you favor the state forbidding women from doing something that they want to do for religious reasons?"

A fair enough question.

My immediate response: Women's freedom may depend upon the separation of religion and state. What one does at home or in one's mosque, church, temple, or synagogue is one thing. But, is it wise to subsidize diverse religious expressions in a taxpayer-supported public school? Especially in the West where the headscarf is as much a symbol of jihad and women's subordination as it is an expression of a modest, religious choice?

In 2004, the headscarf was a burning issue in France when the country passed a law forbidding the wearing of "ostentatious" religious symbols. This meant that no one could wear a cross, a turban, or a yarmulke either but the law was truly aimed at hijab—the wearing of headscarves by Muslim women. Feminists argued both sides of this controvery.

In 2008, the headscarf is again a burning issue in Turkey where an increasingly religious population, including women, is demanding the right to head-veil in university. This is seen as a complete reversal of the enormous gains made by Ataturk in 1921.

It is also a pendulum swing from the various Arab and Muslim feminist movements of that era in which unveiling was a linch-pin issue.

Egypt's Huda Shaarawi must be turning in her grave. I wonder what she would say?

Yes, it's true: Religious families in the West rarely give their children "freedom of choice" when it comes to religious education and practices. Both girls and boys are indoctrinated from an early age. Western law does not intefere with this. On what basis could we do so where only Muslims are concerned? Or rather, like France, are we now willing to interfere in the private religious realm because of new, Islamist "clear and present dangers?"

Ideally of course, tolerating diverse ethnic and religious choices is a great Western virtue. The problem arises when those who themselves are intolerant wish to use such Western virtues in order to achieve separatist, hostile-parasitic enclaves. But, hasn't some degree of separatism been true for every immigrant group—at least in America? Hasn't the genius of America resided precisely in allowing each immigrant group to remain identified in separate ways while becoming identified simultaneously as Americans?

My friend is a religious Jew and is therefore very sensitive to the dangers involved when Jewish religious expression is forbidden. Indeed, even today, the Jews of Europe have been advised by their rabbis to hide their yarmulkes and stars of David lest they be scorned or beaten on the streets—something which has, alas, been happening.

But, said I, with a heavy heart: We can't really compare apples and oranges. Crosses and yarmulkes are not the same as hijab or niqab. With some exceptions, Jews are not only or solely defined as members of their religious group. Most also partake of the public, secular, modern culture. Also, there are less than 15 million Jews world-wide. There are 1.2 billion Muslims and counting. If every single Jew covered every inch of themselves with Jewish symbols it would be as a drop in the sea compared to every single Muslim donning hijab.

Of course, as a religious Jew, my friend is still concerned with the morality involved. From a Jewish point of view, what's good for a Jew should be good for every other religious group since all humanity has been created in "God's image."

But, what about women's rights? Where do we stand on a woman's right not to wear a headscarf? However, what should we do when a woman claims that her right to freely practice her religion is being interfered with if we stop her from veiling? Does the state have the right to force her, against her will, to expose her hair to strange men?

Indeed, this is the subject of a 2007 federal lawsuit brought by the

ACLU on behalf of Jameela Medina. She is a Los Angeles Ph.D student who was riding a commuter train without a proper ticket. For what should have been a minor matter, she was taken off the train, arrested, and kept in jail for several hours where she was forced to remove her headscarf. Medina also claims that she was "intimidated" by a deputy sheriff who accused her of "being a terrorist" and who called Islam an "evil" religion.

No one should be so insulted in America. And, prisoners are actually allowed to wear headscarves in jail—a point which the ACLU is arguing.

I know that many educated Muslim women choose to wear hijab or niqab. But, I also know that many educated Muslim women who choose not to do so are being threatened, pressured, shunned, and even killed for this reason, both in the West and in Muslim countries.

I also know that some feminists have claimed that historically, veiled women on the streets may have been less harassed by men in the Islamic East than unveiled women were at the same time in the West. (No proof exists for this claim.) Today, separate buses and railway cars for women-only have been launched in Hindu India and Mexico in response to the still ongoing harassment of women.

I have been told, over and over again, that many Muslim women do not feel "coerced" into wearing a headscarf in the West as much as they feel called upon to register a permanent, visible, protest against promiscuity and the eroticization of women in the West.

In the 1960s and 1970s, I thought it was poetic justice for former "colonials" to sport their colorful customs all over London. Bangles, nose-rings, turbans, long flowing robes on both men and women—yes! But, by the 21st century, these exotic garments are ominously value-laden; now, they signify a serious cultural, military, political, and theological invasion of Britain and the West.

Quo Vadis my friends? What shall we do in America? Do we allow headscarves or do we ban them? They symbolize or "signal" gender apartheid. Finally, what about the indoctrination into hating Jews and other infidels which begins in childhood and is theologically driven in certain mosques and religious schools? Right here in the USA?

Pajamas Media
1/31/08

- 15 -

Raging Muslim Taxi Drivers in
North American Cities

Are immigrant Muslim taxi drivers heroically selfless "family men" or are they soldiers in an advancing jihadic Army?

As a New Yorker, I have been driven by very friendly and exceptionally courteous male Muslim taxi drivers from Iran, Afghanistan, Pakistan, Egypt, and Somalia, and once, by an enchanting woman driver from Afghanistan—but I have also held on for dear life as ill-tempered, mentally unbalanced, unbelievably misogynistic male Muslim drivers have indulged in full-blown rage attacks as they careened in traffic.

Of course, I've also experienced similarly bad behavior at the hands of home-grown taxi drivers as well. Maybe long hours, low pay, and No Exit will do it every time.

Nevertheless: Aqsa Parvez's father Muhammed, who honor-murdered his daughter because she refused to wear an Islamic headscarf, worked as a taxi driver in Mississauga, a suburb of Toronto. Yasir Said, who murdered his two teenage daughters, Amina and Sarah, because they had become too western, was also a taxi driver in Dallas.

Taxi drivers in England have been known to constitute a network which spies on and actively returns girls and women who are trying to escape being honor murdered. According to a just-released report, UK teachers and police officials are "afraid to take action against so-called honor crimes for fear of being accused of racism." The *Daily Mail* notes that, in addition,

Researchers say taxi drivers, police and government workers

of Asian origin are returning women to the domestic abuse they want to escape.

Taxi drivers again!

In 1997, in New Orleans, a blind woman tried to enter a taxi with her seeing eye dog. The Muslim taxi driver physically attacked her and further injured an already-broken wrist. At trial, the judge described the driver's behavior as a "total disgrace" and sentenced him to 120 days of community service at the Lighthouse for the Blind.

In 1999, a Muslim taxi driver in Cincinnati refused to transport a blind female passenger with a seeing eye dog. The woman complained; CAIR defended him as having acted in accordance with his religious beliefs. (Dogs are considered impure and contact with them is considered to render a Muslim ritually unfit for prayer.)

In 2000, in Edmonton, Canada, a blind woman tried to enter a cab with her seeing eye dog. The driver first claimed "allergies," but then stated that "taking a dog conflicted with his religion." At trial, he failed to produce the necessary proof from an allergist. However, the case against him was dismissed because it had been improperly filed.

In 2005 and 2006, some Muslim taxi drivers in Minneapolis refused to pick up airport fares whom they suspected of transporting alcohol or pork. In 2007, the Metropolitan Airport Commission of Minnesota unanimously voted to crack down on such drivers who "declined to transport passengers with alcohol or pork."

What next? Will Muslim taxi drivers refuse to transport "naked" women? "Naked" as defined by their faces showing?

But, what's true of some Muslim taxi drivers is also true of some Muslim convenience store owners.

For example, in 2003, in Edmonton, Canada, a blind woman tried to enter a convenience store owned by a Muslim and was forcibly ejected by the owner who stated that "this store is also my church because I pray and eat here and my religion will not allow dogs or any animal to come in here." In 2004, at trial, she stated that he started yelling at her and did not allow her to explain why she needed the dog, what the dog meant to her, or to enunciate her legal rights.

In 2005, a blind man in Brooksville, Florida, who tried to enter a store with his seeing eye dog, was similarly thrown out by a raging Muslim.

Other correlates of "raging Muslim" behavior also exist: Poverty, a limited education, (but this is not always so), plus dim prospects for a brighter future—coupled with a culturally and religiously approved zero-frustration tolerance, hostility towards non-Muslims, and supremacist paranoia when non-Muslims are in control.

Please understand: Nothing that I am saying has anything to do with "race." Muslims come in all colors and ethnicities.

If I lived in England, I would now have to describe Muslim taxi drivers who engage in any of the above behaviors as committing "anti-Islamic" acts. By the way, I originally thought that UK officials had lost their last marble when they issued these new, Orwellian directives, but I also understand that these officials are finally getting desperate and want to inspire the hopefully "good" but all-too-silent Muslim majority to protest the jihadists who have, presumably, hijacked their culture and religion.

Let's see if this works.

A final point: Generations of immigrants to the West have "done time" as taxi and truck drivers, dishwashers, small shop owners. There is no shame in this. They have put their children through college and graduate school. I hope that the silent Muslim majority, including the taxi drivers, follow in their august footsteps—and yet, I remain uneasy about this.

Individual taxi drivers are innocent until proven guilty. Culturally different styles do not always rise to the level of a crime—although rudeness and arrogance in public life is always quite disheartening and intimidating. As a group, taxi drivers know city routes; convenience stores and gas station owners control the city's food and gasoline supply. Were even a small group of drivers and shop owners to unite for an Islamist purpose—we would be vulnerable in these specific ways. Muslim citizens would be as vulnerable as non-Muslims.

A number of sites posted my article about "Raging Muslim Taxi Drivers in North American Cities." A comment was posted at *Intellectual Conservative* which I will share.

In February of 2007, a Muslim Somali taxi driver, Ibrahim Sheikh Ahmed, was driving with a suspended permit in Nashville, Tennessee. The comment continues:

> The driver picks up two Christian college students and gets into a discussion about religion, telling them that Hitler was a "good man because he was trying to rid the world of Jews." *Nashville City Paper* reports that when the students paid the cabby they expressed their disagreement by telling him "If

you're going to live in a country like ours, you're going to have to tolerate other people's beliefs." This didn't sit well with Mr. Ahmed who then proceeded to run them down, hitting one of the students, breaking his pelvis and leg. The police who arrested him, testified that Mr. Ahmed told them that he had a problem "managing his anger." He was charged with attempted homicide. Check out the video of the newscast report here: http://es.youtube.com/watch?v=71vdfAgv6fg

According to the *Nashville City Paper*, Sheihk Ahmed pled guilty to two counts of aggravated assault and will serve six years for each count, to be served concurrently. His sentencing hearing will take place on February 7, 2008.

If someone were to do a study of taxi driver incident rates, we might discover that drivers of many religions (and of no particular religion) also get into fights with their passengers. If someone has done such a study, I would welcome the results.

Pajamas Media
2/4/08

- 16 -
Not All Headcoverings are Equal

Why has the *New York Times* published an article today ("Veiled Democracy") written by Harvard Law Professor, Noah Feldman, in which Feldman explains that if Turkey allows Muslim women to wear the Islamic headscarf in universities that Turkey will be that much closer to a liberal democracy?

Isn't Feldman the very man who wrote a long, bitter, and rather shameful article in the *Sunday New York Times* magazine in which he excoriated his own Orthodox Jewish brethren for (accidentally, as it turns out), not including a photo of himself together with his non-Jewish, non-Orthodox, non-convert wife at a class reunion?

Oh, how he carried on about the hard-hearted prejudices of Orthodox Jews (some of whom also wear head coverings). And yet, here he is suggesting that an Islamic religious symbol—a head covering—might be the key to a liberal democracy and, as such, might also render Turkey a worthy entrant into the European Union.

Turkey—but not Israel.

More: Feldman says that allowing the Islamic headscarf is the "best possible refutation of the claim that Islam and democracy are incompatible" and would be a "case study of religious freedom against coercive secularism."

So, Feldman is a passionate warrior for Islamic religious expression but an equally passionate warrior against similar Jewish religious expression.

Why? Does Feldman think that Islam is more liberal than Judaism? Does the Professor understand that Muslims are not allowed to convert, nor can they marry a non-Muslim who does not convert to

Islam? Does Feldman understand that Muslim women are being killed for refusing to wear the headscarf?

Maybe I'm just a bit cranky, what with the Archbishop of Canterbury calling for Sharia law in Britain—a first article of faith in the Church of fundamentalist Liberalism. By the way: Rest assured, Sharia law has already been hard at work in settling many disputes in the UK, ranging from violent crimes to divorces.

Is Feldman entirely out of touch with Muslim-world realities? How about the American woman who was just arrested and strip-searched in Riyadh for the "crime" of sitting in Starbuck's with a male non-relative business associate? How about the two sisters in Iran who were savagely lashed and who are now slated to be stoned to death for the alleged crime of "adultery?"

What is wrong with Noah Feldman? Has the Harvard Kool-Aid had its way with him?

Pajamas Media
2/8/08

- 17 -
I Challenge Noah Feldman to a Debate about the Islamic Headscarf

On Friday, February 8th, 2008 I wrote about Professor Noah Feldman's op-ed piece in the *New York Times* in which he viewed a long-standing Turkish ban on the wearing of headscarves in universities as a ban against religious "freedom." On Saturday, February 9th, I noted here that on the very next day, February 9th, the *New York Times* (page A4) featured an interview with a Turkish woman lawyer, Fatma Benli, titled: "Under a Scarf, a Turkish Lawyer Fighting to Wear It."

Why is the *New York Times* so invested in securing an Islamic religious right (or cultural custom) in Turkey?

Here's an idea: In a gesture towards even-handedness, perhaps The Paper of Record might consider agitating for the right of European Jews to wear headcoverings (kipot or yarmulkes) without risking being cursed, beaten, or knifed to death. Better yet: How about some even-handed agitation for the religious rights, not only of Muslims in Turkey, but of Jews, Christians, Hindus, and Ba'hai, to practice their religions openly in places like Saudi Arabia, Iran, Indonesia—without being arrested and stoned to death?

Yet once again, the *New York Times*, (page A3) featured another article about the Islamic headscarf in Turkey. Granted, this time they quoted some Turks who oppose lifting the ban. These secularists point out that "a woman's right to resist being forced to wear head scarves by an increasingly conservative society—was under threat." (I made this point in my blog on this subject and would welcome Noah Feldman's response to this point.)

Further, this piece, written by Sabrina Tavernise, quotes a member of the Turkish Parliament. "This decision will bring further pressure on women...it will ultimately bring us Hezbollah terror, Al Qaeda terror and fundamentalism." Finally, a former Turkish Justice Minister, Hikmet Sami Turk, says: "(Lifting the headscarf ban has) been presented as a liberty to cover the head, but in practice, it is going to evolve into a ban on uncovered hair."

Noah Feldman: I implore you to listen to such voices. They know something about the Islamic headscarf, namely, that it is an augur of coercion, punishment, and the further subordination of women. Taking a "neutral" position, quoting both sides of the issue, is ultimately tantamount to siding with coercion.

The Islamic headscarf is the not the same as the Jewish kippah, wig or head covering, although I agree that there are troubling signs among a mere handful of ultra-religious Jews in Jerusalem in which the women are being coerced into wearing burqas! and in which long, wide, heavy, dark, and completely unattractive clothing is being forced upon Jewish women in certain ultra-religious sects, both in America and Israel. I view this as an Islamification of Judaism and I fear it both among Jews and among our Muslim cousins.

As I've written before: I believe that mosque and state, church and state, synagogue and state should be separate and that religious women should be allowed to practice modesty and to wear the sign and symbol of their religion at home, and at worship. Doing so on the job, in the streets, and in the classrooms is more problematic—not because there is anything intrinsically wrong with wearing a headscarf or a religious headcovering, but because of the unique and specific nature of Islam. Christians do not kill their own who convert to another religion. Jews do not kill their own who break the ten commandments. Muslims do.

Islam is a totalitarian political ideology, not only a religion, and should be treated as such—at least until such time that the moderates, reformers, and peace-loving Muslims have silenced the aggressive terrorists and haters of freedom who now speak for them.

Pajamas Media
2/10/08

- 18 -

Burqas Come to Bohemia

A friend calls to tell me that suddenly, a completely burqa-ed (or abaya-ed) woman seems to have moved into the legendary apartment building for artists-only in Greenwich Village that my friend calls home. She says: "This woman also wears dark sun glasses so you can't even see her eyes."

Then, another friend who lives in the same building calls me. She says: "This woman is spooky. But I'm afraid to talk to her, to ask her whether she or perhaps her husband are artists. She has some really big men with her. If she were friendly, she might stop and talk to another woman, wouldn't she?"

It's 2008 in Greenwich Village, which has a long and honorable history of radical "attitude"—and my phone caller is whispering.

"Maybe she's engaged in some kind of political theatre," I suggest. "Ask her."

But my colleagues, who are brave artists, do not think this is possible. They accompany each other on a midnight mission to photograph the sign the burqa-ed Lady has on her door. It reads:

"Only Allah (God) deserves to be worshipped. (He is One. He has no partner.) Adam, Noah, Abraham, Lot, Job…Moses, Jesus, and Muhammed (peace and blessings of Allah be upon them) are Allah's slave servants and Messengers. And…Treat others the way you want to be treated."

I have no comment at this time. I am merely the Messenger, passing along this information.

Pajamas Media
3/19/08

- 19 -

Immigrant Millionaire Woman Sentenced to 11 Years in Jail for Enslaving and Torturing Her Female Maids

S ometimes justice is served.

Yesterday, U.S. District Court Judge Arthur Spatt, sentenced 46 year-old Varsha Sabhnani, a millionaire who enslaved and tortured two Indonesian female maids in her Muttontown, Long Island mansion, to 11 years in jail. Her husband, Mahender, will receive a lesser jail term today. One maid, Samirah, arrived in 2002, the second maid, Enung, arrived in 2005. Their passports were immediately confiscated and they became "virtual slaves."

The couple own a world wide perfume business and have both been convicted of "forced labor, conspiracy, involuntary servitude, and harboring aliens." According to Assistant U.S. Attorney Mark Lesko, "This did not happen in the 1800s. This happened in the 21st century." You may see the Sabhnanis, their children, (who claim that no abuse occurred), their lawyer—and the demonstration organized by domestic workers on video.

Varsha, a striking, even beautiful woman, has been dubbed "Cruella de Ville." Both she and her husband are from India and are Hindu Sindhis from wealthy families. According to testimony, Varsha once interrupted one of the maids while the maid was praying and told her: "I am your God. I can make you dead." Varsha, who grew up in Indonesia and married Mehender in an arranged marriage when she was 18, did not take the stand in her own defense. However, she was quoted as saying: "I love my children very much. I was brought to this Earth to help people who are in need."

Clearly, she is not playing with a full deck but whether or not she is mentally ill is irrelevant. According to her lawyer, Jeffrey Hoffman, Varsha once weighed 325 pounds but her decision to starve herself down to 135 pounds made her "angry."

Is this an anti-Twinkie defense? Dan White, the man who shot Harvey Milk, the gay member of San Francisco's Board of Supervisors and the mayor, George Moscone, tried to argue that "the (sugar in the) twinkie" made him do it.

Whether or not starving herself led to a "chemical imbalance" or not, she engaged in criminal actions over a long period of time. Only in America and in the West would such an "employer" be indicted and convicted.

For millennia, female domestic servants have been brutally abused. They have been underfed, overworked, underpaid, never paid, sexually harassed, raped, and impregnated by their employers, tortured, and even murdered—all without recourse. This is still a common scenario in the Middle East, Far East, India, Africa, and in South America. Diplomats, including United Nations officials who hail from these countries, sometimes continue such foul practices when they live and work in the West.

The two Indonesian housekeepers, Samirah and Enung, were semi-starved and therefore forced to eat from a garbage can—but they were then punished for doing so. Their punishments included being beaten with brooms and umbrellas, slashed with knives, burned with boiling water, forced to climb stairs, take freezing showers, digest dozens of hot chilli peppers and then eat their own vomit as punishment when they could not keep the peppers down. They slept on mats on the kitchen floor. Each housekeeper was paid nothing but their families back in Indonesia received $100.00 a month. After years of what federal prosecutors called "modern day slavery," one of the housekeepers escaped. The police found the second housekeeper cowering in a closet.

Federal prosecutors want the Sabhnanis to pay back wages of 1.1 million dollars. Their lawyer has said that $200,000.00 will be sufficient.

I hope this decision makes other Third World immigrant employers or diplomatic families think long and hard before they enslave domestic workers here on our soil. This fine decision is yet one more example of why America remains an exceptional country.

Pajamas Media
6/27/08

- 20 -

In Afghanistan, All Women Are Prostitutes, All Americans Are Infidel-Crusaders

The photo arrests my gaze. It instantly haunts me. It shows two Afghan women chatting while sitting on their heels, close to the ground. They are both wearing iridescent light blue burqas. One seems to be clutching a shopping bag. They are about to be shot to death by Taliban fighters who have accused them of running a prostitution ring that catered to American soldiers. For good measure, the Taliban also accused them of working for the local governor. According to the BBC:

> A spokesman for the Ghazni governor said the dead women were "innocent local people" and the US has also dismissed the allegations. US military spokesman 1st Lt. Nathan Perry said he had never heard of "anything close to that nature." Ghazni officials told Agence France Presse that the women, killed late on Saturday, had no connection with the government.

It is impossible to tell how old the women are. Perhaps they are like some of the women I once knew as servants in Kabul: Hearty, shy, good-natured, energetic peasant women who hid their faces in their long veils when they giggled. These two murdered souls could not have been like the more educated women I once knew in Kabul who were impossibly sophisticated, certainly more knowledgeable about western fashion than I was. The Taliban and the endless, hopeless war has made it impossible for such women to survive and flourish.

The photo, taken on July 12th, 2008 could be an illustration for Khaled Hosseini's *The Kite Runner*. Please recall that this novel, tailored to American tastes, still convincingly shows us how sadistic and twisted the Taliban are. Amnesty International has also documented this and American feminist groups have denounced it as well.

Many say that "Islam" has nothing to do with such behaviors. And yet—the Taliban view themselves as "holy warriors" and perhaps as Saudi-style Sunni Arabs. Thus far, the Taliban has not been publicly denounced as anti-Islam by any of the leading Muslim clerics world-wide.

A few years ago, thousands of Egyptian men went on a "sexual wilding" rampage in Cairo right after they heard a Ramadan sermon in a mosque; they assaulted women who were both veiled and unveiled; they ripped off their clothing. In Algeria, after hearing their mullah denounce the impoverished women who were working as cleaning women for foreign companies in their city of Hassi Messoud, about three hundred men also went on a rampage—only they killed, gang-raped, mutilated, and buried women alive.

In both instances, (in Egypt and in Algeria), "foreign influence" or "colonial-imperialism" did not cause the criminal behaviors. What did? Did Islam do it? Or is this bad behavior a perversion of Islam both by the mullahs and by their followers? And, if it's the latter, where are the Muslim reformers?

We dare not underestimate the Taliban's willingness to kill and die—and to engage in a lifetime of guerrilla warfare. The same Taliban "militants" who executed these two Afghan women in cold blood the evening of July 12th, also managed to get inside an American military outpost in Ghazni province on July 13th that had allegedly only been constructed three days ago. The Taliban killed nine American soldiers and wounded fifteen more.

Historically, each time that Afghanistan has evolved beyond the Middle Ages, it has been plunged back into medieval darkness. What might it take for their cursed country to escape its own history?

Pajamas Media
7/14/08

- 21 -

Damsels of Death:
Female Suicide Killers in Iraq

F our female suicide killers just murdered 57 people and wounded 300 others in Iraq. Many of their victims were on a religious pilgrimage.

This should no longer surprise us. Like men, women are human beings and are therefore as close to the apes as to the angels. Thus, like men, women are as likely to nourish as to destroy. Still, we live in a culture that on the one hand, suspects women of being sneaky, "bitchy," even evil but on the other hand, idealizes women as morally superior to men and as Natural Born Mothers, not as Natural Born Killers.

We are used to hearing that women in the Third World, including the Islamic world, are victims, not killers. Can they be both? Yes, they can.

According to the U.S. Military, in the last five years in Iraq, 43 women carried out suicide bombings. Women hide their explosive belts and bombs under their flowing black abayas—one more reason that such outerwear should be banned in the West. Actually, Muslims kill more Muslims than anyone else does. This latest attack was apparently launched by Sunni Muslims against Shi'ite Muslims. It might be in the interests of Islam to ban such clothing which has been used to disguise both male and female terrorists.

Of course, *The New York Times* suggests that "despair" and "spousal grief" drives women to become suicide terrorists.

Not so fast.

Women who have been despised and abused since birth may be

especially vulnerable to the kind of ideological and religious entrapment which promises them glory (and their families money). Also, due to inbreeding/first cousin marriage and family violence, they may be mentally retarded, already terrorized, or prone to depression and therefore easy to manipulate. Female suicide killers may also be filled with rage—enough rage so that they want to scapegoat strangers to avenge themselves against family intimates.

True, some women are mourning the loss of brothers, fathers, and sons but what about Islamist ideology? What about al-Qaeda handlers who tempt women with glory just as they tempt men? What about the Palestinian members of Islamic Jihad, Al-Aqsa Brigade, Hezbollah and Hamas (al-Qaeda does this too), who exploit depressed, mentally ill, and mentally retarded women into strapping on an explosive belt and blowing themselves up? What about a culture in which being born female is often a capital crime? If someone feels she is already a marked woman—that her family is ready to honor-kill her for some alleged misdeed—why not redeem her shame by going out in a blaze of glory and taking some infidels or the "wrong" kind of Muslims along with her?

Yesterday's huge blasts in Iraq were carried out by four different women and few infidels were involved. These women continued the centuries-old feud between Sunni and Shi'ite Muslims. If anyone still believes that women are more compassionate than men, think about this: According to the *International Herald Tribune*,

> The second (female-launched) attack occurred inside a tent that provided shade and rest for female pilgrims. The female bomber walked into the tent, sat down and, according to a police official, Abu Ali, read the Qur'an with the women sitting inside. When she exited the tent, she left a bag behind, and moments later, it exploded.

The woman sat down and prayed with them and then sent them to their deaths.

I remember two films, one by my friend Pierre Rehov (*Silent Exodus, Suicide Killers*), the other by a promising newcomer, Shaun Beyer. Both filmmakers had interviewed Palestinian female terrorists in Israeli jails. None of the terrorists showed any remorse. Many were proud of their murderous or potentially murderous attacks. They all seemed quite religious. One woman had assumed a leadership position; she and her enforcers policed and punished the other women with enormous

104

cruelty.

These women were ideologically empowered, both politically and theologically, to commit violence. They saw nothing wrong with doing so—just as the families of their culture see nothing wrong with honor murders.

My friends: We are up against a formidable ideological enemy which worships death, despises life, and lives only to fight, kill, and die. We must defeat it.

I would like to acknowledge my colleague, Dr. Nancy L. Kobrin, for her analysis of Arab and Muslim culture in terms of its psychological effect on boys and girls, men and women.

Pajamas Media
7/28/08

- 22 -
A Debate With a Commenter Who Defends Female Suicide Bombers

O h dear, I have a live one here. Emily Brink has now posted three comments which take issue with what I've written about female suicide bombers. In each instance, she misses the boat—as well as the train, the plane, and the camel. She writes:

> The only problem I have with this article is that Chesler assumes that mentally ill people don't know the difference between right and wrong. She also makes some comments about 'inbreeding' among Arabs that I think are just meant to be mean and are not factual. But most troubling to me was the calling of these women mentally ill and thus furthering the stigma that mentally ill people must face all the time.

I see. So Emily defends the moral agency of mentally ill people who, in her opinion, "know the difference between right and wrong." Thus, I have "stigmatized" the female suicide bombers by daring to suggest that they have not made a free and rational choice about blowing themselves and others up. She does not focus upon the ideological indoctrination, or on the exploitation or manipulation of vulnerable women; she sees only free women making free choices.

Emily describes herself as a "mentally ill woman who has a mentally retarded son."

I will take no cheap shots here since I agree that mental illness does exist; that it is painful, and often crippling; and that forced treatments are usually inhumane. However, I also know that when someone is actively hallucinating or is clinically depressed or in a rage that they do not make wise decisions.

In her second comment, Brink minimizes the increase of female suicide killers by saying that girls and women are also increasingly violent in the West. She writes:

> This conversation seems one-sided, examining the crimes of female suicide bombers as if our own culture didn't have its own epidemic of violence by women...Women still want to be equal to men, and sometimes that frustration comes out in the form of violence.

Another comment, by "Fred" addresses Brink's point as well as anything I might say. Here it is:

> But the kind of violence that Ms. Chesler is getting at is more than the usual criminal kind of violence that ensnares women as well as men in our cultures. This kind of violence is ideological, theological, cosmological. It is the act of holding a gun or sword to the heads of other human beings with the aim of exacting "divine" punishment. It says, "If you don't adhere to Allah's demands, we will kill you and indeed we are already in the process of taking your lives. This is POLITICAL violence.

Finally, in her comment today, Brink reveals her hand (and more ignorance). She writes:

> I am ashamed to even be in this conversation. Islam is a noble religion and culture, and several people here have completely dismissed it as backward and invalid, which is exactly the sort of cultural chauvinism that keeps the bombs flying. I'd point out that Islam enjoyed a golden age while Europe was still in the dark ages. Islam pioneered women's rights during this time and made many important advances in mathematics and literature, and jews and christians who lived under the Moors enjoyed complete religious freedom. I think the comments here on Islam are totally racist.

Muslims from many walks of life will tell you it is America's support for Israel that enrages them. I believe that if we stopped that, it would go a long way towards reconciliation. But I know that is not going to happen, because of the large and vocal Jewish population in the U.S.

Ah, Emily. There was never a Golden Age nor has every Muslim or all Islam traditionally behaved in "noble ways." They have been genocidal toward infidels and genocidal towards each other in terms of Sunni/Shi'ite feuding. Perhaps Brink should read the works of Bat Ye'or, Andrew Bostom, Nonie Darwish, Steve Emerson, Ibn Warraq, Daniel Pipes, Robert Spencer, and countless others on this precise point.

A dead giveaway: Brink capitalizes Moors, Islam, and Muslims but presents Jews and Christians in lower case form as jews and christians.

Only leftists and Islamists do this. Or, perhaps Brink might argue, the "mentally ill" do so as well.

Pajamas Media
7/31/08

- 23 -
Pakistani Slave Brides, Underage Forced Marriage in Saudi Arabia

"Shaikha," a 16-year-old Saudi girl, drank bleach in an attempt to kill herself because her father was forcing her to marry a 75-year-old man. And why? So that Shaikha's father could himself marry the elderly man's 13-year-old daughter! Shaikha begged and pleaded not to be forced into this marriage—even her mother supported her plea; all to no avail.

While such normalized atrocities continue in Saudi Arabia and elsewhere in the Muslim world, the publisher, Random House, cancels the publication of a novel, *The Jewel of Medina*, based on the life of Aisha, the prophet Mohammed's beloved wife whom he married when she was either six or seven years old. The marriage was presumably consummated when Aisha was nine-years-old.

Can there possibly be a connection between what Mohammed did and what other Muslim men do? Is the mere suggestion heretical? Is telling the truth about Mohammed heretical?

According to the article in Al-Arabiya, Shaikha might have some redress because theoretically, according to Sharia law, both parties have to consent to the marriage or the marriage may be considered "null and void." However, in practice, girls who resist their family's choice of bridegroom can be killed for doing so.

A Pakistani mother and son unit in England imported a "slave bride" from Pakistan whom the son, "egged on by his mother," violently beat and tormented daily. (Oedipus and Jocasta can't hold a candle to this merged pair).Their fiendish plan was to turn the first wife into the

109

family's "slave" and to procure a second wife with whom to have children. The man, Haroon Ahktar, violently beat 20 year-old Sania Bibi twice a day, sometimes more. She was forced to work 17 hours a day. Her mother-in-law, Zafia Bibi, kept threatening to have her "shot in the head." A sister-in-law threatened to have her put in an asylum and "given electric shocks." Haroon Ahktar threw her down the stairs, smashed her into windows, dragged her by the hair, cursed her constantly. According to Tamara Cohen in the *Daily Mail*:

> (Ahktar) said 'You are not good enough for me' and he would get married a second time and he would have children through his second marriage and I would have to take care of these children.

> The jury of seven men and five women heard that when the teenager arrived in the UK her clothes, shoes, and jewelry were immediately taken from her by her mother-in-law. She was forced to wear pajamas for her housework, and banned from answering the door, or using the telephone.

When Sania Bibi escaped and went to relatives for refuge, they turned their back on her. They told her that family "honor" demanded that she stay with her husband's family.

Miraculously, Ahktar was convicted of five counts of bodily harm. No matter what the sentence turns out to be, the fact that a trial took place and that a conviction was obtained constitutes a powerful triumph of western law over such normalized barbarism.

I hope that the British police understand that Sania Bibi is a marked woman who may need permanent round the clock protection. More: I hope that publishers in the West understand why documenting such truths is so crucial.

Pajamas Media
8/19/08

- 24 -

The Stoning of Soraya M in Iran: Not Caused by Western Imperialism

Phyllis Chesler's Speech for the Women United 9/25 Rally Protesting Ah-madinejad and his Christian Supporters. 5:30pm NYC, across the Street from the Grand Hyatt Hotel, East 42nd St and Lexington Ave.

I wish I could be with you in person this evening but, given my recently implanted titanium steel hip, my days of street rallies may be over. But I am with you in spirit and have sent a colleague to cover the rally for me.

I congratulate you all: the inspired and hard-working rally orga-nizers, the speakers, and those who have gathered here to protest the misogynist, genocidal, and barbaric policies of Iran whose public face is That Man—Ahmadinejad—the mullahs' little errand boy.

You are also here to protest the so-called Christian groups who have assembled inside the hotel to honor this modern day Hitler. They should be ashamed of themselves. However, let me remind us: 55,000 other Christians from 128 nations have demanded that the UN arrest and indict Ahmadinejad over his threats to Israel. (God bless them.)

Khomeini killed more Iranians in his first month in office than the demonized Shah ever did during his entire thirty eight year reign. And the killing has never stopped, it has only gathered steam both in Iran and abroad, in all the places where Iran sponsors terrorism against civilians. However, I've learned that people find it hard to emotionally comprehend large death counts which numb and terrify us.

So, let me tell you a story about one tragic incident that took place in that cursed country in the summer of 1986. Telling this story and listening to it is a way of mourning and of bearing witness. Iranian ex-patriate journalist Freidoune Sahebjam resurrected the facts for us in his jewel of a book, *The Stoning of Soraya M* which is now also a film which stars the great Iranian expatriate actress, Shohreh Aghdashloo. Sahebjam writes that in contemporary Iran, "being born female is both a capital crime and a death sentence." (I wrote about Soraya's fate briefly earlier in this volume.)

The book is a haunting and carefully rendered account of how, on August 15, 1986, a thirty-five-year-old woman was stoned to death in Kupayeh, Iran. Soraya was lynched and stoned to death by the villagers with whom she had lived all her life. Her own father, her two sons, and her greedy, heartless criminal of a husband, Ghorban-Ali, all threw the first stones.

How did this happen? When Soraya was only thirteen, an arranged marriage with the twenty-year-old Ghorban-Ali took place. Soraya was docile, obedient, and fertile. She did everything uncomplainingly. Her husband routinely insulted, beat, and then abandoned her and their children; he also consorted with prostitutes and brought them into the marital bed. Soraya dared not say a word. A "complaining" wife is easy to divorce.

Ghorban-Ali had begun to work with a group of extortionist mullahs in some distant towns and had been well rewarded. He "did not want to live any longer" with Soraya, who had become a "silent, resigned woman who was old before her time and, what was worse, completely above reproach." Ghorban-Ali had a new wife picked out, and although he could now afford many houses, he wanted his old mud house back. For him to get it, Soraya had to die.

He therefore falsely accused Soraya of adultery. Soraya's aunt, Zahra, a village elder (and the author's main informant (who is played by Aghdashloo), loved Soraya and knew she was innocent. But she was powerless and could not save her. Ghorban-Ali tricked Soraya's own father into condemning her. He also had the support of one of the many pederast, drug-addicted mullahs who, under Khomeini, enriched themselves personally by jailing and extorting money from their prisoners and by then executing them and confiscating all their wealth—a process very similar to the European Inquisition in which the Catholic church amassed great wealth in precisely this way.

After Ghorban-Ali denounced Soraya, she was sentenced to die later that same day. Ghorban-Ali was "radiant, jovial. Men slapped him affectionately and heartily…others hugged him." The crowd of villagers began to chant: "The whore has to die. Death to the woman." The villagers—who had known Soraya since her birth—cursed her, spit on her, hit her, and whipped her as she walked to her stoning. A "shudder of pleasure and joy ran through the crowd" as their stones drew blood. According to Sahebjams's account, Soraya died a slow and agonizing death.

When Soraya's aunt Zahra went to retrieve her body for burial, she was greeted by a "hallucinatory" spectacle. On the exact spot where Soraya had been stoned to death, a joyful fire was now burning, and around its flames the villagers were dancing. The strolling performers had started their show. The village women had donned their finest multicolored dresses and were turning in circles."

Afterwards, the mullah declared that the sinful Soraya could not be buried in a Muslim cemetery. He ordered some women to carry her broken body away. They half-buried her near a stream that Soraya loved. But when Zahra returned the next morning, she found that dogs had devoured most of her niece. She sat and wept, collected Soraya's bones, and buried them.

I must again emphasize that this ghastly, local stoning cannot be blamed on the crimes of either America or Israel.

What will it take to stop the stoning of women in Iran? The rape and torture of dissident prisoners in Iran? The lashing and hanging of rape victims in Iran? The forced prostitution and temporary "marriages" in Iran? What will it take to ensure that Iran does not become a nuclear power, does not attack Israel, Europe, America, or other Muslim countries in the region? Iran is a huge state sponsor of terrorism. It has funded Hamas and Hezbollah and conducts military operations against civilians in Gaza, the West Bank, Lebanon, Syria, and Argentina.

What are we willing to do to take Iran down? And please realize that the local village mullahs and the local villagers who played roles in the stoning of Soraya M are collaborators and opportunists. They back the regime. They share the regime's extremist views. The civilian population of Iran is not composed only of peaceful, democracy-oriented, dissidents. Many are as barbaric as their leaders.

Again, I ask: What are we willing to do? Not engaging has not worked. Engaging equals appeasement. Military action is dangerous, unthinkable, inevitable.

I have been asking this precise question for four years now. Your rally brings us one step closer to an answer.

Pajamas Media
9/25/08

- 25 -

Dining with an Egyptian Dreamer

Tarek Heggy's booming voice, Arab charm, and considerable reputation all preceded him. However, I was not prepared for the quiet soulfulness and seriousness with which he graced my home. Tall, trim, warm, effusive, energetic—but also refreshingly business-like, Tarek reminded me a bit, (but only superficially), of Lucette Lagnado's father, Leon, whom she memorialized in her wonderful book, *The Man in the White Sharkskin Suit: My Family's Exodus from Old Cairo to the New World.* Like Leon, Tarek is also a sophisticated citizen of the world and a very successful businessman; unlike Lagnado's cherished Leon, Tarek is a voracious and dedicated reader and the author of many books and countless articles.

Of course, Tarek is a Muslim, not a Jew. He was born in Port Said, Egypt and grew up in the 1950s and 1960s when that city was more cosmopolitan than it now is. Tarek told me that he wept the last time he visited his childhood city because "the women are now all wearing sheets, down to the ground and away from their bodies so that no shape shows," and there is "hate, only hate blaring from the loudspeakers of every mosque."

We dined leisurely and alone so that we might talk at length, and undisturbed. We have been waiting to do so for more than a year. Our long-ago appointment had to be re-scheduled due to his mother's illness and then, alas, her death.

His is a voice of sanity and reason and one that both Arabs and Westerners must heed in these very dangerous times. If we fail to do so, we might inherit a nuclear whirlwind. He is, mercifully, pro-Peace with Israel but he is even more pro-humanity, pro-Arab, and pro-Egyptian.

He wants his country and all Arab countries to enter the modern era and to evolve beyond Muslim-on-Muslim violence, beyond the perennial Arab and Islamic conflict with the rest of the world. He is a dreamer. No other kind of person has ever changed the world.

Tarek Heggy has taught law and modern management in many universities and on many continents. He is a world-class expert in Natural Gas. After working for Shell International Petroleum Company as an Oil and Gas attorney for nearly a decade, Heggy became the first Middle Eastern person to be appointed as Chairman of Shell Companies in Egypt and thereafter in the MRH (Major Resource Holders) countries (Iran, Iraq, Kuwait, Saudi Arabia, Qatar & the UAE). He resigned after a near-decade in order to devote himself full-time to his intellectual and cultural pursuits and to manage his own private company "TANA petroleum."

Not only have I dined with Kings, I may now say that I've also dined with the head of a major petroleum company!

But that's not what drew us together. Heggy's reputation is that of a leading liberal Arab thinker. He has written extensively about democracy, modernity, tolerance, and women's rights and has dared to criticize his own country as well as the entire region in which he continues to live. Heggy has published seventeen books in Arabic and five books in English. Hundreds of essays may be found at his website already translated into English, Arabic, French, Russian, Italian, and Hebrew. Heggy was in New York to meet with many people, including his publisher, Cambridge University Press. They are bringing out a new book of his: *The Arab Culture Enchained.*

We called our mutual dear friend, Nonie Darwish, the author and lecturer, whose new book *Cruel and Usual Punishment: The Terrifying Implications of Sharia Law* will be out early in 2009. The three of us had an excited conversation mainly in English but they also spoke in Arabic at my request. And then we sat down to eat—and talk away the night. Every word Heggy said was said urgently and passionately.

Heggy said that "humanity is heading for a war with militant Islam," that, "The Islamist's mind does not allow anyone to be different, everyone has to be the same, alike." Therefore, he explained, that he "must be cautious. I talk about Muslims not about Islam. Of course, Islam's interpretation needs a reformation."

Heggy also said that "his prognosis is a dark one." He believes that if America "pulls out of Iraq prematurely or in an immature way" that it will "boost the morale of the Islamist movements" and the Middle

East will go up in radical Islamist flames. The Muslim Brotherhood will take over Egypt in the same way that Hamas has taken over Gaza: via the ballot. ("Did you know" he said, "that Hamas was once known as the Muslim Brotherhood/Gaza Branch?") He continued. Iran will battle Iraq even more directly, it will be "imperative for the Kurds to declare independence," Iranian-backed "Hezbollah will take over Lebanon" more completely, the "forces of al-Qaeda will move from Afghanistan into Iraq. We will see a ferocious battle between radical Shia and radical Sunni Muslims. Iraq, which is very fragile, will become greatly chaotic."

When I asked him about Kurdistan he had this to say: "When I visited there last year I found it a very different place than Iraq. For example, girls were the security guards, and of course their hair was uncovered."

On the subject of Jews and Israel, Heggy became thoughtful. Here's some of what he had to say. He confirmed that the Palestinians, both as an issue and as a people, have been badly used by Arabs and to the detriment of the entire Arab world, including the Palestinian people. "Once upon a time, the issue of Palestine was merely a political issue. Now, it's increasingly become a religious issue. Jerusalem was not important to Muslims, but it has increasingly become apparent that Jerusalem is now being treated as a Muslim Holy City."

He said that he "speaks up when Jews are maligned" and tries to remind people that "Jews are the founders of monotheism." Tarek wonders how and why the Jews were able to survive such a long Diaspora and we discussed the Biblical figures of Moses and Joseph, who was also a great dreamer, at great length to our mutual pleasure.

Clearly, the man won my heart. With his permission, I will let him have the last word. He is about to accept Italy's Grinzane Cavour Prize. In the past, the Grinzane Cavour Prize focused the world's attention on writers who would go on to win Nobel Prizes in Literature: Toni Morrison, Wole Soyinka, Nadine Gordimer, Gunter Grass, Jose Saramago, and Doris Lessing. Others who have received this award include Mario Vargas Llosa, Abraham B. Yehoshua, Czeslaw Milosz, and V.S. Naipaul.

Tarek gave me two possible acceptance speeches that he will deliver. I have taken the liberty of joining parts of those two speeches here. Uttering such brave words is a commonplace in the West. Sadly, no one pays the slightest attention. But someone like Tarek can face prison and death for uttering these same words in the Middle East. May these words find favor among his countrymen and women.

Why Do I Write?
By Tarek Heggy

I write in order to instill in the minds and souls of all the Arabic speaking people :

- The fact that although the outside world will harbor animosities towards us at times, and will work to further its own interests most of the time, our problems, in their entirety, originate inside our country and can only be solved internally. We alone are responsible for those problems and for the fact that they remain unsolved. The excessive belief in the conspiracy theory is a confession of our impotence and an admission of the supremacy of others in the face of our ineffectiveness.

- The values of liberalism, democracy, general freedoms and human rights (are) the most noble, sublime and civilized achievements of mankind.

- The value of civil society, (is) the most effective mechanism for public participation in public life.

- That the negative perception of women in some cultures is disgraceful. Not only do women constitute half the population but, far more important, they are the mothers who rear future generations. As such, they are a valuable societal asset, and a society that does not grant its women full rights in all fields cannot hope to realize its full potential.

- That Anwar Sadat's historic choice to move the Arab/Israeli conflict from the battlefield to the negotiation table was the only way to reach a reasonable settlement of a conflict that has been used for too long as an excuse to delay democracy and development.

- That our educational systems are in need of an overall revolution. As it now stands, the system only produces citizens who are totally incapable of facing the challenges of the age. Repeated claims by some that a process of reforming our educational system is currently underway are grossly exaggerated, as borne out by the quality of graduates produced by the system.

- That (a) tolerant and peaceful brand of moderate Islam has been subjected to attacks on many fronts. The attacks came from a trinity made up of the Wahhabi faith, a doctrinaire approach to religion, and the omnipotence of the petrodollar that has funded an interpretation of Islam fundamentally different from the gentle Islam practiced in a number of Arabic speaking societies and which has enabled the sons and daughters of a number of our societies to coexist with others over the years.

- Egypt's Copts and the region's non-Muslims are not second class citizens, they are as entitled to full citizenship rights as its Muslim population and that all the problems they are facing can and must be solved.

- There are shortcomings in Western culture, but it is an essential rung on the ladder of human civilization. To oppose Western culture is to oppose science, development and civilization.

- We have to curb our tendency to indulge in excessive self-praise and to glorify our past achievements. We have to learn to criticize ourselves and to accept criticism from others. We have to try to break out of our subjective culture into a more objective one.

- We (must) learn to engage in self-criticism because unless we are willing to do so, we will not discover the roots of the ills we complain of today.

- The debilitating disease of self-aggrandizement...its most obvious symptoms, (are) vainglorious posturing and a tendency to regard ourselves as distinct from and superior to everybody else, are manifested constantly in our written and spoken words...And what is the role of the Goebbels-style information media in engendering and fostering this negative phenomenon?

- Each Arabic speaking country must concentrate on putting its own house in order by building a strong, successful socially stable and modern educational and cultural infrastructure.

- We must defend freedom of belief, but not in the context of a theocratic culture that places our destinies in the hands of men of religion. No society should allow its affairs to be run by clerics who are, by their nature and regardless of the religion to which they belong, opposed to progress.

- There is the possibility of a new culture of peace, one in which the countries of the region will learn to live together and Israel and its neighbors can work out settlements along the lines of what the French and Germans succeeded in doing less than fifty years after the end of World War II. In promoting the notion of peace, I point out that it is only when the region moves from a dynamic of conflict to one of peace that real democracy will spread throughout the Middle East.

- Knowledge and culture are universal, the common heritage of all humankind, and that opening the door to both is a prerequisite for reform.

- We must end the Goebbels-style propaganda machines operating in Egypt and the Arab world and their dangerous manipulation of public opinion.

- We must instill in the minds of the sons and daughters of our Arabic speaking societies (especially in the minds of the young) that where there is a will there is a way and that, armed with a solid formation and determination, they can achieve anything.

In a word, I write for the sake of a modern, thriving and stable Arabic-speaking region, at peace with itself and with the outside world, integrated into the mainstream of science, innovation, humanity and the civilizing process. The future does not exist as such; it is a product of what we create today.

FrontPage Magazine
10/24/08

- 26 -
The Blood of a 13 Year Old Cries Out to Me

Gentlemen:
My daughter's blood, a child's blood, cries out to me.

Last week, a barbaric gang of Somali Muslim fundamentalists gang-raped a 13 year-old girl after which they stoned her to death. One thousand spectators in the Kismayo stadium cheered the stoning on. The victim's name was Aisha Ibrahim Duhulow.

This atrocious scenario, and similar atrocities, are increasingly familiar in Muslim countries such as Algeria, Egypt, Saudi Arabia, Pakistan, Iran, and Afghanistan. When a Muslim woman dares to allege rape, she is treated as if she herself has committed a crime. And she is not merely shunned or disbelieved—she is punished, tortured, murdered. Her attackers go free or buy their way out of even a light sentence.

Mister Potential Presidents: Do you believe that America has no business interfering with such indigenous behaviors abroad? That this is a fight that we cannot win? Or that the cost of undertaking it is too high in terms of our own blood? After all, America has already been in Mogadishu.

Do you perhaps think that the United Nations will take care of such human rights violations? As you know, they never have and they never will. Instead, they will probably appoint Somalia, a rogue nation filled with pirates who prey upon their neighbors on the open sea, to head a special human rights committee to condemn alleged Israeli atrocities against Palestinian terrorists.

Gentlemen: Are you in favor of economic sanctions for Somalia or are you ready to insist that the men who did this, and the leaders who refuse to punish them, all be brought to stand trial as war criminals?

To student activists and international human rights groups: Are you ready to call for academic boycotts against Somalia? Will you conduct a permanent campaign against Islamic Gender Apartheid in Aisha Ibrahim Duhulow's name?

I would like to thank Amnesty International for documenting this tragic and heartless atrocity.

My daughter's blood, a child's blood, cries out to me.

Pajamas Media
11/3/08

- 27 -
The Lights are Going Out for Women in the Muslim World

The American people are voting in droves today. There are incredibly long lines at all my neighborhood polling sites. Feminists are especially concerned with womens' reproductive rights. They believe that the Democrats share their views.

While this is true, it may be true only for American women, not for women living elsewhere, especially in the Islamic world. Feminists took President Bush to hard task, (and rightly so), for his having de-funded programs that helped women abroad if they also counseled women about abortion.

Islamic fundamentalism is even more dangerous for women. If America is not resolved to stop jihadists, both militarily and educationally, then the lights will continue to go out for women all over the world.

In Afghanistan, the Taliban slaughtered an Afghan midwife in Kandahar whose name was Zarghouna. The Taliban warned Zarghouna to stop giving out condoms (!) and birth control pills since that would lead to adultery. Her fate will be the fate of ever so many more brave Muslim women if the free world allows the jihadists to win.

According to journalist Tom Blackwell:

> The Taliban have also fired off threatening letters recently telling the clinics that they cannot allow male doctors to examine female patients, though often women health workers are simply not available. The clinics do get female guards to interview women patients and pass on the information to the

male physician, but that does not seem to satisfy the insurgents.

I would not call them "insurgents." I would call them dangerously ignorant, reactionary, fascist, terrorist, murderers. But all my name calling will not bring Zarghouna back.

Dr. Fazal Rahman, head of the Afghan Health and Development Service, pointed out that the family planning programs have "helped curb the huge problem here of low birth-weight babies, since fewer children in a family means fewer mouths to feed and better nutrition for everyone. Family planning also aids women who are too weak or sick themselves to go through pregnancy."

Which Presidential candidate is more likely to bring change, not only to America, and not only to the perception of America in the world, but also to the world's women? Even that President may not be able to influence anything that goes on in Afghanistan, Pakistan, or Saudi Arabia.

Pajamas Media
11/4/08

- 28 -

Nonie Darwish: "The Non-Muslim World Must Have No Illusions."

Author Nonie Darwish on Gaza and on the "Terrifying Global Implications of Sharia Law."

Gazan-Egyptian, Nonie Darwish, well known as a "Muslim Sha-hid's daughter," (her father died in battle against the Israelis), is a brave woman who, unsurprisingly, writes brave books.

I am honored to call her a friend and a colleague. Nonie grew up in Gaza when it was under Egyptian control, and then moved to Cairo. She now lives in southern California and is the mother of three children who are 14, 25, and 27 years old. She was formerly a Muslim.

Nonie is just publishing her second book. It's title: *Cruel and Usual Punishment. The Terrifying Global Implications of Sharia Law.*

This book is a landmark event. No American can afford NOT to read this book. Sharia law, which governs every area of Muslim life, is now increasingly infiltrating the West. Europe may be lost, America is now under siege. With profound bravery, Darwish documents the history and nature of Sharia law which is invariably misrepresented and misunderstood, both by its followers and by infidels.

Darwish explains that the Qur'an and other holy works are not always translated accurately into non-Arabic languages and that Muslims are trained, (by that very law), to deny or minimize their own "poisonous" cruelty and to punish anyone who exposes the truth.

Darwish explains that Islam is not exactly a religion in the same way that Judaism or Christianity are; it is, rather a political ideology which seeks world domination and total control over the private lives of each individual. Darwish herself is an escapee from its "prison." She therefore dares to imagine a "2084" in which America has become a to-talitarian Islamic nation which subordinates and persecutes Christians and other religious minorities. Darwish offers practical, specific sugges-tions that Americans must implement in order to defeat this dreadful possibility before it is too late.

In addition, this is a very important book on the subject of wom-en and Sharia law. Darwish explores the internalization of sexism by Muslim women and explains why Muslim women in the free West are so aggressive on behalf of a reactionary status quo; why they insist on veiling as a personal form of virtuous jihad; and what it means when they remain so cold-hearted and disconnected from the female victims of Sharia law who are being stoned, flogged, impoverished, separated from their children, etc. I recently interviewed Darwish. I have edited her answers below.

Phyllis Chesler: What compelled you to write this book?

Nonie Darwish: I had several reasons. Every time I delved into the ills and challenges of Muslim society I discovered that there is an Islamic Law, inspired by scriptures, that stood in the way of any reform or change. Change itself is forbidden by Islamic Law. I also wrote this book to warn the West about what Sharia really is and how devastating it will be for human rights, relationships, and Western democracy. We have recently seen Muslim groups demand the practice of Islamic law (Sharia) in the West and with the blessing and support of some Western intellectuals and journalists.

By writing this book, I have no desire to offend the good and peace-loving Muslims, but the truth must be told. Unfortunately the majority of Muslims do not know what is in their scriptures or their divine Laws that have a huge destructive impact on their society.

PC: What do you hope to accomplish?

ND: My hope is for Western people to understand the threat that Islamic Sharia law poses to their democracy, their concept of equality under the law and their human rights values. The West should never allow Sharia to be practiced in Western democracies. I am also hopeful that my book will inspire Muslims to take an honest look at their oppressive religious laws and reform.

PC: Talk to me about Gaza, your hometown. What, in your opinion, is really going on there?

ND: The world needs to understand the roots of the eternal conflict, which is the Sharia law commandment to kill all Jews. Peace can only happen if such roots are exposed and understood. For decades, Arabs had demanded that Israel end the Gazan occupation, and in 2005, Israel did so, disengaging unilaterally from Gaza. With their demands met, there was no "cycle of violence" to respond to, no further justification for anything other than peace and prosperity. With its central location and beautiful beaches on the East Mediterranean, a peaceful and prosperous Gaza could become another Hong Kong; a shining trade and commerce center. But instead of choosing peace they chose Islamic jihad. Arabs of Gaza rolled their rocket launchers to the border and started bombing Israeli civilians.

The reasons for choosing violence over peace is due to Sharia. Mainstream Sharia books define jihad as: "to war against non-Muslims to establish the religion." (Shafi'i Sharia 09.0). Jihad is not just the duty of the individual Muslim, it is also the main duty of the Muslim head of State (the Calipha): "A Muslim calipha is entrusted to take his people into war and command offensive and aggressive Jihad. He must organize Jihad against any non-Muslim government."

Zia-Ul-Haq, former President of Pakistan, said "Jihad in terms of warfare is a collective responsibility of the Muslim Ummah." These scriptures are taught, preached and promoted as the incontrovertible and eternal word of God and funded by Saudi petrodollars throughout the world, including Western nations such as the U.K. and the United States.

How can a Muslim leader or individual avoid the hundreds of Quran and Hadith commandments to Muslims to kill Jews and Christians? How can a Muslim leader face his devout Muslim subjects with a decision of friendship and peace with Jews when the mosques all over the Middle East recite Mohammed's commandment to Muslims: "The Hour [Resurrection] will not take place until the Muslims fight the Jews, and kill them. And the Jews will hide behind the rock and tree, and the rock and tree will say: Oh Muslim, oh servant of Allah, this is a Jew behind me, come and kill him!" (Sahih Muslim 41:6985, also Sahih Bukhari 4:52:177).

This Hadith, issued by Mohammad was issued in the 7th century, not after the 1948 creation of the State of Israel. It is not a response to modern-day grievances; it is a permanent commandment.

This is the real basis of the Arab/Israeli conflict: not a conflict over land or occupation, but a divine Muslim obligation to destroy neighboring (non-Muslim) Israel, where Jews are no longer dhimmis but are free to rule themselves. We cannot ignore the root of the problem in Muslim scriptures. That is the true force behind the hate and propaganda jihadist machine against Jews in the Muslim world.

Some Muslims tell me that they don't believe in Sharia and question why am I making a big deal about it. My answer is that Sharia is the law of the land in 54 Muslim countries and many Muslim groups are demanding Sharia in the West. In 1990, 45 Muslim countries signed the Cairo Human Rights Declaration which stated that Sharia has supremacy over the UN Universal Declaration of Human Rights.

PC: Thank you, Nonie.

Pajamas Media
1/7/09

Section Three:
Should America Ban the Burqa?

- 29 -
Vindicated by Khalia Massoud, President of Muslims Against Sharia Law

Occasionally, if a thinker-activist lives long enough and keeps in the fight, she might just experience a moment of vindication. For me, an evening in March 2009 was one of those moments.

I completed a Q&A with the *National Review* about honor killings/"honorcides" which appeared there March 12. I also did a long interview with a news service on the subject. Like many other wire services and like the mainstream media, ideas such as mine are usually sidelined, marginalized, attacked, or simply "disappeared."

I now have a number of honorable allies. One surely is NOW-New York State President, Marcia Pappas who is currently being attacked for having linked the Buffalo beheading with "honor killings," with "Islam," and even with "Islamic terrorism." In 2009, Muzzammil Hassan beheaded his wife, Aasiya Hassan, in Buffalo. Pappas was attacked by a coalition of eight domestic violence victim advocacy providers in Erie County where the Buffalo beheading took place.

Lo and Behold: A second honorable ally wrote to me. I want to share what he said. His name is Khalim Massoud, and he is the President of Muslims Against Sharia Law, an international organization. After reading my most recent article, he wrote me as follows:

> There is absolutely no doubt in my mind that (the) Buffalo beheading is a honorcide. We, Muslims Against Sharia, prefer this term to honor murder. Beheading is not just a murder, it's a ritual. It's a form of control and humiliating a family

member who "stepped over the line," in this case, a wife taking out a TRO (order of protection) and planning to divorce her husband.

Ms. Pappas must be commended for her courage to call a spade a spade. (The) PC-climate presents considerable danger for future honorcide victims. Trying to sweep cultural/ religious aspects of honorcide under the rug keeps the problem from being addressed. While most of the media wouldn't touch the issue with a ten-foot pole, (for) fear they would be portrayed as Islamophobic, a few brave women, the true feminists, like Marcia Pappas and Phyllis Chesler are speaking out on the subject just to be slammed by so-called victim advocacy groups because they dare to expose Islamism's dirty laundry. Muslim women in America are at great risk because the Muslim establishment, with help of the media, wants to portray honorcide as fiction.

Honorcide has no place in the modern world, but especially in the West. It must be forcefully confronted; not written off as domestic violence.

Hear, hear!

Pajamas Media
3/12/09

- 30 -
Deadly Disdain, Deadly Denial About The Fate of Muslim Women

Sometimes, I despair of ever being able to convey the disdain for women that one may encounter in the Muslim world.

First, many Americans and Europeans simply do not want to believe it; they absolutely refuse to surrender their belief that all people are both "good" and the "same." Some westerners do not think it is politically correct, or even polite to say so—especially if people really are "different." Thus, for both reasons, westerners will deny the extent to which most women are despised and punished in the Muslim world. Some westerners also say: "Women are oppressed here as well. It's racist to single out an entire culture and people for the ways in which women are mistreated everywhere."

Point taken—but not everything is the "same." Many Westerners have learned how to engage in self-criticism; fewer Muslims have been allowed to do so.

Many Muslims, who live both in the West and in Muslim lands, will deny, outright, that Muslim women are mistreated. First, precisely because this is true, they are well trained to deny it—it is shameful to say so; doing so, disgraces and endangers the family and the Muslim nation. Also, most people are trained not to "see" that which is normalized all around them.

Some time ago, I met with a small group of charming, heartbreakingly sophisticated, educated, assimilated, modern, secular Muslims. They drank, they smoked, they danced with members of the opposite (and of the same sex), they did not limit their friendships to Muslims-only, they were divorced men and women. From an Islamic/Isla-mist view, they were mighty sinners, maybe even "heretics." Of course, I loved them, they were so cosmopolitan.

Nevertheless, they hotly denied that honor killings exist because, in their circles, they had neither seen nor heard of any such thing. In their experience, most Muslims are tolerant and fun-loving. They glided over the facts of polygamy and child marriage because, in their lives, it was a very rare occurrence. They viewed America as the greatest "terror-ist" power and sympathized with Islamic terrorists who had been "driv-en to terrorism because they'd seen either their parents or their children murdered or maimed;" they believed that Islam had been "far kinder to Jews than Christianity had ever been." As for Muslim dissidents and feminists? "They are only a handful of people whom the West rewards for generalizing from their own bad experiences. What they are saying is not true for most Muslims."

Trust me, I more than held my own in this discussion but, emo-tionally and intellectually, it exhausted me. These are the "good" Mus-lims. They are not personally violent, they do not sponsor violence, they move easily in both the Western and Eastern worlds, and yet, their knowledge base is restricted to their own experience and to the main-stream media in the West which encourages precisely such beliefs. Per-haps they are also part of an alarmingly selfish generation which relates everything back to themselves and lacks compassion for others who are not like them.

Pajamas Media
3/17/09

- 31 -
Gender Apartheid – Not Our
Feminist Agenda

The issue of Islamic/Islamist gender apartheid is one of epidemic and global proportions. Although it has reached American shores, the feminist establishment here remains tragically ambivalent about how to deal with forced veiling, arranged marriage, gender separatism, and honor-related violence, including honor killings. Many feminists fear that, were they to tie the subordination of women to a particular religion or culture, especially to Islam, that they would be perceived as "racists," or "Islamophobes." This fear trumps their sincere concern for womens' rights and womens' lives.

The issue is whether or not non-Muslim "white" folks can discuss Muslim-on-Muslim crime or black-on-black crime or whether only people who share the same faith and skin-color are allowed to raise this issue.

Also of concern is whether American feminists really support an American foreign policy, which both President Obama and Secretary of State Clinton have indicated can or should be tied to womens' rights. Feminists viewed President Bush's post 9/11 invasion of Afghanistan and Iraq as morally outrageous and as far more hurtful to Afghan and Iraqi women than was their pre-existing subjugation. Some feminists believed that women had been better off, at least, in Iraq, before the American invasion. We may agree or disagree with this analysis but, nevertheless, why would American feminists hesitate to condemn crimes against women which are being committed on American soil by immigrants, including Muslims, from Third World countries?

The authors have both been speaking out about honor killings in the West and have both described the recent Buffalo beheading of Aasiya Z. Hassan by her husband as an Islamist-style, ritual honor-related killing.

Marcia Pappas, the President of NOW-NYS, has been scolded by national NOW's President and criticized by a coalition of domestic violence advocates for her views about this.

Dr. Phyllis Chesler, the author of thirteen books, including *Women and Madness*, has been writing about Islamic gender apartheid and its penetration of the West for many years. She, too, has been challenged, even condemned, for her views about honor killings in general and for her views about the shocking case of Aasiya Z. Hassan, in particular.

We decided to join forces and write a short piece. However, we discovered that brevity would not serve our goal. The problem is much bigger than honor-related violence, honor killings, or this one case in Buffalo. Indeed, the issue which we still face in 2009, is one that has plagued American feminist leaders for at least 171 years. The issue is that of racism and sexism and the diabolical way in which racism continues to trump sexism among feminists.

A little history lesson is in order.

For a long time, American women had been outspoken leaders in the fight to abolish slavery. However, between 1838-1840, their efforts were increasingly restricted to that of "silent" partners in Ladies Auxiliaries. In 1840, a World Anti-Slavery convention was held in London. American women, including Elizabeth Cady Stanton and Lucretia Mott, both ardent abolitionists, were not allowed to publicly speak out against slavery because they were women. Instead, they were condemned to sit behind a partition and remain silent. Cady Stanton returned home and composed a Declaration of Sentiments, modeled upon the Declaration of Independence. In 1848, three hundred American women and men, including former slave and abolitionist, Frederick Douglass, attended the Seneca Falls Womens' Rights Convention; about a third voted for the Declaration which resolved that women should have the right to vote, control property, sign legal documents, serve on juries, and enjoy equal access to education and employment. This vote and this Convention began the long, slow march towards American female suffrage.

African-American men obtained the vote in 1865. It was fifty five years before American women of any race, color, religion, or ethnicity did. These First Wave feminists and suffragists decided to put womens' rights first. They refused to "sit silently at the back of the (abolitionist) bus," and were sometimes willing to work with anyone, including those who were opposed to abolition, to further their cause. This meant that some of our suffragist foremothers were routinely called "racists."

On the other hand, those men and women who chose abolition over womens' rights were rarely ever condemned as sexists, misogynists, or woman-haters.

Fast forward to the American 1960s when many white women, (many Jews, too), joined the bravest African-American men and women in a non-violent struggle for civil rights. This was a movement against southern and northern segregation, against Jim Crow and for the integration of public places, including lunch counters, buses, and schools. The African-American right to vote—free of intimidation or violence––was also at issue.

Women of many races were also involved in the anti-Vietnam war and in various left-tilted black liberation movements which opposed racism, both here and abroad. But, once again, American women were expected to do the secretarial work, and provide food and sex for the "real" leaders who were always men. In the mid-to late 1960s, we left all that, driven out by Marxist, hippie, and black liberationist sexism. Betty Friedan published the *Feminine Mystique* in 1963 and NOW began organizing in 1966.

Second Wave feminism put womens' rights first and for about fifteen years, we achieved tremendous, dazzling progress. However, by the end of the 1970s, with the rise of the anti-colonialist, anti-imperialist, and anti-Western academy, the ideas of academics like Edward Said, the author of *Orientalism*, took precedence over many feminist ideas. Suddenly, in terms of symbols, women were no longer seen as the most "wretched of the earth," oppressed by both poverty and violence. Now, Arab men of color, "Palestinians," Muslims, took center stage as the world's most noble and oppressed victims.

Caucasian feminists and academics were expected to "atone" for their country's history of slavery, racism, and imperialism by refusing to analyze or protest the fate of non-white women at the hands of their fathers, brothers, husbands, and leaders. To do so would be "racist." Only women of color, (or academics who were women of color), could comment on the fates of women of color. Control of this academic "discourse" was viewed as too valuable a resource—one which should not be plundered by those whose ancestors had been racists, crusaders, colonialists, and imperialists.

In the 1970s, feminism had embraced a universalist philosophy which believed in one standard of human rights for all. By the 1980s, feminism began to devolve into a politically correct "culturally relativist" philosophy in which one standard applied to the West and another standard to the formerly colonized Third World. Because Third World countries suffered from many serious problems, they were seen as blameless innocents who did not deserve to be harshly judged.

Meanwhile, just as left-influenced Western, Caucasian feminists began to view themselves as suspect, and their culture as guilty, they simultaneously began to view Third World barbarians of color as misunderstood innocents. Feminists did not defend the values of the West to which most intellectuals, especially dissidents from Third World cultures, aspired. Just as dissidents abroad cited Enlightenment values against the Third World tyrants who impoverished, tortured, and silenced them at home, western academics, including feminists, refused to "judge" such tyrants and insisted on viewing them sympathetically.

When forced to, western feminists usually condemned the United States and Europe for having contributed to the rise of such tyrants. They absolutely could not imagine that Third World barbarism, including misogyny, might also be indigenous. Nor could they see that they were collaborating with evil tyrants.

Thus, despite great interest in connecting with western-style feminists in Third World countries, and despite genuine interest in the plight of women around the world, by the end of the 1980s, American feminists, especially if they were Caucasian, were highly reluctant to condemn barbarism against women of color by men of color, since such condemnations were, by definition, "racist," or could potentially be used against men of color by white racists.

In 1848, American suffragists decided to focus on the rights of American women only. That struggle was hard enough; indeed, it is still ongoing. However, Second and Third Wave feminists in the latter part of the twentieth century, began to focus on the rights of women globally. To the detriment of feminist movements everywhere, American feminist activists and academics have now recanted, pulled back, apologized, because they have decided that, once again, racism trumps sexism as a feminist concern.

Just as men and women once stood together as abolitionists, we now call upon men and women of all races and religions, including secularists, to stand with us against the subordination of and violence towards women in the name of religion, beginning with Islam or Islamism.

Written with Marcia Pappas

Pajamas Media
3/22/09

- 32 -
Afghan Women Demonstrate in Kabul

When I lived in Kabul, women simply did not rise up, take to the streets, and mount brave demonstrations. Wealthy women wore decorous long headscarves, long coats, and gloves, and were driven around by chauffeurs in expensive European cars. Poor women wore the full burqa and were forced to sit separately from men at the back of public buses; they were also kicked to the back of the line in the bazaar when the male servants of wealthy families came to make their purchases. Occasionally, if a country girl or woman was out working or walking and a male non-relative chanced by, she would swiftly, shyly turn her face away and simultaneously cover it with her headscarf. This was a practiced, perhaps terrified, motion.

Imagine my joy today, nearly fifty years later, when I read that Afghan women just took to the streets to protest a new law which legalizes rape within marriage, requires a husband's permission in order for his wife to be able to work, and requires wives to "dress" as their husbands desire.

The heroic women faced down an angry, dangerous mob of men who called them "whores." "Death to the enemies of Islam," chanted the men. "We want our rights," the women responded. This is not the first time that Afghan women demonstrated such extraordinary bravery. In January, 2008, when the American teacher, Cyd Mizell, was kidnapped (she has never been found and is presumed dead), within weeks, six hundred of her Afghan female students took to the streets of Kandahar to protest this. At the time, I wrote:

"Today, (January 27th-28th), between 500-600 women, many wearing burqas, demonstrated on behalf of the still kidnapped and missing Cyd Mizell in Kandahar. Their husbands gave them permission to do so; still, for women to publicly express their views and feelings constituted an unusual event in this Taliban-infested region. The women gathered in a Kandahar wedding hall. One woman was quoted as saying that the fate of "all Afghan women is at stake" because this kidnapping shows "how dangerous it still is for those who take an active role in rebuilding Afghanistan."

So much for those who say that Afghan, Muslim girls and women do not appreciate American help. And yet, what hope is there, really, for Muslim women who live in the perilous and deadly shadow of the Taliban and al-Qaeda?

In 2009, in Saudi Arabia, the birthplace of al-Qaeda, a seventy-five-year-old woman was punished with 40 lashes because she had been seen in the company of two men who were viewed as not close-enough relatives.

Also, in 2009, the Pakistani Taliban publicly lashed a 17-year-old girl because she had refused to marry a Taliban soldier. These charming monsters, (in videotaped interviews with them, they retain a dignity and a charm that is unnerving), have also been beheading girls, women, and Christians in the Swat Valley which, together with its rich lode of sapphires and other precious minerals, has just come into their possession.

Finally, in 2009, in Saudi Arabia, for the second time, a court in Unaiza upheld the marriage of an eight-year-old girl to a 58-year-old man. (The Saudi Authorities might intervene to make sure that he "does not have sex with her until she reaches puberty.") Now, what can that mean? When the girl first menstruates which can happen when she is only nine or ten?

Left-liberal feminists believe that they should indeed make alliances—but only with those Muslims who blame America first, Islam never. If women are being stoned, veiled, or forcibly married as children against their will—that's because America's foreign and military policies ended whatever stability or progress might have evolved in the country or region. Thus, paradoxically, such western, secular feminists are often most comfortable citing Muslim women who demand their rights—but only within the confines of Islamic religious (Sharia) law; or Muslim women who have honed their anti-Western rhetoric in the West.

Libertarian and conservative feminists believe that the Islamic religion and Muslim culture are, at their very root, intrinsically hostile towards progress, democracy, freedom, and women's rights and that nothing America has done or has failed to do could ever have changed that.

Whether we choose to blame America for its heavy-handedness in the past, for having contributed to the increasing Islamification of Iran, Pakistan, and Afghanistan, or, whether we choose to continue to blame the Qur'an, Saudi (and Western) oil politics and indigenous barbarism for such Islamification—what, exactly, if anything, do we propose to do to help the women of Afghanistan and Pakistan?

I have often said that my fiery brand of feminism was forged in Afghanistan, a beautiful, treacherous country because, when I returned to America, I was a different person. I had seen and experienced Islamic gender apartheid up-close-and-personal; I had also nearly died there.

Despite their relative powerlessness, some Afghan women were exceptionally kind to me. Consider my abiding concern with women's fate in Afghanistan and in the Muslim world as an expression of my gratitude and sense of kinship with them.

UPDATE:

Some very brave Afghan women demonstrated for their rights in Kabul. However, even more Afghan women demonstrated against women's rights and they joined the male mob who cursed and stoned the heroines of Kabul. Such loyalty to the misogynist status quo is typical, not unusual, not only for Afghan or for Third World women, but for women everywhere.

Women have supported their own face and body shrouding as a form of religious modesty or as a statement against "foreign occupation" and "racism." At the demonstrations in Kabul, some counter-protesters shouted "Death to the slaves of the Christians!" Others insisted that foreigners and foreign views were "the enemy of Afghanistan."

My book, *Women's Inhumanity to Woman* (which describes such behavior), is just being re-issued next month with a new Introduction.

Pajamas Media
4/16/09

- 33 -
Woman's Inhumanity to Woman, Terrorist Style

W hile I was enjoying some sunshine in Savannah, World War Four continued to rage blithely on.

Al-Qaeda in Uzbekistan, Pakistan, and North Africa threatened terrorist attacks against Germany and Holland and threatened to kill a British hostage (captured on the border between Niger and Mali), if Britain does not release a radical Muslim preacher.

The Pakistani Taliban shot a couple dead for alleged adultery and their execution in Islamabad was captured on a cellphone.

Egyptian police arrested a Muslim woman for having married a Coptic Christian.

In Lahore, a Muslim husband killed his wife for failing to bear a son; and in the Punjab, a Sikh physician-husband amputated his wife's hand and that of her cousin with whom he suspected she was having an affair.

So much for male terrorists in foreign lands.

Last week, as I smelled the roses in Georgia, there were three carefully organized explosions on one day in Iraq, which killed a total of 80 civilians. One explosion was carried out by a woman in a black abaya, holding a 5 year-old child's hand. She killed herself and 28 other Muslims in a crowded market in a Baghdad slum. The civilians, many of whom were other women, were waiting in line for free flour, cooking oil, tea, macaroni, and other staples that the police were handing out. Police officers died as well.

Many people have written to me, surprised, outraged, perhaps demoralized by the fact that this latest Muslim-on-Muslim atrocity was committed by a woman and mainly against other women.

As the author of *Woman's Inhumanity to Woman*, which is just now being re-released in a new edition with a new Introduction, I am, unfortunately, not surprised. Please recall how quickly the mainstream media covered the "sensational" use of rape by the male members of Al-Qaeda as a way to recruit female human bombs. At the time, people seemed surprised by the fact that Samira Jassim, an Iraqi woman, played an essential role in the further exploitation of these rape victims.

Although women depend upon each other for emotional intimacy and social stability, they are also highly competitive with, mistrustful of, or hostile towards other women. Are women really sexists? Of course they are. A study of 15,000 people in nineteen countries on five continents found that women hold sexist views just as men do. However, some studies suggest that women with low self-esteem are more likely to internalize negative views of women which may account for how such women treat other women: With cruelty rather than kindness.

In addition, women are expected to compete mainly against other women, not against men, and they do so both directly and indirectly (through slander, shunning, and "backstabbing.") In the developing world, especially in war zones, the female-female aggression is far more direct, often fatally so.

I have written a number of articles about Muslim mothers who have participated, both directly and indirectly, in the honor killing of their daughters; and about female Muslim human bombers who have specifically targeted other women and children.

As I previously noted, in 2008, in Iraq, one of four female homicide bombers entered a tent that provided shelter to weary female religious pilgrims. She sat down, read the Qur'an with them, and left a bag behind that, moments later, blew them all up. Please note that she targeted weary, religious Muslim women.

Thus, I was dismayed but not surprised when a Sunni, Al-Qaeda plot emerged, one in which male terrorists raped eighty Muslim girls and women, then turned them over to Samira Jassim who patiently, persistently, "maternally," persuaded the rape victims, (many of whom had been targeted because they were depressed or mentally ill), to "cleanse" their shame by blowing themselves and other Muslims up. Twenty eight women did so.

In an interview with Dr. Anat Berko, the author of *The Path to Paradise. The Inner World of Suicide Bombers and Their Dispatchers*, she pointed out that there is "always a woman" behind the female suicide bomber, who functions like a "pimp or a Madam in a brothel." Potential women suicide bombers are never alone again, they are always accompanied by at least one, usually older woman, who encourages, manipulates, guards, and supports the potential shaheeda—just like a mother might do.

In a culture in which girls are raised by women whose own mothers did not value them as they did boys, women may hunger for attention from an older woman—even one whose sole purpose is to ensure their jihadic death. In Dr. Berko's book, there is a frightening example of how all the jailed, intercepted Palestinian female suicide bombers obeyed and respected one of their own: a woman who was the harshest, angriest, most mentally ill amongst them. Sadly, perhaps this most reminded them of their own mothers.

In a terrible sense, "Madam" Jassim, only exaggerated, by a bit, what is routinely done to many girls and women today in many Muslim countries. Jassim played the Evil Stepmother in a culture which fears, despises, shrouds, genitally mutilates, force-marries girls to their first cousins, and perpetrates honor killings. How different is collaborating in their rape and helping them find glory through jihad? In a sense, some may actually view this as a quantum career leap for women.

Like Madam Jassim, when women are trapped in highly patriarchal cultures, they may gain the only approval and power possible for a woman by vigilantly policing themselves and other women to extol and support the patriarchal status quo. This is true in terms of issues such as veiling which, for women, is the visual shorthand for fundamentalist religiosity. I fear we may see more Evil Stepmother/mothers like Samira Jassim and more raped, traumatized, exploited, ideologically empowered, suicidal-homicidal daughters.

Attention President Obama and Secretary of State Clinton: Supporting the pro-democracy and pro-woman's rights forces within Muslim countries and territories, might go a long way to reversing such ongoing tragedies. If America genuinely believes that women are human beings, now is the time to share that view with the leaders of these countries.

Pajamas Media
4/30/09

- 34 -
Islamic Gender Apartheid: A Speech for the Human Rights Coalition Against Radical Islam

My Speech for the Human Rights Coalition's Rally Against Radical Fundamentalist Islam in Times Square, New York, May 3, 2009.

Radical, fundamentalist Islam is the world's largest practioner of both gender and religious apartheid.

Others are speaking here today about Islamic religious apartheid. I have been asked to focus on Islamic *gender* apartheid.

We who live in the West, and who have learned how to analyze and protest gender inequality here, simply have no idea how much free-er and safer women are in the West than in Muslim countries.

I once lived in the Islamic world, in Afghanistan. What I learned in Kabul rendered me immune to the romanticization of the Third World or to the glamorization of tyrants and terrorists that defined my generation of 1960s and 1970s radicals.

Being born female and Muslim, especially today, under radical Islamic rule, is potentially a capital crime. The warnings and the punishment begin early on and are both relentless and normalized.

Women are viewed as sub-human, half-demon, and sexually "wild"—by men whose own lust knows no bounds. While there are many exceptions, in general, Muslim (and Arab) girls are despised and routinely cursed, beaten, and treated as servants by their fathers and older brothers. Women are hidden, literally suffocated under face and body veils, shrouded, visually buried alive while they are still breathing.

If you have ever worn a burqa you will understand that it is not the "same" as covering your hair with a scarf or a wig. You have no peripheral vision. You can never feel the sun on your face. People cannot see your eyes, your face, your expressions; you really cannot relate to anyone. You cannot comfortably eat in a restaurant or at a family picnic. You are condemned to move in the universe as if you are a ghost.

Today, eight-year-old girls are being married off by their fathers to men as old as fifty—in order to pay off their gambling debts. This is happening as we stand here—it happened in the last few months, in both Afghanistan and Saudi Arabia. Girls are being forced to marry first cousins against their will and if they refuse—they are being honor murdered.

Muslim women are being legally stoned to death; beheaded; scarred and blinded by acid attacks—and not by Jews, Israelis, or Americans, but by other Muslims.

Muslim women are being sexually stalked by "wilding" parties; gang-raped and then lashed almost to death. They are being normatively beaten at home all over the Muslim world—yes in Gaza and on the West Bank as well as in Jordan and Egypt—and normatively killed in honor killings. Physical and sexual child abuse is both rampant and as hotly denied as is homosexual pederasty.

According to recent studies, in Pakistan, 90% of all women are beaten throughout their lives. One million women in Pakistan are beaten every year while they are pregnant. Honor killings are pandemic but the killers are rarely prosecuted. On the contrary. They are usually glorified, heroized.

In the West, woman-battering and femicide are crimes and, while they are not always prosecuted, neither are they glorified or acceptable. Such crimes are not extended family collaborations. Many honor killings are Muslim-on-Muslim or Hindu-on-Hindu crimes, a collaboration of an entire family against their own female blood.

Make no mistake: Such human rights atrocities have fully penetrated the West. If a Muslim girl from a tribal family still bound by honor-and-shame rules in Europe or North America, wants to go to college; refuses to veil; leaves an abusive husband; refuses an arranged marriage; chooses to have non-Muslim friends; acts in ways that are considered too "western," her own family (father, mother, brother, sister, sometimes husband), will kill her. In the last year, this has happened, or been attempted, in Dallas, Toronto, Atlanta, and Henrietta, New York.

Honor murders happen far more often in Europe because the Muslim population is much larger there.

Recently, a Pakistani-Muslim man beheaded his Pakistani-Muslim wife in Buffalo. Beheading takes great strength and planning. The wife's crime? After being beaten and living in fear for years, she finally dared to leave him. More: she dared to keep the children and the home. An order of protection forced him out of his castle. In Pakistan, he would simply kill her for such insubordination. He would not be prosecuted. American feminists and domestic violence workers refused to see this as an honor killing, refused to understand that a beheading is related to fundamentalist Islam, and insisted that if they did so, it would render them vulnerable to being called "racists."

We in the West have also been taught that Islamic barbarism is due to western colonialism, imperialism, racism. We have not been taught to view Islam as the imperialistic, genocidal, slave-owning and misogynist culture which, alas, it is. Today, even saying this is quickly labeled "Islamophobic" and censored as hate speech.

If we do not protect Muslim girls and women in the West from being honor murdered—then their blood will be on our hands too.

Funding shelters, world-wide, for battered Muslim women is long overdue. I challenge the Saudi princes to fund this worthy cause as opposed to their funding of more madrassas or more anti-American and anti-Israel Middle East Studies programs.

I believe we must unite in a vision of human rights that are universal; that long-persecuted Hindus have much to teach the West about Islamic jihad as do Christians, Jews, Buddhists, Zoroastrians, Baha'i, etc., who have been persecuted, forced to convert, murdered, and exiled by Muslims in Asia and the Middle East.

I congratulate the coalition and its leaders for their visionary activism.

Pajamas Media
5/3/09

- 35 -
Muslim Feminist Asra Nomani: Fighting for the Soul of Islam

Asra Q. Nomani, is best known for many things. A former *Wall Street Journal* reporter, she is also the author of *Standing Alone In Mecca: An American Woman's Struggle for the Soul of Islam.* Nomani is a religious Muslim feminist who organized the first-ever woman-led, mixed-gender Islamic prayer group in New York City in 2005, and who made a good faith effort to bring her hometown mosque in Morgantown, West Virginia into the twenty-first century, both in terms of women and tolerance.

Nomani, born in Bombay but raised in Morgantown, West Virginia, is also the last friend whom Daniel Pearl saw before he was kidnapped, held captive, and be-headed on video. Pearl was staying at Nomani's rented home in Pakistan. Currently, Nomani teaches journalism at Georgetown University where she co-leads the Pearl Project.

Nomani will now also be known as the subject of a documentary about her struggle for the soul of Islam, which is airing tonight, June 15th, on PBS, at 10pm est. "The Mosque in Morgantown" is the latest feature in their *America At a Crossroads* series.

Nomani was jolted awake by Pearl's be-heading. In the wake of this tragedy, she chose to become a single mother and went on hajj to Mecca where she experienced a tremendous spiritual "high." Nomani saw that men and women were not separated at Mecca's Masjid al-Haram. When she returned to America, she wanted to bring her own mosque into the 21st century, to transform it into a woman-friendly, "family-centered Islam," not into a hard-hearted "boy's club." She also wanted to moderate, if not eliminate, the forces of hatred within Islam that seem to lead to kidnappings, Jew-hatred, and human bomb terrorism.

Pearl's be-heading forced Nomani to re-examine Islam. Those who had kidnapped Pearl were militant, religious Muslims who believed that their violent acts were sanctioned by the Qur'an. Nomani resolved to take a more activist role in the "battle of ideas, the war of ideas." She wanted to create something that may not yet exist: "A more inclusive and tolerant Islam in the world."

Nomani is precisely the kind of ally that both the West—and the East—urgently need. In addition, to important ex-Muslims (Nonie Darwish, Wafa Sultan), and secular ex-Muslims (Ibn Warraq, Ayaan Hirsi Ali), there is now Nomani: a religious Muslim feminist who wants to redeem, reform, and uplift her religion, as a feminist and as a devout Muslim.

Upon her return home, Nomani was horrified by what she found in the Morgantown mosque. A harsh Arab and Saudi Wahhabi influence had taken over her childhood mosque—the very one that her father had established in the early 1980s. A rude man barked at her to take the back door entrance. This rudeness extended to other women as well.

Finally, Nomani, her mother and a young female relative walked in through the front door and took a place together behind the men's section. But the sermons became more hateful. "To love the Prophet is to hate those who hate him." One man, seen on camera in the film, is very dismissive of Nomani. He says: "She wants to bend the rules her way but the laws are not human laws."

However, as the film documents, extremists, mainly Arabs, led by one rather physically and verbally violent Egyptian, Hany Ammar, took over. At that point, Nomani, on camera says: "I began hearing really scary sermons. An unchaste woman is worthless. The West is on a bad path. We must hate those who hate us. Women should be silent in a mosque. Jews are descendents of apes and pigs. Men should surround (Nomani) and scare her."

Ammar says on camera: "I pray to Allah that you be punished. May Allah get revenge for Ammar"—he physically attacks a young Muslim moderate man—one hears, but does not see this attack. Ammar's wife, Mona, is even more conservative, more aggressive than he is. She minces no words in expressing her contempt, even hatred for Nomani. She, like certain kinds of religious women, is only aggressively empowered to strike down any woman who dares challenge male supremacy or Islamic gender apartheid.

Ammar tried to ban Nomani from the mosque. She began writing about what was happening in her mosque in the media which did not further endear her to them; of course, they accused her of only wanting media attention.

One soft-spoken young man on camera says: "Had (Nomani) gone about this in the right way, (working with moderates like myself), we could have made ten years progress in ten months." However, Nomani's mother insists that "the extremists will never change."

Together with some other Muslim feminists, Nomani then crafted an Islamic Bill of Rights for Women which they posted at her mosque. Included were the following rights: that women have "an Islamic right to enter through the main door;" an "Islamic right to pray…without being separated by a barrier;" "an Islamic right to hold leadership positions." Nomani is quoted on camera: "We are going to change the world starting here."

The Morgantown mosque finally expelled her. However, the film does not make entirely clear whether Nomani was formally or legally expelled from the mosque or whether she left due to the hard line the mosque had adopted.

Not one for inaction, Nomani then organized the first woman-led prayer service—one that had to take place in a church, (St. John's the Divine), in New York City; no mosque would allow it. Dr. Amina Wadud, a distinguished African-American convert to Islam led the service. The service was denounced but it inspired others like it. Nomani also created woman-friendly islands of prayer throughout the country.

Nomani's attempt to turn her mosque into a more tolerant place of worship ultimately failed. She and her parents left the mosque. But, she did not leave Islam. On the contrary. She may be one of the leaders of a movement that is just beginning to arise.

The film portrays Nomani as a brave but lonely figure, a bit high strung, vigilant, principled, determined. She has only one female Muslim supporter at her mosque, Christine Arja, an American woman who converted to Islam and who initially opposed Nomani. Luckily, Nomani has the full support of her parents and of other religious Muslim women around the country.

I "know" Nomani, not only from this film and from her writing, but also from my conversations with her over the years. Yes: I can oppose the mandatory veiling of Muslim women and other aspects of Islamic gender apartheid—and yet honor the work of a religious Muslim feminist. For me, this is not a contradiction. I can respect the hard, uphill work that feminists are doing within each of the major religions—and yet still view many interfaith gatherings as premature. Even if women as well as men participated in such interfaith gatherings (which they do not), I remain pessimistic because women and feminists of both genders have not yet achieved the necessary "critical mass" in leadership positions within orthodox Judaism, Catholicism, Protestantism, Hinduism, Buddhism, and Islam to have their views prevail.

Nomani and other brave religious Muslim women, are just starting down the road that many Jewish and Christian women have traveled before them.

As a religious Jewish feminist, and a co-leader of the legendary, (Original) Jerusalem-based "Women of the Wall" struggle, about which I co-wrote a book, with my colleague, Rivka Haut, titled: *Women of the Wall. Claiming Sacred Ground at Judaism's Holy Site*, I am very familiar with the wrenching realities that a woman and both male and female feminists face as they try to remain connected to a revered tradition which they also view as in need of reformation, transformation, diversity, and tolerance.

Although religious Judaism has had many reformations, many evolutions, and has "split," or diversified into at least four (or more) denominations, misogyny still reigns in many ways. Even though we now have female rabbis, leaders, and Torah (Old Testament) scholars, most religious and cultural Jewish organizations everywhere in the world are top-heavy with men, not with women. The denomination of Judaism which rules the Western Wall (Kotel) and much else in Israel, is Orthodox and ultra-Orthodox.

Today, modern Orthodox Jews gather in all-female groups to pray both in synagogues and homes. Increasingly, younger modern Orthodox Jews pray in mixed-gender egalitarian *minyanim*, (prayer quorums); both women and men read from the Torah. Orthodox girls and women are engaged in tremendous Torah study; some have become leading Torah scholars. Of course, in the Reform, Conservative, and Reconstructionist movements, women are rabbis and cantors and both lead and participate in gender-integrated prayer quorums.

Nomani faces a far more difficult situation. Islam has not yet diversified into denominations—or rather, it has, in part: There are Shi'ites and Sunnis but they are at violent, (not just verbal or legal), war with each other. There are Sufis, more peaceful, mystical, but they are not viewed positively as the soulful leaders they are by either warring sect. No great reform, no great grappling with issues of modernity and hu-

152

man rights has, as yet, influenced religious Muslim views. No major re-interpretations or revisions of the Qur'an and other holy writings have been widely accepted.

I wish Nomani courage, clarity, strength, good health, and support from other Muslims. I congratulate PBS's *America at a Crossroads* for making this film.

Pajamas Media
6/15/09

- 36 -
Sarkozy vs Obama on The Burqa

Frenchmen are back in vogue. Who could ever have predicted that the French president would stand up for women's universal rights and for freedom as a universal right—while the American president would hang back, wait, temporize? It's almost as if we've elected a Frenchman president of the United States—and an American-style president is ruling France.

Please contrast the following two speeches.

On June 22th, 2009, President Nicholas Sarkozy stated that he viewed the full face-and-body burqa and face-veil (*niqab*) as a sign of the "debasement" of women and that it won't be welcome in France. According to the Sarkozy:

> In our country, we cannot accept that women be prisoners behind a screen, cut off from all social life, deprived of all identity … The burqa is not a religious sign, it's a sign of subservience, a sign of debasement — I want to say it solemnly, it will not be welcome on the territory of the French Republic.

France has Europe's largest Muslim population, an estimated 5 million people. Many are hostile to the western enterprise, but some are in the vocal forefront of the fight for women's and human rights. In 2004, France passed a law "banning the Islamic headscarf and other conspicuous religious symbols from public schools," sparking fierce debate at home and abroad.

Now, contrast Sarkozy's words with what President Obama said in Cairo on June 4th, 2009.

Freedom in America is indivisible from the freedom to practice one's religion. That is why there is a mosque in every state of our union, and over 1,200 mosques within our borders. That is why the U.S. government has gone to court to protect the right of women and girls to wear the hijab, and to punish those who would deny it. So let there be no doubt: Islam is a part of America. And I believe that America holds within her the truth that regardless of race, religion, or station in life, all of us share common aspirations — to live in peace and security; to get an education and to work with dignity; to love our families, our communities, and our God. These things we share. This is the hope of all humanity.

This is why I described Obama's Cairo speech as "throwing Muslim women under the bus." Obama is signaling to the Muslim world that they will be able to create a parallel universe in the land of the free and the home of the brave—and will be able to use our laws to do so.

(I know: Obama also threw Israel under the bus—and yet, some say, that his speech was a calculated, careful, respectful—a give-peace-a-chance—kind of speech to an audience that has continually called for "death to America.")

Now, contrast how the two Presidents recently discussed the police and state riots in the streets of Iran.

On June 16, 2009, according to the AP, President Sarkozy denounced the Iranian government's "brutal" reaction to "demonstrators protesting the nation's disputed election. Sarkozy calls the situation in Iran "extremely alarming" and says Iran's clampdown on demonstrators was "totally disproportionate." Sarkozy also said: "The ruling power claims to have won the elections ... if that were true, we must ask why they find it necessary to imprison their opponents and repress them with such violence."

On that same date, June 16th, according to the *Wall Street Journal* here's what President Obama had to say. He "voiced concern about how the election had been conducted, although he fell short of denouncing the vote." What Obama himself actually said was this: "It is up to Iranians to make decisions about who Iran's leaders will be. We respect Iranian sovereignty and want to avoid the United States being the issue inside of Iran." Obama then went on to say that "the world is watching" and described the demonstrators as "inspiring, regardless of what the ultimate outcome of the election was."

155

On June 19th, *CBS News* quoted President Obama again. This time he said:

> The last thing that I want to do is to have the United States be a foil for those forces inside Iran who would love nothing better than to make this an argument about the United States. That's what they do. That's what we have already seen. We shouldn't be playing into that ... now what we can do is bear witness and say to the world that the incredible demonstrations that we've seen is a testimony to — I think what Dr. King called the — arc of the moral universe. It is long but it bends towards justice.

I am not sure what this means but I doubt this is what Attorney General Robert Kennedy and President John F. Kennedy said to Dr. King or to James Meredith's supporters in the 1960s when they were beaten, murdered, and imprisoned in southern jails. In 1962, our government sent 13,500 federal troops to Oxford, Mississippi to quell racist rioting there. True: This all happened on sovereign American soil. But isn't President Obama a citizen of the world, a universalist, someone who prides himself on his knowledge that we all live in a global community?

America has a long history of meddling in foreign affairs, and we have supported corrupt tyrants in the service of a stable, status quo. I am not calling for boots on the ground, for an expansion of the war that America is already waging in Afghanistan and Iraq. I am merely calling for more principled, more "inspiring" words on behalf of freedom and women's rights from our very eloquent American President, our Master Wordsmith. At least that.

And, I am calling for one law for women in America. I hope President Obama supports this view.

As for me: I've already begun to remember my love of French literature, cheese, wine, cooking, perfume, fashion, and art. Ever since Chirac coddled Arafat, and De Gaulle opened the French borders to Muslim immigration (in return for hoped-for oil markets) , I have rarely indulged these guilty pleasures. Now — Viva La France!

Pajamas Media
6/22/09

- 37 -

Islamic Face Masks: Banned in Michigan Courtrooms

I n 2006, in a small claims matter in Michigan, a Muslim woman, Ginnah Muhammed, refused to take off her face mask (*niqab*) while she testfied. Judge Paul Paruk dismissed her case. Muhammed sued and the American Civil Liberties Union (ACLU) backed her. They argued for a "religious exception" to courtroom attire. Although Muhammed's small claims case was against a car rental agency, here's what Michael Steinberg, legal director of the ACLU of Michigan stated:

> The Michigan Supreme Court should not slam the door of justice on a category of women just because of their religious belief...Under the proposed rule, women who are sexually assaulted do not have their day in court if they wear a veil mandated by their religion.

Sexual assault was not at issue nor was the victim afraid that testifying might lead to her death. Leave it to the ACLU to always get it wrong.

Finally, earlier this month, on June 17, 2009, the Michigan Supreme Court, in a 5-2 vote, ruled that a Judge had the power to "require witnesses to remove head or facial covering as (the witness) was testifying." A Judge has the right to see a witness's "facial expressions" to determine her "truthfulness" while she testifies.

Expect many more such cases. Indeed, expect Ginnah Muhammed to appeal this right up to the Supreme Court.

Both the American Civil Liberties Union and the (Muslim Brotherhood's) Council on American-Islamic Relations (CAIR), have gone to court in Florida (2002), California (2005), Michigan (2008), and Oklahoma (2008) to fight for a Muslim woman's right to cover her hair or face—whether it is while being photographed for a driver's license or for a police mug shot; or while working at McDonald's or Abercrombie Kids. In 2007, CAIR wrote a letter on behalf of a Muslim woman in Georgia who refused to remove her headscarf in order to enter a courtroom to plead "not guilty" to a traffic ticket. In 2004, the Justice Department supported a lawsuit brought on behalf of a sixth grade student in Oklahoma who wanted to wear hijab in her public school. That same year, the school reviewed their policy, amended their dress code, paid the student an undisclosed sum, and allowed her to attend classes wearing hijab.

Religious Muslims are outraged that Christians can wear crucifixes, nuns and priests can wear habits, Jews can wear skullcaps or wigs and head coverings, Sikhs can wear turbans, Hindus can wear veils and saris, but that Muslims cannot wear burqas or niqabs.

Of course, only the Islamic female attire masks all five senses and makes human interaction almost impossible. While hijab (head covering) has been discussed, I am only challenging niqab here.

Many conservatives and religious people do not want the government telling them how to dress or limiting their private religious practices. Most progressives, including feminists, view the burqa, (full face and body shroud), niqab, (face mask plus head and body covering), and hijab (headcovering so that no hair, or no hair, neck, and shoulder shows), as either a Muslim woman's religious right or as her culturally sanctioned expression of modesty. In addition, they may see the ban on the burqa as a form of "racial profiling," or as "Islamophobic."

I appreciate but respectfully disagree with both views. I believe that we must ban the burqa and niqab not only for reasons of national security, (something that Daniel Pipes has already argued), but also for health-related reasons—and on the grounds of women's rights and human rights.

Pajamas Media
6/29/09

Al-Qaeda Threatens France Over Burqa

Today, al-Qaeda threatened France over the ostensible issue of the burqa. Tomorrow, America may be in their gun sights on this same issue.

The burqa, niqab—even hijab—are being used as pawns in the power struggle between jihadic Islam and the West. These dress codes are primarily political in nature.

For those people who really and truly believe that the burqa is a religious and not a politically supremacist issue—consider this:

According to the United States monitoring service, SITE Intelligence, al-Qaeda has just announced that it plans to "take revenge on France for its opposition to the burqa, calling on Muslims to retaliate against the country." Abu Musab Abdul Wadud, head of al-Qaeda in the Islamic Maghreb said:

> Yesterday was the hijab (the Islamic headscarf long banned in French schools) and today, it is the niqab (the full veil).. We will take revenge for the honour of our daughters and sisters against France and against its interests by every means at our disposal...for us, the mujahedeen...we will not remain silent to such provocations and injustices. We call upon all Muslims to confront this hostility with greater hostility.

Does anyone really believe that al-Qaeda is a genuinely religious group? Or that their religious pronouncements are holy and should be protected by American or European laws?

In a many months-old video, al-Qaeda's number two man, al-Zawahiri, also condemned the French law (which banned hijab) saying "the decision showed the grudge the Western crusaders have against Islam." Zawahiri claimed to be speaking in Bin Laden's name.

Al-Qaeda now has an Algerian-based Salafist-oriented group which is being encouraged to attack either pro-French Algerians or Frenchmen. Or both.

Le Pauvre Algerienne. For nearly twenty years, Algerian women have been pawns in the power struggle between Islamists and the Algerian government.

According to attorney Karima Bennoune, from 1992 on, Algerian Islamist men committed a series of "terrorist atrocities" against Algerian women. Bennoune describes the "kidnapping and repeated raping of young girls as sex slaves for armed fundamentalists. The girls were also forced to cook and clean for God's warriors… one 17-year-old girl was repeatedly raped until pregnant. She was kidnapped off the street and held with other young girls, one of whom was shot in the head and killed when she tried to escape."

As in Iran, "unveiled," educated, independent Algerian women were seen as "military targets" and were increasingly shot on sight. According to Bennoune, "the men of Algeria (were) arming, the women of Algeria (were) veiling themselves. As one woman said: 'Fear is stronger than our will to be free.'"

According to Bennoune: "Terrorist attacks on women [in Algeria] have had the desired effect: widespread psychosis among the women; internal exile—living in hiding, both physically and psychologically, in their own country." In Bennoune's view, "the collective psychosis" is due to the "escalation of violence" by the "soldiers of the Islamic state."

All of this—and more—was legalized by a series of fatwas (Muslim religious edicts).

According to Meredith Turshen, the Algerian Islamist goal was the implementation of Sharia law as state law. The Islamists frowned upon secular education for women and discouraged women from working outside the home. Separate beaches and separate transporation were part of the Islamist platform.

"A 1994 fatwa legalized the killing of girls and women not wearing the hijab (which in Algeria consists of a scarf that hides the hair and neck and a full-length robe; (a) veil is not an accurate translation; another fatwa legalized kidnapping and temporary marriage ..Muslim women do not have the right to work outside the home, become political leaders, or participate in sports. They should not wear makeup, perfume,

PHYLLIS CHESLER ❧

fitted clothes, or mingle with men in public; they should wear the hijab, 'which not only establishes the distinction between masculine and feminine, but underscores the separation between public and private' ...According to *El Mounquid*, the official FIS journal, the hijab distinguishes Muslims from non-Muslims; it is obligatory for Muslim women and not an individual decision."

I hope that the "muhajideen" are just blowing smoke-rings, rattling their swords. I fear this may not the case. Women in face masks and sheets are Jihad's advance troops.

Pajamas Media
6/30/09

- 39 -
Should America Ban the Burqa?

arlier today, Muslims demonstrated in Antwerp to oppose the banning of headscarves in two schools—and the new Swedish head of the European Union, Justice Minister Beatrice Ask, stated that the "27 member European Union must not dictate an Islamic dress code…(that) the European Union is a union of freedom."

Clearly, this is a major issue in Europe where anywhere from 30-50 million Muslims live. Paradoxically, various European countries have banned or restricted the far less restrictive headscarf (hijab) in schools, universities, and courtrooms—but have not yet restricted the far more smothering burqa. Perhaps hijab is seen as the "nose of the camel," a garment which, if allowed, will lead Europe right down the slippery slope to more oppressively restricted clothing for Muslim-European women.

Could this issue arise in America with its much smaller Muslim population? Is this an issue we must address?

America is a nation of immigrants, one that is dedicated to freedom of religion and to the separation of religion and state. Thus, most Americans are probably inclined to accept that wearing the Islamic burqa, niqab, and hijab is a religious choice and should therefore be protected as a religious right. If not, it is feared, other religious symbols and practices might also be banned; and America would be engaging in religious persecution.

For the moment, I do not want to discuss the politicization of Islamic female attire as a visual statement on behalf of Islamist supremacism and jihad, nor do I want to focus on the headscarf (hijab). I do not yet want to address whether such Islamic female attire (burqa, niqab, hijab) is a free or a forced choice and whether or not it is mandated by the Qur'an.

Religious Muslim scholars and other experts disagree profoundly about this. Some say that such attire is merely a pre-Islamic, desert-based custom that has nothing to do with Islam. For example, in 2009, the Muslim Canadian Congress (MCC) urged Canada's government to ban the burqa. Mafooz Kanwar, a professor and an MCC director stated: "The burqa is not mandated by Islam or the Qur'an and is therefore not religious and protected under the Charter. In Canada, gender equality is one of our core values and faces are important identifying tools and should not be covered. Period."

Other Muslim scholars insist that such attire is an Islamic custom (if not an actual law) which women must follow in order to be "modest."

World-wide, many Muslim women do not mask their faces, shroud their bodies, or cover their hair—but many do, especially if they have been threatened with beatings or death if they are not sufficiently "covered." An increasing number of Muslim women in the West, including educated women, claim that they are freely choosing to wear hijab, the headscarf.

In 2007, Middle East scholar, Daniel Pipes called for a ban on burqas and niqab—not on headscarves. Pipes views the burqa as a security risk and cites literally hundreds of cases in which both common criminals and Islamist terrorists were able to commit robberies, make their escapes or blow themselves and others up, both in the West and in the Muslim world, by wearing a burqa. Male criminals and terrorists did this far more often than their female counterparts. Pipes concludes:

> Nothing in Islam requires turning females into shapeless, faceless zombies; good sense calls for modesty itself to be modest. The time has come everywhere to ban from public places these hideous, unhealthy, socially divisive, terrorist-enabling, and criminal-friendly garments.

I concur. But I would like to explore some other grounds for such a potential ban.

According to French President Nicolas Sarkozy, the burqa is a "moving prison." French-Muslim Minister of Cities, Fadela Amara, views it as "a coffin that kills individual liberties," and as proof of the "political exploitation of Islam."

In a burqa or chadari, one has no peripheral and only limited forward vision; one's hearing and speech are muffled. One's facial expressions remain unknown; social contact and movement are severely limit-ed. A first-time burqa wearer may feel that she cannot breathe freely and that she might slowly be suffocating. She may feel buried alive and may become anxious, claustrophobic. (Try on a burqa, this experience is easy to confirm). Imagine the consequences of getting used to this as a way of life. But maybe one never gets used to it. I have heard many descriptions of what Saudi women do the moment their aircraft leaves the Kingdom's terra firma: they immediately fling off their "coverings."

A burqa wearer, who can be as young as ten years old, must surely experience both isolation and sensory deprivation which are, essential-ly, forms of torture which can lead to depression, anxiety, even a psycho-logical breakdown. According to my colleague, psychoanalyst and Ara-bist, Dr. Nancy L. Kobrin, the burqa may "create an artificially induced autistic-like environment." Covering up the five senses is harmful to the woman in the burqa; making it impossible to recognize or identify such a woman is potentially harmful to others.

There is something else. The sight of women in burqas and niqab is frightening to Westerners of all faiths, including the Muslim faith, as well as to secularists. First, their presence visually signals the forced or accepted subordination of women; the fact that these women acquiesce and collaborate in their own subordination is also alarming, and a bit terrifying. One knows that the people who do this also publicly whip, cross-amputate, hang, stone, and be-head human beings. And, if the "ghosts" are here (my own name for burqa wearers) they are meant to remind us of just such practices. Pipes's "faceless, shapeless" women are meant to terrify and disturb. And they do.

Niqab, which allows the eyes to show but masks the face, reminds Westerners of how a masked robber or a Klu Klux Klan member looks.

Many Westerners, including Muslims, ex-Muslims, and those Christians and Jews who have fled Muslim lands, may feel haunted, "fol-lowed," when they see burqas and women wearing niqab on the western streets. Is their presence a way of announcing that Islamist supremacism and jihad are here?

In the West, the isolation intrinsically imposed by the burqa may be further magnified by the fearful or awkward responses of others. Sev-eral college students have described to me how a single classmate in a heavy burqa and wearing dark, thick gloves makes them feel: "Very sad." "Pushed away." The other students tend not to talk to the burqa wearer. "When she is asked to read aloud she does so but her heavy gloves make turning the pages slow and difficult." The students feel sorry for her and

164

do not know how to relate to her.

Any religious headgear or garments that do not cover the five senses is obviously permissible. Thus, a nun's long, dark habit and headgear; an orthodox or Hasidic Jewish woman's wig, headscarf, and long, dark, clothing; a Muslim woman's headscarf, (as well as various male Sikh, Hasidic, and Hindu attire) all allow the wearer to breathe, hear, see, smell, and speak. Those who wear such attire, are easy to recognise and identify. They can move freely and see clearly. This is not true of the burqa or niqab wearer.

In addition, and for this reason, the burqa (and niqab) may also lead to health hazards. Lifetime burqa wearers may suffer eye damage and may be prone to a host of multiple diseases which are also related to Vitamin D (sunlight deprivation) deficiency e.g. osteoporosis, heart disease, hypertension, autoimmune diseases, certain cancers, depression, chronic fatigue, and chronic pain.

I therefore suggest that we begin a national conversation about whether Americans should consider banning the burqa not only for security-related reasons but on the grounds of human rights/women's rights and for health-related reasons.

Pajamas Media
7/2/09

- 40 -
Conservatives are Feminists,
Liberals are Misogynists

O ver the weekend, Asma al-Ghul, a Palestinian journalist in Gaza was nearly arrested by Hamas policemen for "laughing in public" and for dressing "immodestly" at the beach. The police confiscated her passport. Subsequent death threats have kept her confined to her home.

If Hamas has its way, the women of Gaza will soon be wearing burqas or the Iranian version of them. My question: If Asma immigrates to America, will she be free of such policing? Who will best safeguard her personal rights in America?

Some of my best friends are, or certainly were, leftists and liberals. We have certain memories, friends, interests, and values in common.

Well, maybe we don't anymore.

For example: On the matter of America, Israel, the Jews, and Islam we seem to have parted company. Still, I'm willing to entertain many liberal views; I respect and wrestle with valid points no matter what flag their bearers fly. The same is not true in reverse. Whenever I even hint at a view that does not match theirs exactly, there is tension, yelling, hyperventilating, shaming, a harangue.

This is the behavior of a cult member, not that of a free and well-informed human being.

Why do I even mention this? Because I have been anecdotally polling various leftists and liberals of all faiths and of no faith at all about whether America should restrict or ban the burqa and niqab in America.

A Muslim friend made an interesting point. She said that "if you ban something the hotheads will protest it, you will give them a *raison d'être*, a symbol. If you just leave it alone, it is bound to die on its own."

A Jewish friend immediately yelled at me. He insisted that if I applied the same ban to hasidic and ultra-Orthodox dress that I would consider myself an anti-Semite. "You don't want the government coming in and telling people how to practice their religion."

I pointed out that hasidic and ultra-Orthodox attire does not block the five senses, communication and identification are possible, there is no sensory deprivation involved—although, I conceded, wearing heavy, long, dark clothing works better in nineteenth century Poland on a cold winter day than in The New World (or in Israel) on a hot summer afternoon. I also pointed out that there are only a small number of Jews (14 million) compared to Muslims (1.3 billion), and that hasidic and ultra-Orthodox Jews do not share a religious ideology which has vowed a jihadic war against the West.

I spoke to no avail. Interestingly, this particular Jewish man does not usually defend the rights of hasidic or ultra-orthodox Jews. On the contrary. He continuously attacks them. His brotherly concern seems to emerge only when Muslim dress codes are at issue.

I agree that the subordination, marginalization, disenfranchisement of women may be an issue in all religions. However, there is a difference between an evolved, diversified, and pro-modern Christianity, Judaism, Buddhism, Sikhism, and Hinduism as compared to a medieval and barbaric version of Islam.

In my conversations of the last few weeks, here is how liberal-leftists differ from…myself; I am also known as the "Zionist bitch," conservative traitor," and "Islamophobe," etc.

Left-liberals do not really believe that a war has been declared against the West, that we are in any clear and present danger; but even if we're at war, left-liberals fear that any relaxation of our fundamental civil rights will lead to their permanent loss and will turn into a permanent blot on America's moral reputation. They mean to extend American civil rights to enemy combatants.

Left-liberals do not like the idea of the government telling them how to dress or nosing into their business. Wait a minute. I thought this was a conservative position…and it is. But what left-liberals usually have in mind is clothing, sexual activities, free speech, and the right not to be coerced into a religious practice; conservatives tend to first think about the right to bear arms, family morality, or the right to practice one's religion apart from state scrutiny.

Thus, surely, left-liberals will best safeguard Asma al-Ghul's right to dress "immodestly" at the beach. Ah—not so fast.

Left-liberals tend to view all immigrant groups, especially if they are Muslims, as persecuted victims, not as barbaric oppressors. Therefore, very often, secular or atheistic liberals are willing to believe that the burqa is truly mandated by the Qur'an (it is not) and is a religious right that should be guaranteed in America. Thus, if the equivalent of the Hamas police move here and force or persuade their women to wear the burqa, how will liberals be able to distinguish a free choice from a forced choice when someone else's religious rights are being invoked? Will their feminism trump their multi-culti respect for Islamic *taqiya* (disinformation) and misogyny?

Left-liberals believe in "choice." Thus, they also believe that women have the right to choose: an abortion (I strongly agree with this), to rent out their wombs (I strongly disagree with this), or to work as a prostitute or in the pornography industry. (I am a long-time abolitionist on these last two points). Call me conservative; call me an Old Time radical feminist, because I understand the difference between a "free" choice and a "forced" choice. Fifteen year old girls who have run away from home to escape lives of incest and physical abuse are not freely choosing to sell sex for food.

For such reasons, I cannot persuade most left-liberals that most/ many? /some?/a handful of Muslim women wear the burqa mainly in order to avoid being killed. Western liberals simply do not believe it. Their professors and most beloved journalists have not educated them about the phenomenon. They believe that everyone is like them.

I know: There are all kinds of pro-burqa testimonials one can find in the mass media written by women and by men about "modesty" but I doubt that true modesty requires putting a bag over one's head or dropping a sheet over oneself in public. Surely, as Daniel Pipes has pointed out, there are more "modest" ways to be modest.

Conservatives, who have been accused of misogyny, and former left-liberals who are hawks on certain issues, "get" the burqa problem and do not want women wearing it in America. But that's because they tend to believe that we are, indeed, at war; that Islamic jihad is a serious problem; that Islamic gender and religious apartheid really do exist; that American women live in a more progressive society than Afghan,Saudi, or Pakistani women do (saying so is still heretical in certain feminist quarters); that we may not be able to abolish barbarism abroad but we sure as hell do not have to tolerate it at home.

At this moment, and for these reasons, I wonder whether American left-liberals will support Asma al-Ghul's right to dress "immodestly" at the beach—and whether they'd offer her physical protection against those who might come after her?

Pajamas Media
7/6/09

- 41 -

Palestinian Taliban Arrest Palestinian Feminist: Asma'a Al-Gul in Peril

Asma'a Al-Gul is the Palestinian secular feminist who has written poignant, heartbreaking pieces about honor killings and women's rights in Gaza. Last month, Asma'a quit her job at *Al-Ayyam* because her subject matter got her into "trouble" at work. She is also the journalist who was arrested over the weekend by Hamas's "morality" police, ostensibly for "laughing immoderately" and for "immodest" clothing at the beach.

The beach!

Asma'a, the 27-year-old mother of a four-year-old son, was wearing jeans and a t-shirt. She went into the water fully clothed. Apparently, that was not modest enough for them.

According to Asma'a, with whom I just spoke, the Palestinian police detained her and took her passport away. They also beat up four male friends: two right there on the beach, and all four back in police custody. (One of these men was not sitting with them at the time but came to their aid when the police attacked them). Due to the intercession of a journalist-friend with whom the beach goers were visiting, the police let Asma'a go—but with a warning; they told her "they would be following her case." The police also returned Asma'a's passport to her. In addition, the police wanted to confiscate her laptop but luckily, they were unable to find it.

Since then, Asma'a has received a written death threat. She's been staying home, and has, understandably, had trouble sleeping.

"But," she tells me, "Both my friends and the media have been

170

supporting me." Indeed, Asma'a wrote to thank me for my recent piece which mentioned her plight.

"And" she points out, "yesterday at noon, the government, possibly for the first time ever, announced that they will be looking into this matter."

Asma'a explained that many other such incidents have happened and been covered up. "People are afraid to speak out. But we must speak out in order to stop this. We fear that the government will banish those who speak."

It has been said that the Palestinian people were once the most educated people in the Arab world. Over the years, I have known and worked with both secular and religious Palestinian Muslim and ex-Muslim feminists who are in favor of modernity and women's rights.

Nevertheless, increasingly, Hamas officials have been cracking down on women and on western ways. They have "urged shopkeepers to take down foreign advertisements which show the shape of women's bodies and to hide lingerie which is currently displayed in windows. Officials search electronic shops to check if they are selling pornography on tiny flash drives."

According to human rights activist, Isam Younis, "There's an open, public program to preserve public morals in Gaza...In reality that means trying to restrict freedoms. Hamas denies that any crackdown is under way. But they have failed to take any action against the groups that have been attacking hairdressers and internet cafes."

Under Hamas, women have been increasingly veiling: wearing hijab, wearing versions of the Iranian, Saudi, and Afghani abayas, chadors, burqas, etc.

Asma'a tells me: "Palestinian feminists have not called to support me. They are afraid. Some have told me that I am so 'strong,' (which means that they think) they are not."

Asma'a has written a moving report about honor killings and women's rights in Gaza which she originally published in Arabic in *Al-Ayyam*. She has given me permission to edit and publish it here which I will do in two parts. In it, one of the things she describes is how Palestinian women themselves have internalized misogyny (something that is a global phenomenon and about which I've written in *Women's Inhumanity to Woman*). Thus, women accept, and even support, the punishment and murder of women.

According to Asma'a, at a recent workshop in Khan Yunis, many of the women gathered "were fully convinced that a woman who makes a mistake must be killed. A woman wearing a black folk dress consisting of two parts and only (her) forehead and one of the eyes can be seen through it said: 'She deserves to die…she should be a way to give a lesson to others.' Neither she nor the other women believed that men should be punished for the same crime or for murdering a woman for the sake of 'family honor.'

"You know," Asma'a said, "when my mother was my age she used to wear short skirts and no hijab. I do not wear hijab. But now, the women cover everything, even their faces. I am a secular Muslim. Theoretically, I believe that Islam and secular values can be compatible The government has attached themselves to the most extreme facets of Islam, not to Islam (as it has been practiced in the past). These morality police think they are god."

As to the future—Asma'a tells me: "We don't know. We are waiting."

Asma'a is lucky. Her family supports her. This is crucial. She has friends. She has a college degree and a profession. The media is paying attention. The government, perhaps responding to such media attention, has gone through some pro forma damage control. Asma'a was not arrested. Still, for the first time, Asma'a is now thinking about leaving Gaza.

"Gaza needs liberal and secular people to defend liberty. For this reason, I have never wanted to leave. But after what happened, I am thinking of leaving."

Asma'a wonders whether Hamas would become more flexible, more tolerant, if they were part of a real government. "Now, they are like a caged cat that has become a tiger." I reminded her that the Islamists in Iran and Saudi Arabia also think they are gods and they have full state legitimacy—and they have largely caged and murdered women and dissidents.

Asma'a immediately agreed. But she also said this: "There are no books in Gaza. If you don't give people a chance to learn new things, how will they change?"

I was very moved by Asma'a's article about honor killings in Gaza. She had—and still has—no idea that we share a common passion or that I've been writing about this subject for a long time. With Asma'a's permission, I am publishing it here in an edited form. I will publish Part Two later this week.*

*It is contained in my forthcoming volume on honor killing.

Pajamas Media
7/8/09

- 42 -

Death to the Turbans, No More Stoning:
Free Iran

Defiantly, bravely, they are marching for their freedom in the streets of Teheran. The mullahs' men are gassing, beating, shooting and jailing them.

The people are chanting: "Death to the turbans," "Down with the dictator," "We want democracy." The demonstrators are risking their very lives in order to tell the world the truth about Iran: that it is one gigantic prison in which elections are rigged, children are sacrificed to clear landmines from the fields, and women, intellectuals, and homosexuals are routinely jailed and murdered by corrupt dictators who sponsor terrorism abroad.

We tell children that if they "tell the truth, they will be safe." But this is a lie. Truth tellers invariably get into trouble. Even in the West, whistleblowers get harassed, maligned, isolated, fired. Those who expose family "secrets" are treated as evil or crazy and are often driven out of the family. The evil-doers are protected, those who expose them are punished. This seems to be a fairly universal phenomenon.

While I am no fan of the Islamist Mir Hossein Moussavi or of his Islamist wife, at least Moussavi ran on a platform which promised to ban the stoning of Iranian women.

Last night I finally saw *The Stoning of Soraya M.* The film is both beautiful and terrible, painfully graphic, quite true to Sahebjam's narrative, well worth seeing. I have been writing and speaking about this stoning for about five years now but I was still riveted to my seat. I had to cover my face several times as the actual stoning was re-enacted. This is ironic, given my stand against female cowering/"covering."

Some points about the story and the film which the reviewers may not have noticed:

First, Soraya Manoucheri could have lived—had she granted Ghorban Ali, her husband, an immediate divorce, given up her two sons whom Ali, a frequenter of brothels, had turned against her, and simply accepted her fate as a vulnerable, impoverished women with absolutely no way to support herself and her two daughters other than prostitution which is both shameful and illegal. This small measure of spirit, or outraged dignity that Soraya displayed is precisely what doomed her. It makes no difference that the 40 year-old Ghorban Ali could have married the 14 year-old who had aroused his lust anyway, without having to divorce Soraya. He would still have had to pay some support and this he refused to do. He chose to falsely accuse her of improper behavior with her male employer and to have her stoned to death.

Second, although Soraya and her magnificent aunt Zahra were relatively "spirited" women, neither was capable of effective resistance. To save her life, Soraya would have had to flee immediately—yes, into the same dreadful poverty and prostitution. Failing that, Soraya would have had to wrestle the rifle out of the hands of the man guarding her, turned it on him, and then on herself in order to avoid the most torturous of deaths.

If they are lucky, Iranian prostitutes routinely spend many years in prison, as do rape victims. In 2001-2002, Iranian filmmaker Manijeh Hekmat released a film, *Women's Prison,* which depicts the heartbreaking lives of women behind bars from 1979-1999. Many prisoners have been accused falsely of being prostitutes, or have been forced into prostitution and then punished for it—or have killed their potential rapists or longtime rapists.

In 2007-2008, Mehmoushe Solouki, a Canadian-French-Iranian and a former inmate of Evin Prison, released another film, *The Evil and the Good*, about women in Iranian prisons. Solouki was, and still is, haunted by the cries of other women prisoners, many of whom were women's rights activists who had been arrested for marching for women's rights.

"I heard the cries and yelling of other women prisoners," she says. "I thought that they were terrorists, but when I asked about it, the answer was that they were women activists arrested during the ceremony of March 8 [International Women's Day]. I couldn't tell whether this answer was tragic or comic...I have heard some things about Guantana-

175

mo Bay—that terrorists are kept there." Solouki says. "But I can't believe there could be a place in the world with so many students, intellectuals, writers, and women's rights activists [as Evin prison]."

This is what happens when people tell the truth everywhere, anywhere, but especially in Islamist countries.

The stoning of Soraya M was a cultural honor killing. The people in her village, where she had been born and had lived all her life, were easily convinced that she had shamed and dishonored them and that only by shedding her blood could the villagers themselves be cleansed. These are Ghorban Ali's exact words—and they inspired the murderous sexual rage of the all-male stoning mob. As did the fake mullah's repeated cries of "Allahuakbar." A traveling theatrical-musical company stays to watch the "entertainment" and also joins in by pounding their large drums in a way that excites and thrills the stoners.

I am keeping the brave Iranian demonstrators close to my heart and I am always mindful of Soraya M, whose body was exposed to the dogs to eat and whose bones were then lovingly buried by her aunt Zahra near a stream that Soraya loved.

I want to thank Joy Rose of Mammapalooza for accompanying me down to see this film and for sighing right along with me. No woman should have to sigh alone.

Pajamas Media
7/11/09

- 43 -
Iran Solidarity Day: Maryam Namazie Leads a Stand Against Apartheid

I t has finally happened. Someone other than me and a small handful of others who are also demonized as racists—actually views the Islamic regime of Iran as an *apartheid* regime and is calling for an anti-apartheid-like protest and solidarity movement against the Islamic Republic of Iran.

Please note that this movement has been launched in the UK and amazingly, is not a protest against Israel as an allegedly "racist, apartheid" state.

There is a God after all.

I have been haunted by the information coming out of Teheran, about the murder and torture of so many young Iranians—women as well as men—who are our true allies.

Maryam Namazie, the UK-based leader of One Law For All, is now calling for "people across the world to stand with the people of Iran on July 25th and every day." Maryam Namazie is no novice to organizing. On March 7th, in London, she called for a rally in Trafalgar Square which was followed by a public meeting in Conway Hall. Namazie described the rally as an "anti-racist London rally against Sharia and religious-based laws in Britain and elsewhere and in defense of citizenship and universal rights." She also launched a petition drive which has more than 10,000 signatures.

Iran Solidarity is calling on people everywhere to step up their support for the people of Iran by joining the July 25th demonstrations at Iran's embassies in cities across the globe. Since Iran Solidarity was founded last week, "over 1,000 individuals and organizations have joined, including Nazanin Afshin-Jam, Mina Ahadi, Richard Dawkins, Daniel Dennett and Taslima Nasrin. Iran Solidarity was launched in the House of Lords. The leaders are also calling for:

> ...every day to be a day of solidarity with the people of Iran and are looking to have one person every day in central London for half an hour for the next year starting July 26. We are asking you to volunteer to express your solidarity as you see fit on a day that you are available during the next 365 days. To volunteer to take part, email iransolidaritynow@gmail.com with your name, email and mobile number as well as the dates you are available. We aim to film or photograph all the daily acts of protest and solidarity.

> If you do not live in London and want to take part or organise daily acts of solidarity in other cities contact us so we can help you. You can set up Iran Solidarity groups at your schools and universities, neighbourhoods and workplaces – similar to the anti-apartheid groups that helped get rid of racial apartheid in South Africa.

> We have a responsibility and duty to unite to support a hugely important movement in Iran that will help the people of Iran and the world in heralding a new dawn.

> We can and will make a difference; the future is ours!

I applaud this effort and suggest that we in America, in each great city, also stand in solidarity for the heroic people of Iran.

Pajamas Media
7/21/09

- 44 -

Sudanese Trouser Wearing Hero Lubna Ahmed-al Hussein Forced into Hiding

Today, Lubna Ahmed al-Hussein went to receive her 40 lashes in Khartoum. The world press and scores of female supporters were watching. I was watching, so to speak, from afar. However, the judge delayed her trial until September 7th. He first wants to consult the Foreign Ministry on "whether al-Hussein is immune from the charges because she was formerly a United Nations employee."

The delay disappointed al-Hussein. She refused to claim any UN immunity. Al-Hussein was ready to receive "40,000 lashes if such punishment was found to be constitutional." She is quoted as saying some very bold things:

> I'm ready for anything to happen. I'm absolutely not afraid of the verdict…Tens of thousands of women and girls have been whipped for their clothes these last 20 years. It's not rare in Sudan…I want people to know. I want these women's voices to be heard.

> Whip me if you dare…Flogging is a terrible thing, very painful and a humiliation for the victim. But I will not back down. I want to stand up for the rights of women, and now the eyes of the world are on this case I have a chance to draw attention to the plight of women in Sudan…The acts of this regime have no connection with the real Islam.

What great sin did al-Hussein commit?

On July 3, 2009, Sudan's Morality police arrested al-Hussein for wearing trousers that were allegedly "too tight" and an allegedly "too-transparent" blouse. The fact that she was also wearing a headscarf did not spare her. They publicly menaced, humiliated, and arrested her and twelve other women journalists, mainly Christians from the south, where Sharia law does not even apply, in a restaurant. The police beat all the women about their heads while in custody, then sentenced the women to ten to forty lashes in public for the crime of "indecent clothing."

Ten women opted to receive ten lashes. Al-Hussein, a widow, appealed and then invited 500 people to watch her sentencing and flogging.

Hussein refused to plead guilty. She was put in a cell together with men and forced to crouch down between the legs of the morality police on the way to jail—not very Islamic behavior in her view. She does not believe that the Qur'an or hadith justify flogging a woman or that trousers are religiously forbidden to women. Al-Hussein says:

> These laws were made by this current regime which uses it to humiliate the people and especially the women. These tyrants are here to distort the real image of Islam.

Al-Hussein's bravery is spectacular. She understands that she is dealing with the same rogue regime that has systematically been perpetuating genocide and "gender cleansing" (repeated, public gang-rapes) against the black African people of southern Sudan. She knows what they are capable of doing and yet, despite this, perhaps because of it, she dares to expose and defy this regime.

Please recall that the President of Sudan, Omar al-Bashir, is the first head of state to face an international arrest warrant for war crimes.

If al-Hussein is right about the Qur'an, then surely the country and the world's major imams and mullahs will come forward and support her. I rather doubt this will happen. But, it would be a grand opportunity for moderate religious Muslims to start taking their religion back. If they remain quiet, I would hope that all the interfaith hopefuls draw the necessary conclusions.

For that matter: Will the same American government which insists on telling a sovereign Israel what it can and cannot do, weigh in on al-Hussein's behalf? Will Western feminists come to her aid as readily as Sudanese women apparently have? As my friend and colleague, Barry

Rubin, has just asked: Is the United States even going to comment on any non-Israeli examples of injustice?

"Massive killings of civilians in Sri Lanka, Sudan, and Pakistan? Repression in Iran? Persecution of Christians in Iraq and Egypt? Murder of women for going to school and blasphemy trials in Afghanistan? Repression in Saudi Arabia (wonder if Hillary raised that with the visiting foreign minister); torture of political prisoners in Syria (are U.S. envoys to Damascus raising this issue?); oppression in the Hamas-ruled Gaza Strip?"

Alas, our hero, Lubna al-Hussein, is now moving from one relative's house to another's. Why? Because she was threatened by a man on a motorcycle who told her "she would end up like (that) Egyptian woman who was recently murdered."

I am glad she is taking this threat seriously. The motorcyclist was referring to the case of the popular Lebanese singer, Suzanne Tamim, who was found savagely slashed to death with an eight inch stab wound across her throat in her luxury apartment in Dubai. Her wealthy, married Egyptian boyfriend, Hisham Talaat Moustafa, paid someone to kill her after she dared to break up with him. He is on trial for her murder.

The UN Secretary-General, Ban Ki-moon, is concerned about al-Hussein's case and has said that "Flogging is against international human rights standards."

Sudanese Women Activists signed a petition which urged the Government of Sudan to:

> Cease the use of cruel, inhuman and degrading punishments; guarantee the procedural rights of women accessing the justice system at all times; support and facilitate women's access to the justice system safely and with dignity.

Rogues: The world is watching what you do.

Pajamas Media
8/4/09

- 45 -
Hijab (The Headscarf)—Yes;
The Burqa—No.
Alliances at a G8 Conference in Rome

B anning the burqa in the West might be one way to ban Islamist fundamentalism and the barbaric subordination of girls and women in immigrant communities. Earlier today, French immigration Minister, Eric Besson, called the burqa "debased."

I would hope that the French take their argument further. In the past, they have mainly cited security concerns: Burqa wearing women might be "racially" attacked or burqa wearers themselves might be terrorists or criminals who are planning to attack or rob civilians.

I would hope that the French also argue for such a ban on women's rights/human rights grounds, as I have already proposed. I must emphasize: None of this applies to hijab, the Islamic headscarf, which has already been banned in France in school and is the subject of protest and controversy across Europe.

Perhaps Western governments should not necessarily ban hijab for women; the matter is complicated for girls as we have seen, as city after city across Europe has discovered.

Today, in Holland, in the very country that is putting the very brave parliamentarian, Geert Wilders, on trial for exercising his political free speech—another bright Dutch light, Trouw historian Tineke Bennema has called on "women who were born in the Netherlands to voluntarily put on a headscarf 'out of solidarity' with the hijab wearers." Just like the Danes once wore the yellow Jewish star.

No!

Bennema: This is not the way to atone for all the Dutch Jews whom the Dutch so ~~cheerfully~~ handed over to the Nazis.

One can argue that looking "different," wearing clothing that represents only one religion may, indeed, arouse prejudice and fear and lead to ostracism, especially among children. Visually representing one's religion in the public square may also interfere with one's ability to be seen neutrally in a courtroom, (as a judge, a witness, a plaintiff), classroom, hospital, (as a nurse, doctor, or patient), office, etc. For this reason, an American judge told a priest to remove his clerical collar before testifying in a court case.

However, in order to ban hijab in an even-handed way, one would also have to ban the Catholic hijab worn by nuns, the Jewish headscarf worn by ultra-orthodox and Hasidic women, and the various Hindu and Sikh head coverings. Doing so might interfere with the separation of religion and state that many Western governments hold dear.

But there is another reason to consider not banning hijab for adults. I spent last week in Rome, at the International Conference on Violence Against Women, An Initiative of the Italian Presidency of the G 8. I am deeply grateful to the Italian government, specifically to the Italian Minister for Equal Opportunities, the Honorable Maria Rosaria Carfagna for this opportunity. Here is where I spent time with a dynamic, truly amazing group of religious and secular Muslim feminists. Three wore hijab, two did not, and one wore it sometimes, but not always. Most agreed that headcovering is more of a custom than a religious commandment and that one can be a very good Muslim without it.

My point: They are all modern, eloquent, high achievers; smart, strong-minded, pro-Western, pro-integration, and pro-women's rights. They have won my heart and I view these Muslim feminists who are fifty years old or younger as the true descendents of Second Wave Western feminism. They, too, believe that women's rights are universal. They cannot understand why so many western feminists and academics are willing to sacrifice this principle. And, religious or not, they also believe in the importance of separating religion and state.

I want you to meet them. You will be hearing from them from time to time right here at my site. Allow me the pleasure and privilege of introducing you to some of them and to their work.

Samar Al-Mogren is a Saudi Arabian journalist and novelist. She sometimes gets into trouble, but she remains untroubled, almost sweet-tempered about it. Her latest novel, about women in prison, is a bestseller in Arabic.

Zainab Al-Suwaijis an Iraqi-born American who is the Executive Director of the American-Islamic Conference in DC. She is the grand-daughter of the leading ayatollah of Basra who personally raised her and who supports her world-work. Zainab founded the Conference precisely in order to offer American Muslim students an alternative to the Islamist and Muslim Brotherhood connected Muslim Student Association on campuses.

Seyran Ates is a Turkish born lawyer whose work on behalf of battered Muslim women immigrants in Berlin I discuss in my book *The Death of Feminism.* Seyran was shot by an Islamic extremist and nearly died for her work—which includes her efforts to expose and abolish honor killings. She plans to open a mosque in Berlin where the hijab will not be allowed! Her new book, *Islam Needs a Sexual Revolution*, will be out next month.

Zeyno Baran is a Turkish-born American citizen who is the Director of the Center for Eurasian Policy and Senior Fellow at the Hudson Institute. Baran is an expert on terrorism and oil, and is currently working on a book *The Other Muslims. Moderate and Secular* which will be out in 2010.

Elham Manea, an Egyptian-Yemeni citizen of Switerland, is a professor of Political Science who specializes in the Middle East. She is also a journalist, a novelist, and a human rights activist.

Shada Mohammed Nasser Mohammed is a Yemeni citizen and a lawyer who has handled many high profile cases for women as well as politically "sensitive" cases. For example, she represented Amina Ali Altuhaif and Fatima Badi in criminal cases, and many child brides who sought divorces from forced marriages.

We spent as much time together as possible. Our little group also included the divine and magnificent Italian, Valentina Colombo, who is a Professor of Islamic and Arabic Studies, and the very wonderful Manda Zand Ervin, the founder and Director of the Alliance of Iranian Women, whom I have known for a number of years.

My point is this: Those Muslims in our group who wear hijab are as independent and fabulously feminist as are those who are bare headed. Many are religious, as I am. I think this broke some ice.

Thus: I would not want to blithely support a movement that would force such women to remove their headscarves against their will.

I understand: Many head scarved girls and women are not modern, educated, independent, pro-integration or for women's equality and for them, the headscarf might be the very symbol of all that is holding them back and a way of visually signifying their rejection of modernization and assimilation.

As I said: This is tricky...but let me be very clear especially for those people who might be puzzled by my apparent "defense" of the Islamic Veil.

Here are some problems to solve:

In a world in which girls and women are being beaten and murdered for refusing to wear hijab or for failing to wear it properly enough—how can we safeguard their right not to wear hijab while, at the same time, safeguarding the right of adults to wear hijab if that is their choice? This is something that we must solve in the West.

As we wrestle with this problem, let's avoid cheap comparisons and false moral equivalencies. The bikini is not the same as the burqa. The state is not forcing me to wear a bikini and neither the state nor my family will kill me if I refuse to wear it. Further, no one will stop me from making a fool of myself and, at my age, actually wearing a bikini to the beach.

And, pointing out that women are treated as sex objects in the West does not mean that putting women in body bags proves that they are more respected or better protected. Those who make this argument fail to understand how thoroughly women are sexualized and also sexually abused in the Muslim world.

Pajamas Media
9/15/09

- 46 -
Newspeak vs TruthSpeak about
Female Genital Mutilation:
Elham Manea and Molly Melching

I t is one thing to rail against human rights violations on foreign soil. It is quite another to countenance such violations in one's own Western backyard.

As we know, Europe has allowed immigrant practices to flourish under the rubric of "tolerance" and "multi-cultural sensitivity." In my view, such "tolerance" is actually racist, not anti-racist as it presumes itself to be; inhumane and cruel, not compassionate.

At the G8 conference about Violence Against Women in Rome, which I attended earlier this month, a stellar panel on female genital mutilation took place.

Dr. Elham Manea, a Yemeni-Swiss professor, challenged the western culturally relativist view which leads to "tolerance" for what are, after all, crimes against women and humanity. She said what this really represents is "human rights for westerners only. Women and girls are the first to suffer from such 'tolerance.'"

Dr. Manea then spoke eloquently and movingly about her own mother's traumatic female genital mutilation in Egypt. It happened to her mother when her mother was eight years old. Other women: Neighbors and a female midwife, performed the savage, bloody deed and "the memory has followed her mother all her life."

Dr. Manea stated that it is time "we insist on human rights before religious or cultural rights. And we must not apologize for doing so."

At a time in which we are plagued by non-effective ideologues, we also have in our midst, quiet, practical activists, committed to doing good deeds on earth.

For example, at the G8 panel on female genital mutilation, Molly Melching, a native of Senegal for 35 years, and the Director of *Tostan* ("Breakthrough" in Wolof), described her own successful efforts at stopping female genital mutilation in Senegal. In the beginning, only thirty women stood up to abandon FGM. Others, mainly women, attacked them.

Melching believes that the "power of human rights education" cannot be underestimated. She understood that family and clan networks from which marriage matches emerge, must all agree to stop this practice and to marry girls who have not been genitally mutilated. Melching compared FGM to "ending footbinding in China." She closed by saying "When the women stand up, let us be there at the grassroots level."

Melching took a practical approach and within 12 years, over 4000 communities in West Africa joined the original twelve women. In 1997, a group of women from the Senegalese village of Malicounda Bambara stood up before 20 journalists and "declared their decision to end the practice" of FGM. They had participated in *Tostan's* Community Empowerment Program.

I congratulated her for her good-hearted and practical approach. She said I was the first feminist to do so. "Usually, feminists want me to simply condemn the practice, and to be angry at those who do it. I analyzed the situation differently. These mothers love their daughters and do not want them to be ostracized or to remain unmarried which would be dangerous. What needed to happen was cross cultural, cross-border education and it worked."

Pajamas Media
9/29/09

- 47 -

Egypt Wants to Ban the Burqa, France and Italy Too

F inally, at the midnight hour, some European governments have begun to fight back—not against the Islamification of Europe but against inhumane, even barbaric practices in the name of religion which violate western standards of human rights.

Thus, first France and now Italy have called for a ban on the burqa. Italy's Northern League proposal "aims at amending a 1975 law, introduced amid concern over domestic terrorism, which bans anyone wearing anything which makes their identification impossible.....The Northern League also has the backing of Berlusconi's People of Freedom party. The League's Roberto Cota said: 'We are not racist and we have nothing against Muslims but the law must be equal for everyone.'"

When France's President Sarkozy first called for a similar ban, a self-identified branch of al-Qaeda in Northern Africa threatened to attack France over this.

Predictably, Italian Centre left opposition MPs "criticized the Italian proposal and said it was 'unconstitutional because it infringes on religious freedom and justifying it because of law and order is totally out of place.'"

Not so fast.

Verily, we live in an age of miracles; thus, none other than Sheikh Mohammed Tantawi, the leading religious figure of Al-Azhar, was, just the other day, "reportedly angered" when he toured a school in Cairo and saw a girl wearing "niqab" which means that her face was masked or possibly that she was wearing a full head, face, and body covering.

"Sheikh Tantawi, regarded by many as Egypt's Imam and Sunni Islam's foremost spiritual authority, asked the teenage girl to remove her veil saying: 'The niqab is a tradition, it has no connection with religion.'" The imam instructed the girl, a pupil at a secondary school in Cairo's Madinet Nasr suburb, never to wear the niqab again and promised to issue a fatwa, or religious edict, against its use in schools. The ruling will not affect use of the hijab, the Islamic headscarf worn by most Muslim women in Egypt.

Following the imam's lead, Egypt's minister of higher education is to ban female undergraduates from wearing the niqab in the country's public universities, Cairo's *Al-Masri Al-Yom* newspaper reported. "

Again, don't rejoice too soon.

Even the very influential Sheikh Tantawi has his fundamentalist detractors who have excoriated him for supporting France's ban on hijab in public schools and for shaking hands with Israeli President Shimon Peres. Clearly, the Egyptian government is unhappy about the gathering forces of Islamic fundamentalism which consistently manipulate women and women's clothing as symbolic political statements. Some have even called for more severe Islamic clothing for women in which only one eye (Algerian style) can show. The Egyptian government understands that it is at risk vis à vis Islamic fundamentalists.

Now, some European politicians understand this too.

Follow the burqa. Where it goes, you will probably find normalized wife-battering, serious child abuse, honor killings, polygamy, and a pathological hatred of Jews, Israelis, Hindus, Americans, and all other infidels. There you *may* also find terrorist cells or supporters of terrorism. From this point of view—ban the burqa, and it may lead to an exodus of terrorists back to their fundamentalist-friendly home countries.

I found support from Muslim feminists about this, first at an international conference in Rome, and now in a new book. I've been reading the most elegant book on the subject of the Islamic veil written by Marnia Lazreg; it is titled: *Questioning the Veil. Open Letters to Muslim Women.* It is carefully reasoned and beautifully written. Lazreg is an Algerian Muslim feminist academic and her mother once wore the veil. She is respectful of Muslim women's feelings and of their religious desires. She argues that the veil (face, head, and full body covering) is not commanded in the Qur'an; that it is harmful to women's physical and mental health; and that it is mainly a political statement about fundamentalism and misogyny. She has little patience for feminist academics who themselves are not forced to veil and who "play" at imagining or de-constructing the veil as "liberatory" or as a statement of "resistance." Lazreg is also on record as having objected to the "manner in which Muslim women have been portrayed in books as well as the media," namely, in ways that focus on them only as oppressed victims.

In her last letter, Lazreg implores Muslim women to voluntarily stop wearing the veil. "It is a symbol of inequality...it undermines faith... it objectifies women for (reasons of) political propaganda just like advertising in Western society does: one by covering, and the other by exposing womens's bodies." Lazreg also views the veil as harming Muslim women's employment because "hijab symbolically inserts her into a virtual domestic space" and affects how she is viewed and treated at work. She re-defines "modesty" as related to behavior and character rather than to appearance and opposes "the straitjacketing of a woman's body. "Lazreg does not view having one's face and head uncovered as proof that one has succumbed to the West. She writes:

> Not wearing the veil is not a victory of the 'West,' it is women's victory over a custom that infects their thinking about themselves as human beings. Wearing the veil is not a strike against anti-Muslim prejudice...As long as states mandate or prohibit veiling, as long as political movements advocate for it, as long as organized networks with books, lectures, DVDs, and course packets promote it far and wide, a woman can never be sure she takes up the veil freely...Ultimately, there is no compelling justification for veiling, not even faith...No one is entitled to turn the veil into a political flag.

I encourage you all to read this fine book—especially because Lazreg opposes any state regulations on the matter.

Pajamas Media
10/7/09

- 48 -

Wajeha al Huwaider Leads Veiled
Saudi Women in a Campaign for Freedom

On November 6, 1990, 40 brave Saudi women drove their cars in public in Riyadh to demand their right to drive. They were quickly detained and their passports confiscated; they were also fired from their jobs.

On the 19th anniversary of this event, Saudi women activists, led by prominent activist and journalist Wajeha al Huwaider, are launching the Black Ribbons Campaign. They want to move about in the world freely, without a male minder.

Al Huwaider has called for the abolition of the *mahram* ("guardian") law which requires women to obtain the approval of a male relative for nearly any move they make in their lives. She is also demanding that Saudi women be treated as citizens, just like their male counterparts, and that they be allowed to travel, drive, gain custody of their children, work, study, etc., just like their male counterparts. The Saudi women will not "untie their ribbons until Saudi women enjoy their rights as adult citizens."

But in only nineteen years, how the times have changed! Once, Muslim women chose not to wear hijab—in Egypt, Lebanon, Turkey, Algeria, Morocco, Iran, etc. Today, some Muslim women insist not only on shroud-veiling, but on having male babysitters as well!

For example, the fully-shrouded Saudi princess, Jawaher bint Jalawi, says she must have and cannot part with her male "guardian" who accompanies her wherever she goes. She insists that only he knows what's best for her. In response to Al Huwaider, the (government-backed?)

191

princess has launched a campaign called "My Guardian Knows What's Best for me."

I wonder if she is one of the princesses who immediately shed their shrouds once the plane clears The Kingdom's air space. But the princess's stand is also a perfect example of how a prisoner fears the light, an example of the way in which women internalize sexism and try to enforce the status quo by keeping other women in line. This is a phenomenon that I discuss at length in *Woman's Inhumanity to Woman*.

But Saudi Arabia is a very strange place. For example, a new TV show that discusses issues concerning teenage girls and female university students was recently broadcast with Saudi presenters shrouded in black from head to toe. The show, *Asrar Al-Banat* (The Secrets of Girls), is broadcast on *Awtan TV*, a Saudi religious channel. One broadcaster said: "Basically, this is my hijab and I don't wear it because of the channel."

On the one hand, we have Saudi princesses who insist upon male minders and Saudi broadcasters who do not mind reporting the news covered in black from head to toe. On the other hand, we have highly aggressive women who oppress other women hellishly—in Iran, for example, but now also in Indonesia, where there is a newly created female Sharia police. These humorless and self-important ladies go around Bandeh Aceh reprimanding other women for wearing clothing that they view as "too tight"—but these women have no male minders and are, in fact, also allowed to reprimand men who are not praying at the proper time.

I support the Saudi feminists and yet: Where exactly will the Saudi women wear the black ribbon? Who will be able to see it if they are totally covered up? Probably on their wrists—where I shall wear mine.

I will start wearing a black ribbon on November 6th. Please join me. This black ribbon can become quite a conversation-opener and consciousness-raiser. Remember: We are not really free when others are still in chains, especially if we refuse to hear their cries, and refuse to support their brave, potential liberators.

Pajamas Media
11/5/09

- 49 -
Boycott Burqa Barbie

What will they think of next? A be-headed doll?

I'm talking about the new Burqa Barbie doll which is now on display in Florence, Italy, to celebrate the fiftieth anniversary of the Barbie doll. As my colleague over at weaselzippers wonders: Will clean-cut Ken now come (pun intended, 'tis mine) with four burqa'ed Barbie doll wives?

Ah, I am such a Grinch. After all, the Burqa Barbie is being auctioned off for the Save the Children charity.

Save the Children? Surely, you must be jesting. I would like to save the children from this as well as from every other Barbie doll. (Yes, I know Barbie has diversified and now comes in every color and profession). Even Doctor Barbie is still a pagan goddess or fertility figure but one with absolutely no relationship to female biology or reality.

Barbies are always anatomically impossible: their feet are pre-shaped for high heels, their breasts are high, firm, and perky—like Playboy dolls or surgically enhanced Hollywood stars.

These dolls were so retro—or so I always thought. Well, shut my mouth, those were the good old days of sex, drugs, and rock 'n roll. Now, Barbie is swathed, shrouded, in a burqa; now, she is even more hopelessly retro.

A wonderful Muslim feminist hero just stayed with me for a week. She is a lawyer and an author, her name is Seyran Ates, she is a Turkish-German and lives in Berlin. Ates absolutely opposes the veil in any form. She will not wear a headscarf. Ates is a religious Muslim woman.

Mattel: take Burqa Barbie off the market.

Parents: Boycott it.

Calling all Charities: Save the children from it.

Pajamas Media
11/21/09

- 50 -
Under the Islamic Veil:
Faces Disfigured by Acid

The photos show what happens to real women who wear the Islamic Veil. The images depict horrifying hate and the unbearable suffering it inflicts upon female innocents. The photos were taken by Emilio Morenatti of the Associated Press. The text is based on work done by Nicholas Kristof—of the *New York Times*.

What are we seeing?

The Arabization or the Saudi-ization of Muslims in Afghanistan, Bangladesh, and Pakistan is the hidden hand behind these acid attacks upon women. These poor girls and women have had their lives ruined; some have been forced to undergo surgery 20-30 times in order that they may see a little, or breathe a bit, hear something, perhaps in order to eat or make themselves understood. They look like...monsters. That was what their attackers wanted to accomplish. To render their faces into self-portraits of their attackers.

Why was acid thrown into their faces? The main reasons are because they dared to reject someone in marriage or because they wanted a divorce. The "jilted" suitors (or husbands) took their revenge in this fashion. If he can't have her, no man will; "I will make sure that no man will ever want her." One young girl was gang-raped after which her rapists threw acid on her face. Another committed the "crime" of disappointing her father by being born female, not male. Many were disfigured as a result of a "family dispute."

Thus, the punishment for being born female, for exercising any will of one's own is, Saudi-style, the most horrible punishment. The men

195

tried to make the women loathsome to humanity, to sentence them to painful surgeries, self-hatred, perhaps to lives lived in isolation.

Make no mistake. This tendency to disfigure women—even those who wear the Islamic Veil—is real. And, it might be coming our way if we do not stop the Wahhabi and Salafi influence which is funding our universities in North America as well as the Islamic religious schools.

I will leave aside the question of what must be done and allow the photos to speak to you.

Irum Saeed, 30, was burned on her face, back and shoulders twelve years ago in Islamabad when a boy whom she rejected for marriage threw acid on her in the middle of the street. She has undergone plastic surgery 25 times to try to recover from her scars.

Najaf Sultana, 16, was burned by her father when she was five and asleep, apparently because he didn't want to have another girl in the family. As a result of the burning Najaf became blind and after being abandoned by both her parents she now lives with relatives. She has undergone plastic surgery 15 times to try to recover from her scars.

Kanwal Kayum, 26, was burned with acid one year ago in Lahore, Pakistan by a boy whom she rejected for marriage. She has never undergone plastic surgery.

Munira Asef, 23, was burned with acid five years ago in Lahore by a boy whom she rejected for marriage. She has undergone plastic surgery 7 times to try to recover from her scars.

Bushra Shari, 39, was burned with acid thrown by her husband five years ago in Lahore because she was trying to divorce him. She has undergone plastic surgery 25 times to try to recover from her scars.

Memuna Khan, 21, was burned by a group of boys who threw acid on her in Karachi to settle a dispute between their family and Memuna's. She has undergone plastic surgery 21 times to try to recover from her scars.

Saira Liaqat, 26, was married to a relative when she was fifteen who would later attack her with acid after insistently demanding that she live with him in Lahore, although the families had agreed she wouldn't join him until she finished school. Saira has undergone plastic surgery 9 times to try to recover from her scars.

Words alone cannot express my sorrow and my rage about such heartless barbarism.

Pajamas Media
11/23/09

- 51 -
Battling the Islamification of the World

The other day, a twenty-year-old woman was sold at an open auction in Badani Bhutto, Pakistan. Her brothers divided up the money. No one condemned this shameless and abominable act.

It is an act that haunts me.

For a long time now, similar kinds of people (yes, mainly Muslims) have invaded—no, immigrated to—Europe, where they have continued to engage in polygamy, arranged child marriage, forced veiling of women, honor-related violence, including honor murders (17,000 honor-related crimes of violence have been estimated to occur annually in the UK alone), and female genital mutilation. According to my new (and about to be published) study, honor murders in Europe are especially savage—even more so than in developing Muslim countries.

According to the Dutch *Telegraf*,

> Dutch and foreign intelligence services are at high alert due to a five-day international Islamic conference in Eindhoven, starting today. The intelligence services fear that the congress participants will secretly collect funds for armed Islamic battle. It's also feared that the speakers in the conference will reverse the integration of Muslims in the Netherlands.

In addition, just the other day, perhaps in response to the defacing of a mosque, a British war memorial was defaced with the slogan "Islam Will Dominate the World."

But some of us—Christians, Jews, Muslims, ex-Muslims, Hindus, Sikhs—are fighting back. Yesterday, the American criminal justice system indicted a father for the "honor murder" of his daughter in Arizona. According to the *Arizona Republic,*

> An Iraqi immigrant accused of slaying his daughter in an "honor killing" has been charged with first-degree murder and could face the death penalty, Maricopa County Attorney Andrew Thomas said Monday...Prosecutors have labeled Noor Almaleki's death an "honor killing," saying the elder Almaleki killed his daughter because she dishonored the family by not following traditional Iraqi or Muslim values.

Rather late in the day, perhaps too late, Europe has begun to fight back against being "Islamified." Bat Ye'or, Bruce Bawer, Christopher Caldwell, Oriana Fallaci, Carol Gould, Melanie Phillips, Jean Raspail, Ibn Warraq, Geert Wilders, and I, among others, have all suggested that this is inevitable.

But prithee pause: There are stirrings of resistance yet in the Old World.

In addition to the highly significant convictions of honor murderers in England, Holland, and Denmark, which I wrote about last week, did you know:

That a man in Holland has just been refused welfare benefits because he refused to shorten his beard or to shake hands with women on the jobs that the government found for him?

That a refugee from Afghanistan was about to get married in Denmark when the police broke up the wedding and arrested him? Apparently, his visa had been denied and the police did not want to allow him to gain Danish citizenship in this underhanded way. Apparently, the one thing that Muslim immigrants fear is being deported.

That Denmark is offering to pay Muslim immigrants who do not really want to integrate to leave the country?

That calls for the banning of either headscarves or burqas or both have rung out (like church bells, dare I say) all across France, Belgium, and Germany?

I love Europe. I want it to remain European. It was the land of my bohemian dreams when I was young. I grew up reading poetry, novels, plays, and philosophical treatises by British, French, German, Italian, Spanish, Scandinavian, and Greek authors both ancient and modern. I listened—I still do—to music most divine written by composers from all these countries and by Austrian, Polish, Norwegian, Hungarian, and Russian composers too. I have spent many happy hours viewing European paintings and sculptures.

I used to love the Islamic world as well. I once traveled and lived within it. It called to me. The light, heat, color, sounds, smells, foods, history, music, stories, poetry, charm, and human as well as geographic beauty held me in thrall. That world is now gone. I will probably never again travel to a Muslim country in this lifetime. It, too, has been fundamentalized, Islamified in the worst way. Whatever cosmopolitan tolerance may have once existed is either long gone or is now under siege.

Today, many Muslims are also fighting over who controls their countries and their religion. In Iran, the bravest of pro-democracy and anti-regime activists are marching, marching, to their deaths. All over the Islamic world, in groups and as individuals, Muslims are also marching against tyranny and for women's rights, secular rights, and homosexual rights. Many Muslim dissidents and feminists have also fled to Europe and America where they now live, write, and teach.

I am glad they are here. I hope the "Europe" and the "America" where they sought asylum does not betray them and end up looking and acting like the countries they left behind—the kind of country that would sell a young woman at an open auction.

Pajamas Media
12/23/09

Section Four:
Islamic Homosexual Pederasty and Afghanistan's "Dancing Boys"

- 52 -
Gender, Modernity, and Liberty:
Western Women Travelers to Islam

Reina Lewis, a professor of cultural studies at the University of East London, publishes in the areas of postcolonialism and sexualities, meaning she avidly criticizes Western Orientalism but just as avidly takes interest in the alleged Western eroticization of "Orientalized" women. Lewis has published other titles in this area including *Gendering Orientalism: Race, Femininity and Representation*,[1] and *Rethinking Orientalism: Women, Travel, and the Ottoman Harem*.[2]

Lewis, in brief, is an ideologue, committed to Edward Said's highly biased view about how Western travelers, scholars, and memoirists essentially colonized and objectified their subject and, in so doing, rendered the Orient passive. But Ibn Warraq has definitively challenged Said's interpretation in *Defending the West. A Critique of Edward Said's Orientalism*, and I share his views.

In *Gender, Modernity, and Liberty*, Lewis has collaborated with Nancy Micklewright, a program officer at the Getty Foundation and author of *A Victorian Traveler in the Middle East. The Photography and Travel Writing of Annie Lady Brassey*.[3]

The material itself is fascinating as is their choice of photographs. The authors provide extracts from selected nineteenth- and twentieth-century writings of British, Turkish, and Egyptian women, including Julia Pardoe, Sophia Lane Poole, Emmeline Lott, Melek Hanum,

---

1 London and New York: Routledge, 1995.

2 New Brunswick: Rutgers University Press, 2004.

3 Burlington, Vt.: Ashgate Publishing, 2003.

Annie Lady Brassey, Zeynoub Hanoum, Grace Ellison, Huda Shaarawi, and Halide Edib.

They correctly criticize Westerners for confusing the harem with the brothel—although polygamy and the endless waiting that characterized the secluded, indoor life of Muslim women in *purdah* easily lends itself to such confusion. A harem meant that multiple generations of women and children were off limits to everyone except other women and male relatives. Hence, Western women, but not men, developed a small cottage industry of harem literature.

Although the authors approve of travelers such as Julia Pardoe (1806-62), who "struggled against" the male Western eroticization of the Orient and viewed Turkish women as happier than European women, they typically take every opportunity to view Western women travelers and their harem photographs sarcastically, suspiciously, bitterly. There is almost nothing Westerners can do to avoid their scorn. For example, the fact that indigenous cultures did not educate even elite women in their native languages—while foreign colonial powers did—led to elite Muslim women writing in English and French and not in Arabic, Persian, or Turkish. The authors condemn this. Perhaps Western teachers were not proficient in these languages or were prevented from teaching in native languages.

Lewis and Micklewright reserve their ire primarily for Orientalists and expend no scorn on the indigenous cultures for failing to educate women nor do they critique patriarchy with its concubine-sex slaves and multiple wives. The authors' mission is to rescue Oriental women from other Western writers who are not sufficiently postcolonial, i.e., anti-Western, pro-noble-savage in outlook. This means that they savage most of the extraordinary writers and photographs that they have carefully and lovingly excerpted for this volume.

Contrast this volume with Barbara Hodgson's graceful and beautifully written work, *Dreaming of East: Western Women and the Exotic Allure of the Orient*.[4] Hodgson is no ideologue and in her text, photographs, and drawings, she captures the complexities and charm of Western women traveling eastward. Yes, many heavily-corseted, Victorian-era women did appreciate Muslim women's loose clothing, the charm and politeness of Eastern hospitality, and the fact that, as travelers, they were themselves far freer than they were back home. However, this does not mean that Western descriptions of the Orient are necessarily biased and racist or that the lives of indolent, bored, and illiterate home-bound

---

4 New York: Greystone Books, 2006.

women were anything to envy.

Middle East Quarterly
1/13/10

- 53 -
France Considers a Ban on the Burqa

To the Editor:

Banning the burqa and niqab need not be a case of "Muslim-bashing"; it might also be a statement of support for Muslim women's human rights. The burqa and niqab are isolating garments that interfere with a woman's ability to see, hear, carry on normal conversations and walk safely.

Many Muslim women are not given a free choice about how to dress; some are persecuted and even murdered by their families for refusing to wear the Islamic veil.

Ideally, one does not want the government or the family to tell women how to dress, but the potential French ban on the burqa and niqab is not morally equivalent to the utter subordination of women as practiced by the Taliban and in Saudi Arabia.

Phyllis Chesler
New York
The New York Times
1/27/10

- 54 -
Sixteen-year-old Medine Memi Buried Alive in Turkey—and Under the Burqa

I n Turkey—a country which was nearly accepted as a member by the European Union—a father and grandfather recently buried Medine Memi, a sixteen-year-old girl, alive—and all because she was seen talking to boys. Medine was repeatedly beaten. She ran to the police but they did not help her. When the men buried her she was "alive and fully conscious."

This savage, heartless, primitive act is the ultimate, logical consequence of burying women alive—shrouding them—while they are still allowed to roam above ground. One gets used to being invisible, not-quite-human, as good as dead.

All this past week, I received news of this "buried alive" atrocity in Turkey. I refrained from writing about it. What can one say? There is nothing to say. There is everything to do. No one is doing anything.

But, all over Europe, they are fighting about the Islamic Veil. The Council of Imams in Ireland has just had a press conference. They said that "a ban on the niqab (a face veil) violates personal freedoms guaranteed by democratic systems. They added that "such bans also constitute an obstacle to multiculturalism, integration and human rights."

Well—that will shame the Europeans.

Imams do not have to shame the government in a place like Egypt (or Afghanistan), where Muslim girls and women are already shrouded. Few women are protesting. They have no better, indeed no other option. On January 28, 2010, I ran a photographic series about the graduates of Cairo University. Mid-way though the last century, no female graduate was veiled; by the beginning of the 21st century, many were veiled. And now, a reader has sent me three recent photos of girls and women in Alexandria and Cairo, circa 2009. Most are now wearing hijab; some are face-veiled.

Somewhere in my library, I have a treasured set of late nineteenth century photos taken in Egypt in black and white and then artistically colored in. Graceful, sultry palms, ancient ruins, a Biblical caravan, a party of tourists, the Nile. I always assumed I'd go; I never have.

My reader, "Ann," wrote to me about a trip she took to Egypt a year ago. She noted that:

> Most of the Egyptian women were veiled. They don't consider it a sign of submission but a political statement. A form of Egyptian solidarity and perhaps also a fashion statement. Little girls reportedly can't wait to be old enough to be allowed to wear a veil.

The great Egyptian feminist, Huda Sha'arawi, would weep if she could see these photos of 21st century veiled Egyptian women. The Egyptian girls (really, they are children) seem so eager to please, so excited to dress "up" like their mothers, like adult women. These photos would break Sha'arawi's heart. They break my heart too.

Feminism in Turkey and Egypt was not another form of western colonialism. It was merely modernization. As in Iran, it was also an indigenous movement.

Today, the Islamic forces of darkness are burying women alive, both literally, in the earth, (the Turkish atrocity) and above ground, in burqas and face-masks. This must stop. There is absolutely no Islamic religious requirement that women be face-veiled or shrouded. None. It is *taqiyya*, disinformation, misinformation—jihad. If this does not stop, the West might have to build a wall clear up to the sky to keep such practices out.

Pajamas Media
2/6/10

- 55 -
Heroic Muslim Girls and Women: Nujood Ali and Mukhtaran Bibi— Missionaries to Feminist America?

We have all heard about Nujood Ali, the incredibly heroic ten-year-old girl in Yemen who fled her abusive husband and demanded a divorce. This act was the first of its kind in a country where girls as young as eight are forced into marriage.

We want her as an ally. We want her counterparts in the Muslim world as allies. We want Mukhtaran Bibi on our side. She is the young Pakistani woman who was gang-raped by her alleged social superiors in order to cover up their own crimes. She escaped. She was not silenced by shame. She did not kill herself. Unlike Phoolan Devi, India's Bandit Queen (a girl after my own heart), Bibi did not join a gang of outlaws and then exact personal revenge. Despite numerous death threats, Mukhtaran Bibi legally pursued the criminals—and won.

I wish we had more women like Nujood Ali, Mukhtaran Bibi, (alright, like Phoolan Devi too), here in the West. Their bravery is astounding. Although they have much to lose (their lives for starters), they also have much to gain since they are debased from morning to night from the moment of their birth.

Now, Nujood Ali has written a memoir: *I Am Nujood: Age 10 and Divorced*.

Go to Amazon. You will read this:

I'm a simple village girl who has always obeyed the orders of my father and brothers. Since forever, I have learned to say yes to everything. Today I have decided to say no.

Forced by her father to marry a man three times her age, Nujood Ali was sent away from her parents and beloved sisters to live with her husband and his family in an isolated village in rural Yemen. There she suffered daily from physical and emotional abuse by her mother-in-law and nightly at the rough hands of her spouse. Flouting his oath to wait to have sexual relations with Nujood until she was no longer a child, he took her virginity on their wedding night. She was only ten years old.

Unable to endure the pain and distress any longer, Nujood fled— not for home, but to the courthouse of the capital, paying for a taxi ride with a few precious coins of bread money. When a renowned Yemeni lawyer, Shada Nasser, heard about the young victim, she took Nujood's case and fought the archaic system in a country where almost half the girls are married while still under the legal age. Since their unprecedented victory in April 2008, Nujood's courageous defiance of both Yemeni customs and of her own family has attracted a storm of international attention.

The upcoming National Women's Studies Association should invite Ali and Bibi to keynote their convention in Denver later this year. Their program concerns "Difficult Dialogues" and features panels on "Indigenous Feminisms," "The Politics of Nation," "Outsider Feminisms," and the "Critical and the Creative." They wish to re-position "violence against women" by taking into consideration "nationalism, militarism, religious fundamentalism, land rights, war," etc. They also wish to "effectively challenge nationalistic rescue narratives within and outside the U.S. (i.e. [is] 'saving' Muslim women under the Taliban a justification for US invasion)?"

That is not why America invaded Afghanistan.

I think that Nujood and Bibi would genuinely qualify for and would illuminate, even bless, this gathering of American Women's Studies professors and students.

Pajamas Media
2/15/10

- 56 -

It's International Women's History Month and Where is Secretary Clinton?

Madame Secretary Clinton: Where are you on this? For that matter: Christiane Amanpour, your father is Iranian, you grew up in Tehran, you are proudly "ethnic"—where are you on this? Are either of you working to free the women prisoners of Tehran?

To Secretary of State Clinton's credit, she has issued a video message which repeats the words of her 1995 speech in Beijing: "Human rights are women's rights, and women's rights are human rights. ... Women have made great progress but there is a long way to go."

Madame Secretary: Is issuing your old words—even in Persian— enough? Is hosting an International Women of Courage event (which you're doing later this week), in which one awardee will be from Iran, really enough?

Secretary Clinton knows that nothing short of overthrowing the mad mullahs will open the prison doors in Iran. And she knows that President Obama is not even sitting on the fence about this; he is tip-toeing through the tulips, reading the lines that Stephen P. Cohen, the founder of the Institute for Middle East Peace and Development, pens for him with which to address the Muslim world in Cairo.

Dr. Cohen: Are you proud that America has fought for the right of Muslim girls to wear the hijab?

I don't believe that America can free the entire world, but America even lags behind Europe in terms of understanding and dealing with honor-related violence, including honor killings, which, in the West, are mainly a Muslim-on-Muslim and male-on-female crime. It is a crime that has landed on our shores. At least Europeans are wrestling with issues such as the Islamic Veil. In America, Stephen P. Cohen is proud that America has taken a stand on behalf of the hijab.

I understand how tricky an issue this is and I know that the European Union has just emerged from its enormous stupor to issue a statement on behalf of the hijab etc.—but still. America can do better than this. At least in our speeches. At least in our understanding.

Today, with absolutely no visible moral support from the United States, Iranian women activists wore green overcoats and scarves in Tehran to celebrate International Women's Day. "Peacefully, quietly, without protest and chanting of slogans," they gathered at ten different shopping centers. They say they're "fighting for freedom and gender equality." They write:

> We demand an end to state-led violence and repression, as well as the immediate release of all political detainees in Iran. Iranian women have long demanded freedom and gender equality; they have employed both individual and group strategies, initiated various campaigns, and faced insults, threats, arrests and imprisonment in the process. Many of these women are currently in prison.
>
> Over the past eight months, the protest movement that emerged following the disputed presidential elections has been suppressed by mounting violence. Physical and psychological violence—through arrest, torture, rape, extended imprisonment, and even execution —has been exercised against civil and political activists in Iran. The list of detainees grows everyday. Global solidarity is crucial to giving voice to (our) repeated calls for freedom and equality in Iran.
>
> We invite all women's rights defenders worldwide to demonstrate their solidarity by organizing initiatives under the slogan 'freedom and gender equality in Iran' throughout March 2010.
>
> *Pajamas Media*
> 3/8/10

Death by Hijab: Accident in an Australian Recreational Park

I have gone on record, many times, about how hazardous the Islamic Veil is to women's health in both medical and psychiatric terms. There are other kinds of health risks involved in adopting Islamically "modest" dress. For example, in England, Muslim nurses are now refusing to leave their arms uncovered below the elbow which can potentially lead to spreading hospital superbugs and to the death of patients. The British National Health Service has given in to this demand—but has prohibited short-sleeved nurses from wearing crosses.

Two days ago, a Muslim woman was killed when her Islamic Veil (one account describes it as her burqa) got caught up in the wheels of her go-kart at a recreational park in New South Wales, Australia. Why was she wearing a burqa in a go-kart? Let me guess: Her Wahhabi-Salafi oriented husband, father, brother, demanded that she do so?

Those who specialize in prurient interest have been making the most unsavory comparison between this poor soul, probably from Afghanistan, and the pioneering dancer Isadora Duncan. Duncan defied convention—she did not dance because she was forced to do so. She met everyone of "consequence" in artistic and intellectual circles, stunned thousands of audiences all across Europe and America with her innovative dance—and yes, she also took many lovers. Duncan created modern dance. She did not lead her life in a burqa.

The great dancer Duncan was not forced to wear a veil nor was she wearing one of her many diaphanous dancing scarfs. Duncan only took a shawl along at the last moment because the weather was getting cold.

Duncan's shawl got caught in the wooden spokes of the low-slung con-
vertible automobile—which was being driven by an experienced driver.

What is this almost erotic fascination with the violent death of
women and this unseemly penchant to compare women of great accom-
plishment with unknown women? Are their violent deaths and tragedies of more interest to us than their achievements? Are female victims
to blame for their own violent deaths?

Duncan should be remembered for her pioneering work as a dancer and teacher, not for the few moments in which she died. A Duncan
dancer, Cherlyn Smith, says: "Duncan's legacy is far more important
than the bizarre manner in which she died. Why do people minimize
this American woman's enormous contribution and choose to continuously associate her with the scarf, the car, and the violent death?"

NewsRealBlog
4/12/10

- 58 -
Islamic Homosexual Pederasty and Afghanistan's "Dancing Boys"

Last week, in Quetta, Pakistan, a homicide bomber attacked a prominent Shiite bank manager—and when his friends and relatives followed him to the hospital emergency room, another bomber attacked them, killing eight. The police assume that this was a "sectarian" (Muslim Sunni vs Muslim Shia) attack. This is nothing new; this is the template. For example, also in 2009, in Dera Ismail Khan, Pakistan, a Shiite Muslim leader was shot down; the next day, at his funeral, a homicide bomber killed himself and 28 mourners. The police described this as "sectarian" violence. In 2008, in the same town, after the shooting death of a Shiite Muslim cleric, both the hospital and the funeral were subsequently attacked either by a homicide bomber or by a "planted" device. Muslims take no prisoners. Yesterday, the deputy mayor of Kandahar, in Afghanistan (123 miles away from Quetta), was shot to death while he was praying in a mosque.

What mercy might such people show to infidels and dissidents, or to women, or children, including their own?

None. None at all. Westerners are so confused about this—not only because they are brainwashed and do not want to be called "racists," but also because so many tribal people tend to have such charming and "sincere" faces.

Last night, I watched the saddest little movie, a brave *Frontline* documentary about the "Bacha Bazi," the underage "dancing boys" of Afghanistan. These children are sex slaves to older, powerful Afghan men—in this instance, former Northern Alliance warlords, who have purchased them from their impoverished families or simply taken orphans off the street. When they try to escape, they are found and punished—or they are murdered.

"Dagastir," a former Northern Alliance warlord, who today has hundreds of police officers at his disposal, has an impassive, even kind face. He does not look or sound ashamed or guilty about what he does. Of course, he is married and has two young sons.

The documentary admits that, although such sex slavery is illegal, the police will not make arrests, and that the rare jail sentence is quickly commuted. The police themselves often comprise the all-male audiences who enjoy the dancing boy performances.

And the boys are so very poor and have so few options.

Bacha bazi (dancing boys) are taken and trained in singing and dancing when they are as young as six years old, more often when they are nine or ten. They wear women's clothing, women's jewelry, women's makeup, and are taught to dance with alluring "feminine" gestures. We might call them "transvestites," but that would be an inaccurate comparison. These dancing boys are children, who are forced to dance and then have sex with men old enough to be their fathers and grandfathers.

Homosexual pederasty is epidemic in the Muslim world. Think ancient Greece (Alexander the Great marched through Afghanistan to India); think Ottoman Empire Turkey; think Persia; think Saudi Arabia, where grown men still hold hands in public. The dancing boys are but one expression of this. Nevertheless, the phenomenon is hotly denied, and "homosexuality," as westerners understand it, is strictly forbidden and often savagely punished in Muslim countries. On camera, one man suggests that the practice was learned in Pakistan when Afghan warriors fled the Russian invasion. But homosexual pederasty may also be indigenous to Afghanistan.

The bacha bazi kind of homosexuality is strictly prison-sex: it is sex taken by force and is strictly about money and power. (In prison, this translates into "protection.") The Afghan children have no choice but to make the best of it. Their lives are "ruined," as one boy said on camera. But when they "age out," at eighteen, some hope to set up a stable of dancing boys of their own as their only or best way to earn money.

Other than Radhika Coomaraswamy of UNICEF, we see no woman's face on camera in the *Frontline* documentary. We see Afghan women in chadors prostrate, begging, on the street; we see women in chadors (burqas) scurrying by. Only once do we hear an Afghan woman's voice. It belongs to the mother of a murdered "dancing boy." She sits, in full, eerie chador, at home, right next to another naked-faced son, and talks to the naked-faced interviewer, the very brave Afghan journalist who made this film: London-based Najibullah Quraishi. To his credit, with the help of a former warlord, Quraishi actually manages to rescue one young boy and relocates both him and his family.

The other young sex slaves are left to their own devices. Neither UNICEF nor President Karzai will rescue them.

Wherever women are forced to wear chadors, burqas, niqab, you can be sure that children are also being abused. For men, especially warriors, who are brought up apart from—and taught to fear and despise women—their major erotic and social drives will be male-centric, not female-centric. Homosexual pederasty accompanies extreme gender apartheid in an extreme way.

Pajamas Media
4/21/10

- 59 -

The Female Face of France:
Banned Beneath the Burqa

All across Europe, government leaders are deciding whether to fine, restrict, or ban the wearing of the Islamic Veil. France's President Sarkozy wants a full ban—one that will also apply to Muslim tourists. Belgium wants one too—although it has been warned that doing so "will violate the rights of those who choose to wear the veil and do nothing to help those who are compelled to do so." Recently, a Madrid school expelled a girl for wearing hijab; the government is backing the school, but four of the girl's classmates have been coming to school wearing hijab "as a sign of support for her."

Of course, Tariq Ramadan has condemned Sarkozy's attempt to ban the burqa. On his recent American tour, he said:

> The French...are responding to the burqa, the niqab, by restricting freedom and I think that's not going to work... We have to be very cautious not to translate every sensitive issue into a legal issue...Don't go that direction, speak more about education, psychology, changing mentality. It takes time but...for me, we can do the job as Muslims by saying the burqa and niqab are not Islamic prescriptions.

Clever, isn't he? Ramadan adopts a soft and peaceful tone, one which lulls us into believing that he, personally, will undertake the "job" of educating Muslims that burqa and niqab are not religiously mandatory.

Really, will he? And, how long might such an educational process take? And, why is he suddenly opposed to the rule of law and its educational potential? Is he willing to spurn Sharia law as well for this same reason? Or is it only certain—not all—western laws that he opposes?

According to my French friend and former college-mate, Guy Ducornet,

> One thing is sure. The 'Islamists' have been very clever in testing the weak spots of our democratic system as they keep yelling that they are discriminated against... But they'd be the FIRST ones to abolish the very laws they invoke!!!

Compare Tariq Ramadan to Drancy-based Imam Hassen Chalgoumy, who "dared publicly condemn the wearing of the full veil and who welcomed the idea of outlawing it." The Tunisian born Chalgoumy also acknowledges "the horror of the Holocaust" and has reached out to France's Jews. Chalgoumy works in a very poor suburb of Paris—not in the hallowed halls of Oxford University where Ramadan teaches. Chalgoumy requires two bodyguards.

A final draft of the burqa ban legislation is slated to be approved by the cabinet on May 19.

The West is committed to tolerance—even towards the intolerant. But it is also in favor of women's rights.

Thus, it is no coincidence that the French woman who was fined for wearing her niqab while driving turns out to be one of four wives, all married to the same Algerian-French man who has fathered twelve children. If not this polygamist, then the next polygamist will turn out to have ties to an Islamist group, or will be indoctrinating his French citizen children into Islamism. This French polygamist is also a welfare fraud since all four wives collect government subsidies as single mothers. And, no surprise here, our polygamist is also leading the drive to build a mosque.

And, by the way: The veiled women are not only victims. They are "choosing" not to be honor-murdered or rejected by their communities. But, they are also proudly, aggressively, defiantly, marking out Islamist territory in infidel countries; the fact that they have been brainwashed or not given a free choice makes no difference. These Veiled Crusaders view themselves as superior to an allegedly (and often truly) "racist" infidel population. They are choosing a glorified group identity as opposed to an unknown, difficult, lonely or dangerous individual identity.

Both Marnia Lazreg and Tariq Ramadan warn against secular bans. I hope that they have both read Samia Labidi's chapter in *The Other Muslims: Moderate and Secular*. Labidi herself was indoctrinated into Islamism and into the Islamic Veil by a rabidly Islamist brother-in-law. In turn, Labidi proudly indoctrinated hundreds of other girls to veil "as a feminist gesture against the Western idea of woman as a sexual object." However, once Labidi saw "the full horror of the Islamist strategy," she fled Tunisia and joined her mother in France. She came to understand that "the veil is used as a symbol to spread political Islam among girls," as are arranged marriages which subordinate women.

Labidi never expected that she would "face the same struggle two decades later in the heart of the West." Those Islamists who were expelled from their countries of origin, came to the West and assumed influence or control over immigrant communities. Labidi has now concluded that the Veil oppresses rather than liberates women. She is a feminist Muslim who opposes Islamism and who knows more about how it functions than do most non-Muslim critics of political Islam.

We should listen to her before it 's too late. Yes, I'm suggesting that we include Muslim and ex-Muslim anti-Islamists in our battle against political Islam. I would rather be in the trenches with those Iranian feminists who are risking death to march for freedom in Teheran than with most western Ivory Tower pseudo-fascists.

By the way, Lazreg implores her readers not to veil, but she does so in terms of their making an individual choice. If only Lazreg had Ramadan's platform—I would trust her to educate Muslim women about the Islamic Veil. Ramadan—I would not trust to even spell his own name accurately.

Pajamas Media
4/28/10

- 60 -
Cherchez La Femme (Follow the Woman)
Wearing the Islamic Veil:
Polygamy and Social Welfare

I t gets even better. (Or worse.)

Remember the French woman who was fined for wearing a face mask (niqab) while she was driving? She was one of four wives who collectively had twelve children, all of whom were being supported by the French government; their father, the polygamist, was also on the public dole.

Whatta guy. He's 35 years old, sports a beard, keffiyeh, white cap, and black *djellaba*, and his name is Liès Hebbadj. Formerly Algerian, he became a French citizen in 1999 after marrying a French national. He has also been accused of being a wife abuser and of selling or handing off one of his wives to another man. The charmer has been quoted thusly:

> As far as I know, mistresses are not prohibited in France, nor in Islam. Maybe by Christianity, but not in France. If you lose your French nationality for having mistresses, then a lot of French men would have been stripped of their citizenship.

Now Hebbadj is being sued by a Muslim association for "defaming" Islam! Rachida Benamed, of the Association of Muslims in Meaux and the region, says:

> We were shocked that this man would say that in Islam you

221

can have mistresses. That's completely wrong. To listen to him, our religion is immoral. ... When we saw that nobody reacted, we decided to do something and so filed the complaint. ... This man needs to be convicted for his defamatory statements, we need to put a stop to this type of behavior, he must take responsibility for his actions.

Is she defending polygamy and denying the epidemic of concubinage, prostitution, and sexual slavery among Muslims? In the Qur'an's Sura 4, verse 3, it is written:

And if you fear that you cannot act equitably towards orphans, then marry such women as seem good to you, two and three and four; but if you fear that you will not do justice (between them), then (marry) only one or what your right hands possess; this is more proper, that you may not deviate from the right course.

I have been told that polygamy is actually very hard to practice in "the right way" because a man must treat each wife equally—exactly equally. Since this is impossible, polygamy, by definition, may never have been practiced in "the right way." Also, mainly wealthy men can afford to practice polygamy, a fact which dooms young, poor men to unmarried lives of enormous envy and resentment. In an age of jihad we know where this may lead: They will sexually harass and rape infidel women and kidnap Muslim girls and women as sex slaves. This was done by Islamist paramilitary gangs in Algeria and by the Taliban in Afghanistan. Such resentful and sexually frustrated young men may also become fundamentalists and terrorists. Polygamy makes women and children quite miserable too—but that is the subject for another piece.

Historically, the "right course" among Muslim men has included taking concubines—many, many concubines, both Jewish and Christian, African and European. Muhammed himself did so and this practice has not stopped. Obscenely large harems have existed among Muslim rulers for centuries, although many non-Muslim Africans have "lived large" in terms of multiple wives as well. Jews outlawed polygamy in the eleventh century. Prostitution has always flourished in the world; sexual trafficking is at an all-time high today. Neither Muslim nor African countries are immune to this practice.

Today, the Saudis are known to fly in new planeloads full of European prostitutes each and every week. Are they considered to be "temporary concubines" or even "temporary wives," a practice which is now common in Iran? Female domestic workers in Saudi Arabia are routinely raped by their employers as well as held hostage, underpaid, or never paid.

In other words, poor Rachida Benamed has scarcely a fig leaf to cover the enormous nakedness of Muslim men when it comes to the subject of polygamy, concubinage, and prostitution. I would not recommend trying to justify such misogyny no matter what religion the John may practice.

NewsRealBlog
5/4/10

- 61 -

Women Physically Fight Over the Burqa in Nantes, France

E arlier today in Nantes, France, three women actually came to blows over the burqa. The burqa wearer (actually, the niqab wearer), claims that she heard two women, one a 60-year-old lawyer, make "snide" and "insulting" remarks about burqa wearers. The lawyer and her daughter claim that the burqa wearer physically assaulted them. After which, the lawyer ripped off her veil.

One thing is clear: The shop manager and the burqa wearer's husband "moved in to break up the fighting." Everyone was arrested. The burqa wearer has filed a complaint for "an insult of ethnic, racial, or religious character"; the lawyer and her daughter have filed a complaint for violence.

Both narratives are entirely plausible. Many Westerners are not comfortable around burqa wearers, do not want to see them, and fear that they represent a hostile and intolerant religious fundamentalism that does not respect Western culture or values. Others, including Daniel Pipes, view it as a security risk—homicide bombers and bank robbers may be hiding under that face mask or full head and body covering.

Europe is on fire over this symbol of jihad. Many knowledgeable Muslims and ex-Muslims do not view face veiling as religiously mandated. Egyptians Nonie Darwish and Tariq Heggy remember when there were very few veils in Egypt and mourn the passing of a vibrant modernity and a feminist struggle in their country.

Could the woman in Nantes who wore the burqa have imagined that she was being insulted? Or did she hear correctly?

Europeans did behave in racist ways when they reigned as colonial powers. Their racism continued when they allowed large scale immigration from their former colonies into Europe to do the jobs Europeans declined to do. Now, the European pendulum has swung in the opposite direction. Europeans treat "racism" or even "allegations of possible racism" as crimes; Europe is the multi-culturally relativist capital of the world. Until recently, Europeans refused to condemn polygamy, child marriage, forced marriage, honor killings, female genital mutilation, and burqa wearing. They viewed these practices as "cultural" or "religious" rights—which, when practiced by people who are dark-skinned, might lead to charges of "racism" were such rights condemned, especially by Caucasians, or by former colonial powers.

As the author of *Woman's Inhumanity to Woman*, I am not surprised that the French women came to blows. Many women routinely curse, beat, and mistreat their female servants in developing countries. Wives throw acid at their husbands' mistresses. Mothers-in-law participate in the "dowry deaths" of their daughters-in-law. Co-wives curse, beat, and try to kill each other in polygamous households. Many European women have a very dishonorable history in terms of how they treated women who were Jews, gypsies, "politicals" or homosexuals during the Nazi era.

Just because a woman is kept caged in a movable prison does not mean that she cannot and will not exert great aggression towards others. Her passivity applies only to herself in relation to the men in her family. She can be quite aggressive on behalf of jihad and fundamentalism, both verbally and physically. Indeed, this is the only power she has.

I fear this horrifying scene in Nantes to be repeated all over the continent.

Pajamas Media
5/18/10

- 62 -
Riots over the Burqa in Paris

E arlier today, the French debate over the Islamic Veil again turned ugly, this time in Paris. Pro-burqa supporters "violently thwarted the efforts" of a French Muslim feminist group, *Ni Putes Ni Soumises* (Neither Whores Nor Doormats), which had planned a public debate on the subject.

More than one hundred people (feminists, Islamists, women, lawmakers) came to attend the debate in Montreuil, a suburb of Paris. The debate was "allegedly disrupted by members of Hamas-founder Sheikh Yassin's pro-Palestinian group, forcing the organizers to call for police intervention, as insults turned into fistfights. The rioters had already fled upon the arrival of the police." This successful use of violence to close down an open discussion led Sihem Habchi, the President of *Ni Putes Ni Soumises* to say: "I think those who had doubts before tonight's debate understood, as they left (the meeting), the need for a law that says enough to those who exploit Islam and reduce women to silence."

Manuel Valls, a member of the French Socialist Party, which supports the ban on the burqa, was present "when the riots broke out. According to him, instead of dissuading him, the incident has only given impetus to his belief that the law should be established. 'I for one won't be intimidated,' he said."

Ni Putes Ni Soumises was formed in 2002-2003 in response to the incessant gang rapes of young Muslim girls by Muslim male gangs in the Parisian suburbs and by the brutal murder of 17-year-old Sohane Benziane, who was raped and then burned to death by her ex-boyfriend and his male schoolmates. Sohane had dared to live like a modern French teenager: She wore makeup and she had a new boyfriend. *Ni Putes Ni*

Soumises also rejects the forced wearing of the Islamic Veil, forced early marriage, and forced illiteracy for girls and women.

Wouldn't you know it: French Left feminists describe *Ni Putes Ni Soumises* as "racist" and "Islamophobic,"—even though the founders and members of the group are themselves Muslims or ex-Muslims who seek to assimilate, integrate, Westernize.

The barbarians are not at the gates, they are lodged within the city. In 2005, Gaza-like rioters in Paris and Marseilles burned cars and blocked traffic for days on end. In 2006, a group, literally "The Barbarians," kidnapped and tortured a young, Jewish Parisian North African, Ilan Halimi (may he rest in peace), for three full weeks before he died.

And now today, the Gaza-like riots shut free speech down in Paris. This is one more example of what happens when the world does not stop fascist terrorism immediately, when it is still concentrated in one geographical location. Instead, our world indulges in fantasies of appeasement and scapegoating: Let Hitler have the Sudentenland, sacrifice the Jews for the sake of world "peace." But what inevitably happens is that Gaza migrates. It's Gaza-on-the-Seine, Gaza-in-Mumbai, Gaza-in-Madrid, Gaza-in-London, Gaza-in-Manhattan. Gaza is everywhere now. We have Gaza-on-campuses in both North America and Europe, and Gaza-in-the-streets on every continent in the world.

Most people do not yet understand this. They are sleepwalkers. They say: The fascists have been oppressed, let them speak, give them land, send them money, put those who try to defend themselves against fascist slander and violence on trial as "Islamophobes" and war criminals.

Fascists specialize in threats, curses, and physical blows. They do not debate their opposition. They do not use words. They roar curses, they march carrying hate propaganda, they mask their faces in keffiyas, ski-masks, or in the Islamic Veil. They violently disrupt the free speech of others and they torture and kill those with whom they disagree or whom they simply despise: Women, infidels, Muslims of other sects.

We must stop them. We cannot afford to coddle them, pretend they do not exist, hope that they will simply disappear. The fascists are growing stronger. Russia and Turkey are now both working with an almost-nuclear Iran; Russia is also working with Syria. The White House has decided that the cost of "managing" a nuclear Iran is cheaper than confronting it; why not? We are already living with a nuclear North Korea and a nuclear Pakistan.

Thus far, the West is a Paper Tiger. A nuclear Al-Qaeda or a nuclear Muslim Brotherhood are real tigers whom we must ride sooner if not later.

I hope that Israel has the necessary ties with India well in place. This is an important alliance against all such terrorist tigers.

Pajamas Media
5/20/10

- 63 -
Picture of the Day:
A Woman Votes in Afghanistan

O nce upon a time, long ago, when I lived in Kabul, I was shocked when I first saw a woman wearing a burqa. I was twenty years old but had grown up in New York and considered myself something of a worldly intellectual. The women in my family did not wear burqas—but they did wear attractive head scarves, long coats and gloves. At home, the female servants were not in burqas; they would not be able to work in burqas. Female agricultural workers or female servants on errands did not always wear burqas—but if a male stranger passed by they would quickly, deferentially, turn their faces away and hide their faces in their long headscarves.

And, I was there in the "salad days" when returning Afghan college students were hopeful about the future of Afghanistan, and who even now, in bitter exile, remember the 1960s and 1970s as a time when Afghanistan had flourished and began to modernize.

Well, for what it's worth, democracy exists in Afghanistan. For example, today, women voted there. Below is a photo of a woman registering to vote in Herat. Clearly, she thinks this is an important moment and wants to have a photo to remember it.

Tragic, comic, ironic, pathetic. This is a photo of non-existence, of erasure, proof of invisibility—but also of pride and "agency." This fully burqa-ed woman voted and had someone take a photo of her.

I am tearing my hair out over this one. This photo is the photo of the day at the *London Telegraph*.

A burqa-clad Afghan woman has ber picture taken as she registers for parliamentary elections at a voter registration center in Herat, Afghanistan.

Photo credit: Jalil Rezayee/EPA/Shutterstock

Pajamas Media
6/21/10

- 64 -
Mannequins in Tehran Have No Breasts—
Is a Serial Killer Loose?

D angerous serial killers and sex criminals roam the Western world. In the not-too-distant past, such remorseless killers, such as Jack The Ripper, Ted Bundy, and the Green River Killer, targeted mainly vulnerable women, especially prostituted women, whom they kidnapped, raped, tortured, and murdered. Often, breasts and genitalia were savagely mutilated.

Today, these horrific, individual acts pale in comparison to the barbarism of the Islamist world where similar, but legally approved and publicly shared acts of woman-hatred are carried out by national presidents, religious leaders, Vice and Virtue police—and by mobs inflamed by Friday sermons. In 2001, egged on by their imam, hundreds of men in Hassi Messaoud, in Algeria, physically and sexually attacked any woman they could find, murdering some, sexually mutilating others. Algerian religious paramilitary troops kidnapped young girls off the streets, forced them into domestic and sexual slavery, then murdered and beheaded them when they became pregnant. In 2006, one thousand men in Cairo, Egypt, went on a post-mosque "wilding" in which they attacked both unveiled and veiled women.

The Khomeini- Algerian- and Taliban-era's hot hatred of women, including Muslim women, and of disobedient Muslim girls and women, got heartbreakingly hotter.

Khomeini began by re-veiling the formerly modern and educated women of Tehran. The 1980s Iranian mullahcracy escalated matters; they stoned women to death—but raped them first so that the rape vic-

231

tim would not be able to enter Paradise. The mullahs also forced women into prostitution, then penalized them (not the Johns or the pimps) for it, all the while restricting womens' rights at home, on the streets, and on the job.

Afghanistan (which didn't need much in the way of encouragement) adopted some of the worst Arab customs. They came into their medieval own. Thus, the Afghan Taliban stoned women to death publicly, in large stadiums, with large, blood-thirsty, cheering male crowds. The Afghan Taliban, and after them, the warlords, refused to allow women to work, even when they were war widows and the mothers of dependent children. This forced women into prostitution for which they were jailed. Girls were prevented from going to school, women could not own beauty parlors or wear makeup, polygamy flourished as did the sale and forced marriage of female children, and the kidnapping of orphans of both genders.

Then, the Pakistani Taliban jumped on this bandwagon of misogyny. Roving vigilante squads started spraying acid onto little girls' faces (and shooting them in the head) for the crimes of going to school or simply for allowing their headscarves to slip. They went beyond mutilating the breasts and genitalia of murder victims to scarring the faces of young girls forever.

The control of women and the woman-hating frenzy went viral, crossed borders, and is now quite simply out of control.

For example, in 2009, a militia in a "Muslim region" of the Philippines massacred more than fifty people and sexually mutilated 22 of the murdered women. This is a militia acting in the name of Islam; it is not just one lone savage and psychopathic individual.

In 2010, an Afghan Taliban Court decreed that nineteen-year-old Bibi Aisha's husband should cut off her nose and ears because she had run away from him and his family. Vigilante-style misogyny is now the law of the land.

Recently, a woman's clothing store in Tehran featured female mannequins with their breasts clearly removed, hacked off or filed down, on "orders from the Vice police" as part of the current crackdown on "un-Islamic" or bad hijab practices. This makes perfect, if jarring, sense.

A woman's physical existence is, by definition, sexual and is therefore considered shameful. Living women must be "disappeared" lest their living, breathing, bodies lead men into temptation. Alternatively, one can "practice" eviscerating, mutilating, removing the characteristics that render the female form offensive—on a dummy, a mannequin, and in a store window.

What comes next? And don't tell me that destroying the breasts of female mannequins in Tehran is the same as Western women surgically reducing their breasts for cosmetic reasons. The latter is an individual choice, sometimes for medical or for cosmetic reasons in order to make oneself more, not less, sexually attractive. The case of the Tehran mannequin without breasts is an example of publicly abolishing one of the biological characteristics of being born female.

It is a public warning.

Such woman-phobia, such woman-hatred, always signifies fear and contempt for the life force itself. Thus, the worship of death, the hatred of life, is at the heart of the existential struggle between Islamist terrorists and Israel and between Islamist terrorists and the West. We can measure the terrorist's capacity and willingness to mass murder infidels in a Holy war by their capacity and willingness to murder their own women as well as other Muslims.

Do not expect World War Three to be a short war.

NewsRealBlog
6/23/10

- 65 -
Daughters of Afghanistan:
The Film and the Reality

I n Afghanistan, the women are setting themselves aflame, choosing an awful, fiery death rather than one more awful beating at the hands of a husband and a mother-in-law. Amazingly, when the mainstream media finally writes about this precise tragedy in Afghanistan, it still carefully manages not to use the words "Muslim" or "Islam." For example, see *Time* magazine's recent coverage of this very subject.

In Kabul, when battered women run away, their own families refuse to take them back and the government puts them in jail and treats them as criminals. In a rather moving documentary, *Daughters of Afghanistan*, Sally Armstrong shows us what happened to one young Afghan woman who refused to take the beatings anymore and upon a lawyer's advice dared return to her family of origin. Her own father clapped her up into solitary, perhaps for the rest of her life, to live in a cold, dark room with one bricked-up window.

This happened in 2002, after the Taliban fell.

But the Taliban mentality in Afghanistan long predated the actual Taliban phenomenon. In 1961, I remember meeting a rather genial relative who had come down from the Khyber Pass region to meet me, his first American woman. Apparently, he was a merciful fellow who had married his brother's widow—but then shut her up in solitary. I was told that he fed and clothed her and that this alone saved her from a far more dismal fate. I did not understand then—or now—why this poor widow-wife could not have shared the family tasks and remained among the living. Entombed, buried alive—like Verdi's great opera hero,

234

Aida. Without a name, without even a number, the fate of this unknown prisoner haunts me still.

These tragedies are no longer confined to Third World countries.

Given massive Muslim immigration to the West, we have massive Muslim female resistance to being subordinated, buried alive—resistance which is punished by Muslim-on-Muslim honor killings in the West.

Families of origin carefully plan these murders. Mothers often play a key role in luring their daughters back home, in strangling or stabbing them, and in helping their murderers escape. This was the case in the honor murders of Amina and Sarah Said in Texas (2008), and Noor Al-Maleki in Arizona (2009).

Just yesterday, Aset Magomadova, a Calgary-based mother who strangled her 14-year-old daughter, Aminat, with a headscarf in 2007, finally received a "suspended sentence" and three years probation. The mother is a Muslim refugee and widow from Chechnya; her other child, a teenage son, is suffering from muscular dystrophy, and she herself was wounded in the war—her foot was partly blown off. The girl was allegedly on drugs and suffered from serious behavior problems. Victim advocates are outraged at so light a sentence. The judge did not believe that Magomadova actually meant to kill her rebellious daughter. The judge sentenced the murderer to "counseling for grief, depression, and anger management."

If everyone understood that a Muslim girl is at special risk, especially if she is "wild", i.e. acting in Western ways, if the media used the word "Muslim" where appropriate, perhaps services tailored to Muslim immigrants from war-torn regions might now exist.

This past week, the Canadian "federal government affirmed its zero-tolerance stance against "honor killing," declaring such "barbaric cultural practices" as "heinous abuses" that have no place in Canadian society." They are considering adding "honor killing" as a separate charge to the Criminal Code. Honor killings are referred to as "culturally driven" violence against girls and women. It is true: such violence exists among Canadian immigrants from south Asia who are Muslims and, more rarely, among Sikhs.

Expect such tragic "culturally driven," "South Asian immigrant" and "Muslim" problems to proliferate in the West.

NewsRealBlog
7/17/10

- 66 -

Syria Bans Face Veil, British Minister and American Feminists Defend Burqa

Syria—Bashar Asad's Syria—has just banned full face veils in their universities.

According to Syria's minister of higher education, "All female students wearing the full face veil will be barred from Syrian university campuses … the niqab contradicts university ethics and compromises the government's secular identity."

Amazingly, the Minister confirmed that "hundreds of primary school teachers who wore niqab at government-run schools were transferred last month to administrative jobs."

Other Arab, Muslim countries with long and hard-won secular identities are now also under attack by fundamentalists and Islamists who want to face-veil women or at least to have them wear headscarves. Thus, Egypt, Jordan, Lebanon, and Turkey are now also at risk. Jordan's government has tried to discourage face veils by "playing up reports of robbers who wear veils as masks." Turkey also bans Muslim headscarves in universities, with many saying "attempts to allow them in schools amount to an attack on modern Turkey's secular laws."

Whoa, Nellie!

So, Syria, Venezuela's and Iran's partner—Syria!—is banning the female Islamic face veil. And yet just today, none other than British Minister Carolyn Spelman, the Environment Secretary, the second most powerful woman in the Cabinet, giddily described the burqa as "empowering." Furthermore, she said: "I don't, living in this country as a woman, want to be told what I can and can't wear. One of the things we pride ourselves on in this country is being free, and being free to choose what you wear is part of that, so banning the burqa is absolutely contrary I think to what this country is about. Based on a visit to Afghanistan, she says that she better understands why Muslim women want to wear the chaudry/burqa/niqab: "For them [in Afghanistan], it confers dignity."

Britain is not joining France, Spain, Belgium, Germany, and Italy in proposing any kind of ban on face veils.

In America, as I've written previously, our president is proud of our efforts on behalf of a Muslim girl's right to wear hijab in school. Various American feminists view the essentially non-existent "choice" to wear the Islamic Veil as akin to a feminist choice, a feminist right.

Feminist philosopher Martha Nussbaum, in the august pages of the *New York Times*, recently insisted that burqa wearers are not coerced into wearing the shroud-like garment, nor is it really uncomfortable, dangerous to one's health, or associated with violence against women. She doesn't believe that showing one's face for purposes of identification is even really necessary—and that banning the burqa would be "discriminatory." Nussbaum deftly marshals all her arguments without even getting to the "delicate issue of religiously grounded accomodation." In her view, a ban would be "unacceptable in a society committed to equal liberty. Equal respect for conscience requires us to reject" all the arguments that have been made against face veiling.

In a response to reader comments Nussbaum brings it all back to herself. Once, a nearby construction project filled her office with dust. Allergic, she started wearing a mask and a scarf to protect herself. And she felt just fine, thank you very much. She did not feel as if she'd lost any individuality or dignity.

Martha: Tell that to a non-professor, non-teacher, non-literate ten year old Afghan girl who is being forced to wear the chaudry/burqa. Tell that to someone who has been threatened with being honor-murdered if her headscarf slips or if she refuses to face veil.

Stuart Schneiderman, at his own witty blog, has written a piece called "Burqaphilia." I will let him have the last word here. Schneiderman says that:

> Burqaphilia is a philosophical affliction that besets the mind of an otherwise intelligent feminist, making it impossible for her to support a ban on the most conspicuous modern form of female oppression. When a feminist who has railed against female objectification, both real and imagined, cannot bring

herself to denounce an instrument that reduces women to the status of objects, she is suffering from burqaphilia. A feminist philosopher can explain to you with the most exquisitely twisted logic why miniskirts and lip gloss make women into sexual objects, but when it comes to a cultural practice, enforced by terror, that makes women into social non-entities, she feels that it is beneath her liberal dignity to support a ban on the practice.

NewsRealBlog
7/19/10

- 67 -
Muslim Women:
Harassed in Gaza and Australia

Obediently wearing the Islamic Veil does not protect Muslim women from being raped and beaten within their own families, harassed, assaulted on the streets, or sold into sexual slavery.

In Gaza, the territory that is currently most adored by western artists, "free" thinkers, and flotilla "activists," any woman who refuses to wear hijab, the headscarf, faces new punishments.

In the fall of 2010, Asma'a al-Gul, a Palestinian journalist whom I interviewed, and who has written about honor killings among Palestinians, was literally arrested for not wearing hijab and for wearing jeans; perhaps she was also arrested due to her work which exposed honor killings. In any event, Asma'a now writes that a friend who "refuses to wear the hijab has not been allowed to graduate from university." Asma'a writes:

> In Gaza, you will come across repressive rules, hurtful comments, stupid words and contemptuous looks, and scorn for the women not wearing hijab. In the small world of Gaza, we need someone to defend the rights of women who don't wear hijab, or the jilbab, or the niqab. It's a system that establishes the idea that women should be treated as bodies.

Asma'a goes on to explain that, in Gaza, Christian Arabs are also required to wear hijab.

Although the head of Al-Azhar University recently snatched the

niqab from a girl's face and said that face-covering is not religiously required by Islam—Asma'a decries the fact that the university still
demands that female students wear the hijab, headscarf, if they are to
graduate. And, they must take their official photo wearing hijab, not
bare-headed, even if they are bare-headed in their daily lives.

She writes that young girls are being forced to wear hijab in secondary schools. When they resist, as her younger sisters did, they were
forced into the blazing sun. The headteacher told Asma'a: "I want to receive God's reward because of them."

In Australia, a Muslim woman leader and member of Hizb ut-
Tahrir also defended the right of Muslim women to face-, body-, and
head-cover. Yesterday, in Sydney, a Muslim female speaker addressed a
2000-strong rally which opposes a proposed burqa ban. She said that a
ban is "un-Australian" and that Islamic values are "superior" to "flawed"
western, secular values. According to Fautmeh Ardati:

> The western secular way of life, robs a woman of her dignity,
> honor, and respect, where she is considered little more than
> a commodity to be bought and sold...I feel empowered by
> the knowledge that I am in control of displaying my beauty
> to whom I choose.

It is ironic that so many western "progressive" activists are willing to sign petitions to "free Gaza." But free Gaza from whom? From
Hamas, from rigid Islamist misogyny, or from the Israelis who long ago
left Gaza and who are not now imposing such restrictions on women?

Israel National News
9/21/10

- 68 -
Sexual Assaults of Western Journalists
Covered Up on the West Bank

What is happening on the West Bank reminds me of the American 1960s, when idealistic young white and Jewish women, who thought they were volunteering for Martin Luther King's non-violent movement for black civil rights, eventually found themselves up against sociopathic and sexually violent members of the Black Panther Party.

According to one recent and very disturbing report, foreign American, European, and Israeli Jewish and Christian left-wing feminists are being routinely harassed, raped, and even forced into marriage by the very Palestinians whom they have come to "rescue." More shocking is the alleged pressure brought to bear on those activists who wish to press charges about being raped or abducted into marriage; their own movement pressures them not to do so because the alleged Israeli "occupation" of Palestine is far more important than the violent "occupation" of any woman's body.

Israeli feminist activist Roni Aloni Sedovnik wrote an article titled "The Left's Betrayal of Female Peace Activists Who Were Sexually Assaulted." Yehudah Bello, a pro-Palestinian blogger, confirms that at least one European non-Jewish leftist, one Red Cross worker, and one young Israeli Arab from Yafo all experienced such assaults.

Sedovnik insists that these are not isolated incidents but are part of a systematic pattern—Arabs on the West Bank view all infidel women as prey—but there is also another aim involved, namely that of forcing marriage and conversion to Islam upon them. Sedovnik accuses the media of "complicity" in refusing to report on the matter. She writes:

> How is it that we do not hear the voice of the radical feminists who repeat, day and night, that occupation is occupation, and it does not matter if it is a nation that is doing the subjugation, or a man who is subjugating a woman?

> It appears that there is a gap between the radical-leftist feminist theory about the active resistance to the occupation of the Territories, and the stuttering self-annulment in the face of the violent conquest of women.

In response to the rapes near the towns and villages of Bethlehem, Bil'in, Naalin, and Sheikh Jarrah (Shimon Ha Tzaddik), the Israeli and Palestinian peace activists have urged women to dress modestly and even wear headscarves!

What is more amazing is the failure of such left feminists to support the Palestinian women who are routinely held captive by just such men in Gaza.

NewsRealBlog
9/22/10

- 69 -
The Burqa—Modern Views in the Arab World, Islamist Views in Europe

E very Arab, Muslim, and ex-Muslim feminist and dissident with whom I have worked has criticized the face veil (niqab) as well as the burqa (the full face and body bag). Some have called for state bans; others have implored women not to voluntarily surrender the rights for which their own grandmothers and mothers once fought, rights which they won.

Earlier this month, on October 7, 2010, Rashid al-Marar, a high ranking member of parliament in the UAE, backed France in its ban on the burqa.

As Zeyno Baran has shown, the western media continues to disappear the true faces of moderate, secular, and dissident Muslims. Instead, it glorifies (and hires) Islamists, calls them "moderates," and handily silences the true Islamic dissidents and moderates.

The disappearance of a woman's face in public normalizes Islamic gender apartheid.

Some Westerners beg to differ. Recently, in a British report, Alveena Malik, an advisor to the former Labour government, suggested that "we in Britain need to take a different direction…and to accept the veil as a part of the modern British way of life."

Sweden and Norway have joined Britain; neither has even considered a ban on the burqa. Germany has been debating the issue, and a number of German municipalities have restricted the face veil in schools. Holland first began debating a burqa ban four years ago. A group of parliament members in Italy has drafted a bill proposing that burqas be banned for security reasons. Transgressors would be fined between 150 and 300 euros or, alternatively, mandated to do some kind of community service "aimed at encouraging integration."

France became the first country to ban the burqa. Only the European Union can now challenge the French law which imposes a fine of 150 euros ($190) and/or a citizenship course as punishment for wearing a face-masking veil. Forcing a woman to wear a niqab or a burqa will be punishable by a year in prison or a 15,000 euro ($19,000) fine.

Right now, a woman is on trial in Paris. A French woman, Anne Fontette, currently stands accused of ripping off the full face veil of an Emirati tourist and of biting, punching, and scratching her when she put it back on. If convicted, Fontette faces a possible two-month suspended prison sentence and a 750 euro fine. Fontette denied committing any acts of violence, but she told the media that she felt for a long time that she was "going to crack one day" because she hated seeing women wearing the veil in the "birthplace of human rights." She told reporters that she had once taught languages in Morocco and Saudi Arabia: "I have seen how in those countries women are treated ... walking three meters behind their husbands."

NewsRealBlog
10/18/10

Is the Obama Administration Ready to Consider Banning the Burqa in America—as France and Belgium Have Done?

I can't be sure exactly what Secretary of State Hillary Clinton said the other day in Melbourne, Australia but the reportage sure had me take notice.

According to an Australian news article titled "The Burqa Ban Has Merit," Clinton said that "the belief that burqas should be banned in order to stop suicide bombers disguising themselves is a legitimate one," and she also described the status of women as "one of the biggest pieces of unfinished business in this century." She went on to say:

> In Pakistan, many of the men who are conducting suicide bombing missions arrive covered in a burqa....If you're a Pakistani police officer, respectful of the women of your culture, that causes a real dilemma. So if you are looking at other countries that are understandably nervous about extremist activity, I think it's a close question.

Clinton seems to be straddling two fences. She is suggesting that security concerns may trump cultural or ethnic customs and that the burqa itself may be part of the way in which women are being "persecuted in repressed and impoverished nations."

Do her words represent a small and welcome departure from President Obama's position—that of a respectful dhimmi—vis-à-vis the

Muslim world?

Clinton's words may represent a trial balloon, or they may be entirely spontaneous comments made in the course of a public conversation in Melbourne.

Many Arab and Muslim countries are banning or restricting the face veil and the burqa. They have security and anti-terrorist concerns of their own and they know full well that such clothing is not a religious requirement and that women have not always veiled their faces.

When will the West wake up and smell the bomb?

I am not talking about freeing the women in Afghanistan or Saudi Arabia. I'm talking about banning this visual symbol of political Islam, fundamentalist misogyny, and jihad in our own country.

Gates of Vienna
11/9/10

- 71 -

The Feminist Politics of Islamic Misogyny: Lila Abu-Lughod and Post-Colonial Academy

S tudying honor killings is not the same as sensationalizing them—but Columbia University professor Lila Abu-Lughod disagrees. Moreover, she believes that indigenous Arab and Muslim behavior, including honor-related violence, is best understood as a consequence of Western colonialism—perhaps even of "Islamophobia."

On October 25, 2010, at the American University of Beirut, Abu-Lughod admonished feminists who ostensibly sensationalize honor killings, a position which, in her opinion, represents "simplistic, civilizational thinking." She "warned that an obsessive focus on the so-called honor crime may have negative repercussions" and that "people should be wary of classifying certain acts as a distinctive form of violence against women."

Abu-Lughod opposed the "concept of clear-cut divisions between cultures, which she viewed as a form of imprisoning rural and immigrant communities," and suggested that focusing on "honor crimes" allowed "scholars and activists to ignore important contexts for violence against women: social tensions; political conflicts; forms of racial, class, and ethnic discrimination; religious movements; government policing and surveillance; and military intervention."

What kind of feminism does Abu-Lughod represent? She is a post-colonial, postmodern, multi-cultural relativist, a professor of anthropology and of women's and gender studies who does not believe in universal standards of human rights. However, her allegedly feminist work primarily serves the cause of one nationalism only—Palestinian—

247

and of one tradition only—Islam/Islamism.

Abu-Lughod has long held the positions she expressed in Beirut. According to her 2002 article in *The American Anthropologist*, "Do Muslim Women Really Need Saving?," Abu-Lughod believes that wearing the Islamic veil signifies "respectability" for Muslim women. It can also be "read as a sign of educated, urban sophistication, a sort of modernity."

According to the photo which accompanies the Beirut press advisory and her Columbia biography, Abu-Lughod does not wear a niqab or a burqa.

Abu-Lughod herself and her professor parents are all products of an American academic establishment: Her "Palestinian"-American father, Ibrahim, taught at Northwestern University for 35 years; her Jewish-American mother, Janet Lippman Abu-Lughod, did so for twenty years. Their daughter was raised a Muslim—but in America, not the Middle East. She attended Carleton College in Minnesota and received her Ph.D. from Harvard. Abu-Lughod is married to another Columbia professor of Middle East studies, Timothy Mitchell, who shares her views about "Palestine," Israel, and America. They and others represent an academy which has also sacrificed most real feminist values and curriculum for a hard-left agenda which masquerades as "feminism."

Abu-Lughod suggests that there are many reasons that a woman might veil—and, if she's talking about hijab (a headscarf), I can agree with her. However, wearing a face- and body-covering is not an empowered "feminist" choice. As I've noted before, the growing Islamist pressure to veil is enormous, and women fear being beaten, never obtaining a husband, or being divorced, jailed, or even killed for their failure to do so.

Regarding the benefits of polygamy, Abu-Lughod and others suggest that female relatives, including co-wives, may bond, keep each other company, share isolating and repetitive tasks, and so on. Sounds good—but neither research nor personal memoirs support this theoretical possibility.

Even Abu-Lughod notes that pioneer Iranian feminist Siddiqeh Dawlatabadi "imposed on the nine-year-old daughter of her father's secretary a marriage to her seventy-year-old father when he was widowed. She later ignored the girl's cries when she went into labor and thereafter, when Dawlatabadi's father died, married off the girl to someone else, taking her daughters."

To be fair, Abu-Lughod has also published some interesting work about Muslim women in the Middle East, and about Bedouin women in particular, including *Writing Women's Worlds: Bedouin Stories*. However, Abu-Lughod, like her Columbia University colleague Gayatri Spivak, views a Western-style fight for women's rights in the Muslim world as a dangerous diversion. In *Remaking Women. Feminism and Modernity In The Middle East*, Abu-Lughod criticizes Western "colonial feminism" as attempting to undermine local cultures and recommends that we continue to focus mainly on the "colonial enterprise." Why? Perhaps as a way of reminding Western thinkers—heirs to the colonial adventure—that, given their ancestors' past crimes, they dare not feel "superior" to the Islamic world, and above all, they dare not intervene to free Muslim prisoners from Muslim tyrants, jailers, and murderers.

I am among a handful of Muslim, ex-Muslim, and non-Muslim feminists who humbly but adamantly question this approach. The politicization of the feminist academic world, especially in terms of its "Palestinianization" and its anti-Americanism—has become the universal point of view for feminist academics. Abu-Lughod, Leila Ahmed, Suha Sabbagh, and Gayatri Spivak all share a profoundly negative view of the West and its values. They may study women for complex reasons, but they use their work to condemn the West again and again. Sadly, they are all speaking the same politically correct, presumably feminist language from which a universal concept of human rights for women has been utterly banished.

American Thinker/Campus Watch
11/13/10

Ban the Burqa? An Academic Argument in Favor

S hould Western countries follow the Belgian and French examples and ban the Islamic body and face-covering veil—or more
specifically, the burqa and the niqab? Should the West ban any and all
clothing which obliterates one's identity?

Most Europeans, according to recent surveys, seem to think so.[1]
Still, significant numbers, especially in the United States,[2] and including quite a few feminists,[3] have viewed such a ban as religiously intolerant, anti-woman, and anti-Western. They maintain that the state has
no place in deciding what a woman can and cannot wear—it's her body,
not public property;[4] that given the worldwide exploitation of women as
pornographic sex objects, wearing loose, comfortable, modest clothing,
or actually "covering," might be both convenient and more dignified;[5]

---

1 "Widespread Support for Banning Full Islamic Veil in Western Europe," Pew Global
Attitudes Project, Washington, D.C., July 8, 2010; United Press International, July 17,
2010; *The Toronto Sun*, July 28, 2010.

2 *New Atlanticist* (Washington, D.C.), Mar. 1, 2010; *Los Angeles Times*, July 13, 2010.

3 Martha Nussbaum, "Veiled Threats?" *The New York Times*, July 11, 2010; Naomi
Wolf, "Behind the Veil Lives a Thriving Muslim Sexuality," *The Sydney Morning Herald*
(Australia), Aug. 30, 2008; Joan Wallach, "France Has the Burqa All Wrong," *Salon*,
Apr. 12, 2010; Joan Wallach, "Don't Ban Burqas—Or Censor South Park," *BigThink.
com*, May 21, 2010; Yvonne Ridley, "How I Came to Love the Veil," *The Washington
Post*, Oct. 22, 2006.

4 Marnia Lazreg, *Questioning the Veil: Open Letters to Muslim Women* (Princeton:
Princeton University Press, 2009), p. 62.

5 Wolf, "Behind the Veil Lives a Thriving Muslim Sexuality."

that because of the West's tolerance toward religions, the state cannot come between a woman and her conscience for that would betray Western values;[6] and that women are freely choosing to wear the burqa.[7]

Some Western intellectuals oppose banning the burqa although they understand the harm it may do and the way in which it may "mutilate personhood."[8] For example, Algerian-American academic, Marnia Lazreg, implores Muslim women to voluntarily, freely refuse to fully cover their faces—to spurn even the headscarf; however, she does not want the state involved.[9]

It is arguable that the full body and face cover is not a religious requirement in Islam but represents a minority tradition among a small Islamist minority; that it is not a matter of free choice but a highly forced choice and a visual symbol of radical Islam—one that is ostentatiously anti-secularist and misogynist;[10] that the Western state does have an interest in public appearances and, therefore, does not permit public nudity or masked people in public buildings; and that it is strange that the very feminists (or their descendents) who once objected to the sexual commoditification of women "can explain to you with the most exquisitely twisted logic why miniskirts and lip gloss make women into sexual objects, but when it comes to a cultural practice, enforced by terror, that makes women into social nonentities, [they] feel that it is beneath [their] liberal dignity to support a ban on the practice."[11]

To this may be added that face-veil wearers ("good" girls) endanger all those who do not wear a face veil ("bad" girls). But before addressing these arguments at greater length, it is instructive to see what political and religious leaders in the Muslim world, as well as Muslim women, have to say about the issue.

---

6 Nussbaum, "Veiled Threats?"; Leon Wieseltier, "Faces and Faiths," *The New Republic*, July 27, 2010.

7 Nussbaum, "Veiled Threats?"; Wolf, "Behind the Veil Lives a Thriving Muslim Sexuality."

8 Wieseltier, "Faces and Faiths."

9 Lazreg, *Questioning the Veil*, pp. 62-3.

10 Bernard-Henri Levy, "Why I Support a Ban on Burqas," *The Huffington Post*, Feb. 15, 2010; Samia Labidi, "Faces of Janus: The Arab-Muslim Community in France and the Battle for Its Future," in Zeyno Baran, ed., *The Other Muslims: Moderate and Secular* (New York: Palgrave Macmillan, 2010), pp. 116-9; Melanie Philips, in "Should France Ban the Burqa?" *National Review Online*, July 23, 2010; Elham Manea, in Valentina Colombo, "Europe: Behind the Burqa Debate," Hudson Institute, New York, Mar. 12, 2010.

11 Stuart Schneiderman blog, "Burqaphilia," July 17, 2010.

THE HOUSE OF ISLAM UNVEILS ITS WOMEN

The forced veiling and unveiling of Muslim women, both in terms of the headscarf and the face veil, ebbed and flowed for about a century as Muslim elites strove to come to terms with the demise of the Islamic political order that had dominated the Middle East (and substantial parts of Asia and Europe) for over a millennium.

Turkey's founder, Mustafa Kemal Atatürk, for example, generated a new and vibrant brand of nationalism that sought to extricate Turkey from its imperial past—and its Islamic legacy—in order to reconstitute it as a modern nation state.

Iran's Reza Shah distanced his country from Islam for the opposite reason, namely, as a means to link his family to Persia's pre-Islamic imperial legacy, which is vividly illustrated by his adoption of the surname Pahlavi, of ancient Persian origins,[12] and the name Iran, or "[the land] of the Aryans," as the country's official title in all formal correspondence.[13]

During the 1920s and 1930s, kings, shahs, and presidents unveiled their female citizens, and Muslim feminists campaigned hard for open faces in public. They were successful in Egypt, Lebanon, Tunisia, Algeria, Morocco, Turkey, Pakistan, and Iran, to name but a few countries.

As early as 1899, Egyptian intellectual Qasim Amin published his landmark book *The Liberation of Women*, which argued that the face veil was not commensurate with the tenets of Islam and called for its removal.[14] According to photographs taken by Annie Lady Brassey in Egypt in the 1870s, Egyptian women wore heavy, dark coverings with full niqab (face covering) or partial niqab when possible.[15] In 1923, the feminist Hoda Hanim Shaarawi, who established the first feminist association that called for uncovering the face and hair, became the first Egyptian woman to remove her face veil or niqab.[16] In the following decades, the

---

12 Farvardyn Project, "Pahlavi Literature," accessed Aug. 25, 2010.

13 M. Sadeq Nazmi-Afshar, "The People of Iran, The Origins of Aryan People," Iran Chamber Society, accessed Aug. 25, 2010.

14 Amin Qasim, *The Liberation of Women and The New Woman: Two Documents in the History of Egyptian Feminism*, trans. Samiha Sidhom Peterson (Cairo: American University of Cairo Press, 2000).

15 Reina Lewis and Nancy Micklenwright, eds., *Gender, Modernity and Liberty: Middle Eastern and Western Women's Writings: A Critical Sourcebook* (New York: I.B. Tauris and Co., 2006), pp. 36-7; Afaf Lufti al-Sayyid Marsot, "The Revolutionary Gentlewomen in Egypt," in Lois Beck and Nikki Keddie, eds., *Women in the Muslim World* (Cambridge: Harvard University Press, 1978), pp. 261-76.

16 Colombo, "Europe: Behind the Burqa Debate."

veil gradually disappeared in Egypt, so much so that in 1958, a foreign journalist wrote that "the veil is unknown here."[17]

In Afghanistan, Shah Amanullah Khan (r. 1919-29) "scandalized the [people] by permitting his wife to go unveiled." In 1928, he urged Afghan women to uncover their faces and advocated the shooting of interfering husbands. He said that he "would himself supply the weapons" for this and that "no inquiries would be instituted against the women." Once, when he saw a woman wearing a burqa in a Kabul garden, he tore it off and burned it.[18] However, Amanullah was exiled, and the country plunged back into the past.[19]

Turkey banned the Islamic face veil and turban in 1934, and this prohibition has been maintained ever since by a long succession of governments that adhered to Atatürk's secularist and modernist revolution. Moreover, from the 1980s onward, Turkish women have been prohibited from wearing headscarves in parliament and in public buildings, and this law was even more strictly enforced after a 1997 coup by the secular military.

In recent years, the Islamist Justice and Development Party (Adalet ve Kalkınma Partisi, AKP), which has ruled Turkey since 2002, has tried to relax this restriction, only to be dealt a humiliating blow on June 15, 2008, when the country's Constitutional Court annulled a government reform allowing students to wear Muslim headscarves at university on the grounds that it contravened Turkey's secular system.[20] In recent years, women wearing both hijabs and burqas have been seen on the streets of Istanbul.

As early as 1926 in Iran, Reza Shah provided police protection for Iranian women who chose to dispense with the traditional scarf.[21] Ten years later, on January 7, 1936, the shah ordered all female teachers and the wives of ministers, high military officers, and government officials "to appear in European clothes and hats, rather than chadors"; and by way of "serving as an example for other Persian women," the shah asked his wife and daughters to appear without face veils in public. Ranking

---

17 *Sarasota Herald Tribune*, Jan. 26, 1958.

18 Rhea Talley Stewart, *Fire in Afghanistan 1914-1929: Faith, Hope, and the British Empire* (New York: Doubleday, 1973), pp. 127, 376-8.

19 Rosanne Klass, *Afghanistan: The Great Game Revisited* (New York: Freedom House, 1987), p. 39; idem, *Land of the High Flags* (New York: Odyssey Books, 1964), pp. 202-3.

20 *The Muslim Observer* (Farmington, Mich.), Jan. 31, June 19, 2008.

21 Hamideh Sedghi, *Women and Politics in Iran: Veiling, Unveiling, and Reveiling* (Cambridge: Cambridge University Press, 2007), p. 85.

male officials were dismissed from their jobs if their wives appeared with face veils in public, and the police began breaking into private homes to arrest women wearing chadors there. A report from the city of Tabriz stated that only unveiled girls could receive diplomas.[22] These and other secularizing reforms were sustained by Shah Muhammad Reza Pahlavi, who in September 1941 succeeded his father on the throne and instituted a ban on veiled women in public.

Lebanon has always been the most Westernized Arab society, owing to its substantial Christian population with its close affinity to Europe, France in particular. A Palestinian-Lebanese-Syrian woman visiting the United States said, "In the 1920s, my mother, a university professor, was the first woman to take off her veil in Beirut. She had to remain at home under house arrest for one year due to the violence threatened by street mobs. Then, things changed for the better."[23]

Since 1981, women in Tunisia have been prohibited from wearing Islamic dress, including headscarves, in schools or government offices. In 2006, since this ban was increasingly ignored, the Tunisian government launched a sustained campaign against the hijab. The police stopped women in the streets and asked them to remove their headscarves; the president described the headscarf as a "sectarian form of dress which had come into Tunisia uninvited." Other officials explained that Islamic dress was being promoted by extremists who exploited religion for political aims.[24]

In 2006, in neighboring Morocco, a picture of a mother and daughter wearing headscarves was removed from a textbook. The education minister explained, "This issue isn't really about religion, it's about politics ... the headscarf for women is a political symbol in the same way as the beard is for men."[25] However, the government could only go so far in its ability to restrict the face veil or headscarf.

In 1975, Moroccan feminist Fatima Mernissi described the lives of Moroccan women as circumscribed by Ghazali's view of women, including women's eyes, as erotically irresistible, and as such, dangerous to men.[26] As of 2017, this trend has increased dramatically. In 1987,

---

22 Ibid., pp. 85-7.

23 Author interview with the wife of the Syrian ambassador to the United Nations, New York, 1980.

24 *BBC News*, Sept. 26, 2006.

25 Ibid., Oct. 6, 2006.

26 Fatima Mernissi, *Beyond the Veil: Male-Female Dynamics in a Modern Muslim Society* (Cambridge, Mass.: Schenkman Publishing Company, Inc., 1975).

Mernissi analyzed the Islamic veil in both theological and historical terms.[27] Clearly, as fundamentalism or political Islam returned to the historical stage, "roots" or Islamic identity, both in Morocco and elsewhere, was increasingly equated with seventh century customs that were specific to women and to the Prophet Muhammad's own life.

Public servants in Malaysia are prohibited from wearing the niqab. In 1994, the Supreme Court ruled that the niqab "has nothing to do with [a woman's] constitutional rights to profess and practice her Muslim religion" because it is not required by Islamic law.[28] On July 18, 2010, Syria became the latest Muslim state to ban full face veils in some public places, barring female students from wearing the full face cover on Syrian university campuses. The Syrian minister of higher education indicated that the face veil ran counter to Syrian academic values and traditions.[29]

In October 2009, Sheikh Muhammad Sayyid Tantawi, perhaps the foremost spiritual authority in Sunni Islam and grand sheikh of al-Azhar University, Sunni Islam's highest institution of religious learning, was reportedly "angered" when he toured a school in Cairo and saw a teenage girl wearing niqab. Asking the girl to remove her face veil, he said, "The niqab is a tradition; it has no connection with religion." He then instructed the girl never to wear the niqab again and issued a fatwa (religious edict) against its use in schools.[30]

In 2010, at a time when Britain's department of health relaxed the strict National Health Service dress code by allowing Muslim nurses and doctors to wear long sleeves for religious reasons—despite the high risk of spreading deadly superbugs—the Egyptian ministry of health outlawed the niqab (which often included glove-wearing) for hospital nurses, threatening those who failed to comply with dismissal or legal prosecution. The Iraqi religious authority, Sheikh Ahmad al-Qubaisi, supported this Egyptian decision and issued a fatwa which stated, "People have the right to know the identity of the person they are in front of in order not to feel deceived. The obligation of niqab was only for the Prophet's wives as they were the mothers of all believers."[31]

---

27 Ibid.

28 Nurjaanah Abdullah and Chew Li Hua, "Legislating Faith in Malaysia," *Singapore Journal of Legal Studies*, 2007, pp. 264-89.

29 *BBC News*, July 19, 2010.

30 *The Daily Telegraph* (London), Oct. 5, 2009.

31 Colombo, "Europe: Behind the Burqa Debate."

FREE CHOICE OR FORCED CHOICE?

These examples challenge the increasing number of Muslim women in the West, including converts and educated women, who claim to be freely choosing to wear the burqa and the niqab for religious and ethnic reasons. They are doing so in stark contrast to the ethos and values of their adopted societies at a time when governments in the part of the world where this custom originated have been progressively unveiling their women.

These supposed defenders of women's rights appear oblivious to what is implied by the phrase "to cover," namely, that women are born shamed—they are nothing beyond their genitalia, which can shame or dishonor an entire family—and it is this shame which they must cover or for which they must atone. Qur'anic verse (7:26) states, "We have sent down clothing to cover your shame." Certainly, this applies to both men and women, but patriarchal customs have almost exclusively targeted women. Ironically, this verse also says that "the clothing of righteousness is the best"—a point lost on Islamists and their unwitting sympathizers in the West.

The fact is that Muslim women are increasingly not given a free choice about wearing the veil, and those who resist are beaten, threatened with death, arrested, flogged, jailed, or honor murdered by their own families, by vigilante groups, or by the state.[32] Being fully covered does not save a Muslim woman from being harassed, stalked, raped, and battered in public places, or raped or beaten at home by her husband. Nor does it stop her husband from taking multiple wives and girlfriends, frequenting brothels, divorcing her against her will, and legally seizing custody of their children.[33] A fully covered female child, as young as ten, may still be forced into an arranged marriage, perhaps to a man old enough to be her grandfather, and is not allowed to leave him, not even if he beats her every day.[34]

Moreover, after decades of attempted modernization in Muslim countries, the battle to impose the veil was launched again by resurgent Islamists. The establishment of the Islamic Republic of Iran sent shock

---

32 Phyllis Chesler, "Worldwide Trends in Honor Killings," *Middle East Quarterly*, Spring 2010, pp. 3-11.

33 Phyllis Chesler, *The Death of Feminism: What's Next in the Struggle for Women's Freedom* (New York: Palgrave Macmillan, 2005), chap. 6, 7.

34 David Ghanim, *Gender and Violence in the Middle East* (Wesport: Praeger, 2009), chap. 2, 4.

waves throughout the region and set in motion a string of violent eruptions. These included the 1979-80 riots in the Shiite towns of the oil-rich Saudi province of Hasa, the Muslim Brotherhood's attempt to topple the secularist Syrian Baath regime in the early 1980s, the Algerian civil war of the 1990s, the ascendance of Hezbollah in Lebanon and Hamas in Gaza and the West Bank, and the rise of the Taliban in Afghanistan.

All these developments placed substantial areas under Islamist control and influence with dire consequences for women. As one Egyptian man lamented, "My grandmother would not recognize the streets of Cairo and Port Said. The women are covered from head to toe; the mosques blare hatred all day long."[35]

The Taliban, for example, flogged women on the street if their burqas showed too much ankle while Islamist vigilantes poured acid on the faces of Afghan and Pakistani schoolgirls who were not sufficiency covered.[36] As an Afghan woman noted, "For nearly two decades, we wore no chadors and dressed in modern ways. As the war against the Soviet occupation intensified, women were again forced to wear chadors. Now, even under an American occupation, they are again fully covered."[37]

In Algeria, a leading Islamist group proclaimed that all unveiled women are military targets and, in 1994, gunned down a 17-year-old unveiled girl.[38] In 2010 in Chechnya, roving vigilante bands of men harassed and threatened women for not wearing headscarves. They punched women and taunted them with automatic rifles and paintballs. The vigilante groups have the backing of Chechnyan president Ramzan Kadyrov's government, which also encourages polygamy.[39]

In 1983, four years after the Iranian revolution and the establishment of the Islamic Republic, Ayatollah Ruhollah Khomeini instituted a ban on women showing their hair and the shape of their bodies. The chador, which does not cover the face, is, nevertheless, a severe, dark, heavy, and shapeless garment that has demoralized and enraged what was an essentially Westernized and modern upper and middle class.[40]

35 Author interview, New York, 2008.

36 "Women's Lives under the Taliban: A Background Report," National Organization of Women, Washington, D.C., accessed Aug. 25, 2010; *The Daily Telegraph*, Nov. 12, 2008.

37 Author interview, New York, 2005.

38 "Equality Now Submission to the UN Human Rights Committee: Algeria," United Nations, New York, July 1998.

39 Reuters, Aug. 21, 2010.

40 See, for example, Roya Hakakian, *Journey from the Land of No* (New York: Crown

Thereafter, the Iranian government beat, arrested, and jailed women if they were improperly garbed and has recently warned that suntanned women and girls who looked like "walking mannequins" will be arrested as part of a new drive to enforce the Islamic dress code.[41]

Saudi Arabia does not have to resort to such violence. No Saudi woman dares appear naked-faced in public. In 2002, when teenage Saudi schoolgirls tried to escape from a burning school without their headscarves and abayas (black robes), the Mutawa, or religious police, beat them back. Fifteen girls were burned alive.[42] According to Tunisian-French feminist Samia Labidi, an increasing number of Islamist husbands force or pressure their wives—whose own mothers went about with uncovered faces—to cover.[43] Then, they pressure their new sisters-in-law to do likewise. In the West, some families have honor-killed their daughters for refusing to wear hijab.[44]

A man from Istanbul remembered that his grandmother had fully veiled but not his mother. But, he explained, "It is mainly peer pressure that makes things happen in Turkey. Neighbors tell you to go to mosque; they watch how young girls and women look and behave very closely. The pressure to conform is tremendous."[45]

Westerners do not understand how pervasive such pressure can be. On July 17, 2010, for example, the newspaper *Roz Al-Yousuf* addressed the coercive nature of hijab in Egypt. Wael Lutfi, assistant chief editor writes in the first person feminine:

> Society persecutes women who do not wear a hijab. Of course, I wear a hijab. If I want to be practical and interact with this society while [sustaining] minimal damage, I must wear a hijab. A woman who does not wear a hijab is guilty until proven [innocent]. Why should I waste my time proving that I am a respectable and educated girl?

Lutfi tells "Suha's" story. She comes from a prominent Egyptian family and does not wear a hijab. At work, she is cajoled and harassed

---

Publishers, 2004); Azar Nafisi, *Reading Lolita in Tehran* (New York: Random House, 2003).

41 Associated Press, Apr. 23, 2007; *The Daily Telegraph*, Apr. 27, 2010.

42 *BBC News,* Mar. 15, 2002.

43 Labidi, "Faces of Janus," pp. 117-8. In Baran, *The Other Muslims.*

44 Chesler, "Worldwide Trends in Honor Killings."

45 Author interview, New York, 2010.

by hijab-wearing women who bombard her in person and via e-mail; they give her pro-hijab audio cassettes and invite her to hear a popular preacher whom hijab-wearers follow. Suha loses one marriage proposal after another when she refuses to promise that she will wear the hijab and stop working after marriage. Finally, Suha's married male boss questions her closely, agrees with her anti-hijab position—and then asks her to secretly become his common law wife. He views her as a prostitute because she is not wearing the hijab.

Likewise, Walaa was verbally insulted and her brothers were assaulted by neighborhood boys because she was not wearing a hijab. Now, she dons one when she leaves home, removes it elsewhere, returns home wearing it again. Another young girl wears the hijab because her father has asked her to do so and because her beloved younger brother said that his friends were judging him harshly because she did not do so. She says:

> I wear a hijab because we live in a society that allows the preacher Safwat Hijazi to call women who do not wear a hijab 'prostitutes,' and I do not want to be called a prostitute.[46]

Thus, one can hardly view the covering of one's face as a free choice but rather as a forced choice. One must also realize that non-veiled women, including non-Muslims, who do not veil are then seen by Islamists as "fair game" or "uncovered meat that draws predators," to use the words of a prominent Australian sheikh.[47]

A forced choice is not really a choice at all. One either submits or is punished, shunned, exiled, jailed, even killed. A free choice means that one has many options and freely chooses one of two or one of ten such options.

To be sure, many religious women dress modestly, not "provocatively," because they view this as a religious virtue. Yet only Muslims engage in full face covering to satisfy the demand for modesty.

Many children who are brought up within fundamentalist religions or in cults are trained, by a system of reward and punishment, to obey their parents, teachers, and religious leaders. As adults, if they wish to remain within the community (and the opportunity for leaving did not and still does not exist for most Muslim women), they must

---

46 "Egyptian Newspaper *Roz Al-Yousuf* Criticizes Phenomenon of Compelling Egyptian Women to Wear a Hijab," The Middle East Media Research Institute, Sept. 6, 2010.
47 *The Times* (London), Oct. 28, 2006.

continue to conform to its norms. Most are already socialized to do so and thus, some Muslim women will say that they do not feel that anyone is forcing them to "cover;" they will, in a private conversation, denounce the face veil, the burqa, the chador, and the Saudi abaya.

In the West, young Muslim women may feel they are responding to allegedly racist "Islamophobia" by donning the headscarf or the face veil as a revolutionary act,[48] one in solidarity with Islamists whom they may fear, wish to please, or marry.

EUROPE DEBATES THE VEIL

The Islamist resurgence throughout the Middle East and the Muslim world has triggered a mass migration to the West; Muslim and ex-Muslim dissidents and feminists as well as Christians have exited Muslim lands.[49] Still, it has taken Westerners decades to understand that the battle for Muslim women's freedom as well as for Western Enlightenment values also has to be fought in the West.

Thus, in 2004, France became the first European country to legally restrict Islamic dress by passing an ethnicity-neutral law that forbade the wearing of religious clothing in public schools. Veils, visible Christian crosses, Jewish skullcaps, and the hijab were all forbidden. Also in 2004, eight of Germany's sixteen states enacted restrictions on wearing hair-covering veils, particularly in public schools.[50] Since then, many European governments have debated whether or not to ban the face veil.

In February 2010, the French government refused to grant citizenship to a Moroccan man who forced his wife to wear a burqa;[51] later that year, three women engaged in a physical fight after a burqa-clad woman supposedly overheard another woman making snide remarks about her choice of dress.[52] In Norway, adult neighbors and their children came to blows over the question of whether Muslim women should wear the headscarf,[53] and in March 2010, a ban on the burqa in public places was

48 *Los Angeles Times*, Jan. 12, 2005; *Al-Jazeera* TV (Doha), Sept. 17, 2008.

49 See, for example, *CBN News*, Oct. 15, 2009; David Raab, "The Beleaguered Christians of the Palestinian-Controlled Areas," *Jerusalem Letter/Viewpoints*, Jerusalem Center for Public Affairs, Jan. 1-15, 2003.

50 "Discrimination in the Name of Neutrality," Human Rights Watch, New York, Feb. 26, 2009.

51 *The Guardian* (London), Feb. 2, 2010.

52 *The Daily Telegraph*, May 18, 2010.

53 *Islam in Europe Blog*, Aug. 4, 2010.

proposed although defeated in the Norwegian parliament.[54] On April, 29, 2010, the lower house of the Belgian parliament approved a bill banning the burqa and imposing a fine or jail time on violators;[55] three months later, Spanish lawmakers debated banning the burqa in public although they ultimately decided against it.[56] In August 2010, Sweden's education minister announced his intention to make it easier for Swedish schools to ban the burqa.[57] In July 2010, by a majority of 336 to 1, the lower house of the French parliament approved a religion-neutral government bill that bans face-covering in public, and the bill was approved by the French senate on September 14.

While these bills await ratification, local European officials have already taken concrete steps against the burqa. Since January 2010, the Netherlands has limited the wearing of burqas in public spaces.[58] In May 2010, a local council in north Switzerland voted to introduce an initiative to ban the burqa in public places while, in 2005, the Belgian town of Maaseik passed a law mandating a fine for anyone wearing a face veil.[59] In April 2010, a French woman was fined for wearing a burqa while driving,[60] and in the same month, a girl wearing hijab was sent home from her school in Madrid.[61]

Britain, by contrast, has conspicuously refused to consider banning the burqa. There has, of course, been the odd case when a radical Islamist has been taken to task for unlawful insistence on the Muslim dress code, such as the Manchester dentist who refused to treat Muslim patients unless they wore traditional Islamic dress,[62] but efforts at a ban have gone nowhere in parliament.

In response to the French parliamentary vote of July 2010, Britain's immigration minister, Damian Green, stated that "forbidding women in the U.K. from wearing certain clothing would be 'rather un-British'" and would run contrary to the conventions of a "tolerant and mutually

54 The Foreigner (Raege, Norway), May 28, 2010.

55 BBC News, Apr. 30, 2010.

56 Associated Press, July 20, 2010.

57 The Swedish Wire, Aug. 5, 2010.

58 Benjamin Ismail, "Ban the Burqa? France Votes Yes," Middle East Quarterly, Fall 2010, pp. 47-55.

59 Associated Press, May 6, 2010; "Brussels Burqa Ban Backfires When City Ends up Paying Fines for Muslim Women on Welfare," Militant Islam Monitor, Aug. 26, 2005.

60 The Daily Telegraph, June 3, 2010.

61 Ibid., Apr. 16, 2010.

62 The Daily Mail (London), July 2, 2009.

respectful society."[63] The following month, Baroness Sayeeda Warsi, the first Muslim cabinet minister in the U.K., defended the right of women to choose whether or not to wear the burqa, claiming, "Just because a woman wears the burqa, it doesn't mean she can't engage in everyday life."[64]

Many non-Muslim, Western, female politicians have been cowed by doctrines of political correctness, cultural relativism, misguided beliefs about religious tolerance, and by the fear that if they oppose the burqa, they will be condemned as "Islamophobes" or racists. Ignorance about Muslim jurists' rulings that the full-face covering is not religiously mandated and about the history of the Islamic veil in Muslim lands has led to a curious Western and feminist abandonment of universal human values as they bear on the Islamic veil.

Ironically, powerful Western women, while claiming to represent an anti-colonialist or post-colonialist point of view, are reminiscent of Victorian-era and early twentieth century British colonial administrators who believed that the needs of empire would not be well served by interfering with local customs. This British position was very different from the position of American, Christian missionary women who tried to help, teach, and sometimes save Muslim women from tragedy.[65]

Thus, both U.S. Speaker of the House Nancy Pelosi and Secretary of State Hillary Clinton have donned the hijab when visiting Arab and Muslim countries whereas Arab and Muslim female dignitaries and spouses do not necessarily or always remove the hijab or the niqab while visiting the West. On July 18, 2010, British Minister Caroline Spelman, the environment secretary and second most powerful woman in the cabinet, described the burqa as "empowering." She said, "I don't, living in this country as a woman, want to be told what I can and can't wear. One of the things we pride ourselves on ... is being free to choose what you wear ... so banning the burqa is absolutely contrary to what this country is about."[66]

On July 2, 2009, as Muslims demonstrated in Antwerp to oppose the banning of headscarves in two schools[67]—then-Swedish head of the European Union, Justice Minister Beatrice Ask, stated that the "twen-

63 *ABC News*, Australian Broadcasting Corporation, July 19, 2010.
64 *The Guardian*, Aug. 1, 2010.
65 Penelope Tuson, *Playing the Game: The Story of Western Women in Arabia* (London and New York: I.B. Tauris, 2003), pp. 149-50.
66 *The Daily Telegraph*, July 18, 2010.
67 *Islam in Europe Blog*, July 2, 2009.

ty-seven-member European Union must not dictate an Islamic dress code ... the European Union is a union of freedom."[68]

THE GROUNDS FOR A BURQA BAN

There are a multitude of specific problems associated with the burqa and niqab. Full-body and face-covering attire hides the wearer's identity and gender. In October 1937, Hajj Amin Husseini, mufti of Jerusalem and Adolf Hitler's future ally, fled Palestine donning a niqab as did one of the July 2005 London bombers.[69] From a security point of view, face and body covering can facilitate various acts of violence and lawlessness from petty crime to terrorism. This danger, which has been highlighted by a number of experts, notably Daniel Pipes,[70] has been taken very seriously by some Muslim authorities, who have banned the burqa on precisely these grounds.

In Bangladesh, the largest state-run hospital banned staff from wearing full-face burqas after an increase in thefts of mobile phones and wallets from hospital wards.[71] In a number of Egyptian universities, women were barred from covering their faces during midterm exams and were prohibited from wearing niqabs in female dormitories after it transpired that men had snuck in disguised as women.[72] Abu Dhabi, meanwhile, has banned the niqab in all public offices to fight "unrestricted absenteeism."[73]

There are also numerous cases of bans for security. In Kuwait, for example, female drivers are barred from wearing niqab for "security reasons." The regulation came into effect about ten years ago when the authorities were pursuing sleeper terrorist cells and feared that individual cell members could use the niqab to slip through checkpoints unnoticed.[74] Saudi Arabia's antiterrorism forces have begun a battle against the niqab after discovering that many "Islamic terrorists have used it to hide in order to commit terror attacks."[75] These concerns are not diffi-

---

68 *The Jerusalem Post*, June 30, 2009.
69 *BBC News*, Feb. 20, 2007.
70 Daniel Pipes, "Niqabs and Burqas as Security Threats," *Lion's Den: Daniel Pipes Blog*, Nov. 4, 2006.
71 *The Daily Times* (Lahore), Mar. 23, 2010.
72 *The Daily News* Egypt (Giza), June 7, July 27, 2010.
73 Colombo, "Europe: Behind the Burqa Debate."
74 *Kuwait Times* (Kuwait City), Oct. 9, 2009.
75 Colombo, "Europe: Behind the Burqa Debate."

cult to understand given the widespread use of the burqa and niqab for weapons smuggling and terror attacks, including suicide bombings in Iraq, Afghanistan, and the disputed West Bank territories, among other places.[76]

Beyond these abiding security considerations are equally compelling humanitarian considerations. André Gerin, a French parliamentarian, has described the burqa as a "moving prison."[77] This is an apt definition: In a burqa, the wearer has no peripheral and only limited forward vision; hearing and speech are muffled; facial expressions remain hidden; movement is severely constrained. Often, no eye contact is possible; niqab wearers sometimes wear dark glasses, so that their eyes cannot be seen.

A burqa wearer may feel that she cannot breathe, that she might slowly be suffocating. She may feel buried alive and may become anxious or claustrophobic.[78] Just imagine the consequences of getting used to this as a way of life. But perhaps one never gets used to it. Many Saudi and Afghan women toss their coverings the moment they leave the country or enter their own courtyards.[79] For example, an unnamed Saudi princess describes her experience of the Saudi abaya as follows:

When we walked out of the cool souq area into the blazing hot sun, I gasped for breath and sucked furiously through the sheer black fabric. The air tasted stale and dry as it filtered through the thin gauzy cloth. I had purchased the sheerest veil available, yet I felt I was seeing life through a thick screen. How could women see through veils made of a thicker fabric? The sky was no longer blue, the glow of the sun had dimmed; my heart plunged to my stomach when I realized that from that moment, outside my own home I would not experience life as it really is in all its color. The world suddenly seemed a dull place. And dangerous, too! I groped and stumbled along the pitted, cracked sidewalk, fearful of breaking an ankle or leg.[80]

76 Pipes, "Niqabs and Burqas as Security Threats."

77 *The Daily Telegraph*, June 22, 2009.

78 See, for example, Reuters, July 7, 2009.

79 Edward Hunter, *The Past Present: A Year in Afghanistan* (London: Hodder and Stoughton, 1959), chap. 4, 5.

80 Jean Sasson, *Princess: A True Story of Life behind the Veil in Saudi Arabia* (Georgia: Windsor-Brooke Books, 2010), pp. 94-5.

The burqa is harmful not only to the wearer but to others as well. The sight of women in burqas can be demoralizing and frightening to Westerners of all faiths, including Muslims, not to mention secularists. Their presence visually signals the subordination of women. Additionally, the social isolation intrinsically imposed by the burqa may also be further magnified by the awkward responses of Westerners. Several Ivy League college students mentioned that classmates in burqas and dark, thick gloves make them feel "very sad," "pushed away," "uneasy about talking to them." "When one woman is asked to read aloud, she does so but her heavy gloves make turning the pages slow and difficult." The students feel sorry for her and do not know how to relate to her.[81]

A burqa wearer, who can be as young as ten years old, is being conditioned to endure isolation and sensory deprivation. Her five senses are blocked, muted. Sensory deprivation and isolation are considered forms of torture and are used to break prisoners. Such abuse can lead to low self-esteem, generalized fearfulness, dependence, suggestibility, depression, anxiety, rage, aggression toward other women and female children, or to a complete psychological breakdown.

Wearing the burqa is also hazardous to the health in other ways. Lifetime burqa wearers may suffer eye damage and may be prone to a host of diseases that are also related to vitamin D deficiency due to sunlight deprivation, including osteoporosis, heart disease, hypertension, autoimmune diseases, certain cancers, depression, chronic fatigue, and chronic pain. It is ironic that women in the Middle East, one of the world's sunniest regions, have been found in need of high levels of vitamin D supplementation owing to their total covering.[82]

CONCLUSION

The same Islamists who subordinate women also publicly whip, cross-amputate, hang, stone, and behead human beings. Iran continues to execute women and men by stoning for adultery.[83] The burqa reminds us of such practices. Many Westerners, including Muslims, ex-Muslims, and Christians, Jews, and Hindus who have fled Muslim lands, may feel haunted or followed when they see burqas on Western streets. Does their presence herald the arrival of Islamist supremacism?

---

81 Author interview, New York, 2009.

82 Reuters, June 25, 2007.

83 *The Christian Science Monitor*, Aug. 13, 2010; "Iran: End Executions by Stoning," Amnesty International, Jan. 15, 2008.

Many Muslim governments know something that their Western counterparts are just learning. Covered women signify Islamist designs on state power and control of political, military, social, personal, and family life. Were these designs to be extended to the West, it will spell out the end of modernity, human rights, and the separation of state and religion, among other things; in short, the end of liberal democracy and freedoms as they are now practiced.

Apart from being an Islamist act of assertion that involves clear security dangers and creates mental and physical health hazards, the burqa is a flagrant violation of women's most basic human rights. However, were the government to attempt to ban the burqa in the United States, a team of constitutional legal scholars would have to decide whether to follow the French ethnicity- and religion-neutral approach of no "face coverings," "face masks," etc., or whether to ban outright the public disappearance of women's faces and their subordination in the name of Islam as a violation of their civil rights.

It is impossible for Western governments and international organizations to prevent the acid attacks or honor killings of women in Muslim countries who refuse to cover their faces, but why tie society's hands on Western soil? Why would Western countries prize the subordination of women and protect it as a religious right since historically, many Muslim states historically refused to do so? When it is understood that the burqa is not a religious requirement but rather a political statement—at best merely an ethnic and misogynistic custom—there is no reason whatsoever for Western traditions of religious tolerance to misconstrue the covering of women as a religious duty.

Middle East Quarterly
12/11/10

Section Five:
Muslim-on-Muslim Violence Against Women

- 73 -

A (Merely) Virtual Revolution in Saudi Arabia

Today, there are protests in the streets of Iran, Egypt (again), Bahrain, Yemen, and Algeria. In the last few weeks, there were also street uprisings in Tunisia and Jordan. Iranian riot police are tear-gassing their own people in Tehran, Isfahan, and Shiraz. Egyptians are now demanding that Mubarak's military give them jobs and money.

As I've noted before, the Egyptian women protestors in Cairo were wearing severe hijab; some were wearing face veils. Men and women carried signs against Israel and America. But I saw no signs demanding women's rights.

Thus, the real Arab and Muslim "revolution" is a virtual one—online. One such campaign was recently launched by Saudi Arabian women. The site is mainly in Arabic with some English.

I wrote about this new website yesterday, mainly to applaud the bravery of these women who know full well what can happen to them for demanding their rights. My understanding is that while the site is based outside of Saudi Arabia and the Saudi authorities cannot take it down, they can punish some of the individuals associated with it.

May this not happen.

The comments at this site in Arabic are practical and specific. One woman wants the Saudi King to:

> Drop the requirement that women older than 18 be accompanied by a guardian; open up more jobs and specialties to women; ban child marriage; pay attention to abused wives, grant citizenship to the children of Saudi women, grant women the right to drive.

269

She suggests that "We need to publicize the issue; the more the word spreads the more powerful we'll become."

One comment, in English: "Girls, after Egypt and Tunisia we can demand our rights."

Another comment, also in English: "We all should take an action and stop being treated as slaves. My son was murdered because his father abused him so badly...I will fight to death for my son's right and all the abused children in my country Saudi Arabia. Where is the Saudi Human Rights? Why there is no justice in Saudi? Where does our money go?"

A third woman comments, in English: "AUTONOMY over our own lives is key. The right to gain access to financial and medical services without having to attain permission first."

Another woman also in Arabic wants the King to: "Proclaim that wearing an abaya should be a matter of choice and not a matter of law."

Another woman, in Arabic, calls for "prison time, fines, and public shaming for those who are proven guilty of harassing women." She also wants women to be "granted the right to be members of the King's Consultative Assembly. "

The site's slogans include: 1) "We are demanding the rights granted to us by Islam"; 2) "In the era of the Prophet women straddled horses and participated in wars"; 3) "Yes to granting my rights in accordance with the Islamic Sharia"; 4) and "We insist that our rights be granted but not that they be forced on anyone...Whoever says 'We're OK, we don't need [these rights], we're honored queens, etc.'...[to each her own, just] don't get in the way of [our] legitimate interests."

In other words: I don't want to force my mother to unveil against her will or to drive by herself if this is not her desire.

I understand that it may be absolutely essential to couch such western-sounding demands in Islamic terms. Perhaps, that is the only way that Muslim women in the Kingdom will be able to achieve some kind of reform without being placed under permanent house arrest, divorced against their will, or beheaded in the public square.

Women's rights—as the Saudi Facebook site has enunciated them—have only been gained, worldwide, by using existing secular laws to argue for such rights. Many have viewed religion as one of the chief enforcers of gender oppression. However, there is no concept of secular law in the Kingdom and in many other Muslim-majority countries. Separation of religion and state is a uniquely Western concept.

Asra Q. Nomani, a religious Muslim-American woman who was

born in India, did try to achieve gender dignity and some gender parity in the mosque founded by her own father in West Virginia, but the combination of increasing jihadic-era, Arab male immigrant misogyny coupled with aggressive female submission to such authority made her task impossible. She wrote a very moving book: *Standing Alone in Mecca: An American Woman's Struggle for the Soul of Islam.* She was also featured in a documentary about her struggle.

Nomani also organized a first-ever woman-led and women-only Islamic prayer service. It was led by Dr. Amina Wadud in NYC—but not in a mosque. No mosque would have them, nor would an art gallery which backed out due to a bomb threat. The prayer service was held in a church and filled with media. The worshippers were moved, perhaps even transformed—but the service was still condemned.

I hope and pray that the Saudi women who are behind this website study the attempts of Muslim feminists, both religious and anti-religious, to bring about women's rights. And I hope they draw clear conclusions, canny battle plans, and demonstrate the patience for which their people are well known.

This is a 500 year struggle. Unless, of course, the internet can speed matters up.

NewsRealBlog
2/14/11

What Every Good Cultural Relativist Knows About the 1,000-Man Gang Assault on CBS Correspondent Lara Logan in Cairo

O n February 11th, CBS foreign correspondent, Lara Logan, was publicly gang-raped and beaten for 20-30 minutes by Egyptian men in Tahrir Square who, all the while, cursed her as a "Jew." CBS only revealed this four days later. Writing at the London *Guardian*, blogger Amanda Marcotte chose not to focus on this act of jihadic barbarism because she did not want anyone to draw negative conclusions about Islam, Muslims, Egyptians, or about the so-called Egyptian pro-democracy "revolution." Instead, like many other commentators, Marcotte bemoaned the fact that "rightwingers" might now draw some politically incorrect conclusions. Marcotte writes:

"In this case, rightwingers who have an interest in stoking fear and loathing of Muslims worldwide pounced at the opportunity to smear all Egyptians with this crime."

She dismisses the possibility that any "rightwingers" might have a genuine concern for the victim and condemns them all for using Logan's public gang-rape and beating for "political score-keeping." After all, every good multicultural relativist knows that all cultures, all countries, all religions are equal and therefore are pretty much the same—except for Western cultures which are somehow worse.

Thus, while Marcotte admits that Egypt is well known for its sexual harassment of women, she insists that women in the West, especially in the United States, also endure sexual harassment on the streets.

Marcotte cites one study that shows that "up to 100% of women in the United States are sexually harassed" on the streets and claims that at similarly "jubilant" times, such as fraternity parties on the American college campus, women are also "sexually assaulted."

I doubt that fraternity gang-rapists curse their victims as "Jews." But forgive me: I am about to accuse Islam and Egypt of having an anti-Jewish bias. I also doubt that boozed up American fraternity gang-rapists claim that they are overthrowing a dictator and taking power for the people.

In any event, according to Marcotte, "rightwingers" are also delighted to focus on the vulnerability of female journalists because "rightwingers" want to keep women pregnant and barefoot and out of the job market, certainly far away from war zones.

Well, at least they don't want them to wear burqas. Again, forgive me: I am suggesting that burqas are not a sign of freedom but that burqas and face veils do, increasingly, characterize Islamic gender apartheid today; and that they were all over Tahrir Square.

Ultimately, Marcotte believes that the real assault on Logan is a "rightwing" assault on all women who have ambitions, or who are willing to be out in public while looking attractive. "This response to Logan's attack should make it clear that the US and Egypt differ on the issue of sexual violence perhaps only in degree but not in kind."

On the same day, February 17, 2011, in *The Huffington Post*, Asra Nomani, the co-director of the (Daniel) Pearl Project at Georgetown University, also writes about what happened to Logan.

Nomani, whose work I have quoted several times, reminds us that serious "sexual harassment" of women, including female journalists, goes on in (Hindu) India and (Muslim) Pakistan; and of course, the gang-raping of women has become a "weapon of war" in (non-Muslim) Congo. The words in parentheses are all mine.

Nomani runs a program which trains students to become foreign correspondents. Correctly, she asks whether "uncontrolled environments" like Tahrir Square are safe for journalists and whether what happened to Logan will cause media bigwigs to "man up" and stop sending female journalists into the line of fire. She cautions against this—and then excoriates the so-called "victim blaming" involved in how the Logan Affair is being covered in the media.

Disgustingly, predictably, certain commentators focused on Logan's previous work as a model, her striking good looks, the fact that she was a naked-faced blond infidel, and that she had, perhaps unwisely, decided to return to Cairo despite the fact that the Egyptian police had intimidated and interrogated her the previous week. And then there were Nir Rosen's infamously callous remarks on Twitter. Well, Rosen is a passionate anti-Zionist and pro-Palestinian and was probably pissed at Logan—not at her attackers—because now the Beautiful People might stop to consider that perhaps (some) Muslims, (hard-line) Islam, (some) Egyptians, and the Muslim Brotherhood might be potentially danger-ous, rather than touchy-feely friendly entities.

By the way, the otherwise estimable Nomani does not once use the word "Islam," "radical Islam," "jihad," or the "Muslim Brotherhood" in her entire piece at *The Huffington Post*. In writing about her beheaded friend and colleague, Daniel Pearl, she only refers to those who lured, tortured, and murdered him as "militants." Nomani's opening paragraph declares that Logan was "saved by a group of women and an estimated 20 Egyptian soldiers." Her piece leads off with the actions of the good Egyptians. That kind, brave group of women has been puzzling me for days now. Did women actually take the men on? I doubt it. The best sce-nario I can come up with is this: A group of Egyptian women—but not a group of Egyptian men—went and got the police.

By February 20, 2011, the *New York Times* took it a step further; they always do. Kim Barker writes that being publicly and repeatedly gang-raped and cursed as a "Jew" was not Logan's "fault. It was the mob's fault. This attack also had nothing to do with Islam. Sexual violence has always been a tool of war. Female reporters sometimes are just conve-nient."

No, rape was "not always a tool of war." It was once a spoil of war and only towards the late twentieth century did it become a systematic weapon of war. Think Bosnia. Think Rwanda. Think Congo. Above all, think Darfur. I have called this "gender cleansing."

Barker also points out that male journalists have been beaten and sodomized too. Finally, she argues, correctly, that female journalists can do something that male journalists cannot do: interview "abused wom-en" in Afghanistan, India, and Congo; report on what life is like, not just what war is like, for women.

On the same day, also in the *New York Times*, another journalist, Sabrina Tavernise, tells us that she was never raped in (Muslim) Leba-non, (Muslim) Gaza, (Muslim) Pakistan, (Muslim) Turkey, and (Chris-tian and Muslim) Russia. She had some tricky moments in (Muslim) Iraq but guess what? Tavernise insists that: "In my experience, Muslim countries were not the worst places for sexual harassment. My closest calls came in Georgia with soldiers from Russia." Gori presented the greatest danger for her.

Is it possible that Tavernise has absolutely no idea that Arab Muslims invaded Gori, Georgia in 645AD and were firmly established there by 735AD? True, the Muslim population of Gori is now about 10% of all people. I have no idea who exactly menaced Tavernise but she might have considered adding a little political and religious context to her piece.

On February 20, 2011, journalist Angella Johnson at the *Daily Mail* revealed that she, too, had been groped, leered at, fondled, and man-handled as she covered Tahrir Square. Johnson is not white, nor is she a blonde. But she is a naked-faced foreign journalist, not a doormat, and obviously an infidel as well. Provocation enough. A message is being sent: Leave Muslim territory. If you don't, we will rape your women, sodomize your men, beat you, and murder you to boot.

In America, women do get raped and gang-raped. I delivered the first keynote speech on the subject of rape at the first-ever feminist conference on rape in 1971 in New York City. I have been studying and lecturing on this subject for 40 years. Intimate partner rape is far more common than stranger rape. Rapists "practice" on their own women first—then strike out at women who belong to other races, religions, classes. There is black-on-black rape, white-on-white rape, black on white rape, and white on black rape. The rapists are all men.

No, not all men are rapists nor are all Muslims terrorists; however, all rapists are men, and most terrorists today are Muslims. We must draw some conclusions here.

In America, rape victims are not chosen because they are "infidels," nor are they forcibly converted to their rapists' religion. That only happens in Muslim countries. When one says this, one is immediately accused of "racism" and of inflaming "Islamophobic" sentiment.

I suggest that Marcotte, Nomani, Barker, and Tavernise all read what Ayaan Hirsi Ali wrote in the *Wall Street Journal* on February 18, 2011 about the Muslim Brotherhood. She begins with the credo of the Muslim Brotherhood. "Allah is our objective; the Prophet is our leader; the Quran is our law; Jihad is our way; dying in the way of Allah is our highest hope." She concludes that "the most remarkable thing of all is the way the Brotherhood's motto seduces Western liberals."

While my heart is with the powerless, unorganized secular human rights activists in Tahrir Square and with their counterparts, especially in Iran, my fear is that the Muslim Brotherhood, Islamic Jihad, al-Qaeda, Hezbollah, Hamas, etc. will simply capitalize on the chaos and gladly use the vote to get elected.

Remember: Hitler was freely elected by the German people as was Hamas in Gaza.

UPDATE: According to today's *Daily Mail*, (February 21, 2011), Logan was also whipped and beaten with flag poles and repeatedly bitten in "sensitive" places on her body. She required five days in an American hospital. Of course, the psychological trauma is more serious than the physical injuries. It always is in cases of simple rape. Public gang-rape by hundreds of men who are beating and whipping you as they curse you both as a "Jew" and as an "Israeli"—and when you believe that you are about to die, goes far beyond the usual complex psychological trauma.

NewsRealBlog
2/21/11

- 75 -
A War Crime in Cairo—Censored for Days

S omething is very wrong with the mainstream American media. By now, we all know that CBS did not find it newsworthy that, on February 11, 2011, their own chief foreign correspondent had been gang-raped by a mob of men on the Muslim "Sabbath"—on the very day that President Mubarak stepped down. Instead, they spent four days continuing to celebrate the freedom fighters in Tahrir Square.

Only after CBS finally broke this story did other American media networks come forward with news of their own: Apparently, CNN's Anderson Cooper had also been beaten up by the brave pro-democracy freedom fighters, or by their Muslim Brotherhood opponents, in Tahrir Square and ABC's Brian Hartman had been threatened with beheading in that same allegedly pro-democracy uprising. Even Christiane Amanpour had to be hustled away to safety by her handlers.

Clearly, the American media is so invested in its own political "narrative"—Muslims are a peace-loving people, Americans are brutal invaders and occupiers, Palestinians are the innocent injured parties, Israelis are the brutal aggressors—that they are willing to blindly sacrifice themselves and their staffs to cover events in the Arab, Muslim, and Islamist world.

Before I discuss the war crime committed against Lara Logan—a war crime very similar to those that have been committed against black girls and women by ethnic Arab Muslims in Darfur, and by Hindus in India against women, all women—I want to pose some harsh questions.

Why did Daniel Pearl (may he rest in peace) think that the kind of Islamists whom *Al-Jazeera* had normalized, even glamorized, would not kidnap and behead him? In 2002, why did Pearl, and for that matter,

Nicholas Berg (may he also rest in peace), the young American entrepreneur who was also beheaded in Iraq in 2004, believe that they could "follow the yellow brick road" to The Story or to The Fortune—without becoming the story themselves? Why did they believe that American Jews could safely travel to Islamist war-zones in the 21st century? Why did three American hikers in Iraq and Iran (Shane Bauer, Josh Fattal, and Sarah Shourd) believe that, post-9/11, indeed, in 2010, that central Asia was a beautiful backpacking kinda place? Bauer and Fattal remain imprisoned by the Islamic Republic of Iran, which has accused them of "espionage." Shourd was released but only after fourteen months.

Here is what I am saying. Infidels (non-Muslims) and women (both Muslims and infidels) are treated this way, both now and historically. For example: In 2001, egged on by their imam, and also on the Muslim "Sabbath," hundreds of men in Hassi Messaoud, Algeria physically and sexually attacked (raped, gang-raped) any woman they could find. They also cut off breasts and genitalia; buried some women alive; murdered some. What crime had these women committed? According to the imam, they had been bussed in to work as cleaning women for a foreign company and thus were seen as both whores and traitors.

Lara Logan also worked for a foreign company. She was a blonde infidel and a woman.

But let's return to Cairo. In the fall of 2006, (at the end of Ramadan), perhaps a thousand men conducted a "sexual wilding." They surrounded individual girls and women who were fully veiled, partly veiled, and unveiled, and "groped and assaulted" them. (They probably raped and gang-raped them too but the media was too…polite to say so.) Individuals tried to help these women—who escaped from the male crowds naked and half-naked. The police refused to make any arrests and the Egyptian media did not cover it. I and others only learned of this incident because some foreign journalists blogged about it—and because one brave Egyptian woman spoke about it on a live Egyptian television program.

Journalists are incredibly endangered in the Islamic world. There were more than 140 incidents of journalists being physically attacked in Egypt alone during the so-called 18-day "revolution" in Cairo. Western human rights workers have been kidnapped, held for ransom, tortured, and murdered in Iraq and Afghanistan.

As I suggested previously, the Egyptians in Tahrir Square are not pro-western, pro-modern, pro-democracy, pro-human rights activists; they are Islamist revolutionaries or, if you will, Islamists who wish to "reform" the secular state. The few women in the Square are wearing serious hijab and face-veils.

None other than Egyptian Yusuf Al-Qaradawi, a profoundly and classically anti-Semitic preacher who has an audience of 40 million viewers on *Al-Jazeera*, preached today in the Square to hundreds of thousands people. Yes, he actually says things like: "Oh Allah, take the Jews, the treacherous aggressors. Oh Allah, take this profligate, cunning, arrogant band of people. Oh Allah, they have spread much tyranny and corruption in the land. Pour Your wrath upon them, oh our God." He also approves of female genital mutilation and "light" beating of women. Actually, he is a...moderate. He is also a long time member of the Muslim Brotherhood and has twice turned down offers to be its leader.

According to a number of journalists and scholars who have been covering the Logan atrocity, the jeering, leering, Egyptian gang-rapists kept cursing her as a "Jew." Then again, this crowd also called Mubarak a "Zionist" and had stars of David/Jewish stars scrawled over his face on countless placards.

President Obama has demanded that the Egyptian police hunt down the gang-rapists. This is a laughable request. It will either lead to nothing—or the Muslim Brotherhood will use his demand as the excuse to murder two hundred of their political opponents—the truly secular pro-individual rights activists—and then say that they were the attackers.

President Obama: If you want to do the right thing, bring the Muslim Brotherhood and the interim military government of Egypt to the International Criminal Court in Holland. Outlaw their various organizations and supporters who are right here in America.

Organized feminist groups: Bring some international lawsuits on behalf of Logan, demonstrate outside the Egyptian Embassies, revise your views of how both Muslim and infidel women are viewed and treated in the Islamic world. This barbarism is endemic to the culture, the region, and the religion, it is not caused by American or Israeli wars of "aggression." By the way, the National Organization for Women's website does not mention Logan's gang rape. While they do discuss violence against women, and oppose female genital mutilation, their focus remains largely on abortion, employment, and lesbian rights.

I am not saying that journalists should flee the field. I am not denigrating their choice to bring us the news at considerable danger to themselves. I am suggesting that they start to think realistically, clearly. One does not venture into Islamist mobs without a full platoon of Marines by your side to protect each and every journalist.

And I worry: Who will protect the Marines?

By the way: Many Islamist (and uneducated, illiterate, religious) Muslims view raped women as adulterers who should be stoned to death; or as prostitutes who should be flogged, often unto death. In 2008, a 13 year old girl in Somalia was raped by three men and then stoned to death by a crowd of 1000. In 2011, in Bangladesh a 14-year-old girl was raped by her cousin, then sentenced to 100 lashes. She died after receiving 60 lashes.

FrontPage Magazine
2/21/11

- 76 -
We Are All Lara Logan

Thank you, Amanda Marcotte!

You have given me an opportunity to tear my hair out—yet again; indeed, you have actually driven me to "tweet" in response to your tweet.

I never tweet. You have dragged me, kicking and screaming, into the future.

Ah, Marcotte: You are too thin-skinned. Just because I've criticized your piece in the London *Guardian* about the Lara Logan tragedy does not mean that you have to insult the critic—and in so few words! Why not really take me on at length, but on the issues, not personally? Better yet: Why not consider talking to me? I'd do it.

You have expended a mere 140 characters on Twitter. This is not insulting enough. While you still credit me with being "amazing," you also refer to me as someone who has "what was once an interesting mind." According to your tweet, that mind has been destroyed by "racism."

Ah, Marcotte! Where were you when I began marching for civil rights for African-Americans in the early 1960s and tutoring black children in Harlem? It's not your fault, but you weren't even born yet. Have you read any of my books? If you have, you cannot call me a "racist." Read 'em. Go on, I dare you. Read all or any of my articles about what life is like for women in the Middle East and in central Asia, read my studies about honor killings and about the work I've been doing on behalf of girls and women who have applied for asylum in the United States and who are in flight from being honor murdered.

These girls and women are not white women. They are all women of color. Do you believe that men of color have the right to treat "their" women barbarically? And that we are obliged to collaborate with them in order to be on proper anti-racists?

Marcotte: Your accusation of "racism" constitutes a new and terribly fashionable McCarthyism, one that plagues our world. (Yes, I know: McCarthy was also before your time.)

Today, when real racists (think of the ethnic Arab Muslims in Sudan who have committed genocide and gender cleansing against the African Muslims and Christians in Darfur), real fascists, real totalitarians, real barbarians, want to brand, shame, delegitimize, and silence anyone who dares to expose their racism and misogyny, they simply call her a "racist." The accusation functions as a leper's bell around one's neck. It is meant to keep others away, meant to warn people that if, they, too, say similar things or associate with a known "racist," that they will also be branded as "racists."

The accusation of "racism" is the new, politically correct version of the old accusation of "communism." Today, those who level this accusation tend to be leftists, socialists, "progressives," faux feminists, and real communists.

Your piece in the *Guardian* was written mainly to condemn, protest, the fact that CBS journalist Logan's tragedy was something that "right wingers" might now use to make political hay. You write that "right wingers have an interest in stoking fear and loathing of Muslims." You also write that Egyptian-style sexual harassment is common in the United States and in the West.

It is not. In 2008, the BBC reported the following statistics on sexual harassment in Egypt:

- Experienced by 98% of foreign women visitors
- Experienced by 83% of Egyptian women
- 62% of Egyptian men admitted harassing women
- 53% of Egyptian men blame women for 'bringing it on.'

Marcotte: Have you ever lived in a Muslim country? I have.

The lives of women are…different, harder, not better. And no, American imperialism, colonialism, capitalism, and racism have not caused the shameful and endemic abuse of women in developing Muslim countries. In fact, Islam has quite a history of its own in terms of imperialism, colonialism, capitalism, and racism—and it is the largest practitioner of both gender and religious apartheid.

The bravest Muslim and ex-Muslim dissidents and feminists agree with me on this. There are Muslims, religious and secular, who oppose the kind of Islamism that you seem to support and that the London *Guardian* is willing to publish.

Try building a church, a Hindu Temple, or a synagogue in Saudi Arabia or anywhere else in the Islamic world. Building mosques in the West—yes; reciprocity, tolerance for other religions in the Muslim world—no.

American corporate and military imperialism and Israel's existence have not caused Muslims to force their daughters to marry their first cousins when they are ten years old, nor has it forced Muslims to face veil women, flog or stone them to death if they've been raped, or to honor murder daughters when they are even slightly "disobedient."

Saying so does not make me a racist. Does it?

But here's the point: Your refusal to tell the truth does, potentially, make you a racist. As a feminist, I have one universal standard of human rights for all people, everywhere. While I might favor multi-cultural diversity, I am not a multi-cultural relativist. By your politically correct statements of "anti-racism" (made on poor Lara Logan's back) you are actually holding Arab and Muslim countries to much lower ethical standards. You are condemning their inhabitants, both male and female, to continued Islamist and Islamic barbarism, which includes slavery, racism, and both religious and gender apartheid.

Lara Logan is a naked-faced infidel. Her brutalization was in part caused by the hate propaganda that has poisoned Egyptian, Arab, and Muslim life for many decades. We continue that brutalization by minimizing it or by blaming the victim. We are all Lara Logan. You too, Marcotte.

What my generation of Second Wave feminists discovered about violence against women remains important, pioneering work. Today, I do my feminist work with Muslim and ex-Muslim feminists and dissidents. We work on Islamic gender apartheid. My vision of universal human rights has not changed. I now submit courtroom affidavits on behalf of girls and women who are seeking asylum from being honor murdered. It is quintessentially feminist human rights work.

Islamic gender apartheid is a human rights violation and cannot be justified in the name of cultural relativism, tolerance, anti-racism, diversity, or political correctness. Universal literacy, the separation of mosque and state, the separation of powers, a constitution—and women's rights are all central to the battle for Western values. It is a necessary part of true democracy, along with freedom of religion, tolerance for homosexuals, and freedom of dissent. Here, then, is exactly where the greatest battle of the twenty-first century is joined.

NewsRealBlog
2/22/11

77

Turning a Blind Eye to
Islam's Brutal Treatment of Women:
Honor Killings and Western Feminist Silence

My feminist generation believed in universal human rights—one standard for all. I still do. Therefore, I have taken a strong stand against the persecution of immigrant women and dissidents. I now submit affidavits on behalf of women who've fled the threat of such killings and who are seeking asylum in the United States. Many Western academic feminists are so afraid of being condemned as "racists" that this fear trumps their concern for women's rights in the Arab, Muslim, and Hindu world.

Islamic gender apartheid has penetrated the West. At its most extreme, Islamic gender apartheid is characterized by acid attacks, public stonings, hangings, and beheading of women in Iran, Pakistan, Afghanistan, Somalia and Saudi Arabia.

Feminists should be crying out from the rooftops against these practices. Some are. I am.

I've published two academic studies and hundreds of articles about honor killings, both in the West and in the developing world. An honor killing is a collaborative conspiracy carried out against one victim, usually a young girl, by her parents, brothers, uncles, grandfathers, sisters and male cousins. Her relatives believe that her "impure" behaviour has "dishonored" them.

An honor killing is not the same as a Western domestically violent femicide. Many honorable feminists disagree with me on this point.

They believe that honor killings belong in the same category as Western domestic violence. Understandably, such feminists fear singling out one group for behaviour that may be common to all groups. But if, for reasons of "political correctness," we fail to properly understand a crime, we will never be able to prevent or prosecute it.

These killings are carefully planned by the victim's own family of origin, who have warned her, repeatedly, from childhood on, that they will kill her if she dishonors her family in any way. World-wide, women are honor-murdered based on mere rumors of inappropriate behaviour, for wanting to choose their own husbands, for having infidel friends, for choosing a non-Muslim husband, or a non-Muslim god, or for marrying someone of the wrong caste.

It is rare for a domestically violent Western father to routinely batter, stalk, patrol and murder his own daughter, and to be assisted in this gruesome task by his entire family. In the West, the majority (91%) of honor killings are Muslim-on-Muslim crimes.

Honor killings in the West are also distinguished by their barbaric ferocity. The female victim often is gang-raped, then burned alive, stoned or beaten to death, cut at the throat, decapitated, stabbed numerous times, suffocated slowly, etc. This most resembles what Western serial killers do to prostitutes.

Based on my research, I have increasingly been asked to submit affidavits on behalf of girls and women who have fled being honor killed and who are seeking asylum in the United States or Canada.

My first case was that of an abused Muslim-American teenage immigrant who had secretly converted to Christianity. Lawyers in Florida (she fled there), and in Ohio (her home state), both won her the right to remain in foster care and helped her obtain a green card. The girl now lives in hiding, apart from her family, somewhere in America.

My second case concerns a North African woman who fled a European country to seek asylum in America. Just because a Muslim woman lives in Europe does not mean that she lives in a Western environment. Her large, tight-knit, violent, Islamist family inhabits a parallel universe. As a convert to Christianity, this woman's family would have hunted her down until they found and killed her. They would have never stopped trying.

My third case concerns a graduate student from a prominent family in a southeast Asian country. She has applied for asylum here. She dared, against her parents' wishes, to marry a man whom she loved but who belonged to a different sect of Islam.

My fourth case concerns a woman who was born and raised in the killing fields of Congo. After her father was murdered, her mother fled to a neighboring African country, where she married a Muslim man who insisted on marrying his new stepdaughter off as the fifth wife to an elderly Muslim man; in turn, her chosen husband insisted that she first be genitally mutilated.

Desperate, defiant, this brave soul fled Africa and arrived in the United States with falsified documents. Without going into too much detail, let me say that she languished in jail in Buffalo, NY for more than three months. Recently, a judge ordered that she be deported to Congo. She has six weeks to appeal this decision.

Perhaps the equivalent of a federal witness protection program for the intended targets of honor killings should be created. England has already established just such a program.

The government must issue clear warnings to all immigrants to the West: Honor killings and female genital mutilation will be prosecuted under Western law. Since honor killings are collaborations, both the perpetrators and accomplices should all be prosecuted. European courts have recently begun to do this.

National Post
3/12/11

78

Arab Spring: Male-on-Female Atrocities in Gaza Disappeared by the Western Media

Last month, at least eight Muslim Palestinian female journalists were physically beaten and tortured by male Hamas security forces in the Gaza strip. Their cell phones, laptops, documents, and cameras were confiscated. They were arrested. Some were forced to sign a document "pledging to refrain from covering such events again."

The "events" were a series of pro-unity rallies organized by Palestinian youth on Facebook (!) which demanded an end to the dispute between Islamist Hamas and a presumably more moderate Fatah.

So much for the Arab "spring," and the purposefully misguided Western (and these heroically naïve youthful demonstrators') belief that the increasingly well organized Islamist Middle East will really rise up on behalf of human rights and women's rights—without which there can be no democracy.

But this is not my main point.

The mainstream media did not cover this male-on-female atrocity in Gaza. In the English-speaking world, only a handful of journalists, including two Israelis, one writing in the *Jerusalem Post*, one writing at *Big Peace*, covered it. A few smaller newspapers in America and an English-language Egyptian paper did so as well.

To be fair, Reuters had an article which featured their own agency in Gaza as having been attacked by "armed men." Later on, we learn that these "armed men" were Hamas officials. And near the end of the piece, we also learn that Hamas also beat "photographers and camera men." They do not mention female journalists, nor do they give us their names.

Slate also had an article about how Fatah is undermining Islamism on the West Bank. Parenthetically, later on, they mention that Hamas raided the offices of Reuters and destroyed equipment. They do not mention the attack on the Palestinian women journalists.

It did not happen, it is not important. The mainstream media does not really care about what happens to Arabs, Muslims, or Palestinians—not even when they are fellow or sister journalists, women, and feminists. The media only cares when and if Israelis are allegedly the perpetrators, the murderers, the checkpoint "humiliators." Even when Israelis kill an armed Iranian-backed Palestinian member of Hamas in self-defense, even when Israelis accidentally, with no malice aforethought, kill a British journalist or an American "activist," the Israelis are not only blamed; films, plays, and documentaries are made about the "martyred" American Rachel Corrie or the "martyred" British filmmaker James Miller or British "anti-war" activist Tom Hurndall. Countless demonstrations have been held. In Miller's case the British government insisted on an investigation, and his family brought a civil lawsuit against an Israeli soldier.

The media was all over this even though an investigation strongly suggested that James Miller was killed by Palestinians "from the direction of the populated Rafah." Although people know that Palestinians routinely hide behind civilian hostages, deliberately target Israeli civilians, especially children, create their own "martyrs" (the Muhammad al-Dura case as well as the Rachel Corrie case immediately come to mind)—nevertheless, the media refuses to hold Palestinians accountable and refuses to believe that the Israelis are innocent. The media knows full well that they will be killed or not allowed to "report" in Palestinian areas if they publish anything negative, especially if it's true.

One of the recently beaten and arrested Palestinian female journalists, Asma'a Al-Gul, is someone whom I first interviewed in 2009. Al-Gul is a secular feminist and a journalist who has written brave articles about honor killings on the West Bank and in Gaza. Al-Gul has been harassed and arrested by Hamas before. Why? Ostensibly because she dared to wear jeans on the beach, to laugh (!) and because she entered the sea, fully clothed, to swim. These were her crimes—plus the fact that she was a single woman (divorced, actually), out in public, not wearing hijab, and relaxing on the beach with male friends.

It took the left-wing *Mother Jones* about a year and half after my interviews to find Al-Gul. Guess what the journalist, Ashley Bates, immediately focuses upon? You guessed it. In her third paragraph she writes:

"For three years, Israel has enforced a devastating blockade of the Gaza Strip aimed at isolating Hamas." One might hope that she would leave well enough alone and focus on Al-Gul's heroism and Hamas' Islamist persecution of women. But not exactly. She sees Al-Gul as a heroine primarily because she has remained a "secularist," and of all the things they may have talked about, Bates instead writes this:

> Asma'a wrote her way through the trauma of the 2008-2009 war between Israel and Hamas militants, which claimed the lives of 13 Israelis and about 1,400 Gazans. Often, she slept at her office for fear of getting killed on the way to her home, a mere five-minute walk away.

> 'I felt as if Israeli military planes were blind,' Asma'a recalled. 'They attacked everything and everybody. I saw dead children...As a woman and as a human being, I don't believe in revenge, because it just brings more blood. But people said to me during the war, 'You see? This is your peace.'

While Asma'a has befriended liberal Jewish activists in Gaza, she has never entered Israel. In 2003 and again in 2006, the Israeli government denied her permission to travel through Israel to the West Bank, which is territorially separate from Gaza, to receive awards for her writing.

Yes, we know that *Mother Jones* is a left-wing magazine. But, in case we forget it—the reporter is careful to remind us that, despite Hamas' Islamification, she is pro-Palestinian, not pro-Israeli.

Earlier this week, Artists4Israel and members of the Birthright Israel Alumni Community just did something amazing in Washington Square Park in New York City's Greenwich Village. They erected a bomb shelter and decorated it just as they've done in Sderot, Israel, a city which has absorbed thousands of Hamas rocket attacks in the last ten years, including many after Israel unilaterally withdrew from Gaza. The graffiti artists and muralists spoke about Sderot and about Israel and talked about how people have only 15 seconds to find a bomb shelter after the "code red" siren goes off. They talked about how permanently traumatized the Israeli children are.

Sadly, Artists4Israel were unable to sound the siren every fifteen seconds (to simulate what life is actually like in Sderot and in southern Israel) for more than a half hour. Equally sadly, this brave band of artist-warriors were also forced to contend with an almost immediate, pro-forma counter-demonstrators who shouted, yelled, insulted, and behaved in every way like the Arab Street at its bullying worst. The counter-demonstrators were not respectful, did not engage in dialogue, and did not listen to anything having to do with the suffering of innocent Israeli civilians at the hands of Hamas.

Perhaps they are all journalists or will become journalists when they graduate from college.

NewsRealBlog
4/1/11

- 79 -

Protecting Muslim Girls From Rape is
Now a Crime in Europe

F reedom of speech and women's rights just took a major hit in Denmark earlier today when the public prosecutor found Lars Hedegaard, the President of the Danish (and International) Free Press Society, guilty of "hate speech" under section 266b of the Danish penal code.

Hedegaard's crime was to note "the great number of family rapes in areas dominated by Muslim culture in Denmark."

The prosecutor's crime is far greater. Now, courtesy of this prosecution, it is officially "racist" to tell the truth about sexual violence against women in Denmark, at least when that violence is perpetrated by Muslim fathers, uncles, or cousins.

When feminists first brought rape and incest out of the closet, we were accused of being "strident man haters." We learned to say: Not all men rape but all rapists are men. To our horror, we eventually discovered that women sometimes sexually abuse children. They rarely rape other adults or force unwanted sex on men or on other women outside of a prison setting.

Islam is not a race. Muslims come in every conceivable color. It is not "racist" to describe a tribally barbaric custom. But let's assume Muslims represent a religion.

The Danes, the Scandinavians, all Europe has critiqued and exposed the real and imaginary "crimes" of both Judaism and Christianity. Now, suddenly, Islam alone is to be spared such treatment.

I stand in solidarity with Hedegaard at this awful moment. If the

Danes and the Europeans do not take some very radical measures, it will be just as Bat Ye'or predicted. Post-Enlightenment Europe will no longer exist; Eurabia will.

I am ready to talk to the prosecutor to condemn this utter insanity. And so should everyone else. The real racists, the infidel-haters, the Jew-haters, the woman-haters are not being condemned. Only those who expose them are.

Lars Hedegaard will appeal this dangerous verdict.

NewsRealBlog
5/3/11

- 80 -
Acid Attacks, Stonings, Honor Killings: Muslim-on-Muslim Violence Against Women on Every Continent

I concede that the American mainstream media does print the bad news about gender apartheid—but it does so without drawing any "politically incorrect" conclusions.

Over the years, the American mainstream media has printed articles about Islamic and African female genital mutilation, the public gang-rapes of innocent young girls in Pakistan (like Mukhtaran Bibi) and the repeated gang-rapes of girls and women in Darfur by ethnic Arab Muslims (the *New York Times* simply refused to use the word "Muslim"). The media has covered the disfiguring acid attacks on girls and women in Pakistan, Afghanistan, and Iran. Maddeningly, the media draws no conclusion.

On November 3, 2004, an Iranian man, Majid Movahedi, poured a bucket of acid on Ameneh Bahrami's head as she was leaving work. He did so because she had rejected his many marriage proposals. Poor Bahrami was blinded and disfigured. Since then, she has endured 17 operations, including one in Spain which failed to successfully reconstruct her face. She now has only 40% of her sight and only in one eye.

Under Sharia law, the victim has the right to demand an eye-for-an-eye if other negotiations fail. In this case, the great Islamic Republic of Iran was prepared to have a physician drop acid into Movahedi's eyes—unless his victim forgave him.

On July 31st, 2011, at the last minute, in the hospital, she did so.

Movahedi wept. Maybe poor Ameneh should marry the fiend; maybe Majiid should atone for his crime by supporting his victim for the rest of his life. But Ameneh didn't want him before; how much more repulsive he must seem to her now.

On July 31, 2011, on the same day Ameneh forgave the man who blinded and disfigured her, the *New York Times* ran two pieces on their front page. One article continued its non-stop jihad against the anti-jihadic/anti-Sharia bloggers (whom it blames for the "Islamophobic" Norwegian massacre of mainly ethnic infidel Norwegians). The other article, right beneath it, is titled: "Afghans Rage at Young Lovers: A Father Says Kill Them Both."

"Lovers"? Hardly. These two seventeen year olds have possibly—probably—exchanged glances and perhaps a love letter or two. Maybe they once held hands or even once dared to share a quick, almost chaste kiss. Yes, these two seventeen-year-old Major Muslim Sinners decided it was better to marry than burn in Hell. On their way to their (perhaps secret) wedding, "A group of men spotted the couple riding together in a car, yanked them into the road and began to interrogate the boy and the girl. Why were they together? What right had they? An angry crowd of 300 surged around them, calling them adulterers and demanding that they be stoned or hanged."

The police rescued them from the raging mob but in the process killed a man. The girl's family now want her dead; the mob wants the boy dead too because he is a Tajik and she is a Hazara. The family of the dead man have also sworn to kill her—"unless she marries one of their other sons (in order to pay) her debt."

The reporter, Andrea Elliott, notes that another young Afghan couple who had also fallen in love "were stoned to death (in Kunduz) by scores of people—including family members—after they eloped. The stoning marked a brutal application of Sharia law, captured on a video."

Thus, Elliott's article, while painting a horrifying picture of raging, out-of-control rural Afghan lynch mobs, also praises the Afghan police in Herat for having rescued the young Romeo and Juliet as well as the local clerics for having refused to condemn them. This is surely a point in their favor, but what conclusion does Elliott draw? Does she honestly believe that the police will prevail against the girl's family who have been shamed and are now out for her blood? Does Elliot really understand that such Sharia practices are coming our way, that they are already here?

In 2006, Afghan-Canadians Khatera Sidiqi and her fiancé, Feroz

Mangal, were gunned down in Ottawa by her brother who acted on behalf of his father. Her crime? She refused to allow her father, who had abused both her and her mother, to be involved in the wedding plans.

In 2008, In Henrietta, New York, an Afghan mother persuaded her son to honor murder his sister, Fauzia Mohammad, because she was "too western." (Fauzia wanted to attend college away from home.) Luckily, Fauzia survived the attempted honor killing

In 2009, a high-profile Canadian case in Kingston involved the calculated murder of an Afghan first wife and three Afghan daughters by their Afghan father, brother, and second wife/stepmother.

Please note that I am only listing the honor murder of daughters by their family of origin—something that is typical of Muslims, and to a much lesser extent of Sikhs in the West, and of Hindus only in India. Western domestic violence, including domestically violent femicide, does not usually target daughters.

Islamic gender apartheid has quietly, openly, and fully penetrated the West. Female genital mutilation is going on in North America and in Europe, as is polygamy, forced veiling, normalized daughter-and wife-beating, forced marriage, and honor killing.

This deeply concerns me. It has also alarmed many of the maligned anti-jihadic bloggers. What protection are we able to offer the Muslim girls and women who become citizens of our countries? What kind of prosecutions will we be able to mount against their attackers?

The situation is far, far worse in Europe, including in Norway. Just read Norwegian Hege Storhaug's excellent book on this subject: *But the Greatest of These is Freedom: The Consequences of Immigration in Europe.* According to Storhaug,

> Norwegian government officials who are supposed to help immigrant women enter the work force have instead formed an 'unholy alliance' with those women's husbands. The husbands want the women to stay home, keep house, and raise children; and the employment counselors don't want to harass the women by trying to push them into jobs, since their chances of finding employment are poor anyway. So instead they arrange for the women to take hobby-like courses in subjects like food preparation and needlework. Far from bringing them closer to the work force, these courses ensure that they won't neglect their domestic duties. The government, in short, has made a compromise; it keeps Muslim women busy

within their husbands' strict boundaries and ignores their need to develop into skilled workers— and active citizens."

Storhaug, like myself and a bare handful of other feminists, are all haunted by the Western feminist silence about Islamic gender apartheid in the West. She explains that silence succinctly and accurately.

The feminists are obsessed with their own ethnic Norwegian causes: longer maternity leave, shorter work days for the same pay—in short, everything that can give them a better life, materially and socially. At the same time, many of the classical feminists appear to be old socialists blinded by the multicultural dream—a dream, alas, that has led them to accept the oppression of women in sizable segments of the population.

FrontPage Magazine
8/2/11

- 81 -

Burqa Babes in the Big House -
Love Crimes of Kabul

Forced or arranged marriage is a heartbreaking and soul-crushing tribal (Islamic, Sikh, Hindu, Arab Kurdish and Yazidi) reality. Such concepts of family honor and Arab desert customs are able to break each individual's will in the service of the family, the clan, the patriarch, and tribal custom.

Nevertheless, marrying a ten-year-old to her thirty-year-old first cousin or to a man old enough to be her grandfather—and who already has two wives and grown sons is inhuman. Forcing a girl to marry someone against her will and preventing her from marrying the person of her choice is a crime against the heart. Often, such arranged marriages (and almost all marriages are arranged) include normalized wife-and daughter-in-law beating. The few shelters and jails for battered women and for the intended victims of honor killings in the Muslim world are filled with such stories.

I recently watched an HBO documentary with the catchy title *Love Crimes of Kabul*. The film takes us inside a woman's prison in Kabul. The film is surprisingly "light," given how dark its subject really is. The women in the Badam Bagh prison are commendably feisty. They are surprisingly tough babes in the Big House and their pants-wearing rather butch chief female warden is tougher still. She functions as their respected and protective mother figure.

There is much gruff and playful tenderness among the women who both bond and fight with each other as if they are "family"; they eat and sleep in the same room, communally. The all-female and informal

298

atmosphere is that of a harem, a brothel, and a prison.

The Burqa Babes are surprisingly, refreshingly brash. They are not ashamed of what they've done. They're also funny; they see the comic dimension in their essentially Kafkaesque situations. They are clowns, as self-deprecating as they are aggressive. They are ethnically and racially gorgeous in their diversity. They are from every tribe, every region, and they bear the genetic legacy of every conquering army.

Iranian filmmaker, Tanaz Eshaghian, miraculously managed to get a camera and a crew inside the prison and some of the legal hearings. What crimes have the women committed? Apparently, half the prison population have dared to fall in love, or are suspected of having done so; they have dared to have sex before marriage, have run away from home, or rejected an arranged marriage. These are crimes in Afghanistan. (The other half of the prison population are thieves, smugglers, or murderers.)

Among the "moral" criminals: One woman was sentenced to four years for having run away with the boy she loved. Another woman, the very spunky Kareema, who looks like an innocent child (many of the inmates do), fell in love, had sex, became pregnant—but the scoundrel who had courted her refused to marry her, which would have doomed Kareema to certain death. What did Kareema do? She turned both herself and her boyfriend in to the police. The only way this cad can now get out of jail is if he marries Kareema, who is very pleased that she has managed to turn her potential murder into an inevitable marriage.

Some husband. His name is Firuz and he says, on camera, "I wish I never met her."

Kareema is the one who proposed marriage to him. She is a (Shia) Hazara; Firuz is a (Sunni) Pashtun. The Pashtuns view themselves as a superior caste or tribe—although many Hazaras do not believe in marrying out either. Firuz must marry Kareema. How will Firuz and his family punish this upstart Hazara? Kareema's father says that "she will be their dog, their servant."

Kareema wants to apologize to her father, whose only concern is himself. He believes that Kareema should have married a suitor who could have supported him, the father-in-law, in his old age.

Kareema is now refusing to marry Firuz unless he pays a dowry. She is that spirited. And yes, they do marry in jail but are still found guilty of the crime of premarital sex. They receive a three-month sentence, but the judge says that Islam believes in the family, and thus he decides that the newly married couple will be better off at home than in jail.

And so we see that the scurrying, silent figures beneath the blue burqas are also canny, high-spirited, and daring. They may be oppressed, but they are also incredibly good natured and realistic. And they know exactly what they are up against. A lawyer advises: "A bad husband is better than no husband." The women understand and accept this as their lot in life.

Their female-female conversations are frank, spontaneous, assertive, and sharply to the point. Kareema's mother tells her: "Everyone knows you screwed up."

Another mother-in-law/daughter-in-law-couple, Zia and Alia (or Aleema), are in for rather mysterious reasons. They fight bitterly. Did they run away together from a dangerously violent home? These women say that in their family "people speak with knives." Alia is clear that if she is ever released from prison, her family will "quietly drown" her.

Then there is Sabera, so young, so pretty, so charming, who dared to fall in love. She does not think this is a crime. Although she has been accused of having had premarital sex, a medical exam in prison proves that she is still a virgin. However, she admits to having engaged in anal sex—something that is quite common in Afghanistan both among men and as a birth control device. For this crime Sabera was sentenced to three years.

One woman on camera admits that she finally killed her husband. Naseema is 45 years old and has no regrets. "Men like my husband should all be murdered. He had sex with boys and other women and with a seven-year-old girl. I did the world some good. But it's considered a crime. I have no pain or remorse. I'm glad."

Unbelievably, ironically, the chief female guard says that "women have been given too much freedom." Another prison guard says: "If they were good women they would not be here. They would be home with their families."

No, sir. With their their fighting spirits, defiance, open-heartedness, and philosophical minds, these are very, very good women indeed.

Pajamas Media
8/4/11

- 82 -

The Reluctantly Racist Filmmaker:
Sympathy for the Devil

Films wield great power over people; cinematic images are forever burned into memory and imagination—even if the memories implanted are false, not based on true facts—but on a sophisticated and biased manipulation of reality.

I have just watched *The Reluctant Fundamentalist* twice. This is Mira Nair's new film about a soulful and handsome Pakistani man, Changez Khan, who once believed in the American Dream, succeeded brilliantly as a super-capitalist, but was forced to abandon corporate America, return home to become, perhaps, a "reluctant" fundamentalist. I write "perhaps" because Nair leaves us wondering about whether such a smart and sympathetic fellow would actually order hostage taking, torture, and murder for a "fundamentalist" cause.

Why does her hero leave America and turn against it? Because, immediately post 9/11, Khan, played by Riz Ahmed, is detained and, horrifyingly, strip-searched at the airport; thereafter, he is subjected to anti-Muslim physical and verbal violence on the street; then, he is arrested again by police officers as a potential Muslim terrorist; finally, Changez is exploited and betrayed by Erica, his wealthy American girlfriend-artist, (played by Kate Hudson), who uses their intimate relationship as the subject of her new Art Installation about the exotic Other.

Nair has used every cliché possible to manipulate our emotions into siding with Changez and not with those in Pakistan who are trying to rescue an American professor who has, "perhaps," been kidnapped by Changez and his associates. The journalist, (played by Liev Schreiber),

301

and the murdered American professor are really evil CIA spooks in disguise. We are not meant to sympathize with them at all.

I believe that some Americans harbor anti-Muslim prejudice and that this is wrong; many Americans try hard not to do so. However, it is also true that 97 percent of the FBI's Most Wanted terrorists are Muslims.

Both things are true. We must wrestle with both realities at the same time.

I believe that some innocent Muslim-Americans have been brutally and unfairly targeted, treated with suspicion and hatred, especially right after 9/11 or after the Boston Bombing. This is wrong and it pains me. However, I strongly doubt that each and every kind of relentless, non-stop injustice that Nair's "reluctant fundamentalist" is shown as having endured has been similarly endured by most or even many Muslims in America.

Despite allegations by the Muslim Brotherhood in America (CAIR and ISNA), statistics do not support an escalation in alleged "Islamophobia" here. World headlines do support an escalation of anti-infidel, anti-Western, anti-Israeli, anti-Jewish, and anti-American hatred in the Islamic world—and of the most toxic kind.

Filmmakers keep turning out films that depict America, and most specifically the CIA and American military forces, as cruel, evil, and racist; they glorify the offended dignity of always-innocent Muslims as a way of justifying the nihilistic terror that Muslims are unleashing, globally, first against other Muslims, second, against infidels. Remember *Syriana* (2005), *Kingdom of Heaven* (2005), *Babel* (2006), *The Kingdom* (2007), *Rendition* (2007), and *Amreeka* (2009)?

In Hollywood, the most dangerous Islamists are seen as the new native-American Indians. America is General Custer—but on steroids. If Muslim immigrants engage in sudden jihad syndrome with only the internet to inspire and guide them, (The Ft Hood shooter, the Boston bombers), it is America's fault because we did not help such immigrants assimilate. If the Boston bombers had received even more welfare, scholarships, food stamps, and immediate citizenship, they would not have embraced terrorism as their most powerful form of self-expression.

This is a Big Lie and a dangerous one at that.

If America is always to blame, why did Afghan warlords turn on their own people so barbarically? Why did ethnic Arab Muslims turn on black African Muslims and Christians in the Sudan? Why did Khomeini and his successors turn so viciously against their own people and against

Muslims in Iraq? Why has Assad murdered 70,000-100,000 of his own (predominantly Muslim and Christian) citizens?

The Islamic nations, the world's filmmakers and journalists, the "international community," do not seem to care about the Muslim victims of Muslim terrorism. They care only when Americans or Israelis are the killers.

This is another kind of lethal racism.

If we are truly anti-racists and not merely anti-Western, we would have more sympathy for the millions of innocent Muslim civilians who have been slaughtered and maimed by Islamist jihadists—and less of a need to present Muslims who have turned to military jihad so sympathetically.

The Times of Israel
5/8/13

- 83 -
Outlawed in Pakistan:
The Heroic Kainat Soomro

The American government has just gone into the anti-honor-killing "business." Given my academic and legal work documenting and opposing honor killing, I support this venture. I do find it a bit odd that the U.S. Consulate in East Jerusalem has just launched such a campaign—but for Palestinian-Arab women only.

I wonder: Why not branch out to Pakistan or Afghanistan where honor killing and honor-based violence is, possibly, even more epidemic?

I watched an excellent and heartbreaking *Frontline* documentary by Habiba Nosheen about honor-based violence in Pakistan: "Outlawed in Pakistan." Thirteen-year-old Kainat Soomro was chloroformed, drugged, kidnapped, and then gang-raped for three or four days by four men who threatened to kill or sell her.

Amazingly, Kainat escaped, in her bare feet and without her headscarf.

I am very partial to a story about a girl or woman who escapes a life-threatening captivity in the "Wild East," as I once did, in Kabul, long ago. But, I was a foreigner, an American, and once I got out I had a second chance.

Kainat is now and forevermore a ruined child, an "outlaw," whose family is supposed to kill her for having "dishonored" them. Amazingly, her loving family refused to do so. Unlike so many honor-killing families in which parents and siblings are either hands-on perpetrators or collaborators, Kainat's mother weeps and kisses her. Her father and older brother proudly supports Kainat's search for justice.

This family deserves a prize for having the courage and the sanity to stand up to tribal misogyny.

The Soomros turned to the police, who refused to act. Instead, they said to kill her according to tribal custom. "She has shamed you." The police do no sperm or DNA testing, and do not secure the crime scene. They ensure that charges of rape are almost impossible to prove.

Perhaps the U.S. Consulates in Peshawar and Karachi can donate rape kits to the Pakistani police.

Instead of becoming a bandit queen, as the gang-raped Phoolan Devi did in Uttar Pradesh, India; instead of killing herself—Kainat wanted justice. She wanted these men "sentenced to death" because they ruined her life. And they have. Probably, no one will marry her, and Kainat's plans to become a physician may be permanently on hold. The death threats against this honorable family became so serious, that Kainat's 18-person family was forced to flee their home for two rooms in Karachi.

Men who rape girls in tribal areas feel no guilt. Kainat's accused rapists were enraged when their victim dared speak out. They hotly denied Kainat's charges.

In Karachi, Sarah Zaman, of War Against Rape, a grassroots feminist group, decided to help Kainat and found her a dedicated pro bono lawyer. Zaman knew that powerful village men routinely rape girls and then have them killed for having shamed their families. In Afghanistan, raped women are either honor-killed or jailed as criminals. Kainat bravely agreed to endure a 5- to 10-year legal process, one in which she will be grilled in humiliating ways. The pro bono lawyer who represented the accused men, is also representing the President of Pakistan.

Kainat's lawyer managed to have the four men jailed and held in jail without bail for three years. This is amazing.

Nevertheless, the accused rapists prevail. We see dozens of their village supporters descend on the courthouse yelling that "Kainat is a whore." Their winning defense is ingenious: They claim that Kainat married one of them and he produces her thumbprint on a marriage document and a photo of the two of them, smiling. Kainat repeats that she was drugged and does not remember this. Her presumed bridegroom demands that she return to him.

Kainat was only 13 and did not have the right to consent to a marriage under secular law. However, under Sharia law, if she has reached puberty, she can do so. Sharia law prevails in the matter and the accused are all freed.

Despite claims to the contrary, Sharia law and Sharia courts are dangerous for women.

Still, Kainat's story is a victory and like all such victories, the price is high and the risk is even higher.

For a poor girl and her family to have four powerful men jailed for three years is extraordinary. The price: They allegedly killed Kainat's supportive brother, Sabir. And despite national headlines, the police closed the murder investigation. Kainat quietly says that her "life is a living hell."

Kainat and her family live under police protection. Again, this is extraordinary.

I suggest that the U.S. Consulates consider funding Kainat's education as a physician. Perhaps the entire family should be air-lifted out of the Pakistani Badlands and into America for their safety.

The Huffington Post
5/30/13

- 84 -
Afghan Family Feuds, Wild East Style:
Mohammed H. Anwar's Memoir

Yesterday, *The Wall Street Journal* had a front page story: "As U.S. Pulls Out, Feuds Split Afghanistan's Ruling Family." This title is not "news."

"A Ruling Family feud" is Afghan history and, perhaps, psychology. Afghan Emirs and Shahs seized thrones mainly from their brothers, half-brothers, uncles and nephews. Rulers and pretenders-to-the-throne were routinely tortured and murdered by their relatives.

Afghan rulers have always used their deals with Britain, Russia, and Germany to accomplish their own ends. Stealing from as many Afghan people as possible and sharing it with one's family members is the norm in Afghanistan—as is stealing from your own family. Educated and modern-thinking Afghan men, who envisioned a more progressive and lawful Afghanistan, have been known to rot in jail for twenty years, where their torture was uniquely gruesome.

By definition, business as usual in the Wild East, means hiring only your family members—then spying on them, and assassinating them when necessary. It also means greasing the wheels of commerce by bribing every single gatekeeper. This is considered more civilized than a (selfish) fixed price. Other customs are also seen as superior to those of the West's such as arranged child marriage, first cousin marriage, and polygamy. From a non-Western point of view, marriage is a matter for adult family members to decide, it is too important to leave to children or to the vagaries of "love." Large networks of trustworthy relatives guarantee land and resource consolidation, safety in times of great danger, and a rather large posse with whom to socialize.

They have a point given the neighborhood in which they live.

Mohammed H. Anwar grew up in the slums of Kabul during World War One. His poverty was unimaginable—but he taught himself, he was tutored and mentored and ultimately received a world-class education in America. Anwar would not be surprised by the *WSJ* headline, above, or by any of the recent headlines about Afghan bank corruption, restless, regional warlords, the volatile instability of the central government, cyclical and barbaric civil wars, ruling family feuds, etc.

Anwar wrote an extraordinary memoir (*Memories of Afghanistan*), which was eventually published by his late son, Keith. Author House brought it out in 2004. Anwar describes a life of normalized child abuse, an epidemic of sadistic teachers and mullahs, the totally acceptable and rather savage, pre-Taliban mistreatment of women, the extensive network of royal spies, the repeated "orgies" of public executions.

Anwar describes how a gentle and innocent young boy (who happened to belong to the "wrong" family), was homosexually raped every night in prison—and how he killed himself when he was released; how a gentle mullah, who had an unacceptably open mind, was stoned to death by a large, laughing group of men; how educated Afghans were systematically chosen for torture and death; how homosexual pederasty and boy prostitutes were endemic in Kandahar.

Anwar himself was educated in America and married an American woman. Both escaped from Kabul in 1942-1943. Anwar's wife was also named Phyllis.

Most Westerners (and Afghans who write about themselves), focus on the large Afghan family picnics, warm hospitality, love of poetry, Nature, God, and kite-flying. That is true too—but if you are held captive, none of that matters.

All cultures, including those we wish to romanticize, are characterized by injustice and cruelty; while the Wild East may be charming and beguiling, and while its individual citizens may be humane and sympathetic, Afghanistan has never been ruled by law or experienced a peaceful transition of rulers; its tribal feuds are fierce and never ending; its educated intelligentsia and its women have always been endangered. Afghanistan has a history of barbarism that is truly breathtaking—and one that existed long before the Taliban came to town.

The Huffington Post
7/2/13

- 85 -

Why Are America and The West Funding an Increasingly Fundamentalist Afghanistan?

H ow long is the West going to obligate itself to keep doing that which is impossible?

President Hamid Karzai's government is considering bringing back stoning for adultery—and imposing 100 lashes (which is a death sentence) for unmarried people who have had sexual relations.

Thus, Afghan men can marry female children, keep male children as sex-toys, maintain four wives, and visit prostitutes from dawn to dawn. But it's a capital crime if an Afghan man dishonors another Afghan man by having relations with his female "property;" and, if he has raped someone's wife, she is to be stoned. Worse yet, if two young Afghans meet and fall in love on their own and have sexual relations, but do not marry—they, too, will be committing a capital crime.

Just imagine what it's like to live in a world where a woman cannot divorce a man, no matter how violent or cruel he and his family may be; where a girl is maritally raped or forced into prostitution by her mother-in-law (these things happen all the time in war-ravaged Afghanistan).

Understand that if a bride is bold enough to run away, she will be jailed—that's if she's lucky. Otherwise, her family of origin and her husband's family will kill her for dishonoring them.

This reality is surreal, actually worse than Margaret Atwood's dystopian novel *The Handmaids' Tale*. Such customs are indigenous, tribal, and pandemic—and have not been caused by Western colonialism, imperialism, militarism or even Zionism!

In fact, Afghans are very proud of the fact that they have never

309

been colonized, not by Great Britain and not by Russia.

Why are America and the West funding a country which is so clearly headed back towards the darkest days of the Taliban in the 1980s, and to the even darker days of the bitter battles between warlords which massacred so many innocent civilians in the 1990s? Do Americans really believe that we can wean the Sunni Afghans from gender and religious apartheid?

Why is America funding humanitarian projects and training an Afghan Army when Hamid Karzai, presumably America's puppet, is in reality just another wily Afghan who needs to posture against the infidel West in order to keep his conservative countrymen from assassinating him; who breaks promises as fast as he makes them and considers this clever diplomacy, Afghan-style; whose family has grown very rich allegedly as opium dealers as well as bankers and landlords.

Karzai has just now even gone against the wishes of his own *Loya Jirga* (mass meeting of elders) by deciding that he would not sign the agreement with America that he promised to sign.

The entire civilian world is being held hostage by this style of terrorism and asymmetrical warfare i.e. a war in which soldiers are dressed as civilians and there is no "front." A suicide bombing can happen anywhere and everywhere.

Author Rajiv Chandrasekaran tells a story about an Afghan farmer who observed American do-gooders at work in the 1950s. The farmer said: "The land upon which (the Americans) were standing was cursed because the infidel had touched the land."

The fear, envy, and hatred of infidels, especially the Jew, is pandemic and will not be easy to uproot and transform.

Please draw all the necessary parallel conclusions about Israel's chances of transforming a heavily indoctrinated Palestinian-Arab Muslim population. I wrestle with the commandment that, as a Jew, I must bring light unto the nations—but I am also evaluating the high cost of doing so in terms of blood and treasure.

I know that if Western boots on the ground leave Afghanistan, that every humanitarian project will disappear overnight and the country will become a Living Hell. And yet: If the ideal cannot be translated into reality at this historical moment, how long are we morally bound to attempt to do that which is impossible?

Israel National News
11/27/13

- 86 -
Fawzia Koofi and the Stunning Bravery of Afghan Women

Although Muslim women are increasingly endangered by fundamentalist misogyny, in Muslim-majority countries, it is crucial to note that many such women (and men) are incredibly heroic in ways that westerners can barely comprehend or match.

Anti-Islamist Muslims and ex-Muslims risk death for expressing ideas that we in the West take for granted. Resisting tradition is considered a crime. Helping someone flee from being "honor" murdered is a capital crime.

In 1950, Maga Rahmany, an Afghan teenager, walked out alone without a male escort in Kabul. True, she was wearing a burqa but her independence caused tongues to wag. When she accompanied her father, a recently released political prisoner, to the cinema, she removed her burqa in order to watch the film. Relatives threatened to beat them both.

Finally, Maga went too far: she dared attend her all-female class at Kabul University without wearing a burqa. For this act of defiance, the government placed Maga under house arrest, where she stayed for three and a half years.

It took five more years before the government officially unveiled the women of Afghanistan, in 1958. In the 1960s and 1970s, many city women did not wear the burqa, although some did. However, the Soviet infiltration and invasion led to the rise of western and Pakistani-backed mujahideen who morphed into the Taliban, Al Qaeda, and into vicious warlords who attacked civilians without mercy. The persecution of women and other living beings became surreal.

During these dark days, Dr Sima Samar, an Afghan Hazara, opened medical clinics. She also refused to veil her face. When the Taliban told her to close her schools for girls or face death, she replied: "Go ahead and hang me in a public place. Then tell the people my crime: I was giving papers and pencils to girls. I won't stop doing what I am doing." Instead of killing her, Taliban members secretly began to bring their mothers and wives to her for care. Since 2005, she has remained chair of the Afghanistan Independent Human Rights Commission.

Afghan women, doing what women routinely do in the West, have been routinely threatened with death by their male relatives, sexually harassed by their male colleagues and shot at by "insurgents." Yet they continue their work.

Consider Fawzia Koofi, who is running for the presidency of Afghanistan (I'd vote for her if I could). In her book, *Letters to My Daughters*, she writes: "During the latest elections, there were even more threats on my life: gunmen trailing my car, roadside bombs laid along my route, warnings that I would be kidnapped."

In the summer of 2012 Hanifa Safi, the acting head of women's affairs in eastern Afghanistan, was killed by a bomb that exploded under her car. Undaunted, Najla Sediqi took her place. In December of 2012, Sediqi was shot dead on her way to work. The bravery of these women is stunning and their executions tragic and infuriating.

One by one, these brave souls, especially Afghan female police officers, have been assassinated: Malalai Kakar in Kandahar, in 2008; Islam Bibi in Helmand in 2013; "Negara" two months later, also in 2013. Please note: other women quickly took their places.

In the 21st century, against all odds, Afghan women and western humanitarians staffed shelters for battered women and rape victims, relocated girls in danger of being honor murdered, and worked as teachers, doctors, lawyers, social workers and police officers.

I believe that only western "boots on the ground" have allowed such humanitarian work to take place. I also believe, as the West departs, we leave behind a perpetually endangered population—endangered by their own traditions and customs, not western imperialism.

The Big Issue
11/27/13

Section Six:
The West Must Stand with Muslim Feminists

- 87 -
Multicultural Relativism, Islam and Child Sex Slavery

Soeren Kern has published an article about child sex slavery in the UK. He focuses on a new report about the large-scale "grooming" of non-Muslim girls (ages 11-16) by gangs of Muslim men into sex slavery. These men do not prey upon Muslim girls. The government, police force, and media have been "multi-culturally correct" and very reluctant to expose this phenomenon or to arrest these men.

I am sure that many feminists would say that men all over the world buy and sell women, kidnap or trick them into prostitution. And they're right. But they are wrong to refuse to focus on Pedophilia and Sex Slavery wherever and whenever this monster rears its ugly head.

The report is meticulous. It documents that "officials in England and Wales were aware of rampant child grooming—the process by which sexual predators befriend and build trust with very vulnerable children in order to prepare them for abuse—by Muslim gangs since at least 1988."

Rather than taking steps to protect non-Muslim British children, however, police, social workers, teachers, politicians, neighbors, deliberately downplayed the severity of the crimes perpetrated by the grooming gangs in order to avoid being accused of "Islamophobia" or racism.

How can we prevent such crimes and prosecute such criminals in the West if we are busy falling all over ourselves trying not to appear "racist?" Can't we expose and prosecute everyone, women as well as men, Muslims and anyone else, who ensnare children into lives of sex slavery?

Islamic doctrine, Islamic history, and individual Muslim interpretations of the Qur'an support the sexual use of non-Muslim girls and women as "easy meat." It also supports a tax on infidels (*jizya*) which some may say is now being exacted in the West in the form of state welfare, housing, education, health care, etc.

Read the report, read Kern's summary of the report—then think about the times in which you live.

When one tries to talk about normalized Muslim-style daughter and wife beating and stalking, western feminists quickly point out that male domestic violence is a global phenomenon and not confined to one ethnicity or religion. Here again, they are wrong. While male domestic violence is a global tragedy, the Islamic version of it is different and worse.

Most western fathers do not spy on their daughters, have their sons stalk them, threaten them with death, or beat them into submission daily. Many—not all—Muslim fathers do just this.

Israel National News
3/26/14

- 88 -
The Shame of Brandeis University:
Dishonoring Ayaan Hirsi Ali

We all know that Brandeis University was about to bestow an honor on the elegant author, Ayaan Hirsi Ali, best known for her critique of Islam, her decision to leave Islam, and her championship of Muslim women's rights.

One might understand why an apostate intellectual might be in danger in Somalia, the country of her birth, or in Saudi Arabia, where she once lived.

However, she has just been dishonored by Brandeis University, which withdrew its offer of a awarding her an honorary degree because the Muslim Brotherhood in America, known to us as the Council on American-Islamic Relations (CAIR) and its national student group, the Muslim Students Association, which is also allied with the Islamic Society of North America (ISNA), mounted a successful campaign against the award. Both CAIR and ISNA are unindicted co-conspirators in the Holy Land Foundation terrorist financing case.

CAIR provided the Muslim Student Association (MSU) at Brandeis with outdated, out-of-context, and highly inflammatory quotes from Hirsi Ali. They did not provide her thought-provoking, stirring, moving passages—of which there are many. Brandeis caved in to the lynch mob.

This is a terrible moment for academic freedom and critical inquiry on the American campus.

Yale University drove the first nail into the coffin of academic freedom, critical inquiry, and freedom of thought when Yale's University Press refused to publish the Danish "Mohammed" cartoons to accompany Jytte Klausen's 2009 book on the subject: *The Cartoons That Shook The World.*

Yale drove a second nail into that coffin when it ousted Dr. Charles Small, who dared to focus on the victims of contemporary Islamic, as well as Western, anti-Semitism; he did not merely focus on safely dead Jews. Dr. Small's major international conference on this subject in 2010 had more than 100 speakers and 600 in attendance.

However, official Palestinians and student Palestinians insisted this was an "Islamophobic" conference. A campaign was mounted and Yale administrators and professors ousted Dr. Small's Institute although it was independently funded.

Brandeis University, the "Jewish" university, (in terms of liberal values), has now driven the last nail into the coffin of academic freedom and intellectual diversity, when it bowed to student and faculty pressure and rescinded their offer to Hirsi Ali.

I understand that peaceful Muslim students at Brandeis may not wish to be associated with the hate propaganda and terrorist atrocities being committed in Islam's name. They should be standing outside the mosque that indoctrinated the Boston bomber with signs reading "Not in my Name," criticizing the gender and religious apartheid that characterize Islam today, and denouncing the Muslim-on-Muslim and Muslim-on-infidel violence being committed in the name of a religion that is dear to them. They should be holding teach-ins at mosques and within Muslim communities about human rights in Islam and wrestling with the question of whether radical Islam is compatible with modern Western values.

Students should hear what Hirsi Ali has to say. Instead, Brandeis and the Muslim Student Association have taken a Sharia-like position about apostates and the anti-Islamist position she has adopted. The Brandeis MSA student Facebook page is filled with an attitude of offended Islamist supremacism and rage over alleged "Islamophobia."

Ironically, none other than Brandeis Professor, Jytte Klausen, the author of *The Cartoons That Shook the World*, published her views in the Brandeis student newspaper *The Justice*. In her (Stockholm-syndrome?) view, giving Hirsi Ali a degree "undermines years of careful work to show that Brandeis University promotes the ideals of shared learning, religious toleration and coexistence, irrespective of religion."

Klausen was joined by Brandeis Professors Mary Baine Campbell and Susan Lanser of the English Department. Campbell told *The Justice* that "Hirsi Ali represents values that Brandeis, in naming itself after Justice [Louis] Brandeis, ... was founded in noble opposition to." Professor Susan Lanser said that Hirsi Ali's (outspoken views on Islam) foment an intolerance that is "wholly antithetical to Brandeisian values."

Women's and Gender Studies Professor, Mitra Shavarini, told *The Justice* that offering this award to Hirsi Ali is not in line with the University's mission, unless it wishes to "incite hate, mistrust and division among its community." She further stated that Hirsi Ali's approach to discourse "collapses thought in obscure, non-contextualized allegations that have no intellectual merit."

I have been told that more than forty professors signed a petition against honoring Hirsi Ali.

American campuses have long welcomed critiques of Judaism, Christianity, Mormonism etc. on the grounds of misogyny and Biblical-era atrocities. Secularists, atheists, and anti-religionists have been lionized. Great thinkers have, historically, condemned religion—all religion. Think of Voltaire, or Bernard Russell.

Over the years, Brandeis has awarded honorary degrees to a wide variety of worthy people. The awards are wide-ranging, balanced and reasonable.

In 1987, the award was given to Adrienne Rich who said: "With initial hesitation but finally strong conviction I endorse the Call for a U.S. Cultural and Academic Boycott of Israel." Although I am an admirer of her poetry, I believe that some of her awards, perhaps not this one, were given in recognition of the presumably "bold" stand she took on boycotting the Jewish state. In 2000, Brandeis also gave this award to Desmond M. Tutu, who has been quoted as saying that the "Jewish lobby" is too "powerful and scary." In 2006, Brandeis gave this award to Tony Kushner who is on record saying that he can "unambivalently say that I think it's a terrible historical problem that modern Israel came into existence."

One can openly criticize the Jewish state and be lionized. There was no groundswell of protest against these awards; if there were, they were not successful.

The conclusion: One can criticize Judaism, the Jewish state, America, real apartheid in South Africa, but one cannot criticize Islam, Islamic jihad, Islamic supremacism, and Islamic gender and religious apartheid without being attacked and silenced.

Newsmax
4/10/14

- 89 -

Brandeis Feminists Choose to Be "Islamically Correct" and Fail the Historical Moment

The Brandeis professors who demanded that Ayaan Hirsi Ali be "immediately" dis-invited wrote that "we are filled with shame at the suggestion that (Hirsi Ali's) above-quoted sentiments express Brandeis's values." The professors also castigated Hirsi Ali for her "core belief of the cultural backwardness of non-western peoples" and for her suggestion that "violence toward girls and women is particular to Islam." The professors note that such a view "obscure(s) such violence in our midst among non-Muslims, including on our own campus."

This is exactly what these professors are teaching the more than four thousand Brandeis students who signed a petition to rescind Ayaan Hirsi Ali's award.

Eighty seven professors, or 29% of the Brandeis faculty, signed this letter. These professors teach Physics, Anthropology, Near Eastern and Jewish Studies, English, Economics, Music, Film, Computer Science, Math, Sociology, Education—and Women and Gender Studies. Four percent of the signatories teach Anthropology, 6% teach Near Eastern and Jewish Studies, 9% teach Physics—and 21% teach Women and Gender Studies. These Brandeis feminists, both male and female, are defending Islamist supremacism, (which is an ideology, not a race), and are attacking a dark-skinned African Somali woman, who happens to be a feminist hero.

Feminists have called Hirsi Ali an "Islamophobe" and a "racist" many times for defending Western values such as women's rights, gay rights, human rights, freedom of religion, the importance of intellectual diversity, etc.

Over time, women no longer mattered as much to many Western feminists—at least, not as much as Edward Said's Arab men of color did. The Arab men were more fashionable victims who had not only been formerly "colonized" but who, to this day are, allegedly, still being "occupied." Feminists became multi-cultural relativists and refused to criticize other cultures, including misogyny within those other cultures.

They are guided by the same false moral equivalencies which the above Brandeis professors share. It is similar to the kind of false moral equivalence that author Deborah Scroggins made when she compared Hirsi Ali to one Aafiya Siddiqui in her 2012 book: *Wanted Women: Faith, Lies, and the War on Terror: The Lives of Ayaan Hirsi Ali and Aafia Siddiqui.* Scroggins is far more sympathetic to the Pakistani-born, American-educated Aafia Siddiqui, who became an Islamist terrorist and a rabid Jew hater (she is known as Lady Al Qaeda), than she is towards the Somali-Dutch feminist and apostate Ayaan Hirsi Ali, who eloquently opposes Islamic jihad and gender and religious apartheid. Hirsi Ali also supports the Jewish state.

Siddiqui married the nephew of Khalid Sheikh Mohammed (KSM), one of the masterminds of 9/11. She disappeared into Pakistan for many years. She was found wandering in Afghanistan, where she was arrested by American soldiers after they found her carrying bomb-making and chemical warfare instructions. Once captured, she picked up one of the soldiers' guns and shot at him.

Siddiqui received a Ph.D. in Neuroscience from Brandeis University. The university is certainly not to blame for her actions. However, according to Scroggins, as a student in America, Siddiqui joined the infamous Muslim Students Association and fell under the spell of one of bin Laden's own mentors who ran a Muslim charity in Brooklyn, New York. This is the same Muslim Student Association (a Muslim Brotherhood- and Hamas-related enterprise in America) that has just played such a prominent role in the Brandeis campaign to dis-invite Hirsi Ali.

Nevertheless, Scroggins views Siddiqui as a victim. Siddiqui is a religious Muslim, veiled to the eyeballs, and she has been sentenced to 86 years in prison. Many Muslims view her as a freedom fighter and, therefore, as unjustly imprisoned.

Scroggins—and the "dis-invite her" Brandeis professors—represent your typically misguided left-wing point of view. The West has allegedly caused jihad due to its imperialist, colonialist, racist, and capitalist policies. Scroggins, like so many left feminists, has absolutely no idea about the long and barbaric history of Islamic imperialism, colonialism, racism, slavery, and its practice of gender and religious apartheid.

Hirsi Ali championed the West and its values over and above the Islam that she had been exposed to in the Middle East. She became an apostate, a member of the Dutch Parliament, and ultimately, a woman who needed round-the-clock security against all the Islamist death threats against her.

Nevertheless, throughout the book, Scroggins shares Aafiya's political analysis and condemns and challenges Ayaan's views. Only on the very last page of her book does Scroggins admit that the entire premise of her "morally equivalent" comparison is flawed. She writes:

> That is not to say they are equivalent figures, morally or otherwise. They are not. Ayaan…fights only with words whereas the evidence leads me to conclude that Aafiya was almost certainly plotting murder during her missing years and perhaps prepared to further a biological or chemical attack on the United States on a scale to rival 9/11.

I wonder if the above Brandeis professors would also sympathize with Aafiya Siddiqui. I mourn the loss of an activist, vibrant, intellectually independent, and politically incorrect feminist Academy.

Israel National News
4/16/14

- 90 -

Nigeria's Boko Haram and the History of Child Rape in Jihad

On April 14, 2014, Boko Haram (whose name either means "Western education is forbidden" or "a colonialist fraud being perpetrated against us"), captured three hundred Christian and Muslim Nigerian schoolgirls to become their sex and domestic slaves. The Muslim fundamentalists swooped down upon them as they were learning in a "forbidden" secular government school. Some girls managed to escape. Two hundred and seventy six girls are still missing.

The world media calls this a "kidnapping." It is not a "kidnapping." It is the face of jihad, the way of jihad. Boko Haram are not holding these girls for ransom, they are not willing to return them for money. They already view the girls as their God-given booty, and as sale-able property.

The girls are between the ages of twelve and fifteen. The Christian girls will be raped, converted to Islam, and then, like the Muslims girls, "married" to one of their captors. Some will be trafficked into the sex trade, which is pandemic throughout Africa and the Muslim Middle East. Sharia law allows men to purchase the sexual favors of a female child or a young woman for one hour, a week, or a month. Private and public brothels exist as well.

Boko Haram are the Nigerian Taliban. Like their Pakistani and Afghan counterparts, they oppose education for girls and would rather marry and impregnate them instead—for Allah's sake.

Boko Haram's behavior is typical of any armed Muslim force beginning with Mohammed. The Prophet's warriors went on raids and systematically massacred the Jewish tribes in Arabia. The men were beheaded—and then the Prophet divided the women, children, houses, and chattels among the Muslims. The women were forcibly converted and kept as "wives" or slaves.

Thereafter, Muslim warriors in search of power, land, and gold, did much the same thing.

Contrary to the politically correct intelligentsia, who focus only on Western sins, Islam also has a long and ongoing history of imperialism, colonialism, gender and religious apartheid, conversion by the sword, sex slavery (of both boys and girls), polygamy, sex trafficking, and the brutal subordination and cyclical massacres of religious minorities.

Westerners either do not know this, do not want to know this, don't care all that much, or misunderstand this.

Journalists still believe that Boko Haram and other such groups are crying out against injustice and poverty, against government corruption and ineptitude—all of which do exist.

But that is not Boko Haram's major concern. They want to assert an Islamic state in Nigeria, similar to that which exists in Saudi Arabia, Iran, and Afghanistan. Such Muslim extremists, both Sunni and Shi'a, want Sharia law to dominate public and private life. This means that the state will have the power to stone people to death for adultery and apostasy, to amputate limbs for theft, to lash and jail for "blasphemy," to tax and hold hostage, jail, murder, or exile infidels.

Male polygamy will be legal, marriage will be forced, women will be veiled, normatively beaten and raped without recourse, honor killed for the slightest perceived disobedience. Women are breeders and housekeepers—an education would ruin them.

Nevertheless, the world is momentarily mobilized, we have a "teachable moment." Petitions have been signed, tweets tweeted, articles written, offers of military support tendered.

The capture of girls is horrifying but the Western intelligentsia say, let's not forget that there are many moderate Muslims who believe in women's rights and the Western enterprise. True—but this all takes the focus away from the way in which historical Islam views and treats women.

In 1971, hundreds of thousands of women were raped during the Bangladesh Liberation War. Pakistani Muslim soldiers publicly and repeatedly gang-raped and tortured Muslim (future Bangladeshi) women. These women became known as "Birangona," or "brave women." At the time, many killed themselves or, if pregnant, their families killed them in honor killings. Forty years later, those who survived are still traumatized and shamed by what was done to them. Many were humiliated by their relatives, rejected by their husbands.

At the time, the West paid no attention.

From 1992 on, Islamic paramilitary troops enslaved young Muslim girls in Algeria both sexually and domestically; they just grabbed them off the streets. If they tried to escape, they would be shot dead; the same was true when they became pregnant. Their names are lost in history.

At the time, the West paid no attention.

And then there was 2004, in Sudan, a long and ugly war in which ethnic Arab Muslims engaged in what I call "gender cleansing" when they publicly and repeatedly gang-raped mainly Black African Muslim, Christian, and animist women. I suggested setting up Women's Talking Tents where the raped girls and women could come and speak of their pain, see they were not alone, learn that it was not their fault.

Western governments did nothing.

I wonder what will happen to those poor Nigerian girls who survive this ordeal. Will they be rescued and embraced? Will they be able to one day see themselves as war heroes, not victims? Will they all be found?

Mainly, will the world finally take a strong stand against such barbaric Islamic groups?

Breitbart
5/9/14

327

- 91 -

The Boko Haram Girls May Already Have Been Genitally Mutilated

The entire world is momentarily focused on the captured Nigerian girls, many scenarios have been envisioned—and yet there is at least one issue no one has raised: That it is entirely possible that these poor girls have also been genitally mutilated. If so, that means that their rapes will be doubly torturous and traumatizing.

And make no mistake: They will be raped by their captors on their "wedding" night and/or over and over again by strangers if they are trafficked into a brothel.

Nigeria is both an African and an increasingly Muslim country. Experts have warred over whether female genital mutilation (FGM) is primarily pre-Islamic and tribally African or whether there is a basis for it in Islam. Both points of view have merit.

To the extent to which Boko Haram are following the rules of Islamic jihad, they will not think of rape as "rape." This is what women are for: to be used, to be profitable, to produce children and be domestic slaves. A Boko Haram warrior will have no conception of how this intimately violent act affects his victim—whom he does not think of as a "victim." This is a Western and infidel concept.

Boko Haram are, no doubt, using rape, not as a spoil of war, and not as a weapon of war, but as a form of gender cleansing, possibly a form of religious or ethnic cleansing when the victims are not Muslims.

This kind of jihad-rape was widely practiced in Sudan. Black African girls and women, sent out to forage for firewood and water, were publicly, repeatedly, gang-raped by ethnic Arab Muslims; some children

328

were as young as five or six years old.

Rape shames its victims, it breaks them; they can offer little resistance and become resigned to a life of self-blame and suffering. Many rape victims become clinically depressed and suicidal.

Imagine the pain of being forcibly penetrated when you have been sewn shut and thick scar tissue exists where there was once a clitoris, labia, and a vagina.

According to UNICEF, the U.S. State Department, and a variety of medical reports, either there are 30 million genitally mutilated women in Nigeria, or 41% of the female population has been mutilated. One report guesstimated that between 10-90% of women in the state of Borno, where Boko Haram are based, have been genitally mutilated.

In 2007, Thomas von der Osten-Sacken and Thomas Uwer wrote in the *Middle East Quarterly*, "there are indications that FGM might be a phenomenon of epidemic proportions in the Arab Middle East" and are being perpetrated, not for African tribal reasons, but for Islamic reasons.

In 2013, Shereen El Feki, in *Sex and the Citadel: Intimate Life in a Changing Arab World*, documented the epidemic nature of FGM in Egypt where more than 90% of the women have been mutilated. Increasingly, doctors and nurses perform the procedure. El Feki writes:

> Those who support FGM believe they have God on their side...that the practice is obligatory for Muslims....the Prophet Muhammad is said to have advised a female practitioner in Medina to 'not cut too severely as that is better for a woman and more desirable for a husband.'

Whether FGM is truly a "Muslim" obligation or whether it isn't, what matters is that so many Muslims believe it is and therefore act accordingly.

I hope that U.S. Navy Seals are on the ground and about to find these poor Nigerian girls. I fear their fate was sealed long ago when radical Islam arose in the world again and the West, for many reasons, did nothing to stop it.

Breitbart
5/12/14

- 92 -
Boko Haram: West Wakes Up,
Media Still Asleep

For weeks, I have been wrestling with the question: Should America and the West take on Boko Haram or not?

Now, France—not the United States—has convened a meeting of five western African states in Paris. American, British, and other European diplomats attended what was primarily a regional African alliance (Nigeria, Niger, Cameroon, Chad, and Benin). The Africans were, no doubt, assured of technical and behind-the-scenes Western assistance in order to take down Boko Haram. Israeli and Western experts have been on the ground for some time now.

French Prime Minister Hollande has done the right thing.

Americans do not really grasp what is going on in Nigeria. Our media are reluctant to publish the word "Muslim" or "Islam" when they cover terrorism; they justify or deny the Muslim hatred of Jewish Israel and allow the Muslim persecution of Christians to fly far beneath their radar. In fact, where Muslims are in the numerical "minority," as in India, the mainstream media have viewed them as "persecuted." No articles appear about the persecution of Hindus and Christians in Pakistan or about the ongoing illegal waves of Muslim jihadists and criminals into India.

Muslims are clearly waging a classic, military holy war (*jihad*) against Christians—as Boko Haram is doing in Nigeria; Time magazine presents it very differently.

In *Time* magazine's current (May 26) issue, Belinda Luscombe puts Boko Haram's "abduction" of 276 schoolgirls in a politically correct context. Her article, "Bring Back All Girls," minimizes and "disappears" the fact that capturing infidel girls for sex is a legitimate act of jihad. Instead, the 276 Nigerian schoolgirls are shown as only a very small part of the kind of "forced labor" that exists in the world. Luscombe writes:

> The most conservative abolitionists estimate that 21 million people are currently in some sort of involuntary servitude, while others say it is closer to 30 million....According to the U.N., victims from 126 different countries have been found in 118 other countries having been taken there against their will or through deceit. China, India, and Pakistan have the most slaves, followed by Nigeria.

A pull quote reveals the article's political intentions: "Move the spotlight that is currently trained on Borno almost anywhere else in the world and it will reveal trade in human beings."

Time presents a map which shows us rates of "slavery" "sex trafficking" and "forced labor" in Thailand, Australia, India, China, Russia, Africa, Mexico, the United States and South America. Entirely missing from this map is the Arab Muslim Middle East.

The article goes on to describe how awful ordinary life is for Nigerian girls in terms of being sex-trafficked, forced into early marriage, etc. Luscombe does not add that many Nigerian girls are also genitally mutilated—somehow, she missed that.

The first time that *Time* mentions religion is when poverty is discussed. Ultimately, *Time* says, the country's wealth is "unevenly spread" because it is "concentrated in the southern, predominantly Christian south...the north, where Boko Haram operates, is excruciatingly poor and mostly Muslim." The article concedes, once, almost in passing, that Boko Haram wants to establish a "separate nation under Sharia" but, that "many experts believe the conflict in the north is more about economic desperation and thuggery than faith."

The article drives home these main points again and again and closes with a quote from a Nigerian nun: "This is not just a Nigerian problem anymore. This is happening everywhere."

It is true: Sex trafficking and varieties of indentured servitude and wage slavery exist globally. As does jihad. The point here—one that PM Hollande obviously understands—is that terrorized civilians, both Muslim and infidel, have proved unable to defend themselves and that global jihad is getting stronger, not dying out. Since the entire world is, for a brief moment, paying attention to the face of jihad in Nigeria, this might be a good place to start the necessary and inevitable push back—even if it is only "symbolic," even if it only (!) manages to rescue a few hundred girls.

Let Boko Haram and other jihadists know that innocent civilians and inept governments have had enough—and that the West is ready to place its technical and special forces expertise on the line to tackle barbarism.

Breitbart
5/18/14

Stopping the Flood of Female Genital Mutilation: Egypt Brings Historic Case

For the first time in Egyptian history, an Egyptian physician, Dr. Raslan Fadl, will stand trial for the female genital mutilation of a thirteen-year-old girl—not only because he broke the 2008 Mubarak-era law against such practices, but because the girl died.

Dr. Fadl claims she had an allergic reaction to the penicillin used for the procedure.

Her family will probably settle for compensation for her death, as they cannot accuse the physician of undertaking a procedure that they themselves had not asked him to perform.

Doctors have actually been seen as the solution to this intractable problem. Long ago, African and Muslim feminist activists decided that since the practice had such widespread support, that a physician (ideally in a hospital, ideally using anesthesia, and ideally performing a minimal mutilation, not the more common maximal versions) would be safer than an illiterate peasant woman with her rusty razor blades and knives.

According to UNICEF, 91% of married Egyptian women between 15-49 have been subjected to FGM.

I first learned about female genital mutilation (FGM) in 1976, when my esteemed feminist colleague, an American in exile from her native South Africa, Dr. Diana Russell, published her proceedings of a legendary International Tribunal on Crimes Against Women. One woman from Guinea testified about FGM.

What she said was horrifying. Adult women, including the victim's female relatives, held down girls of twelve and "without any anesthesia or regard for hygiene" attacked their genitalia with "the neck of a broken bottle... when the clitoris had been ripped out, the women howled with joy." This witness also said that in other countries, "this savage mutilation is not enough; it is also necessary to sew the woman up...leaving only a small space for the passage of blood and urine."

Another witness, from France, testified about the side effects and complications of this procedure: "Hemorrhage, tetanus, urinary infection and septic anemia are not infrequent results. The perineum (tissue) of those who survive hardens, and will tear in childbirth." She explained that some women experience agony if their clitoral area is even gently touched. And those who give birth may develop fistulas (urinary and bowel incontinence) and may be rejected by their families because of their foul odor. This practice is pandemic all over the Arab Middle East and among Christians, Muslims, and animists in black Africa.

This issue remained relatively unknown until 1979-1980 when I worked at the United Nations. In 1979, Fran Hosken, an Austrian-American scholar, published The Hosken Report which exposed the barbaric custom. Some African and Muslim feminists who were connected to the UN immediately condemned Hosken as a "white imperialist" whose outrage and exposé might hurt their within-system work to have physicians at least minimize the danger and the trauma involved in such mutilation.

In the late 1970s and early 1980s, I also learned about FGM from my Egyptian colleague, Nawal El-Sadawii, a physician herself, as well as a leading feminist. She is also a novelist and a very good one. El-Sadawii wrote about her own traumatic clitoridectomy when she was six years old. She was terrified, in physical agony, but she remembers that her own mother smiled during the procedure. When El-Sadawii heard similar stories from thousands of her female patients, she began a crusade against this atrocity.

El-Sadawii rose to become the director of Public Health in Egypt but, in 1972 when she published her book, *Women and Sex* (which discussed FGM), she was dismissed. El-Sadawii was subsequently jailed for three months for running a gynecological clinic under the "Law for the Protection of Values from Shame."

In 1983, the African-American novelist and poet, Alice Walker, published a book and a movie, both titled *Warrior Marks*, about her campaign against FGM in Senegal, Gambia, and Burkina Faso.

In 2008, Egyptian President Hosni Mubarak criminalized FGM in the penal code.

In 2011, Egyptian President Mohammed Morsi, a leading member of the Muslim Brotherhood, said that "this (FGM) is a private issue that he will not actively combat."

In July 2013, General Abdel al-Sisi, the former head of the Egyptian Army and now the Deputy Prime Minister (running for the Presidency), overthrew the Muslim Brotherhood and designated it a terrorist organization. Al-Sisi remains an independent.

Full circle back to the beginning of this piece. It is on al-Sisi's watch that this unprecedented trial against a physician is now taking place in Egypt—based on a 2008 Mubarak-era law.

Just today, a group of scholars and experts wrote an Open Letter to Democratic Senator Patrick Leahy and other Senators protesting the Senate decision to block "the $650 million in military aid to Egypt that the Administration has agreed to release. Egypt is and continues to be America's strongest ally in the Arab world and has been a key partner in the war on terrorism. Egypt is now facing a war with an al-Qaeda affiliate in their (own) backyard and they need America's full political and military support as they face the same enemy that declared war against the United States so many years ago."

Signatories include Robert C. MacFarlane (National Security Advisor to President Reagan), Donald Rumsfeld, Dr. Walid Phares, Katharine Gorka, and numerous retired military personnel and scholars.

No one in Egypt believes that the physician will be seriously punished. Few people believe such a trial will convince other physicians and non-medical personnel to stop performing such mutilations. Men whose own mothers and grandmothers endured FGM will not marry girls who are not genitally mutilated, and no daughter's father wants to be responsible for her permanent upkeep—unless they can be persuaded otherwise.

Breitbart
5/22/14

- 94 -
The Real War on Women:
The Stoning of Farzana Iqbal in Pakistan

I just appeared for a rather intense hour on the BBC on the *World Have Your Say* program to talk about three separate cases in the news: the Pakistani woman who was just stoned to death for daring to marry the man she loved; the massacre in Isla Vista, California, fueled by a violently misogynistic manifesto; and the German tabloid exposure of Kate Middleton's bottom.

I appeared with some very wonderful speakers in Pakistan, the United States, and the UK on this issue.

As to the first story: Early today, a 25-year-old woman was stoned to death by twelve—yes, twelve—male relatives, beginning with her father and including her brothers and possibly cousins. They did so right outside the High Court in Lahore. This is a brazen statement about the refusal to abide by secular Pakistani law.

This victim's blessed name was Farzana Iqbal and bravely, tragically, she refused to marry her cousin and instead married the man she loved. One of the Pakistani women on the BBC program pointed out that none of the many bystanders rescued her or stopped these men from killing her.

A crowd gathered. No one dared intervene. The bystander phenomenon coupled with cultural approval for this act of barbarism, coupled with some vicarious enjoyment involved in seeing an "uppity" woman punished, coupled with the fear that if one intervened they, too, would be stoned, stayed the hand of one and all.

According to one news account, Farzana's husband claimed that her family had wanted money from him and, failing to get it, they killed her. This suggests that the family may have been poor. However, wealthy families in Pakistan also commit brazen honor killings.

In 1999, in a high-profile case in Pakistan, twenty-eight-year-old Samia Imran was shot to death in her feminist lawyer's office for having initiated divorce proceedings from a violent husband, a man who was also her first cousin.

Samia's parents were wealthy. Her father, Ghulam Sarwar Khan Mohammed, was one of the most successful businessmen in the North West Frontier and the president of the Peshawar Chamber of Commerce; her mother, Sultana, was a gynecologist. They prided themselves on being modern and liberal. Thus, they told Samia that she could leave her violent husband and return to school; they even had a hand in banning her husband from the home. Samia's parents were adamant: Whatever she did, she could never, ever get divorced. This meant that, at twenty-eight, Samia would have to resign herself to a life without intimate companionship. An affair would be out of the question. Samia told others that she feared her parents "would kill her" if she disobeyed them.

Samia decided to initiate divorce proceedings. She made an appointment with two leading feminist lawyers, Hina Jilani and Asma Jahangir. Within five minutes of Samia's entering their offices, her mother came in, accompanied by a hired hit man who shot Samia to death. Unbelievably, Samia's paternal uncle was there, too. The hit man proceeded to kidnap at gunpoint a woman, Shahtaj Qizalbash, who worked in the law office building.

Many Pakistanis were not angry that the Sarwars had murdered their own daughter. On the contrary, violent demonstrations broke out against her feminist lawyers—whom the police and the courts refused to protect. The lawyers received death threats from religious extremists. Imran's family organized a meeting of the Peshawar Chamber of Commerce which supported the murder and issued fatwas demanding that the lawyers be punished. Samia's father considers himself a "liberal." He is also a realist. He is not in a position "to change society. Everyone must have honor."

Please note: Her mother carried this murder out in person; contrary to myth, women are also perpetrators and collaborators when it comes to the honor killing of their own daughters. And also note: Absolutely no one has been prosecuted for this heinous crime.

Pakistan is a terrible place. Honor murders are committed without fear of prosecution. Even if an arrest is made, jail sentences are rare. The tribal concept of family honor trumps all western concepts of universal human rights.

I stayed on the BBC to discuss 22-year-old Eliot Rodger's massacre in Isla Vista, California. He killed six men and women and wounded fourteen. He then committed suicide. There was an extraordinary internet outpouring from women about their own experiences of similar sexist verbal abuse, sexual harassment, rape, near-rape, domestic violence, etc. The murderer's manifesto was hateful towards women (whom he wanted to punish for rejecting him) and toward sexually active men (for living a more enjoyable life than he did). It is too chilling to quote in full.

A culture in which verbal and sexual harassment and rape are both glorified and criminalized, a culture in which the eroticization of young girls as well as prostitution and pornography flourish as never before—such a culture is bound to profoundly influence the loose cannon, the mentally ill, the evil, the haters, those who have access to guns or drugs, who will then unpredictably act upon such propaganda with impunity.

Some American feminist voices on the BBC program spoke about feeling relief that so many other women were responding to the hashtag #yesallwomen; they also felt anxious and fearful of so much misogyny. Some said that internet activism was fully underway. Said I: It is only the start. Often, when one tweets something, that is the end of it. No legislation gets crafted and passed. One merely expresses oneself and feels stronger that one is not alone. I am counting on the coming generation of feminists, both men and women, do more than that.

Our last topic was the German newspaper's publishing Kate Middleton's exposed bottom when the wind blew her dress up. Poor taste, beneath contempt said I—but proof, yet again, that no woman, however royal, is really spared this culture of public shaming. All women are equal in terms of eroticized body parts when it comes to providing fodder for tabloid rags.

Breitbart
5/27/14

- 95 -

Muslim Women's Liberation:
Nadia Shahram in Seneca Falls

On July 18-19, 2014, a group of Muslim women, led by attorney Nadia Shahram, will hold a convention in Seneca Falls to issue a "Declaration of the Equalities for Muslim Women."

Symbolically and historically, this is an important event, one that may only be possible in the West.

In 1776, in bold and stirring words, fifty-six men signed the American Declaration of Independence. I was not there—but because of this document, I have not grown up in a colony of the British Commonwealth, and I pay no taxes to the queen.

In 1848, American feminists launched their Declaration of Sentiments in Seneca Falls. I was not there, either. However, my life as an American woman has been immeasurably improved by their work. Sixty-eight women and thirty-two men were signatories.

Elizabeth Cady Stanton, Lucretia Mott, and Susan B. Anthony were all abolitionists; Mott had not been allowed to speak at an anti-slavery conference in London because they were women. They called a meeting in Seneca Falls and presented their Declaration, which drew upon the language of the American Declaration of Independence. "When in the course of human events," the feminists began, continuing on to "we hold these truths to be self-evident."

Thereafter, they parted company with our august ancestors and addressed the specific "disenfranchisement of one-half the people in this country" who are therefore "aggrieved, oppressed, and fraudulently deprived of their most sacred rights." This included the right to vote, own property, receive decent wages, obtain a higher education, merit custody or "guardianship" of their children, be allowed to practice law, medicine, and theology, and participate in the affairs of the church.

The nineteenth century feminists did not view religion as a primary stumbling block. On the contrary. Therefore, when Elizabeth Cady Stanton and a committee of 26 women published The Women's Bible (Part One in 1895, Part Two in 1898), criticizing both the Old and New Testaments, they were formally denounced by the National American Woman Suffrage Association. The question of God or of organized religion divided the early feminists.

Today, Muslims are also divided.

In 2007, I was privileged to chair the opening panel of the Secular Muslim Summit in St. Petersburg, Florida. They issued a Declaration, which nine Muslim men and five Muslim women signed. Chair Ibn Warraq called for "an age of Enlightenment. Without critical examination of Islam, it will remain dogmatic, fanatical, and intolerant, and will continue to stifle thought, human rights, individuality, originality, and truth."

The secularists affirmed an "inviolate freedom of individual conscience;" saw "no 'Islamophobia' in submitting Islamic practices to criticism or condemnation when they violate reason or human rights"; demanded a "separation of religion and state"; called upon the "governments of the world to reject Sharia law, fatwa courts, clerical rule, and penalties for blasphemy and apostasy." They also demanded "the elimination of practices such as female circumcision, honor killing, forced veiling, and forced marriage." These dissidents called for "the release of Islam from its captivity to the totalitarian ambitions of power-hungry men and the rigid strictures of orthodoxy." They concluded, "We say to Muslim believers: there is a noble future for Islam as a personal faith, not as a political doctrine."

Even these staunch secularists left the door open for religion as a private matter.

Now, seven years later, a group of Muslim women will gather to discuss and sign a Declaration of Equalities for Muslim Women. The document also reads, "When in the course of human events ... we hold these truths to be (not self-evident) but indisputable."

The Declaration of Equalities begins and ends with quotes from the Qur'an. It interprets these verses as signifying the God-given equality of women and men. While this Declaration is global and universal in intention and language, there are some very specific areas that concern

340

Muslim and, I must add, Hindu, Sikh, and, in some areas, Jewish women, as well.

The Declaration calls for the "right of self-determination for all women." It demands "that women have the opportunity to gain permanent custody of children." This is a major problem for women, both in Sharia courts and in religious Jewish courts. Based on my research over the years, custody is still a problem for women in American secular courts. Please read my updated 2011 edition of *Mothers on Trial: The Battle for Children and Custody.*

The Muslim women's Declaration demands that women not be killed in the name of "honor" and that crimes against women be swiftly prosecuted; that women be allowed to gain access to an education, employment, gender-neutral inheritance, citizenship, and nationality rights.

So far, all rights demanded apply to women of all faiths. Then, there is this, which is addressed in this Declaration: "We insist that crimes such as stoning, burning, acid pouring, and mutilation not only be illegal and punishable, but the perpetrators be publicly prosecuted by the courts."

Such crimes are almost unique to Muslims, and I hope and pray that this Declaration is taken seriously far and wide, beginning in the West.

The heroism of Muslim and ex-Muslim women is astounding. Think of Nudood Ali, Malala Yusufzai, Ayaan Hirsi Ali, and the countless Afghan women who stand up to extraordinary misogyny and barbarism. Imagine if they could gain further momentum from Muslim women living in the relative safety of the West. The organizer Shahram told me:

> My hope is that this movement will continue over the next decade and grow into a world community. We want to be able to add new declarations aimed at improving the lives of Muslim Women. My dream is that we generate enough signatures and support to have some influence on foreign governments and courts to amend discriminatory laws. I also want to change the attitudes and perceptions of Muslim women living in the U.S. and the West. They often succumb to the pressures of the community to conform. That is the biggest problem in Muslim communities today, conformity to antiquated men-made laws.

Please go to Seneca Falls. Meet the speakers. Agree or discuss, respectfully. But above all, Be on record supporting this next great wave of global feminism.

Breitbart
6/10/14

- 96 -

The West Must Stand with Muslim Feminists Against Sexual Violence

I was recently asked to advise a young Arab Muslim woman on her doctoral dissertation. Her work concerned violence against women—honor killings in particular. I said it would be my "honor" to do so. However, this feminist, from a wealthy family, made the mistake of announcing her intentions to her family. They—her husband, father, brothers—stopped her and gave her a choice: Leave graduate school or work on another subject entirely. (I am purposely not identifying the country she lives in.)

The message is clear: Exposing the crime is shameful—not the crime itself. If an Arab or a Muslim writes about normalized sexual and physical violence against women, gays, and political dissidents, with some exceptions, he or she risks severe punishment, even death.

Ironically, a similarly intense kind of censorship also currently exists in the Western academic world. Families are not enforcing tribal values; the professors are. Last week, I heard from another doctoral student based in Europe, who risks losing many years of work if she does not follow a party line position against Israel. No Ph.D—or she must positively cite anti-Israel sources such as Noam Chomsky and Judith Butler. It does not seem to matter that the dissertation is not about the Middle East.

We live at a time when people, including our presumed intellectual leaders, demand that everyone salute one flag, in one voice, and avoid any and all thought crimes lest they be shunned by everyone they know. Here, I am talking about the once and future Free World.

This reality makes the heroism on the ground in Muslim countries all the more praise-worthy.

For example, late last week, in Tunis, Tunisia, activists, both men and women, staged a silent march to protest the honor killing of a 13-year-old girl. Her crime? She was walking home from school with a male classmate. Her father burned her alive.

We have all seen the enormous violence against women in India among both Hindus and Muslims. Women are gang-raped to death; women are sexually harassed constantly; they are also, heartbreakingly, raped and hung from trees. The level of misogyny is stunning, surreal. And yet, simultaneously, a Muslim women's organization in India has just demanded a complete ban on polygamy and child marriages.

> The draft law proposed stipulates that a Muslim marriage should be solemnised only when the bride is at least 18 years old and the groom 21. Further, there should be 'an unambiguous consent' by both, and neither of them should have a living spouse. Polygamous marriage should be strictly prohibited and marriages should be compulsorily registered, payment of maintenance to the wife and children must be made mandatory during the marriage, or in the event of separation and divorce.

Similarly, we have seen the male mobs in Cairo strip and gang-rape any woman, almost to death, who dares to simply walk out in public. Even if she is "properly" veiled, the Islamist imams have empowered men to view her as "fresh meat," prey, who exists to be to devoured by men.

President al-Sisi made a point of visiting the hospital bedside of just such a victim of a rape spree in Tahrir Square—and so far, seven men have been arrested for having sexually assaulted up to fifty women.

Despite the potential danger involved, Egyptian-American journalist, Mona Eltahawy, has just penned an op-ed piece (dateline, Cairo), in which she recounts her own sexual assault at the hands of the Egyptian police and insists that such police violence against women existed under the Muslim Brotherhood and still exists under President Al-Sisi. She writes: "It does not matter where you stand on Egypt's political spectrum; if you are a woman your body is not safe. We need a comprehensive campaign that tackles sexual violence."

Six years ago, my friend, the German-Turkish feminist lawyer,

Seyran Ates, wrote a book: *Islam Needs a Sexual Revolution*. And then she called and asked whether she could stay with me in New York City. I immediately agreed. She told me that the Berlin (!) police had told her to leave town for "for a while." Ates had nearly been assassinated for her work with Turkish immigrant women; one of her clients was shot dead and Seyran had to spend years in rehab.

Seyran, who has a large and supportive family in the West, decided that it might be necessary to keep a low profile and work on other, less dangerous projects for the time being.

We are all connected. The barbarism that is raging in the Middle East and Central Asia is also here. We read about it, we view it online. Muslims have turned Malmo into the rape capital of Sweden but it is not politically correct to say so. More and more immigrant girls who live in Sweden are genitally mutilated. Interestingly, the newspaper fails to tell us what nationalities or religions are involved in perpetrating what is a crime in Sweden.

Breitbart
6/23/14

- 97 -
Self-Defense Forbidden to Women in Iran Which Jails and Executes the Children Who Dare

They rape and torture women in Iran: First, at home; then in a state prison.

Iran publicly executes women for daring to kill their attackers in self-defense. They do so publically in order to terrify others, ensure that they understand that when the authorities come for them, no one will intervene on their behalf. A public execution is a fine way to keep a civilian population permanently cowed.

And yet, there are things that will not allow one to go on, brutalities on a daily basis that are, perhaps, even more sickening than a public execution.

Rayhana Jabbari has been sentenced to hang for the crime of killing the man who was attempting to rape her. She has already been in jail for seven years. Even the United Nations has called for a "fair trial." Her execution was postponed but she remains in danger of being hung at any moment.

As does an Iranian child bride, Razieh Ebrahimi, married at 14, and who now faces imminent execution for killing her violent and abusive husband when she was 17 years old. She has been languishing in prison for the last four years.

Farzana Moradi was also accused of murdering her husband. She was married to him when she was 15, became a mother at 16, and wanted "out" by the time she was nineteen. "Out" did not exist for her. "Out" meant killing her husband. Despite an international campaign on her behalf, the Islamic Republic of Iran hung her on March 4, 2014. Farzana was 26 years old.

Interestingly enough, if a murderer's family is willing to pay "blood money," the victim's family has the power to spare his life. This is true, even in Iran. Safar Anghouti's family raised fifty thousand dollars via an internet campaign—and he was freed.

I am not familiar with a woman's family buying her life or a murdered man's family accepting money for his death.

Iran is the world's most notorious executioner of children. They hang homosexuals. They routinely rape female and male prisoners.

Our government believes it can and must make alliances with this country—the same country that has threatened Israel with genocide and has funded Hezbollah, its Islamist striking force in both the Arab Middle East and in South America.

The United States did not act to support The Greens when they marched in Tehran and both they and we will surely reap the whirlwind.

I was first in Tehran in 1961, when I was on my way to visit Kabul. The Iranian women whom I met were elegant and sophisticated. They wore expensive western clothing and perfume, smoked cigarettes, talked in French and English. No one was veiled.

Yes, the poverty was shocking—still, the smells of the bazaar were enchanting, and I loved the food, the architecture and the wide open sky.

Fifteen years later, I was involved with an organization known as CAIFI, Students Against the Shah. Their leader, Reza Baraheni, an author and intellectual, had a standard talk about having been tortured by SAVAK because he had opposed the monarchy and yearned for liberation. He flew home after Khomeini's "revolution," ecstatic about the possibility of "freedom."

A year later, my friends, Kate Millett and Sophie Kier, were in Iran for International Women's Day—invited by Baraheni. Guess what? Khomeini arrested the two feminists. For days, we agonized about how to get them out. Amazingly, Khomeini decided to let them go!

The very next year, Baraheni invited me to Tehran to speak on International Woman's Day. "You understand the Muslim soul, you can bring feminism in a soft and feminine way." Needless to say, I did not go and within years, Reza himself was lucky enough to flee the Monster Mullah regime and find asylum in Canada.

Today, the women are garbed in fierce black. They scowl. They are forced to wear chadors while on bicycles and in swimming pools.

And yet: The Iranian women I have met who live in exile are exceptionally feisty and fierce for freedom. They claim Zoroastrian roots, as well as Ba'hai, Jewish, and Muslim roots. In general, they are very accomplished women.

Once, I was asked to join a panel of Iranian and Afghan women associated with the United Nations. Although I had vowed never to return to the UN, I made this one exception. As the panel began, a force of six to eight Iranian women all in heavy black chadors came in and sat down all in one row in battle readiness. They were here to intimidate the speaker. One of the Iranian women panelists immediately jumped up, pointed them out, pointed to them and then said: "We know who you are. We know why you are here. You do not scare us and you cannot silence us. Just tell your Masters back in Tehran that, one day, women will bring them down."

I was stunned and impressed. Shortly thereafter, the Iranian women, on a signal from their leader, all walked out.

Oh, how I wish our government would take a lesson from this brave Iranian women panelist and behave in similar ways.

Breitbart
6/24/14

- 98 -

The National Organization for Women Tables a Resolution Which Considers Sharia Law

I just realized that, with one or two exceptions, none of my left-liberal feminist compatriots of nearly fifty years have said a word to me about Hamas's kidnapping-murder of three Israeli teenagers. Not a word in the 18 days while they were missing. Silence since their bodies were found.

This silence was not a surprise after a career observing American feminists' relationship to the Middle East. Very few American feminists, for example, have understood my work on honor based crimes, including honor (horror) killing. Luckily, Muslim and ex-Muslim feminists and dissidents, North American and European prosecutors, detectives, and conservative intellectuals rely upon this work. But not feminists. Not yet.

So what are some American feminists doing right now?

This past weekend, the National Organization for Women (NOW) held a Strategy Summit in New Mexico. Please understand: I am more than sympathetic to many items on the women's rights agenda ranging from reproductive freedom to equal pay for equal work to the criminalization of violence against women.

NOW considered a series of resolutions. They passed those in favor of a "Paycheck Fairness Act," the "Expansion of Pregnant Women's Rights," the elimination of "Debtor's Prisons," "Pay Equity for Tipped Workers," "Reframing Abortion Rights Advocacy," "Creating a National Monument To Honor Our Foremothers"—and then their resolutions descended into a dreadful mire of politically correct madness.

Child care and parenting issues were nowhere to be found. A series of politically correct slogans were passed, with some demanding immediate compliance.

For example, NOW passed a resolution about "Dismantling White Privilege." This one requires that each chapter report "must include verification of participation in racial justice actions." In terms of Women With Disabilities: "Be it resolved that NOW conference events and discussions will include presenters who are women with disabilities." Okay, fair enough.

The two Resolutions that NOW did not pass are even more interesting than the ones they passed.

Believe it or not: Someone—bless whoever it was—actually tried to pass a Resolution against "Culturally Oppressive Laws Against Women and Girls." All the resolution called for was a public education campaign. However, it specifically singled out Sharia law and listed the human and women's rights violations performed in its name.

> Whereas, one of NOW's official priorities is to eliminate violence against women…we urge NOW members to educate law enforcement, educators, medical professionals, and community leaders to the danger of Sharia law.

This resolution was tabled for further discussion.

Had anyone at NOW asked me (and no one has for a very long time), I would have broadened this idealistic Resolution to include any and all "cultural" practices that violate American law. I would not have focused only on Sharia law. The French law which banned the burqa was ethnically and religiously "neutral." Face masks are banned. One's identity must be visible.

Breitbart
7/1/14

- 99 -
The European Court Upholds French Burqa Ban

On July 1, 2014, the European Court of Human Rights upheld the 2010 French burqa ban, a religion-neutral piece of legislation which eliminates face masks. By a "majority" vote of seventeen judges with two dissents, the Court found that the ban did not violate "Article 8 [the right respect for private and family life of the European Convention on Human Rights] and [there was] no violation of Article 9 [the right to respect for freedom of thought, conscience and religion]." No further appeals are possible.

I applaud this decision, on the grounds of security, and as a matter of women's human rights. The obliteration of female identity is not a Western value.

Criminals and terrorists wear masks. Men have been known to dress in flowing burqas in order to rob jewelry stores or escape after committing a terrorist act. In an interview, scholar Daniel Pipes said:

> France leads the way in banning a repugnant garment from the public square that restricts young women's rights, poses a criminal and terrorist danger to the society, and does yet other forms of damage. In this, Americans should emulate the braver and wiser French.

In addition to the very real danger of terrorism and ordinary crime, there is also a human rights violation involved in face-masking. As previously noted, veiled women are confined to an isolation and sen-

351

sory deprivation chamber; isolation and sensory deprivation are forms of torture and health hazards.

It is important to understand that the French ban is not specific to Islam. The French law is ethnicity- and religion-neutral and refers only to a generic "face-covering." In 2004, France became the first European country to legally restrict all religious clothing in public schools: Veils, visible Christian crosses, Jewish skullcaps, and hijab (headscarves) were forbidden, not in public, but in public *schools*.

I also understand that the matter is complex and usually poorly understood.

First, Westerners have little knowledge of the century-long struggle which took place in Muslim countries to abolish the Veil in Afghanistan, Iran, Turkey, Syria, Egypt, Iraq, and the Maghreb.

Second, Westerners naively believe that face veiling is an Islamic religious requirement and thus, under our belief in freedom of religion, that we must permit whatever someone says is a religious requirement.

However, Muslim religious scholars and intellectuals, as well as feminists, have explained, over and over again, that the Qur'an only requires that men as well as women dress "modestly" and that women cover their bosoms.

Third, so many formerly cosmopolitan societies have, in the last fifteen-twenty years, been conquered by radical Islamist jihad. Today, the face veil often—not always, but often—signifies radical Islam, jihad, and the most extreme misogyny. It sets Muslim women apart who are living in the West; often signifies the existence of parallel, non-integrated communities; reinforces the tribal and ethnic customs which discourage Muslims from befriending infidels. Most importantly, if women refuse to face veil, or if their headscarf (hijab) comes undone, they may be beaten or ultimately "honor" killed for such disobedience.

Here is what makes the matter tricky. Sociologist Marnia Lazreg, in her book, *Questioning the Veil: Open Letters to Muslim Women*, implores them to voluntarily refuse to veil. Lazreg views this as a far better alternative than having the government tell women what to wear and what not to wear. But realistically, women who are subjected to normalized beating and stalking and who are expected to obey in all ways may not be capable of "resisting" this oppression. In this matter, Resistance=Death.

Where the matter is at its most tricky is in terms of western views about individual liberty and religious freedom.

Religious Muslim and feminist activist, Raquel Evita Saraswati, wears hijab (a headscarf) and her scarves are exceedingly glamorous and friendly. She fully understands how face veils (niqabs) and burqas are "tools being used to render women invisible." Nevertheless, Saraswati views such a ban as an "affront to Western values and women's liberty." Her main point: "Compulsion in matters of religion and expression works against both the promise of secularism and the best parts of faith."

In my view, as long as one woman in the West is "horror" killed for refusing to veil, the West has a duty to remove this as a temptation to murder.

It is impossible for Western governments and international organizations to prevent the acid attacks or honor killings of women in Muslim countries who refuse to cover their faces, but why tie society's hands on Western soil? Why would Western countries prize the subordination of women and protect it as a religious right at a time when many Muslim women in the West refuse to face veil? When it is understood that face masks (niqabs) and the burqa are not religious requirements but are, rather, political statements—perhaps merely ethnic, tribal, and misogynistic customs—there is no reason whatsoever for Western traditions of religious tolerance to misconstrue the face-covering of Muslim women as a religious duty.

Breitbart
7/2/14

- 100 -
New York City Artists Favor Face Masks

Two Upper West side artists think New York women should try wearing face masks, also known as "niqab." Their names are Saks Afridi and Quinza Najm. They are calling upon women to don black face masks and take a "selfie."

The political art project began as a private experiment when Najm began wearing niqab (erroneously referred to as "hijab," which is just a headscarf) in her neighborhood; she encountered some hostile responses. "Go home!"

At that point, Najm decided that concealing her facial identity was an act of assertive liberation and a challenge to a presumably "tolerant" America. She launched a hashtag #DamniLookGood and asked other women, both Muslim and non-Muslim—men too—to don niqab as "an exercise in tolerance."

Some women who tried on the black niqab and close black head covering found it "sexy" to be concealed. Najm also points out that you can wear "crappy clothes" underneath and be very "comfortable." (Here she must be talking about a full body covering as well).

The two artists claim, on their website, that a woman can "choose" to wear niqab and when she does she is "in complete control of her sexuality, and ultimately that's what makes her so beautiful."

Western adventurers and artists have a long history of "slumming." They go "native," both politically and in terms of couture. Lawrence of Arabia and Isabelle Eberhardt both dressed the part of Arabs. European and American leftists marching against America and for "Palestine" often don keffiyas which they wear around their necks but which can also be worn as face and head masks.

354

I wonder what Afridi and Najm would have to say to all those girls and women who have been honor murdered for refusing to face-veil, or because their wore their veils improperly; or to those fifteen Saudi teenage girls who tried to flee the fire burning down their schoolhouse but were pushed back in to their deaths because the Morality Police did not want them to survive if they were, even temporarily, naked-faced, and bare-headed.

These artists and all who agree with them are treating what is mainly a forced choice in the Muslim world (and in Muslim communities in the West), as a potentially free choice. They are, in essence, donning the equivalent of "black face," or slave chains, and saying that this feels good—in New York City, where they are only play-acting, and can remove their face veils without any negative consequence.

In our times, the Islamic face and body veil signify the utter subordination of women. It is also the flag of jihad.

"Tolerance" and religious reciprocity would consist of these two New York City artists being able to drive by themselves in Saudi Arabia, naked-faced and without a male escort; being able to practice Christianity without being stoned to death or executed in Sudan; being able to run a shelter for battered women in Kabul or Herat, naked-faced, without being shot dead; being able to demand an education for girls without the Pakistani Taliban shooting a bullet into your brain. While I am glad that Malala Yusufzai just won a Noble Peace Prize for her extraordinary heroism in this regard, I must point out that it is Westerners, not the Pakistani Taliban, who gave her an award.

We must be careful that our "tolerance" for the "intolerant" does not lead to even more "intolerance."

Otherwise, we are merely play-acting, just like these two New York artists are doing.

Breitbart
10/14/14

- 101 -
British Officials Uncover Hundreds of New Cases of FGM in the UK

The British National Health Service—in a first-of-its-kind, just released study—has documented 467 "newly identified cases" of girls and women who had been genitally mutilated. Half live in London.

Previously, 1,279 such girls and women were known to be receiving post-mutilation treatment. However, estimates suggest that up to "170,000 women and girls living in the UK may have undergone FGM."

This is simply not acceptable.

As I've previously noted, female genital mutilation (FGM) is not at all like male circumcision. It is often a life-threatening and life-ending procedure with routinely terrible consequences. And then there is a life-long post-traumatic stress disorder that normally accompanies the experience of having been forced into such suffering, usually by your mother or grandmother, and at the hands of a female butcher.

Matters are far worse in non-Western countries. Earlier this year, the World Health Organization estimated that 125 million women have been genitally mutilated. They confirmed that this hellish procedure renders absolutely no health benefit and, on the contrary, harms its victims beyond measure and violates their human rights. As we know, the practice is common in the Arab Muslim Middle East and in parts of Muslim, Christian, and animist Africa.

This particularly heinous crime is perpetrated—not only in England but also in America. A lawyer who deals with immigrant families in New York City, believes that it is the "capital" of FGM in America. She told me that "Doctors usually see it when the women go into labor and they do not know how to deal with the tremendous scarring.

My colleagues, Ayaan Hirsi Ali and Soraya Mire, have each written harrowing, literary accounts of their own mutilations. Both have campaigned against it—as have many other Muslim and ex-Muslim women who are both Left and Right in orientation, including Dr. Nawal el-Sadawii.

One must ask: Why does this custom persist?

Some insist that it is due entirely to the patriarchal refusal to have their sons marry "unclean" (un-mutilated) girls who might sexually stray. Thus, if the men and their parents of a given tribe can be otherwise persuaded, the custom might cease. Molly Melching, with whom I worked in 2008 at a G8 conference in Rome, has done very creative work in this regard in Africa. She persuaded the families of eligible grooms to accept uncut girls in marriage.

The custom persists in cultures where the value of a woman's life is unimaginably cheap. Neither her existence nor her suffering—proper penance for the crime of being born female—count.

In the West, misguided concepts of "multi-cultural relativism," soft racism, sexism, and fear of offending an increasingly hostile Muslim and African immigrant population has condemned those girls and women who live among us and who deserve their rights under Western law. This practice must be prevented in the West. This is hard to accomplish because the practice is done in secrecy, sometimes on a "vacation" to one's home country, sometimes by a certified physician in the West in a private office, or in one's country of origin. One might have to assume that all girls of a certain ethnicity or region will be subjected to FGM from the time they are five years old and act pre-emptively, thus running the risk of being accused of xenophobia, Islamophobia, or racism.

Failing that, those who perpetrate this crime and who live in the West must be prosecuted. And that, too, is complicated. If the mother and father are responsible and the girl and all her sisters are removed from her home—who will her extended family and community be? How well would a state home treat them?

Breitbart
10/17/14

- 102 -
Punished for Being Raped and For Accusing Rapists: Women's Burden Under Sharia

I SIS has just be-headed a woman in Baquba because she dared to resist being raped. In the process of struggling to defend herself, she actually killed her would-be rapist, an ISIS warrior. The woman was at home recovering from a medical illness.

This is precisely the crime that led to Reyhaneh Jabbari's execution in Iran at dawn this past Saturday—except that the Iranian regime first jailed and tortured her for five years. Her life might have been spared if her victim's family had forgiven her, but that did not happen. Her would-be rapist was a former member of Iran's Intelligence Ministry.

And thus we learn that under Sharia law the penalty for resisting rape is torture and death for women.

What happens when a woman does not or cannot resist being raped?

In 2008, in Somalia, 13-year old Aisha Ibrahim Duhulow was accused of adultery ("zina"—in her case, sex outside of marriage). She had reported being gang-raped to the controlling jihadist group there, al-Shabab. The very act of accusing her rapists condemned her—but not her rapists—to a brutal death-by-stoning at the hands of fifty men. She begged for mercy, crying out up until the moment of her death.

Sharia courts in Pakistan have punished thousands of raped women who dared accuse their attackers of the crime with long term imprisonment. Bangladesh has flogged, beaten, and imprisoned raped women.

Families of rape victims in Afghanistan have honor-murdered their daughters for having been raped. Most recently, in 2014, one ten-

358

year-old victim who was raped by a mullah in a mosque was saved, temporarily, by an Afghan and international woman's group which has, so far, successfully persuaded her family not to kill her.

We have all heard about Aisha Bibi aka Muhktar Mai, who reported her more powerful Pakistani gang-rapists and managed to get some convicted. She lives with permanent death threats—she also shelters other such rape victims and their families. A haunting opera has been written and performed about her bravery.

We have witnessed the mass male sexual assault of veiled and unveiled women in Tahrir Square in Cairo. Human Rights Watch refers to this Square as "Rape Central." Journalist Judy Bachrach, who lived in Cairo, documented the extraordinary level of normalized street harassment of infidel girls and women in Cairo.

I have previously written about an atrocious three day "pogrom" perpetrated by three hundred Algerian men against thirty nine impoverished women in 2001. Their crime? They had dared to work as cleaning women and secretaries for an infidel company. The imam had denounced the women as "evil," the male mob stormed out of the mosque after Friday services, yelling "Allahu Akhbar"—and attacked the terrified and helpless women.

In many Muslim countries—and Hindu India—women have been viewed as tempting men; the men are not viewed as licentious, promiscuous scoundrels but as helpless victims. This used to be true in the West as well and to an extent, it still is. However, rape is now understood as a crime and is prosecuted, not normalized, in the West.

However, if the rape is known to a Muslim woman's family in a Muslim country, it may mean her death sentence. If she and her family report the rape to the authorities, the rape victim (and sometimes her family as well) may be further victimized. Death threats are common. The rape victim is usually jailed and once in custody will be routinely raped and sometimes impregnated by police officers and interrogators.

What must we understand about such barbaric misogyny?

First, that to be born a woman in certain parts of the world is to be born guilty; being female is a capital offense. Girls and women must keep proving that they will not shame their families by a level of obedience and subordination that Westerners cannot truly comprehend. Memoirs by women—Somali Ayaan Hirsi Ali, Punjabi Aruna Papp, Iranian Marina Nemat, to name only a few—share details of daily, sometimes hourly terrorization and punishment within the family and at the hands of the state and religious authorities.

Second, when men from tribal cultures immigrate to the West, these attitudes and customs do not change. By now, we know that vulnerable, pre-adolescent and adolescent Caucasian girls were kidnapped, gang-raped and forced into prostitution by Muslim gangs in Britain; the authorities looked the other way. Why? Because they did not want to accuse Muslim men of perpetrating crimes lest they, the authorities, be accused of Islamophobia or racism.

Third, as Islamic fundamentalism gains territory and followers, life will become much harsher for women.

For example, in October of 2014, acid attacks by men on motorcycles against "improperly veiled" Iranian women have increased on the streets in 25 cities, including Isfahan, Kermanshah, and Teheran.

The Women's Freedom Forum of Iran has informed me that "demonstrators compared these attackers with the terrorists of ISIS" and described the Iranian "regime as Godfather to ISIS when it comes to such crimes." Laws have been passed to protect the acid throwers, and the Iranian regime has been "intimidating the families of the victims and hospital nurses and staff. Reporters are also prevented from going to hospitals to see the victims." The Freedom Forum finds this "ominous," and a sign that the regime "will allow these attacks to continue."

On one hand, there is really little Westerners can do about this short of making common cause with the brave dissidents. President Obama has showed no signs of doing so. In fact, he is seeking common ground with the regime, not with its victims, and not with anti-Regime demonstrators in Iran.

Breitbart
10/28/14

- 103 -

A Race Against Time: Yezidi-American Women Strive for a Global Rescue of Their People

Two young Yazidi women are heroically negotiating for the survival of their people in Iraq. They are talking to the media, planning to lobby Congress, and they tell me that they have interested at least three countries in providing political asylum for the Yazidis—if they can be rescued militarily.

Adoul Keijan and Gulie Khalaf are Yazidi-American cousins. They view themselves as advocates and front-line soldiers for their people because they can speak English and are safely away from a horrifying war-zone.

As we know, ISIS has conducted a scorched-earth march across Iraq. On August 3rd, ISIS began slaughtering all those Yazidis who refused to convert to Islam. They also kidnapped many Yazidi women and kept them or sold them as sex slaves.

For five days in August of this year, 40,000 Yazidis were stranded atop Mount Sinjar without food or water. On August 8th, American forces dropped humanitarian supplies and created a safe passage down the mountain for many thousands of Yazidis.

Adoul Keijan's aunt was among them.

However, Adoul tells me, "a week after being rescued, my aunt called crying and begging for help. She had one gun to protect them from ISIS, but had to sell it in order to get food and water."

In recent weeks, Adoul has not been able to contact anyone in her extended family.

On October 20th, ISIS renewed their assault on the Yazidis, forcing the remaining Yazidis up Mt. Sinjar.

And there they remain—again without food or water and without a second American air-strike in view. I do not understand what President Obama is waiting for.

Adoul Keijan escaped from Iraq when she was nine, together with her parents. She grew up in refugee camps in Syria where Yezidis were routinely persecuted. Her cousin, Gulie Khalaf, who lived in the same camp with Adoul, writes, "We were treated as second class citizens both in school and at the camp. Every year the Christians and the Muslims would get free gifts from the government during their major holidays, such as Christmas and Eid. None of our holidays were recognized. In school if we didn't read Qur'an we would get lower grades and in middle school if we didn't participate in Qur'an class we would fail." In the refugee camps, she says, "it was a rough life. There was no running water... Sometimes fights would break out because water was scarce." Their luck with food was no better: "We would get our bread from the local baker, and many times the bread had bugs in it."

In 1999, when Adoul was sixteen years old, she and her parents were granted political asylum in America. Luckily, Gulie's family was also brought to America at the same time.

Since then, Adoul has become an American success story. She is now an EMT paramedic and a pilot who owns a company—North American Aerials—which is devoted to humanitarian rescues. People pay to take aerial tours and Adoul and her partner, Daniel Kairys, donate the funds to charity. Adoul says, "We started a Humanitarian Relief Effort campaign on September 1st. Anyone who buys an aerial photography shoot or an airplane ride from us has the option of having all the proceeds go toward this cause."

Now, three weeks later, about 5,000 women, children, and the elderly remain on Mt. Sinjar, stranded. As of October 20th, more Yazidis are being forced back up the mountain.

According to the United Nations, over 200,000 Yazidis were displaced within 48-hours in August. Many others have been kidnapped or murdered.

The Yazidi people have roots in common with Hinduism and Zoroastrianism; they believe in reincarnation. The Yazidis may have migrated from India 5,000 years ago. Their native language is Kermanji Kurdish, but Adoul also speaks Badini Kurdish, Arabic, and English.

She tells me: "Gulie and I have stayed in touch and we both are working very closely together to raise funds and awareness about the situation our people are facing in Northern Iraq."

Together, they have interested Sri Sri Ravi Shankar, an Indian Guru, in helping them by negotiating political asylum in India for those Yazidis who can be rescued. But, they have not stopped there. Adoul tells me that negotiations are now also under way with Kurds and Israelis for additional sites of political asylum—until a better time.

They are quintessential Americans—grateful to America for having given them political asylum and yet still loyal to their people, who are living in a bloody inferno of hate.

Breitbart
11/1/14

- 104 -
Yazidi Slave Trade Video Latest Proof of Radical Islamist Cruelty Towards Women

What exactly is a "barbarian?"

A barbarian is someone who finds joy in inflicting pain and death. Doing so makes them laugh. Literally. Thus, culturally and psychologically, Islamist barbarians are the equivalent of Western-style sadistic, sociopathic serial killers—only the barbarians do not work alone or in secret. They work in large theological-military paramilitary gangs and they do their grisly work quite openly.

Western serial killers are hunted down and not valorized. Groups like Al-Qaeda, the Taliban, Al-Shabaab, Hamas, Boko Haram, and ISIS are considered fearless and heroic warriors, religious freedom-fighters by their followers and by a strong minority—some say a majority—of Muslims worldwide who have called for Sharia law. What these terrorist groups are doing obeys the tenets of Sharia law—a law which has never been refined, modified, or re-interpreted to render it compatible with Western, modern concepts of human rights and jurisprudence.

By making and releasing videos, such groups wish to terrorize onlookers as well as their captives. Terror is meant to subdue the opposition.

Beheading helpless captives and then playing football with their severed heads is a sport to them. Giving severed heads to children, forcing children to watch the beheadings (so as to de-sensitize them to the suffering of others), positioning guns in the hands of five-year-old boys and photographing them as future warriors—all creates a torture- and death-oriented culture. Such behaviors characterize not only ISIS but

364

also Hamas and the Taliban.

This year, both ISIS and Boko Haram released a series of videos. Beginning in August, ISIS released four videos which showed the beheadings of four Westerners—men whom they had tortured for months or years beforehand. They beat them, water-boarded them, starved them. They probably laughed when they did this, perhaps referred to Abu-Ghraib (so tame by comparison, so exaggerated by Western media), or to Gitmo; perhaps they also referred to the waterboarding of Al-Qaeda's Khalid Sheikh Mohammed by Americans.

Note the difference: Khalid Sheikh Mohammed was a warrior, one of the master-minds of 9/11, and the clock may have been ticking in terms of other planned terrorist attacks. All the Westerners whom ISIS tortured and beheaded were civilians: humanitarians, journalists.

One ISIS video was released on November 3, 2014. In it, we see men laughing and joking about the Yazidi girls and women who are about to be sold at a slave auction. These men are enjoying themselves immensely. They know that such a video will discomfort all Yazidis who may see it as well as all Westerners and other non-barbarians.

These men are doing exactly what Mohammed himself did and said was the right thing to do. Conquer, expand, convert; behead the men in full view of their womenfolk—and then either marry the women "in your hand" or sell them as sex slaves. Share them among the warriors. They are the just spoils of war. The Quran (4:24) states that:

"And [also prohibited to you are all] married women except those your right hands possess. [This is] the decree of Allah upon you." The Hadith give us numerous examples of what Mohammed himself did, examples which are revered and followed.

For example, Mohammed ordered the slaughter of an entire Jewish tribe in Northern Arabia as their women stood watching. He then ordered his warriors to take the women as wives or concubines. He himself took one Safiya Bint Huyayy, whom he "married," no doubt against her will, and whom he probably converted against her will. According to Bat Ye'or, in *The Dhimmi: Jews and Christians Under Islam*:

> ...whenever the Muslims besiege an enemy stronghold who agree to surrender on certain conditions that will be decided by a delegate, and this man decides that their soldiers are to be executed and their women and children taken prisoner, this decision is lawful.

365

Bat Ye'or describes and analyzes jihad. She explains that "it is not prohibited to kill non-white Arabs who have been taken prisoner... women and children must not be executed (unless they have taken part in battle). The imam will retain a fifth of the booty captured by Muslims in the course of warfare and he will share the remaining four-fifths among the soldiers."

According to Ibn Warraq, in his 1996 work, *Why I am Not A Muslim*, the Quran "enjoins all Muslims to fight and kill nonbelievers." (47:4) "When you meet the unbelievers, strike off their heads; then when you have made wide slaughter among them, carefully tie up the remaining captives." And in (5:51:) "Believers, do not take Jews or Christians as friends. They are but one another's friends."

As long as these beliefs are not "abrogated," abolished, outlawed, punished, they will continue to characterize political Islam.

The most recent ISIS video should—but may not—convey to Westerners, especially Western feminists, the sub-human status in which Islamist barbarians view women—their own and infidel women especially. ISIS warriors are talking about the preference for "green" or "blue" eyes, for a mouth full of teeth, for fifteen-year-olds. It is as if they are talking about horses or cows—and to them, that is what women are. Beasts of burden, slaves, and "fields" in which the sons of men are to be planted.

Here's another example of what characterizes a "barbarian." In a May 2014 video, the leader of Boko Haram in Nigeria, Abubakar Shekau, talks at length, in Hausa and in broken English, about having married off, sold, and converted the mainly Christian girls he'd kidnapped. He is defiant, taunting, and very happy to crush the families of the kidnapped girls. Here is what he says:

> Just because I took some little girls who were in western education, everybody is making noise. Let me tell you: I took the girls. Girls: Go and get married. We are against western education and I saw 'stop western education'. I repeat, I took the girls, and I will sell them off. There is a market for selling girls.

> In every nation, every region, there is a decision to make. Either you are with us, I mean real Muslims, who are following Salafism. Or you are with Obama, Francois Hollande, George Bush, Clinton...I haven't forgotten Abraham Lincoln. Ban

Ki-moon and his people generally. And any unbeliever. Kill, kill, kill. This war is against Christians.

He clearly states that Boko Haram opposes "Western education;" states that girls (whom we may consider children but whom Islamist warriors consider almost too old to marry), must, indeed, be married off and always against their will. Abubakar Shekau names all the Western leaders, beginning with Obama and including Francois Hollande, George Bush, Clinton, Ban-Ki Moon. All are to be killed, killed, killed.

Saying so makes him happy. He is not grave nor is he introspective. He makes no "rational" demands. He is not negotiating. His goal is to subdue the world and turn everyone into a Muslim. His goal is to turn the global clock back to the 7th century.

President Obama, Secretary General Ban Ki-Moon: Are you listening? Do you understand that you are on Boko Haram's hit list because you are infidels? What do you plan to do about the Sunni barbarians? And after you have solved that problem, what do you plan to do about the Shi'ite barbarians, funded by Iran, and active in Syria, Lebanon, and Gaza? Will you at least publically condemn their colonialism, imperialism, and apartheid?

If you do not act now—and act decisively—it will mean that the barbarians will command more weaponry, more oil, more territory and more slaves and will be harder, not easier, to defeat.

Breitbart
11/5/14

- 105 -

17-Year-Old Saudi Girl Wins Case Against Father After Being Tricked into Marriage with a 90-Year-Old

A Saudi teenager, told she would marry a handsome young man whom she had been allowed to meet, was shocked when she discovered that her father had tricked her and that her groom was a man in his nineties. She is 17 years old.

Amazingly, the girl bolted and called the police. Headlines and a social media campaign condemned her father, accusing him of "selling his daughter to an old man." A court just ruled the marriage "null and void."

This news is both depressing and inspiring. Depressing because fathers are still arranging inappropriate matches for their daughters and sentencing them to lifetimes of misery. Depressing because, according to Sharia law, in the case of a divorce, custody belongs to fathers, not mothers. This girl was living with her father whose authority is traditionally considered supreme. She was, or so it seems, a child of divorce.

But the news is very inspiring because the girl actually fled her father's choice (which is unheard of), other Saudis supported her on the internet, and a court upheld her right not to be duped in this way.

This case follows another similar case in which a fifteen-year old Saudi girl "locked herself in her bedroom on her wedding night after being forced to marry a 90-year-old Saudi man." Social media condemned this arranged marriage, calling it "child trafficking and prostitution." The elderly man said he paid 10,767 pounds for her—and later insisted that both the bride and her parents had set out to "swindle him."

One must understand that the "selling" of girls into marriage is not seen as barbaric. On the contrary, it is viewed as taking care of one's daughter, protecting her reputation, ensuring that an (under-valued, useless, potentially dangerous) daughter is fed, clothed, and housed and not at her father's expense. In poverty-stricken, illiterate countries and cultures, marriage is a woman's only alternative other than prostitution.

It must be noted that Mohammed himself married a six-year-old girl when he was in his fifties and consummated the marriage with Aisha when she was 9 years old. The Prophet's life is considered a role model for Muslims. According to the Center for the Study of Political Islam, the Qu'ran specifically notes "91 times that the Prophet's words and actions are considered to be the divine pattern for humanity." Thus, a 44-year difference between a husband and wife is not considered abnormal and might even be viewed as "divine." Mohammed himself had eleven wives and two sex slaves. In Islam today, men are allowed four wives—and any number of dalliances with prostituted women and sex slaves.

Muslim women are (dishonorably) killed if they are suspected of having sex with someone who is not their husband or not the man chosen for them by their fathers. No one is exempt. In 1977, a Saudi princess, Misha'al bint Fahd al-Saud, was executed because she chose her own husband and tried to flee the Kingdom with him. Her love-match husband was also executed.

Given this kind of tribal and Sharia-based culture, it is nothing short of a miracle that, in 2014, two Saudi teenaged girls fled the marriages arranged for them by their fathers; were supported by others in the Kingdom; and, in one case, protected by a Saudi Court. Apparently, neither girl has been killed by her father for having dishonored the family.

It is a time of small miracles. Recently, King Abdullah's Advisory Council proposed a bill that would allow women to drive cars—but only during the day and only if they refrain from wearing any makeup. Let's see if this bill passes.

Breitbart
11/14/14

- 106 -
Female Genital Mutilation in the West:
A Crime Against Humanity

Tomorrow, on November 20, 2014, an Egyptian doctor, Raslan Fadl, will, for the first time in history, be sentenced because his 13-year old patient died during a female genital mutilation (FGM) procedure; he claims she was allergic to penicillin.

This girl died—but she was probably among the lucky few who have real physicians perform the mutilation in a clinic, as opposed to a midwife or tribal elder who performs the mutilation on a mud floor and with a rusty knife or razor blade.

Recently, a photographer was present at the FGM "ceremonies" of four teenage Kenyan girls of the Potok tribe. They look terrified.

But we also know that Western authorities have failed to stop it here. Last week, Detective Chief Supt Vanessa Jardine of Manchester stated that the genital mutilation (FGM) of girls in England should be treated as a form of "child abuse and not as a cultural issue." In other words, it is a crime and perpetrators should be prosecuted. It is not a tribal, ethnic, racial, or cultural issue to which Western law enforcement should continue to turn a politically correct blind eye. Jardine stated that "this is about protecting a child, not (about) being a racist."

FGM has been viewed as a violation of girls' and women's human rights by international treaties. This has changed nothing. UN Secretary Ban Ki-Moon has announced a global campaign to end this atrocity within a decade.

I doubt this will happen. A number of countries have banned FGM, including Egypt, in 1959 and again in 2008. It did not stop this practice.

In 2008, a 12-year-old Egyptian girl died during a clinic surgery. That alone—her death—is what led Egypt to again ban FGM. In other words, the life-long agony and negative medical consequences which FGM inflicts upon girls and women does not matter. The fact that she will never be able to experience any sexual pleasure whatsoever does not matter.

A woman is meant to suffer—little enough punishment to pay for the crime of being born female.

We may not be able to stop such crimes if they take place in Somalia, Sudan, Kenya, or Egypt. But we can and must stop such crimes if they take place in any Western country—even if the parents send the girl back home to be mutilated.

What might deter this practice? I fear that laws and treaties per se will not be able to do so. Here's what might. If the parents of a mutilated girl are themselves deported and if their entire extended family is also deported, this alone might give pause to the next set of parents who live in the West but whose hearts remain in the Middle East or Africa.

This is a radical suggestion. I would recommend it for honor killings in the West as well. A family can be "shamed" by having a non-mutilated daughter or they can be "shamed" for having mutilated their daughter and thereby responsible for the deportation of their entire extended family. The choice is theirs to make.

Breitbart
11/19/14

- 107 -
China Becomes Latest Nation to Impose Burqa Ban in Muslim Western Capital

C hina has just banned the burqa in the mainly Muslim province of Xinjiang's capital, Urumqi. The government has also banned Islamic head coverings and beards in an effort to contain restive Islamic fundamentalism ("political Islam") from turning into a full-scale jihad against the state.

"Beijing blames Islamist separatists for several deadly bomb and knife attacks that have killed hundreds of people in the past two years," Reuters notes. According to experts and exiles, China's "heavy-handed policies" may be the cause of ethnic and religious unrest.

Communism still views religion as the "opiate" of the people and as having the power to divide a citizen's loyalty between private faith and the state. Thus, China has controlled permitted religious practices—but it has also jailed clerics, instituted bans, and restricted certain religious practices entirely. In neighboring Tibet, occupied by China, Buddhist monks, nuns, and former nuns have immolated themselves to protest the "brutal repression" of their religion.

While I do not agree with many of China's policies, their ban on face veils, body bags, and beards in public may make sense. Many European cities and countries have also banned the face veil (with varying degrees of success).

Communist Russia was unsuccessful in holding back the tide of political Islam in Afghanistan. Although they did offer education and other benefits to impoverished and illiterate people, including women, the Afghan mode of resistance was associated with the burqa, the turban, and the beard. China is well aware of this.

Do followers of radical, political Islam who believe in holy war (jihad) against "unbelievers" tend to face-veil their women? According to Paris-based, Tunisian born activist Samia Labidi, the answer is yes.

If someone is living in France or China, what does it mean that they want to look as if they are living in the Arab Middle East? Does it mean they are signaling a hostile separation from the state—one that inevitably seems to lead to, or enable, jihad terrorism?

China is not known as a bastion of religious freedom or of other human rights. The atheist, communist, Chinese government has been persecuting, outlawing, and limiting Protestant, Catholic, Buddhist, Fa-lun Gong, and Taoist practices for many years.

Islamic practice have been similarly treated. There are anywhere from 21 to 50 million Muslims, mainly located in four northwest provinces of China: Ningxia, Quinghai, Gansu (where Hui/Han and some Uyghur Muslims live), and Xinjiang (where mainly ethnic Uyghur Muslims live).

Many Uyghur Muslims were once part of Eastern Turkistan.

As Westerners, we value the post-Enlightenment principle of freedom of religion as well as freedom from religion. Islam does not honor anyone who leaves the faith and views doing so as a capital crime. For this reason alone, Islam is radically different than other world religions.

Breitbart
12/15/14

Muslim Women Sue in US Courts for Right to Wear Islamic Garb on the Job

The Supreme Court has just agreed to hear a case concerning the rights of a woman to wear hijab, a headscarf, while working at Abercrombie and Fitch. This case began in 2008, in Tulsa, Oklahoma on behalf of then seventeen-year-old Samantha Elauf and is known as Equal Employment Opportunity Commission vs Abercrombie and Fitch Stores, Inc.

Our own federal government has brought the suit against Abercrombie and Fitch Stores, Inc.

At least ten "friends of the court" briefs have been submitted by religious and civil rights organizations, including The American-Arab Anti-Discrimination Committee, the American Jewish Committee, the National Jewish Commission on Law and Public Affairs, the Becket Fund for Religious Liberty, and the Council on American-Islamic Relations aka the Muslim Brotherhood in America and an un-indicted co-conspirator in the Holy Land Foundation lawsuit.

The issue is framed in this way: Can an employer be liable under Title VII of the Civil Rights Act of 1964 for refusing to hire an applicant or discharging an employee based on a "religious observance and practice"—if the employer has no actual knowledge that a religious accommodation was required and the employer's actual knowledge did not result from direct, explicit notice from the applicant or employee?

Similar right to wear hijab cases have been brewing all across America for the last decade.

In 2004, the U.S. Justice Department supported a lawsuit brought on behalf of a sixth grade student in Oklahoma who wanted to wear hijab in her public school. That same year, the school reviewed their policy, amended their dress code, paid the student an undisclosed sum, and allowed her to attend classes wearing hijab.

In 2006, in a small claims matter in Michigan, a Muslim woman, Ginnah Muhammed, refused to take off her face mask (niqab) while she testified. Judge Paul Paruk dismissed her case. Muhammed sued, and the ACLU backed her. They argued for a "religious exception" to courtroom attire. Although Muhammed's small claims case was against a car rental agency, here is what Michael Steinberg, legal director of the ACLU of Michigan stated:

> The Michigan Supreme Court should not slam the door of justice on a category of women just because of their religious belief…Under the proposed rule, women who are sexually assaulted do not have their day in court if they wear a veil mandated by their religion.

Sexual assault was not at issue nor was the victim afraid that testifying might lead to her death. Leave it to the ACLU to almost always get it wrong.

On June 17, 2009, the Michigan Supreme Court, in a 5-2 vote, ruled that a Judge had the power to "require witnesses to remove head or facial covering as (the witness) was testifying." A Judge has the right to see a witness's "facial expressions" to determine her "truthfulness" while she testifies.

Both the American Civil Liberties Union (ACLU) and the Council on American-Islamic Relations (CAIR) have gone to court in Florida (2002), California (2005), Michigan (2008), and Oklahoma (2008) to fight for a Muslim woman's right to cover her hair or face—whether it is while being photographed for a driver's license or for a police mug shot or while working at McDonald's or at Abercrombie Kids.

In 2007, CAIR wrote a letter on behalf of a Muslim woman in Georgia who refused to remove her headscarf in order to enter a courtroom to plead "not guilty" to a traffic ticket.

Religious Muslims are outraged that Christians can wear crucifixes, nuns and priests can wear habits, Jews can wear skullcaps, stars of David, wigs and head coverings, Sikhs can wear turbans, Hindus can wear veils and saris, but Muslims cannot wear hijab, burqas or niqab.

They have a point. However, the face mask (niqab) and the burqa mask all five senses and make human interaction impossible. But what's wrong with hijab (a head covering)?

Over the years, I have interviewed a number of religious Muslim women who are completely westernized, educated, modern, and anti-jihad. They "cover" their hair for religious and ethnic reasons. It is a statement of "who they are" and what they believe in. This sometimes includes a desire to publicly signify a belief in God and to separate themselves from a secular, promiscuous world in which women dress provocatively.

Religious people do not want the government telling them how to dress or limiting their religious practices. Many secular feminists have viewed Islamic "coverings" as either a Muslim woman's religious right or as her culturally sanctioned expression of modesty. In addition, many progressives see the ban on the burqa (not to mention discrimination against hijab) as a form of "racial profiling," or as "Islamophobic."

Some people fear that if America legally accepts hijab in the public square that doing so may represent the proverbial "nose of the camel." Once the camel's "nose" is permitted in the tent, that soon enough, the demands for halal food, separate classes for boys and girls, separate swimming facilities, breaks for prayer, prayer rooms, and the recognition of Muslim holidays in tax-funded public schools and in government employment may soon follow.

Some counter-terrorism experts fear that permitting Arab and Islamic clothing on the job, at school, in the United States at this time in history may not be the same as allowing Christians, Jews, or Sikhs to wear head coverings. Why? Because no other religious ideology calls for supremacy over infidels ("kafirs"), or for violent jihad against infidels and against other Muslims who do not adopt extremist views. None of the other religions mentioned view the state and religion as one or view non-co-religionists as beings who deserve to be subordinated, taxed, persecuted, and converted via the sword. Islam is also the only religion in which believers are commanded to kill all those who leave the religion. In addition, since global jihad is upon us, permitting head coverings at work may frighten or offend some customers and may not comport with the expected dress code on the job.

I am not suggesting that any individual hijab-wearer would kill anyone.

The Supreme Court will have to carefully balance the separation of religion and state; freedom of religion; the nature of the public square, business bottom lines, and individual civil rights—over and against the meaning that the Islamic headscarf may have in such dangerous times. I eagerly await the oral arguments and the Supreme Court ruling.

Breitbart
12/18/14

Section Seven:
As ISIS Brutalizes Women, a Pathetic Feminist
Silence

- 109 -
Sultan of Brunei Bans Christmas, Brother Runs Private Brothel

Sultan Haji Hassnal Bolkiah of Brunei has banned Christmas in his Kingdom. This latest ban was implemented "after a number of people were reportedly spotted wearing clothes resembling Santa Claus at Christmas time."

Businesses that openly displayed Christmas decorations were asked to remove them. A government spokesman explains: "Muslims should be careful not to follow celebrations such as these that are not in any way related to Islam, for it is feared that this could lead to *tasyabbuh* (imitation) and could unknowingly damage the *aqidah* (faith) of Muslims."

Muslims in the West are erecting an increasing number of mosques, praying most visibly in the streets and at work, and veiling Muslim women more and more prominently—arguing that Western laws allow for such religious freedom. However, it is clear that Muslims, Muslim leaders, Muslim mobs, and Muslim jihadists do not allow non-Muslim religious practices in their countries and have been persecuting most horribly all kuffars (infidels), especially Christians and Jews.

It is also clear that Muslim jihadists have taken their religious anti-infidel Crusade into the West by targeting infidel women for rape and sex trafficking and targeting Jews, not only in Israel, but in bloody incident after bloody incident, all across Europe and especially, most recently, in France.

In the spring of 2014, Brunei's Sultan introduced Sharia law. This means that "fines and jail terms can be imposed for failing to attend

Friday prayers, indecent behavior, and pregnancies outside of marriage." The second phase, which was implemented later in 2014, "prescribes flogging for Muslims who consume alcohol and, for property crimes, flogging and amputation." In late 2015, the third phase will "allow for death by stoning for gay sex and adultery."

Please recall that in 2014, the West Coast branch of PEN, the author's association, canceled their annual benefit gala at the Beverly Hills Hotel—because the hotel is owned by the Sultan of Brunei's Dorchester Collection.

A Jewish American woman, Jillian Lauren, an ex-stripper and teenager, spent some time in the drunken and highly competitive "harem" of the Sultan's brother, Prince Jeffri Bolkiah, which consisted mainly of paid Western prostitutes. Lauren and other prostituted women shopped 'til they dropped; Lauren claims that she personally broke "two of the (anti-Sharia) offenses" with the Sultan himself "as we looked down on the lights of Kuala Lumpur from a penthouse suite."

This is interesting because it suggests that the Sharia law being imposed is meant for everyone else but the royal rulers of Brunei. This also confirms what we already know—think of what ISIS is doing to Yazidi girls and women, and what Boko Haram is doing to Christian girls and women—namely, that infidel women are to be used for male sexual pleasure.

According to the January 8, 2015 Brunei government announcement, it is now also a crime to "propagate" religions other than Islam; those who "insult the Qur'an or the prophet Mohammed will be stoned to death."

Europeans have endured a series of lawsuits, assassinations, and assassination attempts against those who have been seen as "insulting" Islam. We have just witnessed a jihad assassination in Paris against those who were seen as "insulting Islam." Sharia law has gone global.

These kind of attacks will continue. They are cheap. One or two jihadists can perpetrate massacres with their cars, knives, and automatic weapons. Such attacks may, in the long run, prove counter-productive since they will eventually alert Westerners to the danger we face.

However, UN Secretary-General Ban Ki-moon says he's "relieved that the French terrorists have been killed and is urging all people around the world 'to enhance the level of tolerance and respect for the belief and religions and tradition of others." Ban said all differences of views on religion and other issues can be resolved through dialogue. But he said the tragedy in Paris was not about religion. "This is a purely unacceptable terrorist attack, criminality," Ban said. "This kind of crim-inality must be brought to justice in the name of humanity."

As long as such leaders, which include French President Hollande and American President Obama, continue to insist that jihadic terrorism has "nothing to do with Islam," the West will fail to go on the necessary war footing. As long as Hollande and Obama allow Muslim immigrants to come and go at will—including those on no-fly lists who have been trained as jihadists in Syria, Iraq, and Yemen; as long as America fails to stop Iran and other state sponsors of terrorism, the infidel West will inherit the whirlwind and risk becomes "dhimmis," or converts to Islam.

Breitbart
1/10/15

Yazidis Forced to Give Blood to Wounded ISIS Fighters: Report

Tonight, BBC Arabic will air a new documentary, *Slaves of the Caliphate*, which documents the horrendous plight of captured Yazidi girls and women. This film will be broadcast on BBC World on January 17, 2015.

The first Yazidi sex slave to reveal her identity—Hamshe—talks about what happened to her and to others. Disclosed for the first time: in addition to being forced to sexually service ISIS jihadists, these girls and women were also forced to "give blood to wounded fighters."

Activist Nareen Shammo has been keeping track of hundreds of kidnapped Yazidi; she has tried to locate them and negotiate their return.

In December, 2014, Amnesty International released a report about the "abducted hundreds, possibly thousands of Yazidi men, women, and children who were fleeing the ISIS takeover….younger girls and women were forced to convert to Islam under threat of death. Some as young as 12 were separated from their parents and older relatives and sold, given as gifts or forced to marry fighters and supporters. Many have been subjected to torture and ill-treatment, including rape." According to Amnesty, about three hundred of those abducted have escaped captivity. Amnesty interviewed 42 such women and girls.

Amnesty considers what ISIS is doing to be "war crimes."

According to *The Daily Mail*, "it is estimated that over 2,600 women remain captive… (However), the Yazidi community in Iraq says that 3,500 of its women and girls are still being held by ISIS."

These girls and women are being sold as sex slaves for both pitifully small and outrageously large sums of money. Girls who are beaten and injured are allowed to recover and are then re-sold. ISIS's Department of Research and Fatwas issues legal/religious documents, posts them online, and gives them out in pamphlet form after prayers. This concerns the Sharia basis for the taking of captives and slaves. According to MEMRI, quoted in Newsweek, the pamphlet is titled: "*Su'al wa-Jawab*," ("Questions and Answers on Taking Captives and Slaves").

ISIS justifies capturing the women based on their unbelief in Islam: "Unbelieving [women] who were captured and brought into the abode of Islam are permissible to us." This can occur as soon as a woman is captured: "If she is a virgin, [her master] can have intercourse with her immediately after taking possession of her...A female captive cannot be sold, however, if she has been impregnated by her 'owner.'" The pamphlet ends with these lines:

> Before Satan sows doubt among the weak-minded and weak-hearted, remember that enslaving the kuffa (infidels) and taking their women as concubines is a firmly-established aspect of Sharia.

Some will insist that this interpretation of Sharia law is a "deviant" or a "perverted" form of religion. Some Arabists will tell us that the masses do not really understand Sharia law and that the experts who do are afraid of reining in their followers lest they be fired from their pulpits and shamed.

Western human rights experts are very clear that such behaviors are barbaric and legally constitute "war crimes."

If we do not stop ISIS in the Middle East, they may soon be coming our way. And even if we *do* stop ISIS, they may soon be coming our way.

Breitbart
1/13/15

111

Four Saudi Princesses in Solitary for Life: Obama Mum on Plight of Muslim Women

P resident Obama, who chose not to join France's march for freedom, cut his state visit to democratic, nuclear India short in order to visit Saudi Arabia Tuesday to pay his respects to the new king, Salman al-Saud, upon the death of King Abdullah.

Is this an urgent state matter or a matter of Realpolitik? Not necessarily. During a 2009 G-20 conference, Obama shocked people when he bowed down quite low to King Abdullah, 5'11". On that same visit, Obama didn't bow to Queen Elizabeth, 5'4".

Perhaps the president's visit is better seen as part of what he has said, many times, is his mandate to reach out to the Muslim world.

Obama has refused to call ISIS "Islamic," or to connect jihad or terrorism with Islam. His administration has been obsessively concerned with the false concept of "Islamophobia."

And, while our president has frequently spoken out on behalf of African-American and Muslim men, he has been all but silent about African-American and Muslim women.

Now it is urgent that he break this silence. There are Muslim and ex-Muslim dissidents and feminists who are desperate to hear supportive words from the leader of the free world.

Four such women are now in harsh captivity in Saudi Arabia.

In 1972, when he was 48, King Abdullah took a 15-year-old Jordanian-born wife, Alanoud Al-Fayez. The marriage was arranged; she was one of 30 wives. In four years, she produced four daughters—infuriating the king, who wanted more sons. (He only has seven sons—and 15 known daughters.)

For this crime, Abdullah divorced Alanoud. But he beat her, too, and prevented her from taking care of her daughters when they were ill. In 2001, she fled the kingdom, hoping that as a father, Abdullah would treat his own daughters with more kindness.

She was wrong. In addition to having a mother who "got away," these daughters, Sahar, Maha, Hala and Jawaher Al Saud, now in their late 30s and early 40s, dared speak out for women's rights. Their punishment has been extreme and long-lasting.

For 13 years, the unmarried princesses have been confined in pairs, isolated from outside contact—beaten, drugged, deprived of food and water for periods of time, slowly starved, subjected to heat without air-conditioning in the desert climate.

According to their mother's account, and to a video that Sahar and Jawaher smuggled out, the princesses claim that their "half-brothers beat them with sticks" and "yell at us and tell us we will die here."

Sahar also told *The Post*, "My father said that after his death, our brothers would continue to detain us and abuse us." (The London-based Alanoud maintains a Twitter account: @Freethe4.)

It's not just princesses who are at risk in the kingdom. Allegedly disobedient women at every social level are beaten daily, shunned, honor-killed or sometimes sentenced to solitary confinement in padded cells for the rest of their lives. No relative dares visit.

In 1990, 47 brave Saudi women drove their cars in Riyadh, to demand the right to drive. They were quickly detained, roundly condemned, their passports confiscated—and, they were fired from their jobs.

When I was held captive in Kabul by my own family long ago, US embassy personnel would not help me. Once my American passport was taken, I instantly became the citizen of no country and the literal property of a wealthy, polygamous, Afghan family.

This experience, which I write about in *An American Bride in Kabul*, turned me into a lifelong advocate for women's lives.

The battle for women's rights is central to the battle for Western values. It is a necessary part of true democracy, along with freedom of religion and freedom of dissent. The greatest battle of the 21st century is one against barbaric misogyny and totalitarianism.

Mr. President: As Pete Seeger sings, "Which side are you on?"

There is a new king on the throne. Couldn't you have asked him to release these women, and given them a ride to freedom on Air Force

One? It's not too late to make the request—to show that America actually stands for something.

New York Post
1/27/15

ISIS Manifesto for Women: "Emasculation of Muslim Men … Tearing Society Apart"

I SIS has released a Manifesto on women and girls. Titled *Women in the Islamic State*, it is far more extreme than even Hitler's vision of women as belonging in the nursery (Kinder) the kitchen, (Küche) and the Church (Kirche).

ISIS believes that girls can marry adult men when they are only nine years old; that "pure" girls should be married by the time they are 16 or 17; that motherhood is the sole purpose of female existence. The Manifesto was posted in Arabic last month on a Jihadist forum and crafted by ISIS's female militia: Al-Khanssaa Brigade.

Face and body veiling are mandatory for women—which is just as well since beauty parlors and shops selling fashionable clothes are the "instruments of the devil and must not be tolerated."

A girl's education must end when she is fifteen—and that education will mainly focus on religion, Quranic Arabic and science, the Sharia laws about marriage and divorce, as well as knitting and cooking.

There are some puzzling exceptions. "A woman may leave the house if she is going to study theology, if she is a woman doctor or teacher, and if it has been ruled by fatwa that she must fight jihad or holy war."

One marvels at the prospect of women doctors and teachers who are only allowed an eighth or ninth grade education. Or, will all the doctors be men? Will traditional Afghan rules apply—namely, when a woman is ill, her husband would visit the doctor on her behalf and describe her symptoms? Based on that description, the doctor would diagnose and prescribe. Edward Hunter, in his wonderful book, *The Past*

Present: A Year in Afghanistan describes just such customs—and worse. And he was there in 1959, long before the Taliban arose.

Paradoxically, the Manifesto also rejects "Western values, including financial systems and scientific research… 'the study of brain cells of crows, grains of sand, and fish arteries' as a distraction from the fundamental purpose of humanity, to worship God." Yet, it states that certain scientific research, "that help facilitate the lives of Muslims and their affairs are permissible" such as "medicine, agriculture, and architecture."

However, the Manifesto talks about having captured "hospitals that are 'full of modern medical technology that could treat all those suffering from chronic diseases, including cancer.'"

The ISIS Manifesto identifies the root cause of the world's ills—and the "emasculation of Muslim men"—as due to the "Western program for women." The "blurring of the lines between the roles of each sex has caused people to forget how to worship God properly…and is tearing society apart."

In other words, Muslim-on-Muslim religious wars, poverty, illiteracy, shame-and-honor tribalism, barbarism, terrorism, corruption, unemployment, non-productivity, are all caused by the increasingly limited freedoms that Muslim women enjoy—mainly because they have been corrupted by Western ideas.

If anything can wake up Western academics, liberals, leftists, and especially feminists, this Manifesto should do it. I doubt that it will—although it is a direct hit on women's rights, human rights, and Western civilization.

Breitbart
2/6/15

- 113 -
Why are Jihadis so Obsessed with Porn?

Recently, London Mayor Boris Johnson described jihadists as "porn driven losers" who have "low self-esteem and are unsuccessful with women." He's on to something important and profound.

According to Syrian doctors in a report in the British media, ISIS fighters are buying frilly underwear for their wives and sex slaves—and subjecting them to abnormal and sadistic sexual practices. They may well have learned this from pornography.

The Navy SEALs who killed Osama bin Laden found a fairly extensive stash of modern pornography in his possession.

The 9/11 jihadists visited strip clubs, paid for lap dances, and for prostitutes in their motel rooms in Boston, Las Vegas and Florida.

Anwar Al-Awlaki, the American-born imam who fled to Yemen in 2004 and was later assassinated by a US drone, ate a lot of pizza and visited a lot of prostitutes in the months after 9/11.

As a presumably "holy man," Al-Awlaki mentored at least three of the 9/11 hijackers, the Fort Hood shooter, the would-be Times Square bomber (Faisal Shahzad) and the underwear bomber.

In the years since 9/11, police raids of terrorist cells in the United Kingdom, Italy and Spain have yielded countless images of hard-core child pornography.

Not only did jihadists use porn for pleasure, they also embedded secret coded messages into shared pornography and onto pedophile Web sites.

In 2011-2012, German police found more than 100 al Qaeda documents concerning terrorist plots embedded within a porn video hidden in suspect's Maqsood Lodin's underwear.

According to NSA documents made public by Edward Snowden's leaks, countless "radicals" have called for jihad by day but watched porn by night. One damaging piece of evidence shows a "militant" using "sexually explicit persuasive language when communicating with inexperienced young girls."

This year's Paris jihadists Amedy Coulibaly and Cherif Kouachi both kept child-porn photos on their laptops, which included "sickening pictures of young boys and girls involved in sexual acts with adults."

Why does the jihadis' porn obsession matter?

Pornography is literally what prostituted women are forced or paid to do. It is derived from the Greek *porni* ("prostitute") and *graphein* ("to write").

Porn is a global phenomenon, produced and consumed everywhere and increasingly by people of all ages—deforming the sexual development of young viewers. Watching it desensitizes the viewer to sexual aggression and strengthens existing beliefs that support violence toward women.

It is routinely very violent: 82 percent of the top-rated porn scenes involve physical aggression (slapping, spanking, gagging); 49 percent contain verbal aggression (name calling, insults). The perps are male, 94 percent of the targets are female.

It's easy to imagine pornography's empowering effect upon would-be jihadists, who may unable to afford the price of a wife or a prostitute, who are young, without normal sexual outlets and already predisposed to violence towards women—and to pedophilia.

Yet, while most of the Muslim world is profoundly sexist (and while porn is everywhere there, too), few Muslims approve of porn. Indeed, its leaders often castigate the West for exposing women in a sexually explicit way.

Consider the divide in Western Europe, revealed in a 2008 Gallup poll: 43 percent of the general French population found viewing porn "morally acceptable," but only 16 percent of French Muslims did.

In Germany, it was 58 percent of the general public but only 18 percent of Muslims. In Britain, 35 percent of non-Muslim Brits viewed pornography as acceptable, but only 1 percent of British Muslims did.

Muslims may lie to poll takers about sex, but if they are telling the truth, the way to de-heroize bin Laden and all the other jihadis is not to call them "terrorists," but rather to describe them as "porn hounds."

Maybe Muslims are opposed to pornography—but jihadists are not.

New York Post
2/17/15

Syrian Doctors: ISIS Jihadists "Demanding Viagra," Lingerie for Wives and Slaves

I SIS fighters are "buying their wives kinky underwear," demanding Viagra to better their performance, and subjecting their wives, concubines, and sex slaves to sadistic sexual practices, according to Syrian doctors forced to treat jihadists in conquered territories.

The Daily Mail reports that doctors have been able to relay their witness testimonies through the advocacy group "Raqqa is Being Slaughtered Silently." Their eyewitness accounts of being forced to treat Islamic State terrorists echo reports from the Iraqi city of Mosul, where doctors are often forced to treat wounded jihadists returning from the front lines.

These men are living day-to-day in an almost post-Holocaust desert of their own making, and yet—perhaps therefore—they are obsessed with sex, frilly underwear, their own impotence, and an insatiable desire to have as many orgasms as possible.

There are their captive brides, beaten for failing to cover even their eyes, prohibited from attending school, shrouded in black ambulatory body bags, and expected to act the part of prostitutes in order to please their brutal and demanding husbands or masters. The women subjected to such tortures range from the hundreds of known Yazidi girls and women to Western Muslim converts traveling to Syria and Iraq to fulfill the work of a "jihad bride."

Jihadists from Bin Laden on have developed a reputation for being known pornography addicts. ISIS fighters may be learning some additionally savage tricks from pornography. The proliferation of both child porn and sadistic adult porn has essentially mainstreamed prostitution, as has the popularity of depicting increasingly young women in revealing clothing outside of pornography.

Now, a devil's host of angry men, losers, porn addicts, and ex-convicts have an outlet to express their sadism towards women. Fighters may be flocking to join the ranks of ISIS not only to bring about a potential Caliphate or to express their hatred towards infidel ways, but also to achieve Paradise Now. Instead of having to become human homicide bombs in order to merit 72 eternal, heavenly virgins, ISIS fighters can have an endless number of virgins right here on earth.

They can treat the Madonna as the Magadalen as a form of revenge against Christianity. They can treat tender virgin Muslim girls as whores—and no one can stop them. They have paid good money for their brides. They have no roots in the neighborhood and thus, there is no extended family with whom the bride's family can negotiate.

Joining ISIS might be the best deal in town for sexually starved, sexually ignorant, sexually repressed, unemployed, unemployable, and impoverished men.

All praise to President Al-Sisi for bombing ISIS on behalf of the 21 beheaded Egyptian Christians. All praise to the Gulf States who are involved in doing "something." All shame is America's, whose President is still "leading from behind" and refusing to admit that the Islamic State (ISIS) has anything to do with Islam.

Breitbart
2/17/15

- 115 -
Feminist Muslims Fight Genital Mutilation's Growing Popularity

As Islam conquered what was formerly a Jewish, Christian, Hindu, Buddhist, and Zoroastrian Middle East and central Asia, Islam also conquered a pagan, animist and Christian Africa, and what was formerly a Hindu and Buddhist Indonesia and Malaysia.

As an Arab-and African-style Islam spread via the sword, customs that may or may not have been religiously mandated also spread.

According to a recent report, female genital mutilation (FGM), long associated with Muslims and Africans, is becoming more popular in Malaysia. Some Malaysians believe this is religiously required by the Qur'an; others believe it is an important Muslim custom. A spokeswoman for a local women's rights group, Sisters in Islam, insists that *sunat* (Malaysian for circumcision) is not mentioned in the Qur'an."Previously, it was a cultural practice," she says, "but now, because of Islamization, people just relate everything to Islam. And when you link something to religion, people here follow it blindly."

Increasingly, Malaysian Muslim physicians, often female, are performing FGM procedures (which range from very mild to very severe). According to a 2012 study conducted by Dr. Maznah Dahlui, "93 percent of Muslim women surveyed had been circumcised." Some gynecologists admit that they perform "a more drastic version with needles and scissors;" other Malaysian physicians claim "less invasive procedures."

FGM is not banned in Malaysia, although the government has issued medical guidelines for the procedures. Malaysian hospitals are not allowed to perform FGM surgeries. Therefore, many private Muslim clinics have arisen. Some Malaysians are outraged that internationalal organizations, such as the UN, the World Health Organization, and UNICEF are telling Malaysians what to do.

According to Abdul Khan Rashid, a professor at Penang Medical College, "The problem with the West is that it's so judgmental. Who the hell are you to tell us what to practice and what not to practice?"

Interestingly, last year, in response to Bill Maher, Reza Aslan, the author of *No God But God: The Origins, Evolution, and Future of Islam* and *Zealot: The Life and Times of Jesus of Nazareth*, claimed that FGM is primarily "a Central African, not a Muslim problem." However, many experts disagree with Aslan. Egypt, Sudan, and Somalia may be located in North Africa, but they are definitely Muslim-majority countries.

Contrary to Aslan's point, women from Kurdish Iran, the UAE, Oman, Indonesia (a fact that UNICEF tried to bury), Thailand, parts of India and Pakistan, as well as women from Malaysia have undergone FGM.

Musawah—"equality" in Arabic—is a global Muslim feminist movement which believes that misogynist custom, not divine religion, is behind anti-woman practices. Marina Mahathir, the daughter of Malaysia's former Prime Minister, has been active in this movement.

According to Iranian Nobel Peace laureate Shirin Ebadi, culture can be changed "through law." Before Khomeini, polygamy was "legally restricted in Iran and became culturally unacceptable. When legalized after the revolution, polygamy became more acceptable."

As medieval Islam spreads its dark shadow like a demonic hawk on the wing, those Muslim feminists who seek freedom and dignity through re-interpretations of the Qur'an are facing an important but uphill battle.

Breitbart
2/23/15

- 116 -
Palestinian Journalist Asma'a Al-Gul Chronicles Brutal Life of Muslim Co-Wives

Polygamy is widely practiced in Gaza—and the women (or "sister wives") are not happy about it.

So says Asma'a Al-Gul, who has just exposed this practice in an article for *Al Monitor*. Al-Gul is a heroic feminist Palestinian journalist who, in 2009, was fired for her work which exposed honor killings on the West Bank and in Gaza; she was harassed, threatened, and nearly arrested by Hamas for this work.

Now, she reports that polygamy is practiced by both rich and poor in Gaza. Anecdotally, she describes "hostility" and "hatred" between a pair of "sister-wives" who visited a beauty parlor together. She also quotes a financially independent and professionally successful woman who chose to become a second wife but who now says:

> Becoming the second wife is the worst decision that a woman can make. She will always live with the guilt of taking what was not hers. In most instances, the second wife discovers that 90% of the things her husband told her about his circumstances and his first wife were lies.

Another woman, a first wife, describes the enormous "pain and humiliation" that she felt when her husband sprang a second wife upon her.

Polygamy is legally sanctioned by Sharia law, by the Hadith, and by custom. A man is supposed to treat each woman "equally," something that is humanly impossible to do. The classic arguments in favor of polygamy are as follows: A man does not have to remain in an unhappy marriage—but he does not have to divorce the mother of his children for whom he remains responsible; if a woman has been widowed or has no husband and if she cannot support herself, a married man can extend the kindness of "protection" by marrying her; if she is poor and cannot afford a dowry, becoming a dowry-less second, third, or fourth wife will afford her the chance of marriage and childbearing; and, if a man's first wife cannot bear children, polygamy allows her to remain part of an extended family where she may "mother" her husband's children.

This does not always work out. One might remember how Mohammed Shafia's second wife, Tooba Yahya, tormented his first wife, Rona Amir Mohammed, who was infertile. Mohammed, Tooba, and their biological son honor-murdered Rona and three of Tooba's biological daughters who were all seen as "too Western" for Afghan girls who lived in Canada.

It is also clear that in poor families, everyone lives in close quarters and the first wife uses and abuses the second wife as her indentured servant—until or unless the second wife begins producing high-value sons. Then, the tables may turn. Also, the half-siblings are in a dead heat competition for their father's affections, attention, and for whatever inheritance there may be.

It is also clear that male lust, both for sex and for as many children as possible, is a factor in the practice of polygamy.

This practice is hardly confined to the West Bank and Gaza. It is rampant in Europe, especially in the UK, where the number has been estimated to be at least 20,000 such illegal unions. This often means that the second, third, and fourth wives do not enter into legal unions but are married under Sharia religious law only. They have no rights—and they scarcely understand the situation they are in. This also means that polygamous families, which are illegal, may nevertheless be all living on the dole.

In 2008, the estimate for polygamous unions in the United States was even higher and ranged from 50,000 to 100,000. However, a Palestinian woman, now a second wife, explained that when she got divorced, she became a "pariah" in her Muslim community in New Jersey. Thus, marrying again, even illegally, solved her problem within the community.

A Muslim-American woman from Senegal confirms my own observations. She says that her father married four women and she had 19 or 20 siblings: "'Sometimes he doesn't know who's who, and he forgets the name' of his children and wives."

This practice is not slowing down. Recently, at the end of 2014, a UK-based matchmaking site appeared for "Muslim polygamists." It is called "The Second Wives Club."

Many women have set up accounts at this site—including those who live in the United States.

Breitbart
3/23/15

- 117 -
"Sex Work" Is a Faux Feminist Phrase Utilized at the UN

P rominent Indian anti-prostitution activist Ruchira Gupta was about to receive a Woman of Distinction award at the United Nations this past March when she was told not to use the word "prostitution" in her acceptance speech. Doing so would "put UN Women on the spot." According to a PassBlue report, Gupta revealed: "I was surprised that the UN was trying to censor [me and told] me not to speak on prostitution, when my work was with victims of prostitution."

At the UN, the politically correct phrases are: "trafficking," "sex slavery," "sex work," and "sex workers." This is Orwellian doublespeak—something the UN has honed to a high art when it comes to Islam, critiques of Islam, and Israel.

Employing the phrase "sex work" represents a faux feminist or a liberal feminist point of view in which women are seen as having "agency," and therefore as being able to freely choose to be sex workers. The phrase "sex work" is an attempt to mainstream prostitution as just another form of work. Doing so utterly obliterates the fact that prostitutes are most often unwilling victims who suffer from a much higher rates of post-traumatic stress symptomatology than combat veterans do. It hides the fact that Johns often want—and get—under-age children. Legally, a good deal of prostitution is pedophilia or legalized rape.

Imagine the nature of prostitution in the Muslim world—especially in an era of jihad, and in war zones. Imagine the nature of sexual violence towards women in Third World countries. Actually, it is unimaginable.

Therefore, the UN's world view is outrageous, corrupt and ludicrous given that Gupta's work is with children as young as seven years old and whose families have sold them to pimps. Gupta describes what happens next in the brothel quarters of Mumbai, Delhi, Kolkata, and other cities.

> 'The pimps would hand over these little girls to the brothel keepers…and the girls were locked up for the next five years [...] Raped repeatedly by eight to ten customers every night.' By their 20s, Gupta said, their youth is gone and bodies are broken, and they 'are thrown out on the sidewalk to die a very difficult death because they were no longer commercially viable.'

Prostituted women have protested the UN Women policy of avoiding the word "prostitution." They view themselves as victims of prostitution and as survivors who were trapped. In a letter demanding this and signed by 61 different organizations, they write, "we can never accept our exploitation as 'work.'"

They are right. The label "sex work" applied to a great deal of the world's prostitution trade legitimizes violence against women.

The UN should be ashamed of itself not only because it does so little to save mortally endangered women—but because it is trying to censor heroic women, such as Gupta, who are doing just that.

Breitbart
4/1/15

- 118 -
ISIS's Nazi-Style 'Jihad Bride' Propaganda an Alluring Trap for Western Girls

F oreign girls who are lured via the internet to join ISIS are being misled by a glamorized vision of women posing with AK-47s and in martial arts positions—in essence, a vision of women performing forbidden, male-only holy tasks.

ISIS propaganda is capitalizing on the allure of such adventure coupled with a Western desire for High Romance, and a girlish desire for love, marriage, and children. Quilliam Foundation think tank researcher Charlie Winter notes that such online propoganda provides "a false image based on targeted obfuscation and exaggeration." He quotes Glasgow runaway, Aqsa Mahmood, who writes that "the women you may have seen online are all part of propaganda."

The reality for ISIS "brides" is dull, domestic, and dangerous. Food and electricity are minimal, there are no schools, but there are constant air strikes and gun fights. Women police and punish other women. They do not engage in battle.

The all-female Al-Khanssaa Brigade holds an anti-feminist ideology in which women's rights are seen as part of a corrupt and material West that has led to the emasculation of men.

The brides lead isolated lives spent mostly indoors without electricity or clean water. They wear heavy head-face-and-body covering in 100 degree weather—and they are monitored, harassed, and punished by a sadistic all-female brigade if their burqa slips. "When their (arranged marriage) husbands are killed, they are expected to celebrate their 'martyrdom' and quickly marry other fighters."

According to ISIS internet recruiter and former Australian, Dullel Kassab, "Reality hits you when you celebrate a *walimah* (marriage banquet) and console a widow on the same day."

Then, there is the scarcity of medical care. The wife of an ISIS fighter was totally ignored as her blood pooled on the hospital floor during a painful miscarriage. According to Kassab: "She wasn't offered a chair or a bed and nobody even returned to check on her...the *muhajireen* (migrants) are also subjected to mistreatment and discrimination by the locals."

In February of 2015, ISIS released a Manifesto which states that girls can marry at nine; their education, which must consist mainly of Qur'anic Studies and home economics, must end when they turn fifteen; they must be fully face-, head-, and body-veiled; and motherhood is the sole purpose of female existence.

This is reminiscent of Hitler's Nazi, Stepford Wife-style of "Bride Schools," in which office workers and career women were taught how to be wives. Propaganda photos consisted of smiling groups of women in a hayfield, carrying baskets of flowers, "chopping vegetables in a kitchen, and singing along to another woman's accordion playing."

This country idyll promoted a six-week course in which women learned household skills such as cooking, ironing, gardening, child care, and interior design. They were taught how to clean a husband's uniform, to pledge their loyalty to Hitler "until death," and to raise their children "in accordance with Nazi belief." This meant they would "promote racial values in the family."

Traditional domesticity: confinement to the home, child care, and devotion to a political religion ("Kinder, Küche, Kirche") were presented as a female warrior's task.

ISIS may have taken a page from Hitler's playbook—but they are also following the harshest and most traditional interpretation of the Qur'an: "A woman's highest achievement is motherhood;" "Women must be veiled;" "The majority of inhabitants in Hell are women;" "Women are less intelligent and spiritually inferior to men;" "Women are an affliction to men."

Perhaps many Westerners, both men and women, cannot handle all the choices and responsibilities that freedom entails. Perhaps they want an all-purpose Program to contain their anxieties. Many Western male prison-converts to Islam have found that by embracing a communal identity they can better control their antisocial tendencies—plus, they can now have four wives. Arguably, Western women converts to

Islam may idealize "surrender," (this is what Islam means), as both erotic and elevating, as a way out of a humdrum and demanding existence.

A serious effort must be made to reveal these motives and the grim reality of marrying an unknown ISIS warrior to young Western girls. The problem is that girls in the West also want adventure through romance, love through bondage. Think of the popularity of *Fifty Shades of Gray*. Western girls have also been brought up on fairy tales and believe in Happy Endings. They do not understand that they are walking into a dangerous situation from which there may be No Exit.

Breitbart
4/8/15

Author Zainub Priya Dala Beaten, Sent to Mental Hospital After Praising Rushdie

Zainub Priya Dala, a South African Muslim author and psychologist, was "violently attacked for expressing admiration for Salman Rushdie." After countless phoned-in threats to recant, Dala was also placed under psychiatric care where she was "drugged until I could not walk" and advised to adopt a proper Muslim lifestyle.

Dala recently published her first novel, *What About Meera*. Last month, at a literary festival in Durban, she said she "admired the writing of Arundhati Roy and Rushdie."

Three days later, three men forced her car off the road, held a knife to her throat, banged her face with a brick and broke her cheekbone. They called her "Rushdie's bitch." Had a taxi not passed by, she is sure she "would've been stabbed."

Immediately thereafter, Dala was placed under intense pressure. The Muslim community, her father, and her husband all demanded that she "recant, repent, and say prayers." Her phone rang repeatedly late at night.

And then things got worse. In classic Soviet style, Dala was admitted to a psychiatric facility in Durban. Initially, genuinely stressed, she consented to this admission; soon enough, she understood that her treatment (or punishment) would consist of learning how to become "a good Muslim woman, stay covered and silent."

Dala tweeted from the institution that she was "not dragged kicking and screaming here," but that "a religious leader" suggested she should be interned at a mental institution to "reflect on my religion."

Dala was drugged in order to "break her" and force her into "submission." She said that she had been "broken down into submission." She was harangued to renounce her admiration of Rushdie's works. She says: "I could just as easily burn my Oscar Wilde collection because some homophobes came calling."

Many of us have compared Islamic totalitarianism with its Soviet and Chinese counterparts. What the Muslim community of Durban and the doctors at St Joseph's Mental Hospital there are doing is incarcerating a healthy person—even if, as *The Guardian* notes, she was admitted "voluntarily" after being pressured by family. The family and the Muslim community may not command state power in Durban—but for a Muslim dissident, they do. This mistreatment is precisely what Soviet Russia and China have done to many of their dissidents.

According to Richard J. Bonnie, LLB, in *The Journal of the American Academy of Psychiatry and the Law*, this is a "particularly pernicious form of repression because it uses the powerful modalities of medicine as tools of punishment, and it compounds a deep affront to human rights with deception and fraud."

PEN, the international literary and human rights organization, mounted a campaign on her behalf. Dala was just released this past Sunday evening. She thanked PEN for their efforts and issued this statement:

> I would like to thank PEN Centers in South Africa, America, and the U.K. a million times over for mobilizing so quickly and working so hard to secure my release from St. Joseph's psychiatric hospital. I felt myself slipping into a deeper depression while there. I felt cut off from the world and that my faculties were compromised by excessive medication. I am now home with my family, laughing kids and overgrown garden.

Please note: Dala does not venture her opinion on any literary matter.

In my expert opinion, and with all due respect to PEN's efforts, Dala might still have not been released unless she was able to demonstrate some genuine remorse and a willingness to either publicly recant her views about Salman Rushdie's "literary style" or to keep quiet about the matter. A tweet she sent from the mental facility in which she claims her comments on Rushdie were misquoted seem to indicate that may be precisely the direction she will take in publicly addressing the matter.

Now, she knows what her family and her community will do to her if she steps out of line.

Breitbart
4/14/15

- 120 -
Yazidi Girls Tortured by ISIS Warriors

According to Kurdish media network Rudaw, seventeen-year-old "Suzan," a Kurdish Yazidi girl was kidnapped, gang-raped, enslaved, and impregnated by ISIS warriors. Incredibly, she managed to escape and has told her story to Delal Sindy, a Swedish-Kurdish activist living in a Kurdish region.

"Suzan's" story is surreal but alarmingly typical. She and other female sex slaves were lined up naked every morning, "smelled," and then chosen either by ISIS militant Al-Russiyah, or by his bodyguards. They were beaten and gang-raped daily. When "Suzan" was sold to Al-Russiyah, she was held in a hotel in Mosul in a building full of half-naked girls and women.

The virgins were highly prized; as such, they were examined to make sure that their hymens were intact and then taken to a room filled with 30-40 men who chose among them.

Based on "Suzan's" and other reports, sexually repressed jihadic misogynists are treating innocent, virgin children as if they are sophisticated prostituted women, the kind of women that jihadists watch, addictively, in pornography. Among the recently released 216 Yazidi women, there was a nine-year-old Yazidi girl who was pregnant; she had been raped by at least ten Islamic jihadists.

ISIS fighters are also torturing the girls as if sadistic torture is synonymous with normal sexual behavior or with male-female relations. They are killing the girls, even burning them alive, when they resist or cannot perform.

"Suzan" reports that she was forced to "say things from the Quran" during the rapes. If she refused, they whipped her or burned her thighs with boiling water. ISIS fighters cut off the legs of one girl who tried to escape.

"Suzan's" father is dead and she cannot find her mother, but her uncle has threatened to honor/"horror" kill her "if he finds out that she has been sexually abused or her honor 'tainted.'" The raped Kurdish and Yazidi women and their Sunni Arab babies will never be accepted—not even though the "highest Yazidi cleric [has urged] families to accept and welcome the women who had fled ISIS."

Rape is no longer merely a spoil of war. It has become a major weapon of war. Think Bosnia, Rwanda, Sudan, and Nigeria. The repeated public gang-rapes of female children and women is meant to drive these victims into madness—which it often does. They become depressed, insomniac, and suicidal. "Suzan" is haunted by flashbacks and wishes she was dead. "I want to kill myself," she says.

According to United Nations' Special Representative on Sexual Violence in Conflict, Zainab Bangura, although women are required to cover their heads under sharia law, ISIS fighters "have reportedly banned the captive girls from using headscarves after some of them used the scarves to hang themselves."

This barbaric behavior during war is not new. According to Algerian-American attorney Karima Bennoune, from 1992 on, Algerian fundamentalist Muslim men committed a series of "terrorist atrocities" against Algerian women. Bennoune describes the "kidnapping and repeated raping of young girls as sex slaves for armed fundamentalists."

Such rape is "gender cleansing." The intended effect of rape is always the same: to utterly break the spirit of the rape victim, to drive her out of her body and out of her mind so as to render her incapable of resistance.

According to Bennoune: "Terrorist attacks on women (in Algeria had) the desired effect: widespread psychosis among the women; internal exile—living in hiding, both physically and psychologically, in their own country." In Bennoune's view, "the collective psychosis" was due to the "escalation of violence" by the "soldiers of the Islamic state." According to Michael Curtis, M.D., an American volunteer-physician for Doctors Without Borders, "In Bosnia's Tuzla camp, the leading cause of death [was] suicide, probably the only refugee camp in the world where that is the case."

But some Muslim families refuse to demonize or kill the rape victim. As I've previously noted in chapter 83, in 2007, in Pakistan, thirteen-year old Kainat Soomro was chloroformed, drugged, kidnapped,

410

and then gang-raped for three or four days by four men who threatened to kill or sell her. Kainat escaped, in her bare feet and without her head-scarf.

Amazingly, her loving family refused to kill her. On the contrary: Kainat's mother wept and kissed her. Her father and older brother proudly supported Kainat's search for justice. This family deserves a prize for having the courage and the sanity to stand up to tribal misogyny.

For a poor girl and her family to have four powerful men jailed for three years is extraordinary. The price: The rapists allegedly killed her supportive brother. And despite national headlines, the police closed the murder investigation. Kainat quietly says that her "life is a living hell."

As of 2013, Kainat and her family still lived under police protection.

Breitbart
5/28/15

- 121 -

Hijab at Abercrombie and Fitch Heard in the Supreme Court

On June 1st, the Supreme Court "reversed and remanded" Samantha Elauf's high profile lawsuit concerning her right to wear a hijab at work back to the Tenth Circuit's appeals court for further proceedings. Elauf, represented by the Equal Employment Opportunity Commission, had been awarded $20,000 by a jury at the trial level; that award was vacated by the appeals court. Now, when the appeals court revisits the case, they may reinstate that jury award.

The Supreme Court decision states that a private employer must "accommodate" an employee's religious rights on the job:

> An employer may not make an applicant's religious practice, confirmed or otherwise, a factor in employment decisions... Title VII gives favored treatment to religious practices, rather than demanding that religious practices be treated as no worse than other practices.

On the one hand, this decision is a superb example of how American law protects religious freedom. Unlike French law, in which a neutral, secular state is envisioned as the best way to level the playing field among private religious differences, American law is grounded in "accommodating" the religious differences among immigrants and their descendants who wish to enjoy the American dream of freedom from tyranny and the right to exercise religious beliefs without coercion or punishment. The decision explicitly rejects a "neutral" policy: "Title VII

412

requires otherwise-neutral policies to give way to the need for an accommodation."

Thus, Sikhs wearing turbans, nuns wearing habits, Muslims wearing beards, prayer caps, and headscarves (hijab), Jews wearing kippahs, side-locks, and other head coverings, have now trumped private enterprise dress codes such as the one previously enacted by Abercrombie and Fitch—the employer whom the Equal Employment Opportunity Commission sued on Elauf's behalf.

The Qur'an mandates "modesty" for both men and women. This has, variously, come to mean headscarves, face veils (niqab) and full body bags (burqas) for women, and beards and skull caps for men.

On the other hand, one wonders if religious "accommodation" might next be claimed for the Islamic face mask. The decision states that "Samantha Elauf is a practicing Muslim who, consistent with her understanding of her religion's requirements, wears a headscarf." Somewhere, surely, there must be a Muslim woman who believes that face-masking is also, "in her understanding," a religious requirement. What then? Will courts rule that such an "understanding" must be "accommodated" or will that be trumped by an American definition of human and women's rights—and by the public's need for security?

I have one other gnawing fear. It is to America's credit that we believe in "accommodating" religious freedom. However, when we extend such blessed tolerance to a religion such as Islam—many of whose contemporary leaders are religious supremacists and religiously intolerant, and some who convert via the sword, and execute infidels and apostates—what sort of whirlwind may we be unleashing?

Breitbart/Middle East Forum
6/2/15

122

Injustice as Usual: Malala's Would-be Assassins Secretly Acquitted in Pakistan

I n 2012, the world was up in arms when a Pakistani Taliban gunman shot fifteen-year-old Malala Yousafzai in the head for having promoted education for girls. She survived dangerous and delicate surgery, moved to Britain with her family for reasons of security—and, along the way, received the Nobel Peace Prize, Europe's Sakharov prize for Freedom of Thought, and was named one of *TIME* magazine's most influential people.

But Pakistan—the country that sheltered Bin Laden for years—allowed the world to believe that justice was possible in this lawless country, that all the men who conspired to murder Malala and who wounded two other school girls had been convicted and sent to jail for 25 years each.

In reality, the Pakistani courtroom proceedings were secret. Despite what reporters were previously told this past April, (that ten men had been convicted), Pakistani authorities secretly acquitted eight of the men charged with conspiracy and attempted murder in the case. Today, the judgement of the secret military court was revealed together with contradictory explanations. Some sources said that there had not been enough evidence to convict all ten; others claimed "misreporting" for the confusion.

According to an unnamed security official, cited by *The Independent* and pegged to the *Daily Mirror*, "This was a tactic to get the media pressure away from the Malala case because the whole world wanted convictions for the crime." However, this view is upheld by the BBC's

Ilyas Khan, who wrote that "even if Pakistani officials did not purposefully spread misinformation, they allowed it to stand."

The Guardian quotes yet another unnamed army officer who believed that there "had been enough evidence to convict all of the men" but due to "longstanding weaknesses of Pakistan's judicial system," eight men were acquitted. This officer reported that witnesses were "intimidated into not giving evidence and the court dropped many of the charges against them." This same officer "denied claims made by the *Daily Mirror* that any of the men had been released. He said they were still being held and would be brought back to court."

The Guardian also claims that the ten men were part of a "group tasked by Pakistani Taliban leader Mullah Fazlullah with killing a series of high-profile people, including Yousafzai."

NPR's reporter, Philip Reeves, believes that it is "common for police to respond to public pressure by arresting large numbers of people who turn out to be unrelated to the crime in question, including relatives of suspects."

Pakistan is a tribal, highly corrupt, very violent Islamist country, in which Christians and women are severely persecuted. Pakistani honor killings are usually unpunished and are rarely reported. Pakistan is strategically located between India, Iran, and Afghanistan. It also happens to be a nuclear power.

Thus, it is America's ally.

But, if you think that reporters are not on the same page about what happens in Pakistan, just imagine the thin ice upon which diplomats skate.

In 2013 and again in 2015, Secretary of State John Kerry confirmed our alliance with this Wild East state. On a visit to Pakistan, Kerry announced "the reinvigoration of a Strategic Dialogue with Pakistan to foster a deeper, broader, and more comprehensive partnership and [to] facilitate concrete cooperation on core shared interests ranging from energy to counterterrorism."

Good luck to us.

Breitbart
6/5/15

123

As ISIS Brutalizes Women, a Pathetic Feminist Silence

Oh, how the feminist movement has lost its way. And the deafening silence over ISIS's latest brutal crimes makes that all too clear.

Fifty years ago, American women launched a liberation campaign for freedom and equality. We achieved a revolution in the Western world and created a vision for girls and women everywhere.

Second Wave feminism was an ideologically diverse movement that pioneered society's understanding of how women were disadvantaged economically, reproductively, politically, physically, psychologically and sexually.

Feminists had one standard of universal human rights—we were not cultural relativists—and we called misogyny by its rightful name no matter where we found it.

As late as 1997, the Feminist Majority at least took a stand against the Afghan Taliban and the burqa. In 2001, 18,000 people, led by feminist celebrities, cheered ecstatically when Oprah Winfrey removed a woman's burqa at a feminist event—but she did so safely in Madison Square Garden, not in Kabul or Kandahar.

Six weeks ago, Human Rights Watch documented a "system of organized rape and sexual assault, sexual slavery, and forced marriage by ISIS forces." Their victims were mainly Yazidi women and girls as young as 12, whom they bought, sold, gang-raped, beat, tortured and murdered when they tried to escape.

In May, Kurdish media reported, Yazidi girls who escaped or were

416

released said they were kept half-naked together with other girls as young as 9, one of whom was pregnant when she was released. The girls were "smelled," chosen and examined to make sure they were virgins. ISIS fighters whipped or burned the girls' thighs if they refused to perform "extreme" pornography-influenced sex acts. In one instance, they cut off the legs of a girl who tried to escape.

These atrocities are war crimes and crimes against humanity—and yet American feminists did not demand that President Obama rescue the remaining female hostages nor did they demand military intervention or support on behalf of the millions of terrified Iraqi and Syrian civilian refugees.

An astounding public silence has prevailed.

The upcoming annual conference of the National Organization for Women does not list ISIS or Boko Haram on its agenda. While the most recent Women's Studies annual conference did focus on foreign policy, they were only interested in Palestine, a country which has never existed, and support for which is often synonymous with a genocidal anti-Israel position. Privately, feminists favor non-intervention, non-violence and the need for multilateral action, and they blame America for practically everything wrong in the world.

What is going on?

Most feminists are, typically, leftists who view "Amerika" and white Christian men as their most dangerous enemies, while remaining silent about Islamist barbarians such as ISIS.

Feminists strongly criticize Christianity and Judaism, but they're strangely reluctant to oppose Islam—as if doing so would be "racist." They fail to understand that a religion is a belief or an ideology, not a skin color.

The new pseudo-feminists are more concerned with racism than with sexism, and disproportionately focused on Western imperialism, colonialism and capitalism than on Islam's long and ongoing history of imperialism, colonialism, anti-black racism, slavery, forced conversion and gender and religious apartheid.

And why? They are terrified of being seen as "politically incorrect" and then demonized and shunned for it.

The Middle East and Western Africa are burning; Iran is raping female civilians and torturing political prisoners; the Pakistani Taliban is shooting young girls in the head for trying to get an education and disfiguring them with acid if their veils are askew—and yet, NOW passed no resolution opposing this.

417

Twenty-first century feminists need to oppose misogynistic, total-itarian movements. They need to reassess the global threats to liberty, and rekindle our original passion for universal justice and freedom.

NY Post
6/7/15

- 124 -
Not to Act Against Evil is to Act

C hristians, Kurds, and Yazidis are being ethnically cleansed—massacred, exterminated—in Iraq and Syria and neither President Obama nor any stable, allegedly moderate Muslim regime (is there one?) has done anything to stop it.

ISIS and Boko Haram have been kidnapping, torturing, and turning Muslim, Christian, Kurdish, and Yazidi girls into sex slaves and, despite his professed pro-Arab, pro-African, and pro-Muslim biases, the American President has not stopped this nor has he come up with a viable strategy to do so.

Ten to twenty million refugees have fled the war-ravaged region of the Middle East's "Arab Spring," adding to an estimated number of sixty million refugees, world-wide. Many Middle Eastern, North African, and Central Asian refugees are trying to enter Europe and are dying in the process. Nevertheless, global leaders, the media, and the United Nations continue to focus on an artificially inflated number of Palestinian refugees—and are failing to confront or resolve the greatest and most complex refugee stories of our times.

President Obama and his European allies are about to unleash the Iranian bomb, a fact which they are presenting to us, Orwell-style, as the only way to stop the Iranian bomb. As we know, Iran and the Iranian bomb are a direct and existential threat to Israel as well as to the entire civilized world.

Those who dare to say so are demonized as "racists." We are not allowed to speak the truth in universities, human rights organizations, or in the left mainstream media, at least not without police protection and a capacity to endure hostility, interruptions, and lies.

One pays a price for speaking out, yes. In Muslim countries, dissidents are forced into exile, or jailed, tortured and executed. In the West, one's career as an academic or public intellectual is ruined. One is defamed, shunned, sued, censored, death-threatened, and may require round-the-clock police protection.

But, what is the cost of remaining silent? I asked this question in a previous column and now wish to expand upon it.

Evil always triumphs when good people do not oppose it. The failure to resist and overthrow barbarism always, always means more suffering, more deaths, more despair. Surviving victims are always more haunted by what the "good" people failed to do than by what the "bad" people did do. They cried out—no one rescued or believed them, few helped them bring their torturers to justice.

When good people do nothing to stop radical evil—a soul-eating despair enters the world as well as an enormous cynicism.

The jihadists know they can keep going for a very long while. No one has stopped them. The Arab and Central Asian Christians being slaughtered in their beds and churches know that the Western Church will not save them. The untold millions of Syrian refugees know that America does not have their back. The girls and women raped and impregnated by ISIS and Boko Haram know they are on their own.

Despite 9/11, 3/11, 7/7, I fear that the West has not yet paid the price for failing to stop far-off genocides. Today, we watch the jihadist propaganda and, in viewing their death pornography, we become passive collaborators, complicit.

Our President refuses to name or understand this evil that is coming our way—an evil that is already here. Only incredible vigilance has stopped hundreds if not thousands of jihad attacks.

Evil triumphs when good people do not stand against it. Like Europeans and Americans in the Nazi era—privately disagreeing with Hitler's policies did not save eleven million people. One must resist—or the Devil wins. Covering up Stalin's crimes—40 to 50 million died—is not resisting the Devil.

According to Dietrich Bonhoeffer, "SILENCE in the face of evil is itself evil, God will not hold us guiltless, NOT to speak is to speak, NOT to act is to act."

Israel National News
6/18/15

- 125 -
World's Yazidis Rally for International Community to Stop ISIS Genocide in Iraq

The Yazidis are holding worldwide rallies and Memorial Services tomorrow in Oldenberg, Germany; on August 2nd in Lalish, Iraq (the Yezidi spiritual heartland), and in France; and on August 3rd in Geneva, Armenia, Berlin, and in cities in Sweden, Turkey, Iraq, Syria, and the United States (Lincoln, Nebraska; Houston, Texas; and perhaps Buffalo, New York).

On August 2nd in Lincoln, Nebraska, the Yazidi community is sponsoring an Art Walk with prizes for the best art work that illustrates their people's historical and contemporary story. Houston-based Yazidis are holding a Remembrance Service at the University of Houston.

Yazidis are remembering and protesting the seventy four genocides that their people have endured in the Middle East. These massacres have taken place from the seventh century on and were perpetrated by Arab Muslims, Mongols, Persians, Kurds, Turks, Ottomans, etc.

August 3, 2015 marks the one-year anniversary of the most recent of these genocides—perpetrated by the Islamic State (ISIS or ISIL); it is a 21st century disaster that remains ongoing.

According to Yazidi-American activist Gulie Khalaf, who is also the treasurer for Yazidis International, in an interview, ISIS has "killed over 3,000 civilians, including women, children, elderly, and the disabled. They have kidnapped at least 5,000 civilians, most women and girls, who were targeted for sexual enslavement. After being taken from their parents, many young boys were brainwashed and trained as child soldiers to fight for ISIS's jihadist objectives. In some cases, ISIS jihadists buried Yazidis alive or burned them inside their religious temples. ISIS destroyed over 20 Yazidi shrines and religious sites and, with explosives, forcefully displaced 350,000 Yazidis in an attempt to permanently ethnically-cleanse them from their traditional homeland as a way of discouraging the community from ever attempting to return."

According to Murad Ismail, co-founder of Yazda, a global Yazidi Organization, and another interviewee, "Our hostages are still living under terrible conditions. Girls and women are being sexually violated on an hourly basis. ISIL wants to destroy our people and our culture. And the international community has allowed this to happen."

Some Yazidis have escaped. Some have been rescued. Many more have been murdered. According to Ismail, the Yazidis who were brought to Houston and Lincoln were people who had worked in some capacity for the American government or military. Once settled, they brought their relatives; their neighbors gravitated to where Yazidi community existed.

However, many Yazidis still remain trapped in refugee camps or remain in ISIS's clutches. Both Yazidi and Christian girls and women have been taken as sex slaves by ISIS. Many young Yazidi boys have been trained to hate their own people, to study the Qur'an, and to train as warriors. According to today's *Daily Mail*, one four-year-old Yazidi boy had to learn Sharia law and was "given a sword to behead his own mother." (Amazingly, both he and his mother escaped.)

Last week, *The Telegraph* published yet another heartbreaking interview with Rozin Khalil Hanjool, a 17-year-old Yazidi girl living in England. Rozin has launched a Change.org petition on behalf of the captive girls which now has 110,000 signatures. Hanjool wants the UK government to rescue their girls.

According to Gulie Khalaf, "governments might not yet recognize this officially as genocidal, but we want August 3rd as a remembrance day for the sake of those who were attacked and who passed away."

Khalaf also shared some troubling information with me about American do-gooders who take money and promise to help rescue specific Yazidis by name—and then disappear or present other Yazidis with the exact same name but who are unknown to their anguished relatives. She says, "We are pursuing one particular man who has promised to return our money but, if he does not, we may not be able to afford to take him to court. We also do not wish to be sued ourselves."

According to an article in *Rudaw*, a Kurdish media network, a claim was made about some Evangelical Christians handing out Bibles to traumatized Yazidis, praying with them, telling them that Jesus can save them, and "asking the refugees to convert to Christianity in order to start a new life in the West."

However, according to Sinjari-born Murad Ismail, the co-founder of Yazda, "such allegations against Christians have been exaggerated in the media." Ismail knows of one, maybe two such cases. Otherwise, he says, "Christians are helping us enormously. There is a lot of corruption in the programs provided to refugees, not all the money gets into the hands of the refugees, but organizations have a huge overhead."

Recently, in Copenhagen, I interviewed Hans Erling Jensen, the International Director of the Hatune Foundation. They are rescuing mainly Christian as well as Yazidi girls and women, bringing them to Europe, and trying to help them deal with their agonizing traumas and losses.

Murad Ismail explained that the American air strikes and food drops over Sinjar last year were very successful. Otherwise, "50,000 Yazidis would have been killed or enslaved." However, after last August, there were opportunities to rescue hostages in Kocho and Talafar but this did not happen. The international community failed their obligation to stop genocide in the 21st century.

Since President Obama has a way with the UN Security Council and is committed to multi-lateral actions: Why not persuade the world to stop genocide in the 21st century? We failed the former Yugoslavians, the Rwandans, the Sudanese, the Nigerians, the Iranians—and the Yazidis are certainly not the only endangered peoples today, but why not start somewhere? Let's do it. Let's do something noble and important and in doing so, we will be fighting back against barbarism and misogyny.

Breitbart
7/31/15

- 126 -

UK Police Declare War on Female Genital Mutilation as "Cutting Season" Approaches

The summer is known as the "cutting season." This means that infants as young as two or three months old are being taken out of the UK to be genitally mutilated in their countries of origin, such as Malaysia, whose customs, like those of Iran, have become increasingly Arabized and Africanized.

The UK has banned such procedures, but Malaysia, Middle Eastern Muslim, and African Muslim-Christian countries have not done so.

Female citizens of Europe, Canada, and the United States have also been taken on "vacations" to visit with families in Somalia, Egypt, Kenya, Nigeria, Sudan, Sierra Leone, Eritrea, Yemen, Afghanistan, Kurdistan, Indonesia, and Pakistan; these vacations are, essentially, medical nightmares. Innocent, often very young, girls are subjected to FGM—female genital mutilation—a procedure which is known to cause life-long agony and which is usually not reversible. If a girl is lucky, she may be anesthetized and the procedure hygienic, but that is not always the case.

A genitally mutilated woman will never be able to experience sexual pleasure. This is seen as the best way to keep women chaste and faithful to their husbands. However, it may also mean (as I've written before) that she will urinate and menstruate in great pain, experience childbirth as agony, may die in childbirth, risk life-endangering infections, or develop a fistula (which requires major surgery but which is not always available), etc. She might die from the mutilation or from any of its consequences.

The United Nations estimates that 100 million to 140 million women who are alive today have been genitally mutilated or "cut."

The good news: The UK police are getting admirably aggressive in this area. Last month, they stopped girls and their mothers and grand-mothers who were bound for Somalia on "cutting" vacations. Today, Scotland Yard is investigating a Type 4 procedure (the clitoris is pricked) performed on a two-month-old girl.

Ignorance of the law is no excuse, nor is the belief that religious custom demands this barbaric procedure. According to Detective Chief Superintendent Keith Nevin: "If anybody thinks it might be legal over-seas and they can go there to get it done and they will not be prosecuted here, they are wrong… If they have a footprint in this country they are vulnerable to the law."

The UK police have come in for deserved criticism in terms of not breaking up the rings of South Asian men who trafficked mainly white female children for more than a decade and for failing to believe and protect certain girls, such as Banaz Mahmud, who said she was in dan-ger of being honor killed.

However, the UK is quite advanced in terms of locating female cit-izens who have been tricked into visiting their home countries (mainly Pakistan), and trapped there in an unwanted marriage. If they can locate the woman and if she wishes to leave, they will return her to the UK. The UK police also provide protection and aliases for women who have coupled or married against the wishes of their families, who now want to honor ("horror") kill them. Finally, the UK does prosecute honor kill-ings.

I would like to see European families prosecuted for genitally mu-tilating their daughters and granddaughters, but also for forcing them into first cousin or unwanted marriages—especially when the girls are underage; for the practice of normalized daughter- and wife-beating and stalking; for practicing polygamy; and for forced face-veiling.

If Europe fails to do this—and if it continues to fail to bring Eu-ropean law-and-order into the so-called "no go zones" across the conti-nent, European civilization will die out and a radical brand of Islam will take over.

While in Scandinavia recently, I met with some of the brave people of the International and Danish Free Press Society. They told me this story. In Sweden, Mona Walter, a Somali-Swedish dissident, is known as Sweden's Ayaan Hirsi Ali. Reporters demanded that she walk through a bad neighborhood in Malmo naked-faced so that they would see what might happen. She insisted that she would be attacked but, accompa-

425

nied by a reporter and a police officer, she set out. She was attacked, as were the reporter and the police officer. They all fled for their lives. The reporter was not allowed to file this story for his newspaper. The truth was seen as too "incendiary," "provocative" and as not "politically correct."

If European countries do not turn this way of thinking around—and very quickly—they are doomed.

Breitbart
8/3/15

- 127 -

Situation in Refugee Camps Dire—
the Hatune Foundation to the Rescue

E ven as the Western intelligentsia continue to focus upon the fake and inflated refugee crisis among Palestinians, the world's real refugee crisis—Christians and Yazidis persecuted by ISIS—has become both overwhelming and hidden in plain sight.

There may be sixty million refugees and "internally displaced people" in all, primarily from Syria, Somalia, Sudan, Afghanistan, Congo, and other countries. Nine and a half million"refugees" and "internally displaced people" are Syrians. Some now live in refugee camps in Jordan, Israel (where they are also treated in hospitals), Lebanon, Iraq, and on the Syrian-Turkish border.

Half are children. Most of the children are no longer in school; worse, unvaccinated, they remain in deadly danger of contracting polio and measles in addition to other camp related diseases such as dysentery. Families are destitute and cannot afford the emergency surgeries that will save young lives, limbs, or eyes.

One young Yazidi girl, "Dilleen," has been suffering from retinal blastoma which, according to her advocate, Gulie Khalaf, "has moved to her other eye and, without surgery, will move to her brain. She is unable to see from either eye." Surgeons will perform the operation in Dohuk and her advocates are trying to raise money for it.

Many children are also starving and at best, severely undernourished. "Lucky" young Muslim virgin girls are being given in marriage to much older Muslim men in Jordan and the Gulf States in the hope that they will be fed and cared for. "Unlucky" Christian and Yazidi girls and

427

women are being kidnapped and used as sex slaves by ISIS.

President Obama's "international community," beginning with the United Nations, has not taken responsibility for any of this. Individual countries have accepted refugees, but they do not have the resources to accept them all–and to feed, house, educate, and integrate them. Europe is terrified of being overwhelmed by refugees who are illiterate, dependent, and hostile to the Western enterprise; some of whom may be jihadists; and whose predecessor-refugees are already known for their high crime rates, refusal to become "Western," and for their creation of lawless or Sharia run "no-go" zones all over Europe.

Enter individual heroes.

Sister Hatune Dogan and Hans Erling Jensen, the International Director of the Hatune Foundation, have been rescuing Christian and Yazidi girls and women from Iraq and bringing them to Europe for medical and psychological treatment. Last month, I was privileged to meet with Jensen in Europe. He described the work he and Sister Hatune are doing and I was very moved and excited. In a 4-minute interview he conducted with Sister Hatune, she described her monthly visits to the rescued girls in this way: "I give them my shoulder to cry on. There is little more relief we can offer until we get them to Europe."

Since January of 2014, the Hatune Foundation has freed "317 Christian and Yazidi girls from the hands of ISIS." In addition, with the help of "partners," the Foundation has been involved in "280 additional releases." As of this moment, "200 women and girls are now under professional care in Germany where "they now live in a safe environment while they are trying to get back to life after their traumatic experiences as an Islamic State captive."

Sister Hatune is five feet tall. She wears a nun's black habit and a large cross. She does so in places where Christianity is not only despised and under siege but where, over the centuries, it has been decimated by Muslims. Christians now comprise only 4-5% of the population in Middle East and Central Asian countries, where Christianity began and once flourished. Sister Hatune is particularly passionate on this subject.

She is doing God's work and believes that God will protect her.

This past July, she flew to Istanbul, where she and her team provided "financial support to more than 400 people... and psychological support to 32 who really needed this." She went to eastern Turkey and provided financial support to some Christian villages who needed "food, medicine, and clothing." Undaunted, she then went to the refugee camp Chanek in Iraq where "51,000 Yazidi families live among 500,000 other people."

Sister Hatune encountered "catastrophic medical conditions." She found children with "black blisters in their faces caused by flies—flies, that infected the children after they had spent several days with their dead relatives in hiding from ISIS. There was a woman with worms in her foot that came out of large black holes."

She believes that a mobile clinic is necessary and has launched a campaign to fund it.

This brave soul then went to the Sinjar Shingal mountains. "Thirteen Yazidi fighters covered her" as she went to "the front lines." She reports that "right now, there are 30,000 Yazidi fighters trying to stop the expansion of ISIS in this area. They live in 2,000 tents, in open camps in the mountains. They get neither support from the West nor from the Kurds."

In her latest newsletter, Sister Hatune thanks her Foundation's Director and friend Hans Erling Jensen, and all those who have helped. She writes: "Without [their] support, I would be a bird without wings."

You may donate to this heroic cause and to the mobile clinic.

You may donate to help defray the cost of eye surgery for the Yazidi child who will become blind.

May God bless you for upholding and representing the very best of Western values.

Breitbart
8/17/15

128

Hans Erling Jensen, a Hero Working to Rescue ISIS's Core Victims

"**I**'ve been raped 30 times and it's not even lunchtime," cried one young Yazidi woman in a dangerous and desperate call.

Chillingly, she begged the man on the line, someone embedded with the Kurdish Peshmerga fighting ISIS: "If you know where we are, please bomb us. There is no life after this. I am going to kill myself anyway."

That request was made a year ago. So far, no brothel has been bombed, no slave auction interrupted.

She personally interviewed a young Yazidi girl who had been held captive by ISIS for two months. She was 14. "She was raped five to 10 times every day. She couldn't express what she had been through. 'I was dead—killed—hundreds of times,' she says. She knew of many girls that had jumped from a high rock to kill themselves because they could not live on with the shame."

This young girl is now safe. She has joined others who had been sold on the slave markets in Mosul and Rakka where girls are being sold again and again. One girl who is now with Sister Hatune had been sold eleven times.

Last month, I met with Jensen in Europe to talk about the work he and Sister Hatune are doing. She described her monthly visits to the rescued girls this way: "I give them my shoulder to cry on. There is little more relief we can offer until we get them to Europe."

Since January 2014, the Hatune Foundation has freed "317 Christian and Yazidi girls from the hands of ISIS." In addition, with the help of "partners," the foundation has been involved in "280 additional releases."

Right now, "200 women and girls are under professional care in Germany" where they can safely recover. Most of these girls are without family.

Many have seen their loved ones brutally murdered. The task is huge.

Hans Erling Jensen met Sister Hatune and became director of the Hatune Foundation last year.

They agreed to mount a Web platform as a way of campaigning for the rescue of Christians and Yazidis. Sister Hatune got special permission from the Archbishop of the Syrian Orthodox Church to work outside the church.

Jensen tells me: "They have all been raped, sold as slaves countless times ... Our long-term goal is to offer them security and comfort in life. We have bought three houses close to the foundation's headquarters [in Germany] and we intend to design them for these girls when they have finished treatment."

The Foundation is located in Germany because there is a large, active Yazidi community there—and, Jensen says, because Germany is "into Christianity much more so than many other European countries."

The Yazidi women are not waiting for Western feminists or Western military men to come their aid.

A Yazidi singer, Xate Shingali, with the permission of Kurdish President Masoud Barzani, just formed an all-female brigade to fight ISIS. They have been equipped with AK-47s and wear military fatigues. Shingali says: "While we have had only basic training, we are ready to fight ISIS anytime."

She adds, "ISIS will never go to heaven. We will kill them."

NY Post
8/20/15

129

Dukhtar: Award-winning Film Highlights Struggle of Tribal "Badlands" Women

In the wild, wild East, in the tribal "badlands" between Pakistan and Muslim India, few girls or women willingly risk being honor killed for refusing an arranged marriage or for wanting to leave an exceptionally violent husband.

Women do not usually run away in search of freedom. No one will help them. It is their own families who will punish them—and women are viewed as the property of their families. Whoever dares help a runaway, allegedly "disobedient" women immediately becomes prey as well.

This is precisely what happens in Afia Serena Nathaniel's very beautiful, very gripping, and very tragic film: *Dukhtar* (Daughter). The award-winning film, which opens in New York October 9th and in Los Angeles on October 16th, is a road-trip thriller about a heroic Pakistani mother, Allah Rakhi, who risks almost certain death in an attempt to spare her ten-year-old daughter, Zainab, from having to marry a tribal warlord old enough to be her grandfather; Zainab's own father, Daulat Khan, has arranged this in order to end a blood feud.

The film is fast-paced. It is like a fable or a folk tale, fraught with forbidden potential romance and ever-present danger. However, despite exceptions such as Samia Sarwar, Mukhtar Bibi, and Malala Yousefzai, our heroine, however inspiring, is fictional and does not represent your average Urdu or Pashto-speaking tribal woman.

On the contrary.

Shockingly, in a new study of mine, just out in *Middle East Quarterly*, I found that female accomplices play an essential role in such family conspiracies. Equally significant: Worldwide, the (female) accomplices are arrested significantly less often than the male or female hands-on perpetrators.

While there are an amazing number of feminists in Pakistan and Afghanistan, there are also a far larger number of women who have internalized the values of a shame and honor culture and function as enforcers—as a matter of survival.

Like men, women internalize tribal shame-and-honor codes. The honor killing family views their crime as one of "self-defense." Had they not murdered the girl, no one would marry their other children. They would be shunned both socially and economically. And, this is all true.

Honor killings—family-of-origin conspiracies to kill a "disobedient" daughter or wife—are very common among Pakistanis, both at home and in the West. The disobedience can range from "looking at a boy on a motorbike" to wanting a divorce from a more-violent-than-usual first cousin. The fictional ten-year-old, Zainab, believes that if "you look at a boy you get pregnant." Absolutely no freedom of choice in terms of a marriage mate is allowed. A woman's virginity and fertility are resources that belong to her family and tribe, not the woman.

Tribal councils in Pakistan consider honor killing justifiable; mostly, the local police turn a blind eye. If ever questioned, families say: "She is missing, "she ran away," or "she killed herself." In Pakistan, honor killing is sometimes used as a pretext for other crimes. According to Muhammad Haroon Bahlkani, an officer in the Community Development Department in Sindh, Pakistan, a "man can murder another man for unrelated reasons, kill one of his own female relatives, and then credibly blame his first victim for dishonoring the second. Or he can simply kill one of his female relatives, accuse someone rich of involvement with her, and extract financial compensation in exchange for forgoing vengeance." Bahlkani has a name for this: the "Honor Killing Industry."

In Pakistan, many honor killings are known as karo-kari killings, which literally means "black male" and "black female" in Urdu and refers to cases in which adulterers are killed together. However, according to Bahlkani, there is an escape clause, but only for the men who can run away, hide, or pay restitution. Women are confined to the home, and few people will shelter a female runaway.

The film challenges this reality by imagining a rebel: A mother who loves her daughter enough to risk being killed for violating the honor codes; a daughter who loves her mother enough to risk being killed for running away from her father's house. Finally, in *Dukhtar*, a former (and very soulful) mujahid, Soheil, is initially duped into rescuing both mother and daughter; over time, he actively decides to protect them.

Clearly, his character has come a long way.

Allah Rakhi is an inspiring heroine—and a surprising one too. She is illiterate, and was herself subjected to an arranged marriage to a much older man when she was fifteen years old. The film reverses reality—and challenges tribal imagination by portraying three generations of spirited heroines and woman-loving women: Allah Rakhi, her daughter, and her daughter's maternal grandmother.

The filmmaker was inspired by a story of a Pakistani mother who once kidnapped her two daughters to ensure a better future for them. It took ten years for Nathaniel to write, produce, and direct this amazing film; she shot it in 30 days, working 12-14 hours a day, "under freezing conditions mostly in the disputed territory between Pakistan and India." There were also "bomb blasts and sectarian killings" along their route as well as "extreme weather conditions and warlord threats." The film is unique in many ways: It is a unique co-production between the United States and Pakistan and one directed by a woman with a 40 man crew.

The acting is superb (thank you Samia Mumtaz, Mohib Mirza, and Saleha Aref) and the cinematography breath-taking. Cinematographers Armughan Hassan and Najaf Bilgrami capture the awesome and treacherous beauty of the South Asian mountains, narrow mountain passes—and the sheer grandeur of the sky.

Breitbart
9/14/15

- 130 -
Sister Hatune Disappeared from British Film She Facilitated

I n 2014, Sister Hatune Dogan had been rescuing Christian and Yazidi girls from ISIS captivity for eight months, but she was desperate. If only the world could see the harm being done, understand that rescues were possible, people would open their hearts and their wallets.

Sister Hatune and her international director, Hans Erling Jensen, found an independent British filmmaker, Edward Watts. In an email dated February 6, 2015, Watts's producer, Rosie Garthwaite, wrote: "Hatune you will be the lead story in a documentary about women living under ISIS."

Watts spent nine days in Germany, Turkey, and Iraq with Sister Hatune, who introduced him to Sheikh Khaire, the head of the powerful local relief organization Ezdan Humanity, and to his co-workers, Sheikh Hassan and Khalil. The girls and their families would never have agreed to talk to him, or to be filmed, without Sister Hatune's having persuaded them that doing so would allow her to rescue more girls. She also served as Watt's interpreter.

However, Watts removed the nun from his prize-winning film, *Escape from ISIS*. He did not tell viewers to send funds to the Hatune Foundation to help with further rescues.

Watts decided that the rescues could take a back seat while he set up his own online charity to build a psychiatric center in the UK, to do the work that the Hatune Foundation had already been doing for years.

At one of his many sites, Watts claims to have raised 37,000 pounds.

Until his own charity is up and running, Watts directs people to the Amar Foundation. He also names one of Sister Hatune's go-betweens, Khaleel, and directs that funds be sent to him via the Amar Foundation, via Western Union (!), or to a Jerusalem-based foundation, The Springs of Hope, which, he alleges, sends couriers into ISIS territory with money.

On November 13th of this year, Watts wrote to me: "Anyone looking for information on how to help the rescues and contribute to the rehabilitation of the freed women can find information on my blog: www.edwardwattsfilms.com/blog and look for the two entries marked 'Donations.'"

Is Watts simply out to personally capitalize on human tragedy? That's been known to happen. Has he cut a deal with one of Hatune's "fixers" or go-betweens? That's also been known to happen in this part of the world.

Or, is this a matter of political differences trumping a matter of life and death and riding roughshod over the truth?

That seems to be the case.

On July 29, 2015, two weeks after his film aired in the United States on *Frontline* on PBS and in Britain on Channel 4, Watts testified before the Committee on Foreign Affairs of the American Congress. He told the Committee that: "It's worth noting that ISIS's extreme interpretation of Islam is not shared by the majority of Muslims in the territory under their control." Watts said that only Yazidis are kept as sex slaves because they are not considered People of the Book as Christians are.

This is a lie. Muslims have been kidnapping, torturing, enslaving, and murdering Christians merely because they are Christians for centuries, both in Iraq and in other Muslim countries. Sr. Hatune fled Muslim persecution in Turkey where the Muslim genocide of Christians (Armenians) took place.

Sister Hatune does have a different view of ISIS and of Islam.

According to Hans Erling Jensen the film's producers explained that "her prominent statements about Islam and ISIS would shift the focus of the discussion about the film and would overshadow the relief work."

Sr. Hatune said that "Islam is ISIS and ISIS is Islam; they would have a lot in common, even though ISIS pursues them with more barbaric means." Sr. Hatune also mentioned that "atrocities like beheadings and crucifixions [are] justified by verses in the Qur'an, and have been going on in Iraq long before ISIS. Saudi Arabia is also conducting beheadings and other draconian punishments."

I just spoke to producer Rosie Garthwaite who, after claiming that Hatune herself had refused to be seen on camera (not true) and that her foundation did not "meet the requirements of a UK charity" (probably true), admitted to me that Hatune had to be cut out of the film because "her views are viciously anti-Muslim, anyone can Google her and see that and we felt it would hurt the film."

Clearly, Watt's and Garthwaite's concern was all about the film, not about the girls.

The Hatune Foundation accepts donations.

FrontPage Magazine
11/18/15

National 'Woman's Studies' is Betraying
Women Under Sharia Law

L ast week, the National Women's Studies Association member-
ship voted to boycott Israel. The resolution reads, in part:

> As feminist scholars, activists, teachers, and public intellec-
> tuals ... we cannot overlook injustice and violence, including
> sexual and gender-based violence, perpetrated against Pal-
> estinians and other Arabs in the West Bank and Gaza Strip,
> within Israel and in the Golan Heights, as well as the colo-
> nial displacement of hundreds of thousands of Palestinians
> during the 1948 Nakba.

This vote is an utter betrayal of both reality and of women—especially women who live under Sharia law.

In 1970, I taught one of the first Women's Studies courses in the
country. What I had envisioned for the discipline has nothing to do with
today's anti-American, anti-Israel, post-colonial, faux-scholarly feminist academy.

Today, Women's Studies has been Stalinized and feminist professors are less concerned with the "occupation" of women's bodies worldwide than they are with the alleged occupation of a country that has
never existed: "Palestine."

So I wasn't surprised that the association held a plenary panel
last year on that crucial feminist issue: "The Imperial Politics of Nation-States: US, Israel, and Palestine." Panelists included communist

Angela Davis, the recipient of the Lenin Peace Prize; Rebecca Vilkomerson, the executive director of the infamous anti-Israel Jewish Voice for Peace; and Dr. Islah Jad of Birzeit University, who seems to focus only on Palestinian women.

They vowed to get the association to boycott Israel. Now they've succeeded.

But these "Feminists for Palestine" are in denial about Islam's long and ugly history of imperialism, colonialism, gender and religious apartheid, anti-black racism, conversion via the sword, executions of apostates and slavery.

The association doesn't condemn, for example, the atrocities being practiced by Hamas, ISIS, Boko Haram and the Taliban against Muslim women, children and dissidents and against Christian, Yazidi, and Kurdish women whom ISIS has captured as sex slaves.

This Women's Studies group isn't boycotting the honor killings among Arabs in Israel, on the West Bank, in Gaza and among Muslims in the West. They aren't condemning the forced face and body veiling of women in Saudi Arabia and Afghanistan, or the forced wearing of the hijab and heavy coverings in Iran and Nigeria.

The association doesn't focus on the pervasive nature of female genital mutilation in Egypt or on the increase in child marriage across the Arab and Muslim world. There's little mention of the terrible fate of women—even royalty—who dare to choose their own husbands.

Israel may not be flawless—what society is?—but it's still a modern democracy that protects the religious rights of all its minorities. These rights simply don't exist in the Arab Middle East or in Muslim Central Asia where Christians must hide their religious identities and risk being crucified. By now, the ethnic cleansing of Jews in the Muslim world is almost complete.

By contrast, according to Israeli feminist lawyer Frances Raday, Israel's Declaration of Independence was one of the "earliest constitutional documents in the world to include sex as a group classification within a guarantee of equality in social and political rights."

Today, Israeli women not only vote; they're elected to the parliament—right now 23 percent of Knesset members are women. Women also serve as judges on the Israeli Supreme Court. Women constitute 34 percent of all soldiers and 57 percent of all Israel Defense Forces officers. The majority of students studying at universities are women.

In addition, Arab citizens of Israel not only vote, but also serve in the Knesset and as judges on the Supreme Court. While they may be intimidated by Islamist death threats of "disloyalty" if they praise their Israeli citizenship, few would trade it to live under Hamas in Gaza.

Israel isn't a feminist paradise. Women are seriously limited by the ultra-Orthodox control of marriage and divorce, and control of public holy places. However, Jewish women have been successfully fighting for our religious rights in the Israeli Supreme Court.

I suspect that were our feminist counterparts to do so in Mecca, Mogadishu, Tehran, Islamabad or Kabul, their fate would consist of being jailed, raped, tortured, beheaded, stoned or murdered in some other way.

NY Post
12/6/15

132

Tashfeen Malik, Lady Al-Qaeda, Maryam Jameelah, and Boston "Bomber's Widow" All Wear the Islamic Veil

A number of journalists initially claimed that a woman was behind the San Bernardino massacre, and that Tashfeen Malik radicalized her husband Syed Rizwan Farook.

Anyone who has studied Islamic terrorist killers and radical Islamic culture knows that this is very unlikely.

Samia Labidi, a French-Tunisian dissident and former Islamist, describes how Tunisian Islamist men infiltrated her family "very softly, by means of marriage." They also infiltrated universities by promising men to "restore their masculine dominance." Docile wives and polygamy in a post-feminist age might seem very attractive.

Radical Islam appeals to many men for this reason, among others.

According to Labidi, once an Islamist penetrates a single family, "the next step is to marry off the remaining sisters to Islamists." As a girl, her brother-in-law had Samia, her sisters, and their mother face-veil and subjected them to nightly at-home "political" meetings based on the Qur'an. They were indoctrinated to believe that Islamic law "takes care of women and protects them" and that "what is good for Western women is not good for Muslim women."

Chillingly, Labidi writes that when such Islamists were exiled from their countries of origin they entered Europe and the internet to continue their work on a "global scale."

Labidi views the Western feminist embrace of a woman's alleged "religious" right to the burqa as a "betrayal" of feminism.

I totally agree. In my view, whenever burqas, heavy face veils, and dark, Iranian-style head, shoulder, and shapeless body coverings appear in the West, we must consider this as a symbol of radical Islam—or of Islamic jihad.

Katherine Russell, an American convert to Islam and the widow of one of the Boston bomber's, wears very heavy head and body coverings as well as dark glasses.

Female jihadists themselves are often heavily head-, shoulder-, and body-covered, if not face-veiled. Pakistani-born Aafia Siddiqui, "Lady Al-Qaeda," was a neuroscientist and wore dark head- and body-coverings; Pakistani-born Tashfeen Malik, studied to be a pharmacist. Her hijab is dark, heavy, and decidedly unfriendly.

Perhaps the most interesting (and most mentally unstable and dangerous) female jihadist was American-born convert Margaret Marcus (Maryam Jameelah), who fled to Pakistan to become a propagandist and translator for Maulana Abul Ala Mawdudi, who adopted Maryam. She helped him as an editor and translator in his influential work which argued the case for militant Islam against the West and which justified Sharia law. Maryam wore an Afghan-style burqa.

Daniel Pipes has argued that the West should ban the burqa for reasons of security, which include crimes committed by men wearing burqas. I have argued for such a ban on the grounds that the burqa and niqab are sensory deprivation isolation chambers and, as such, violate the wearer's human rights. In addition, the increasing appearance of heavy hijab, niqab (face veils) and burqas on Western streets, psychologically rattles infidel and secular women. First, they cannot free these women—who also function as a warning: If radical Islam succeeds, this can happen to them.

While I don't think that women are the masterminds behind male jihadists, I do think that our myths about female pacifism or passivity are dangerous. Women suicide killers and human bombs have a long history of killing civilians, including children, for nationalist and religious purposes.

FrontPage Magazine
12/14/15

Section Eight:
The American Gulag

133

The Other Face of Jihad: Muslim Gangs Sexually Assault Civilian Women

O n New Year's Eve, large gangs of Arab and North African Muslim men sexually assaulted women in a large number of cities in both Germany and in Austria.

These attackers, often a thousand strong, simultaneously stuck their fingers into every female orifice; groped, licked, hit, and terrified every vulnerable woman who was out celebrating the holiday.

The traumatized women did not all report these assaults to the police because they *were* traumatized and because many could not identify their attackers; there were so many of them. The media also under-reported these rapes. Not until one hundred German women in the city of Cologne, a number that grew to close to 400 by the weekend, reported their assaults to the police, did the matter become public.

Some media, including feminist media, refused to name the perpetrators as being of Arab or North African descent or as "Muslims." They did not wish to be demonized as "racists" or "Islamophobes," but there is, potentially, also a legitimate feminist reason.

European men rape European women every single day. Gang-rape often characterize rapes perpetrated by young men in the West. But the pattern of sexual harassment and rape in the Muslim and Hindu worlds in general is vastly different. Muslims in Sudan and Nigeria have perpetrated similar horrific attacks upon Christian, animist, and Muslim women. Similar atrocities took place in the former Yugoslavia, perpetrated by both Serb and Croat Christians and Muslims. Nevertheless, in an Islamist era, such Muslim-perpetrated attacks have assumed monstrous proportions.

Recall the roving gangs in Egypt in Tahrir Square in 2011, the mass groping and the assault of blonde American journalist Lara Logan. Realize that hundreds, perhaps thousands, of Egyptian Muslim and Christian women were also groped and sexually assaulted, whether or not they were wearing headscarves or face masks.

I am haunted by an Algerian story which took place in Hassi Messaoud in the summer of 2001, which I've previously described in this volume. A rampaging mob tortured, stabbed, mutilated, gang-raped, buried alive and murdered these innocent but vulnerable women. Unsurprisingly, some of the women who survived became mentally ill.

Algerian-American lawyer, Karina Bennoune, writes: "Terrorist attacks on women in Algeria have had the desired effect: widespread psychosis among the women; internal exile—living in hiding, both physically and psychologically, in their own country." In Bennoune's view, "the collective psychosis" is due to the "escalation of violence" by the "soldiers of the Islamic state." (This is pre-Daesh in Iraq and Syria).

In addition to what happened in Germany and Austria, similar male Muslim group gropings and assaults of women on New Year's Eve have now been widely reported to the police in Finland and Sweden.

If Germany and Austria—if all Europe--does not find, prosecute, and deport all the men who took part in the recent New Year's Eve atrocities, they will soon discover that such attacks might become regular features of European life and will occur on most holidays; that, like Muslim women, European women will increasingly live in fear; begin to stay indoors; and that female citizens will increasingly suffer from post-traumatic stress symptoms. A European woman's quality of life and efficiency at work may decrease. This will be true for women of every ethnicity and religion.

How can one educate a barbarian lynch mob? In my opinion, only through the mosques and the Islamist media.

That is not likely to happen any time soon.

Until it does or, failing that—elimination of the growing threat to the West will be required., That will only begin to happen when people realize that such mass public gang rapes represent the normalization of "Islamist" ways and are also another face of jihad.

Israel National News
1/9/16

- 134 -
Iranian-Ordered Hijab in the US Navy

As I look at the photos of the American sailors captured by Iran, many things about the entire incident vie for my attention.

The shameful postures of surrender that the Iranians demanded of our innocent sailors—is, in and of itself, unacceptably shameful. There they are, on their knees, with their hands clasped on or behind their heads.

The fact that the Iranians brazenly violated the Geneva Convention which requires Iran to protect prisoners against "insults and public curiosity" is criminal—although again, not surprising, as is their seizure of the American boats' GPS equipment.

Iran's demand—what else could it be?—that at least one American sailor "apologize" on video for their "mistake" and thank their Iranian captors for their great hospitality—is disgusting but so useful for the Iranian propaganda mill. It bears no relation to the truth of the matter.

The fact that President Obama failed to mention that his sailors were in captivity even as he addressed the nation in his last State of the Union speech—is beyond shameful but alas, is merely more of the same.

The fact that Secretary of State John Kerry would have us believe that his conversations with Foreign Minister Mohammad Javad Zarif actually played a significant role in Iran's decision to release the sailors unharmed and quickly—is as shameless as everything else—such as the fact that the American administration has gone along with the pretense that the sailors had either done something "wrong," or that their boat had somehow mis-functioned.

Then, there is at least one other thing.

Dr. Walid Phares, on Facebook, called my attention to the fact that the single American female sailor in the photos is....wearing hijab.

What? Is that regulation American Navy attire for women? Is this American sailor perhaps a religious Muslim?

No. Iran is demonstrating that it is prepared to enforce its version of Sharia law, even upon infidels, when it has the power to do so.

America, like other Western countries, including Israel, has been busily integrating women into a previously all-male military.

Iran will have none of it. Iran will not recognize the sovereignty of foreign vessels, diplomats, journalists, or the military.

Formerly sanctioned money is flowing into the country and this has empowered Iran, not to become more open and conciliatory, but rather, to show more of its true barbarian colors.

Iran will put women in their place wherever and whenever it can as a way of declaring war upon despised Western customs such as that of gender equality.

King Obama is making no principled moves, none at all.

Israel National News
1/15/16

- 135 -
How Academia Whitewashes Muslim Honor Killings

The whitewashing of Muslim honor killings in America has seeped into academia. And the PC police have found a new scapegoat: Hindu Americans.

In January, the *Journal of Family Violence* published "An Exploratory Study of Honor Crimes in the United States" authored by Brittany E. Hayes, Joshua D. Froelich and Steven M. Chermak. It was an act of cowardice as well as a shoddy piece of research. It broke absolutely no new ground, either theoretically or statistically, and is so "politically correct" that it completely misses an entire forest for a tree.

The study's first error consists of comparing violence against women in general with femicide. Being battered is not the same as being murdered.

A classic honor killing is a family conspiracy mainly against a young daughter; fathers, mothers, sisters, brothers, aunts, uncles and cousins—sometimes even grandfathers—may join in. Westerners don't often kill their teenage daughters—and especially not in a conspiratorial pack.

The reason Hayes et al. place honor killings within the broader context of "violence against women" is clear. They don't want to be accused of "Islamophobia" or of targeting any ethnic or religious group.

They don't tell us the names of any of the 16 honor-killing perpetrators or the names of their victims. The phrase "Muslim perpetrator" and "Muslim honor killing" appear nowhere. In 10,000 words, only 14 are related to "Islam," "Muslims," "Arabs" or "Middle Easterners."

Three times, Hayes et al. rail against "Western media coverage." They write: "Significantly, media reporters in the United States may be more inclined to cover honor crimes, especially those committed by Middle Easterners, compared to other fatal crimes because they may be perceived as more 'exotic' and news worthy." They insist, "Reporters may search for an honor crime angle when the victim and/or offender are of a particular ethnicity or religion ... there is a need to study honor crimes in the United States that involve victims and perpetrators from other cultures, like India, or extremist ideologies."

Wrong.

The New York Times, for example, has published a series of articles on Hindu honor killings in India and has published very few articles about Muslim honor killings in the United States, in North America or in Europe.

These authors seem not to be familiar with the 2012 study which compared Hindu honor killings in India with Muslim honor killings in Pakistan and Hindu versus Muslim honor killings worldwide. Hindus absolutely perpetrate honor killings (and some of them are quite gruesome), but they do so mainly in India; they don't bring the custom with them when they emigrate to the West. (Or those who emigrate are not honor-killing tribalists.) That is why one cannot study them here.

Also, many honor killings in India are perpetrated by Muslims as well as by Hindus.

That study showed that most Hindu honor killings are caste-related and that Muslim honor killings are triggered by many more reasons, e.g., girls have been killed for looking at boys, allowing their veils to slip, being seen without their veils, refusing to marry their first cousins, insisting on divorcing their first cousins, developing non-Muslim friends, having a non-Muslim boyfriend, being suspected of having an affair, wanting a higher education, etc.

Ironically, this comparison of Hindu and Muslim honor killings may actually support a politically correct view: The origin of honor killings seems to reside in shame-and-honor tribalism, not necessarily in a particular religion. I don't understand why other scholars have not yet absorbed this point.

The Qur'an does not command that a woman be honor-killed. It does, however, demand male and female "modesty" and female "obedience," and it allows husbands to physically chastise wives. Perhaps extreme misogynists have allowed superstitious and illiterate people to believe that committing intimate family femicide is religiously sanctioned.

Neither Islam nor Hinduism, as religious institutions, has worked very hard to abolish honor killing. The Indian Hindu government has tried to do so. The Pakistani government has not.

Nevertheless, Hayes, Freilich and Chermak bend over backward not to single out any one ethnicity, religion or nationality—except, perhaps, India.

New York Post
2/22/16

- 136 -
Veiled Betrayal:
Western Celebrities Don Hijab

The stewardesses of Air France are outraged and have just refused to don headscarves when they fly into Tehran, as the mullahs have demanded.

Viva La France!

The French stewardesses have more dignity, more sobriety and more self-respect than many American and European women do, beginning with trendsetting celebrities, female diplomats and first ladies, who have all donned headscarves (hijab), face masks (niqab) or full burqas when visiting Muslim countries—and as carefree fashion statements.

For example, Madonna, three Kardashian sisters, Rihanna, Selena Gomez, Katy Perry and Nicole Ritchie have all recently posted photos of themselves in Islamic "drag," either on visits to Dubai, Abu Dhabi or Morocco or just because it suited their fancy. They've posed wearing filmy, long scarves (Katy Perry), a heavy black hijab (Kylie Kardashian, Rihanna), niqab or face masks (Madonna), a heavy hijab plus abayas (Gomez) and almost full burqas (Kim and Khloe Kardashian).

Such female celebrities may influence Western girls more than female Western political leaders can. They don't understand that they are "slumming"; they can remove their exotic Islamic garb and pose naked whenever they choose to do so. This isn't possible for Muslim girls and women who are forced to wear the Islamic veil (headscarf, or face mask or full head, face and body covering) and who risk death when they resist.

452

Being forced to adopt a custom that subordinates women; being forced to "pretend" that one is a Muslim when that isn't the case; being made to feel shameful, shameless, if one is naked-faced, is an act of psychological warfare.

Remember the sole female Navy sailor who was recently forced to don a hijab on board while Iran held American sailors in captivity? It was an outrage, and reminiscent of how Barbary pirates once treated their captured Christian female slaves.

Why, then, are female non-Muslim Western leaders sometimes willing to comply?

Daniel Pipes has been keeping a careful list of such compliant Westerners. For example, in 1996, Britain's Princess Diana donned a headscarf when she visited Pakistan; in 1997, First Lady Hillary and Chelsea Clinton both donned a hijab on a visit with Yaser Arafat; in 2005, Secretary of State Condoleezza Rice wore one on a state visit to Tajikistan; in 2007, journalist Diane Sawyer did as well when she interviewed Iranian tyrant Mahmoud Amadinejad; also in 2007, Speaker of the House Nancy Pelosi wore a headscarf on a visit to Damascus, Syria; and in 2007, First Lady Laura Bush wore hijab on a state visit to Saudi Arabia.

In 2012, a high-ranking UN official on climate change, Christiana Figueres, donned a hijab on a visit to Qatar.

In 2015, Australian Foreign Minister Julie Bishop wore hijab on a state visit to Iran; and Secretary of State Hillary Clinton wore a hijab on a state visit to Pakistan.

Some of the same American and European Christian leaders also chose not to wear a hijab as well. There seems to be no rhyme or reason to their decisions.

In 2008, Rice and Bush did not wear a headscarf in Saudi Arabia; in 2010, German Chancellor Angela Merkel made a bare-headed visit to Saudi Arabia; in 2012, Clinton wore no hijab when she visited Saudi Arabia. When Michelle Obama attended the late Saudi king's funeral, she wore no hijab.

If you're representing America, it's fine to find ways to respect the customs of the country you are visiting. But please note: American male diplomats don't wear traditional Saudi male attire—the *bisht* or *thobe*, the *keffiya* and the *ayal*.

But some very brave westernized Muslim girls and women have also paid a high price for their decision to dress Western-style. They've been threatened with death, battered, imprisoned at home, rushed into forced marriages, escorted to and from school—and have been the victims of honor killings.

As long as women are forced to wear face masks and burqas, or even to wear the heavy hijab, it renders naked-faced women vulnerable, both in Muslim lands and in the West.

New York Post
4/6/16

- 137 -
How Many Bodies Will It Take?

A fghan-American Omar Siddeque Mateen was relentless as he shot down the living beings in a gay club in Orlando, Florida. He claimed that he did so as an ISIS fighter.

The question I and others have raised since 9/11 was: "How many bodies will it take for Americans, especially the intelligentsia, including the feminists, including gay people, including our elected officials, before they understand that we: (the West, America, Jews, Christians, Hindus, secular Muslims and ex-Muslim dissidents) have a very real enemy?" It is radical Islam or Islamism, Islamic jihad or, if you prefer, Islamist jihad; and it is not going away anytime soon.

This is precisely what Israel alone has been up against since its founding in 1948. Actually, long before that, Jews suffered the most profound Islamic anti-Semitism. Buddhists in Afghanistan were murdered or forcibly converted. Hindus in India were slaughtered by Muslims by the millions—simply because they were Hindus and because they refused to convert. Christians have long been persecuted by Muslims for the same reason; that persecution continues today.

Clearly, more than 3,000 bodies on 9/11 were not enough. Obviously, the many millions of Muslims murdered by Muslim jihadists have not been enough. Will the murder of 49 gay Americans finally be "enough?"

Somehow I doubt it but I certainly hope so. Sure, yes, let's ban assault rifles completely. That will not stop someone like Omar Mateen. But the handguns and the rifles are not as important as banning and abolishing the routine hate of women, the "wrong" kind of Muslim, ex-Muslim apostates, homosexuals, infidels—hatreds that are intimately part of historic Islam.

How many deaths before we become effective in identifying potential jihadists? Within our borders? Arriving as refugees and immigrants? How many deaths before we are willing to use the word "Muslim terrorist" without fearing we will be demonized for doing so?

In response to this jihad atrocity, gay websites are more focused on general "hate" against gays and the need for gun control than they are focused on the nature and the danger of radical Islam. Gay communities have been willing to march against Israel—but never against jihad.

Long ago, Natan Sharansky asked me if I thought I could "turn the feminists, the leftists, the gays around." I told him that I doubted it, but that I would try.

Will these 49 dead and 53 wounded start that "turning?"

We shall see.

If Mateen turns out to have been at war with his own homosexuality, the gay rights movement in America may claim him as "one of their own." Thus far, gay websites have not mentioned Islam's position on homosexuality—or on terrorism.

What does it mean if a Muslim jihadist, like Omar Siddeque Mateen, is ambivalent about his own homosexual longings? Can we blame his murderous massacre on self-hate, on his frustration about having to be "closeted," and/or on "homophobia" writ large?

Or must we begin to understand that jihad is the approved and all-purpose solution to severe and normalized child abuse and a consequent abiding sense of shame and paranoia; an ambition to become "famous," both among other Muslims and among infidels; heterosexual or homosexual frustration; a desire to conquer the world for Islam; and as the only way that Muslim sinners may enter Paradise.

This is primarily a religious war. However, someone's motives do not really matter when they are shooting at us. We must stop them first, try understand them later.

Phyllis Chesler Organization
6/13/16

- 138 -
The American Gulag

For years, beginning in 2002, I have personally faced both censorship and demonization. When I began publishing pieces about anti-Semitism, anti-Zionism, and Islamic gender and religious apartheid at conservative sites, (my formerly left-liberal venues would not publish what I was writing), I was almost instantly seen as having "gone over to the dark side," as having joined the legion of enemies against all that was right and good.

Thus, I learned, early on, about the soft censorship of the Left, the American version of the Soviet Gulag. One could think, write, and even publish one's thoughts, but it would be as if one had not spoken—although one would still be constantly attacked for where one published as much as for what one published.

Since then, Left censorship has only gotten worse. (There is also censorship on the Right—but the Right does not control as many media outlets and does not share the Left's reputation for distinguished and objective "truth telling.")

A week ago, a colleague of mine was thrilled that a mainstream newspaper had reached out to him for a piece about the violent customs of many male Muslim immigrants to Europe. He discovered, to his shock, that his piece had been edited in a way that turned his argument upside down and ended up sounding like American Attorney General Loretta Lynch's view, namely, that home-grown terrorists need "love and compassion," not profiling or detention.

I told him: One more left-liberal newspaper has just bitten the Orwellian dust. He could expose this use of his reasoned view for propaganda purposes—or wear out his welcome at this distinguished venue.

"But," I said, "on the other hand, what kind of welcome is it if they change your words and the main thrust of your argument?"

That same week, right after the jihad massacre in the Orlando gay club, another colleague, long used to being published—and published frequently at gay websites. He counseled gays to understand that the issues of gun control and "hate," while important, were also quite beside the point, that "homosexuality is a capital crime in Islam."

His piece was rejected by every gay site he approached. One venue threatened him: If he published his piece "anywhere," that his work would no longer be welcome in their pages.

I welcomed him to the American Gulag.

He told me that he finally "had" to publish the piece at a conservative site.

Gently, I told him that what he wrote was the kind of piece that was long familiar only at conservative sites and that he should expect considerable flack for where he's published as well as for what he's published.

Another gay rights activist told me that when he described Orlando as a jihad attack, he was castigated as a "right-wing hater." He, too, had to publish what he wanted to say at a conservative site.

I published two pieces about Orlando. I said similar kinds of things and I privately emailed both articles to about 30 gay activists whom I know.

The silence thereafter was, as they say, deafening. I was not attacked but I was given the Silent Treatment.

For a moment, I felt like gay activist Larry Kramer might have felt when, in the 1980s, he tried to persuade gay men to stop going to the baths and engaging in promiscuous sex, that their lust and promiscuity was literally killing them. Kramer was attacked as a spoilsport and as the homophobic enemy of the gay lifestyle. Alas, Kramer had been right and many gay male lives were lost to AIDS.

Thus, gay activists see their collective interests as best served by marching, lock-step, with politically correct politicians who view "mental illness," "gun control," and "American right-wing hatred of gays"— not jihad—as the major problems. Such gay activists also prefer "Palestine" to Israel. It makes absolutely no difference to such ideologues that Israel does not murder its homosexual citizens and that in fact, Israel grants asylum to Muslim Arab men in flight from being torture-murdered by other Muslim Arab men.

A number of European activists have recently visited me. They have described what has been happening to women who undertake the journey from Iraq, Syria, Afghanistan, and Turkey; along the way, the girls and women are continually groped and sexually assaulted, even penetrated in every possible orifice, by gangs of male Muslim immigrants. If they want to live, their husbands and fathers can do nothing.

So much for Muslim immigrant women on the move.

And now, or so I'm told, European women are being told to "dye their hair black," stay home "after 8pm," "always have a male escort at night;" a group of German nudists, whose tradition goes back 100 years, have just been told to "cover up" because refugees are being moved into the rural lake community.

Where will this all end? In Europe becoming a Muslim Caliphate dominated by Sharia law and by all its myriad misogynist interpretations? In Muslim immigrants assimilating to Western ways? In Europeans voluntarily converting to Arab and Muslim ways? In non-violent but parallel Muslim lives?

Bravo to England which has just taken its first, high risk steps to control its borders and its immigrant population.

The Phyllis Chesler Organization
6/27/16

- 139 -
Q & A: Burqas and Burquinis

Q: Does a democratic government have the right to legislate what women wear?

Chesler: In my view, neither a government nor a woman's family, both of which are patriarchal entities, should be entitled to legislate what a woman can and cannot wear. It is therefore very dispiriting that so many Western "progressives," including feminists, are rushing to uphold Sharia law and reactionary Islamist interpretations of the Islamic Veil, even as they remain silent about Sharia based gender and religious apartheid. Even more ironic, is their silence about how freedom-loving Muslim and ex-Muslim dissidents, feminists, and gays are being persecuted, tortured, and murdered by Muslim Islamists.

In my view, as long as any woman can be beaten, death-threatened, or honor murdered in the West because she refuses to wear any version of the Islamic Veil—for this reason alone, the Western democracies should consider banning it. Doing so, will not protect us from Islamic terrorist attacks nor will it necessarily help foster integration—two very essential priorities, but it may help save the lives of women living in Western-style democracies.

Such bans reflect my concern with women's human and civil rights; her right to sunlight, (without which she will contract all the diseases associated with a Vitamin D deficiency); her right to see, hear, and walk—or swim—easily; her right to be comfortable in the heat by wearing light-weight clothing; her right to see and be clearly identified by others in the public square or at work.

Banning the Islamic Veil is one way of refusing to collaborate with such misogyny.

There is another reason a ban on the Islamic Veil might be essential. Remember the alarmingly high rates of Muslim male gang-gropes and gang-rapes of naked-faced women all over Europe, both infidel and Muslim? Not wearing the Islamic Veil (burqa, chador, niqab, hijab) is often interpreted as: "The woman is fair game, she's an infidel and a prostitute." Thus, wearing Islamic head, face, and body-gear targets those women who are not "covered." And, by the way, many "covered" women have, nevertheless, been assaulted anyway.

Does a democratic, post-Enlightenment government have the right to extend the rule of law to all its citizens, including female or immigrant citizens? I'd say that it has the absolute moral and legal obligation to do so.

Q: So what is your problem with the burquini?

Chesler: On the one hand, this is a false issue. Far more important is finding Islamic terrorists before they attack in Paris, Nice, Brussels, and elsewhere in Europe and North America. Far more important is naming, fighting, and winning the War of Ideas, the Islamic religious war against Western freedoms which has led to terrorist attacks. Far more important, is either finding ways of integrating non-hostile immigrants or of stopping "the hostiles" at the border.

However, my concern with the burkini as follows: It does not seem all that comfortable to be swimming in so much yardage; it is not safe to have one's ears blocked while swimming either. Not to be able to feel the water directly against one's skin is equivalent to wearing a monk's hair shirt. Women are not being permitted the simple God-given pleasures of our sensory beings. Why? What crime have women committed to be so punished?

Q: Why do you think France made an issue of this when there is so much other Muslim evidence of takeover? (Maybe they are afraid of doing anything else, as Giulio Meotti has written, and this is their weak and symbolic way to "fight" Islamization.)

Chesler: Perhaps Giulio is right and yet, France has a long tradition of "secularism" or *lacite*. They have banned the hijab (headscarf) in certain settings (schools, government offices), and they've banned the burqa (or face mask) entirely. Banning the burkini is just another such

461

challenge on the long and difficult road to integration.

The burquini and the burqa are also on a continuum of demands and challenges which face Europe and America. It is not an isolated instance in which foreign cultural norms are being injected into Western culture. Where does it stop?

Female genital mutilation, (which leads to terrible and continual consequences which require burdening the state in terms of medical coverage); polygamy, (which often means that multiple wives are each living on the dole); child marriage, forced marriage, first-cousin marriage, (which often delays or prohibits female education, employment, and potential integration); honor based violence and honor killing (which again burdens the state with either the cost of rescues or of lengthy and costly prosecutions or both)—all, all, have gathered force in the West, both under-the-radar and more visibly. Sexual assaults of women mainly by young Muslim men are on the rise and the state is increasingly burdened by the extra cost of police protection or of prosecution.

Muslim attacks on infidels, especially of Jews in Europe, and of critics of Islam, characterize how Islamic religious apartheid is being imported from the Arab Middle East, North Africa, and Central Asia. This burdens the state with the cost of extra police protection, and also burdens individuals with the cost of private security. The demand for halal food in public secular schools, demanding that Muslim holidays be recognized as if they were national holidays, etc., demands for separate prayer rooms and time-outs for prayer three to five times a day, burden both schools and places of employment and are all part of this continuum.

Praying, eating halal food, taking holidays, is not the problem. Acting as if such observances must be sanctioned and paid for by the state which, in the West is separate from religion, is the problem.

The Burqa is the proverbial "camel's nose" foreshadowing all these additional issues.

Israel National News
9/1/16